COMPUTER SYSTEMS IN THE
AND CATERING INDUSTRY

Other Hotel and Catering texts available from the publisher

Hotel and Food Service Marketing
Francis Buttle

Food Service Operations, Second Edition
Peter Jones

The Management of Hotel Operations
Andrew Lockwood and Peter Jones

People and the Hotel and Catering Industry
Andrew Lockwood and Peter Jones

The Management of Catering Operations
Paul Merricks and Peter Jones

The Hotel Receptionist, Second Edition
Grace and Jane Paige

Principles of Hotel and Catering Law
Alan Pannett

Computer Systems in the Hotel and Catering Industry

BRUCE BRAHAM, FHCIMA, Cert.Ed., R.Dip.

Senior Lecturer in Hotel Accommodation Management
Department of Service Industries
Bournemouth University

CASSELL

Cassell Educational Ltd
Villiers House, 41/47 Strand
London WC2N 5JE

First published 1988
Reprinted 1992, 1993

British Library Cataloguing-in-Publication Data

Braham, Bruce
    Computer systems in the hotel and catering
    industry.
    1. Hotel industries. Catering industries.
    Hotel & catering industries. Applications
    of computer systems
    I. Title
    647'.94'.0285

ISBN 0-304-31502-8

Typeset by Fakenham Photosetting Ltd, Fakenham, Norfolk
Printed in Great Britain by
Redwood Books, Trowbridge, Wiltshire.

Contents

Acknowledgements 8
Preface 13

1 Catering Computers Then, Now and in the Future 15

What are computers? 15
The evolution of catering computers 18
References 38

2 Computer Applications in Food and Beverage 39

Computers and food and beverage 39
How can computers help the operation of a restaurant? 41
Computers and kitchens 59
Computers and hospital catering 71
Computers and bars 89
Computers and vending 101
References 106

3 Computer Applications in Hotel and Catering Administration 107

Computers and reservations 107
Computers and the front desk 121
Electronic funds transfer at point-of-sale (EFTPOS) 133
Guest history 136
A computer as an aid to sales and marketing 141
Conference management 153
Back office computerized accounts 157
Telephones and computerization 170
Security 183
Computers and the housekeeping department 200
Mini-bars or in-room refreshment centres 201
Energy management systems 204
Television provision 209
References 230

4 Selecting a Computer System   231

Introduction   231
Why contemplate using a computer?   232
The selection process   235
The suppliers   238
Computer installation   241
Physical alterations that a computer might necessitate   242
Clean electricity   244
67 days to install a restaurant computer system   245
Support   255
The importance of computer maintenance   256
Where can the caterer go for impartial advice?   260
References   264

5 Computer Hardware and Software   265

Hardware selection   265
Software selection   307
References   314

6 Overcoming Computer Jargon   315

'Computerspeak'   315
How to conquer 'technofear'   317
The importance of training   318
References   322

Appendix Glossary of computer jargon   323

Index   332

TO CHUBBY, DAN AND ANIKA

Acknowledgements

The author is grateful to the following individuals and organizations who have provided considerable assistance in the production of this book:

ACOM Computer Systems Ltd, 11275 Cote de Liesse, Suite 202, MTL (Quebec), H9P 1G7, Canada – Kevin Reath, Vice President (back office computer systems).

ADP Hotel Services, Innsite House, Park Lane, Cranford, Hounslow, Middlesex, TW5 9RW – Michael R Howes, Marketing Director (ADP Innsite integrated systems).

Anglo Manufacturing Ltd, Ronsons Way, 214 St Albans Road, Sandridge, St Albans, Herts., AL4 9PY – Richard Langrick, Sales and Marketing Director (Optronic electronic drinks dispenser system).

Auditel Lodging Management Systems Inc., 2100 Hwy 360, Suite 104/105, Grand Prairie, Texas 75050, USA – David R. Maurice, Executive Vice President (integrated hotel microcomputer systems).

Bar Vender, 2555 Veterans Drive, Posen, Illinois 60469, USA – Daniel J. Fox, Vice President, Sales & Marketing (Bar Vender minibar system).

BellSouth Advanced Systems Inc., 2001 Park Place, Suite 1200, Birmingham, Alabama 35203, USA – Melisa Heard, Lodging Industry Manager (Lodging Industry systems).

Besam Ltd, Unit 3, Blackburn Trading Estate, Northumberland Close, Stanwell, Staines, Middlesex, TW19 7LN – I. R. Straughan, Sales Manager (Besam automatic door systems).

Bournemouth Department of Tourism, Westover Road, Bournemouth, Dorset, BH1 2BU – Ken Male, Tourism Officer.

Chart Software Ltd, AEC Business Systems, Hiscock Offices, Eastheath Avenue, Wokingham, Berks, RG11 2PN – Ann E. Clegg (Check-In integrated hotel system).

Comdial Corporation, 1180 Seminole Trail, P.O. Box 7266, Charlottesville, VA 22906–7266, USA – R. A. Kutzenberger, Product Manager Station Apparatus (Hotelephones with built-in dataports).

Computerized Security Systems Inc., 138 N. Moon, Suite C, Brandon, Florida 33511, USA – Fred A. Crum, Vice President Sales and Marketing (Saflok electronic door locking system).

Delphi Management Systems, Inc., 44 Newmarket Road, Durham, New Hampshire 03824, USA – Beverly Valentine, Administrative Assistant (marketing and sales software).

Dynamic Logic Ltd, The Western Centre, Western Road, Bracknell, Berkshire, RG12 1RW – Mike McHugh (telephone management systems).

EECO Computer Inc., 7 Airlinks, Spitfire Way, Heston, Middlesex, TW5 9NR – Jeff Thomas, UK Sales Executive (hotel PMS computer systems, Guestrak and Self-Chek).

ERS Technologies Inc., Suite 120, Shellbridge Way, Richmond, British Columbia, V6X 2W8, Canada – Bret Conkin, Marketing (Night Clerk automated guest registration system).

Falcon Lock Company Ltd, North West Industrial Estate, Mill Hill, Peterlee, County Durham – Graham Hammond, National Sales Manager (Gibraltar 2000 electronic locking system).

Fortronic Limited, Royal Mint Level, Europe House, World Trade Centre, London, E1 9AA – Ramesh Juneja, Sales Executive (hotel and catering EFTPOS terminals).

Fretwell-Downing Computer Group, Brincliffe House, Eccleshall Road, Sheffield, S11 7AE – Richard Plumb, FHCIMA, Director (catering management information systems).

GiroVend Cashless Systems (UK) Ltd, City Gate House, 399–425 Eastern Avenue, Gants Hill, Ilford, Essex, 1G2 6LS – M. Kobeissi, Sales Director (cashless systems for vending and catering).

Hotel Information Systems Inc., 400 Ellinwood Way, Pleasant Hill, California 94523, USA – Crystal Page, Manager, Advertising Programs (software for the hospitality industry).

Hugin Sweda, 18–30 Clerkenwell Road, London, EC1M 5NN (hotel information management systems).

Inn-Ventory Computers Ltd, Westwood House, 80 Warwick Street, Leamington Spa, Warwickshire, CV32 4QG – David J. Robinson, Sales Manager (computerized stocktaking systems).

Intelpost, Room 323, Royal Mail Marketing Department, 33 Grosvenor Place, London, SW1X 1PX – Malcolm Cutting, Intelpost Manager (international communications).

International Datel, British Telecom International, Facsimile and Datel Marketing, Holborn Centre, 120 Holborn, London, EC1N 2TE – Phil Grace, Datel Marketing Manager (international data communications).

I.V.S. Enterprises Ltd, 54 Warwick Square, London, SW1V 2AJ – Carol Dukes, Television Services Executive (satellite TV).

JB Computer Catering Systems Ltd, 47 Granville Road, St Albans, Herts., AL1 5BE – Phillip Saunders (computerized labelling systems).

Kaba Locks Ltd, Woodward Road, Howden Industrial Estate, Tiverton, Devon, EX16 5HW (Kaba Nova electronic locking system).

Kronos Inc., 62 Fourth Avenue, Waltham, Massachusetts 02154, USA – (Time Accounting systems).

Lodgistix, Two Brittany Place, 1938 N. Woodlawn, Suite 1, Wichita, KS 67208, USA – Gail Haywood, Marketing Relations Manager (integrated hotel systems). UK Office – Savoy Hill House, Savoy Hill, London WC2.

Megabyte Ltd, P.O. Box 32, B'Kara, Malta – C. T. Galea, Director (hotel computer systems).

Micro Scope plc, Vanwall Business Park, Vanwall Road, Maidenhead, Berkshire, SL6 4UN – David Bennett, UK Sales manager (Videotex systems).

Micros Systems Inc., 1200 Baltimore Blvd., Beltsville, Maryland 2075–1384, USA – Katherine A. Quinn, Manager, Marketing and Communications. In UK: Micros Systems Ltd, Station House, Harrow Road, Wembley, Middlesex HA9 6DB – Andrew Prince, Sales Manager (catering control systems).

Monitor Auto-call, Unit 2, 13 Distillery Road, London, W6 9SE – Margaret Hughes (radio and hard-wired hotel communication and auto-call systems).

NCR Ltd, 206 Marylebone Road, London, NW1 6LY – P. W. Pruden, Retail Information Services (POS and integrated computer systems).

Nixdorf Computer Ltd, 125–135 Staines Road, Hounslow, Middlesex, TW3 3JB – Philip Summons, Account Manager Retail and Leisure Division (integrated hotel computer systems).

Norand (UK) Ltd, Cutbush Park, Lower Earley, Reading, Berkshire, RG6 4XA – John Murray, General Manager (EPOS restaurant systems).

Norton Telecommunications Group plc, 347–349 City Road, London, EC1V 1LJ – Joanne Gorry, Marketing Assistant (communication systems).

Prologic Hotel Systems, 1 Shortlands, Hammersmith, London, W6 8DR – Gary T. Francies, Director (integrated hotel systems).

Remanco Systems Ltd, Remanco House, Church Street, Twickenham, Middlesex, TW1 3NJ –
(restaurant management systems).

Schlage Lock Company, 2401 Bayshore Boulevard, San Francisco, California 94134, USA –
(Intellis electronic security systems).

Synerlogic Inc., 1680 128th Street, Suite 200, Surrey, British Columbia, V4A 3V3, Canada – Ken
Harrap, Vice President, Product Marketing (integrated hotel systems).

Systems Reliability plc, 400 Dallow Road, Luton, Beds., LU1 1UR – (Hotel-Tag and Tel-Tag
telephone management systems).

Tandata Marketing Ltd, Albert Road North, Malvern, Worcs., WR14 2TL – M. A. Green,
Market Development Manager (Viewdata systems).

Thorn EMI Champs Systems, Meudon Avenue, Farnborough, Hampshire, GU14 7NB – Anne
Kennedy and Tony Lucas, Sales and Marketing Manager – (CHAMPS integrated hotel
systems).

Tiger Systems, Stone Lane, Wimborne, Dorset, BH21 1HD – Diane M. Priday (telephone
management systems).

Uniqey (Europe) Ltd, Unit 21D, Horseshoe Park, Pangbourne, Reading, Berkshire, RG8 7JW –
Donald A. G. Palmer, Deputy Chairman (electronic door locking systems).

Vista (Satellite) Ltd, Swiss Centre, 10 Wardour Street, London, W1V 3HG – Bob Johnson, Field
Services Manager (satellite TV).

Westminster Cable Television, 87/89 Baker Street, London, W1M 1AJ – Biba Hartigan, Media
Operations Manager (cable TV).

Yaletronics, Yale Security Products Ltd, Wood Street, Willenhall, West Midlands, WV13 1LA –
(hotel security systems).

Zettler UK, Brember Road, Harrow, Middlesex, HA2 8AS – C. E. Illman, Product Manager,
Building Systems (fire detection and emergency alarm systems).

The author is additionally grateful to the following individuals and publications who have given
permission for the reproduction of material within this book:

Accountancy, 40 Bernard Street, London, WC1N 1LD.

Banking World, Athene House, 66/73 Shoe Lane, London, EC4P 4AB.

British Hotelier & Restaurateur, 40 Duke Street, London, W1M 6HR.

Caterer & Hotelkeeper, Business Press International Ltd, Quadrant House, The Quadrant,
Sutton, Surrey, SM2 5AS.

Communications/Communications International, International Thomson Publishing Ltd, 100
Avenue Road, London, NW3 3TP.

Computer Fraud & Security Bulletin, Elsevier International Bulletins, Mayfield House, 256
Banbury Road, Oxford, OX2 7DH.

Computer Solutions for Hotel & Catering, Patey Doyle (Publishing) Ltd, Wilmington House,
Church Hill, Wilmington, Dartford, Kent, DA2 7EF.

Computer Systems, Techpress Publishing Company Ltd, Northside House, 69 Tweedy Road,
Bromley, Kent, BR1 3WA.

Concise Oxford Dictionary, Oxford University Press, Walton Street, Oxford, OX2 6DP.

Acknowledgements

Cornell Hotel and Restaurant Administration Quarterly, Statler Hall, Cornell University, Ithaca, New York 14853–0223, USA.

D.P. Media Services, 21 Horseshoe Park, Pangbourne, Berks, RG8 7JW.

Gardner Merchant Limited, Information Services, Unit 7, Parkway 4, Fourways, Longbridge Road, Trafford Park, Manchester, M17 1SN – Martyn J. McReynolds, Systems Manager.

HCIMA Yearbook, Sterling Publications Ltd, Garfield House, 86/88 Edgware Road, London, W2 2YW.

Mark Jones, Computer Training Adviser, HCTB Micro-Systems Centre, HCTB, P.O. Box 18, Ramsey House, Central Square, Wembley, Middlesex, HA9 7AP.

Hospitality, Wordsmith & Company, 35 Albemarle Street, London, W1X 3FB.

Hotel & Catering Technology, Seymour House, 30/34 Muspole Street, Norwich, Norfolk, NR3 1DJ.

Hotel & Motel Management, 7500 Old Oak Boulevard, Cleveland, Ohio 441330, USA.

Kate McDermid, 112 Ravenscroft Road, Beckenham, Kent, BR3 4TW.

Frank Mezulanik.

Mind Your Own Business, 106 Church Road, London, SE19 2BU.

Practical Computing, Reed Business Publishing, Quadrant House, The Quadrant, Sutton, Surrey, SM2 5AS.

Restaurants & Institutions, 1350 E. Tuohy Avenue, P.O. Box 5080, Des Plaines, IL60017–5080, USA.

Roux Restaurants, 539 Wandsworth Road, London, SW8.

Which Computer, EMAP, Abbot's Court, 34 Farringdon Lane, London, EC1R 3AU.

Marian Whitaker, Department of Business Management, Brighton Polytechnic, Moulsecoomb, Brighton, BN2 4AT.

Cynthia Yeadon, Barnfield College, New Bedford Road, Luton, LU3 2AX.

Preface

Several people have asked me why I decided to write a book about computers for caterers. The answer is quite simple. Some time ago I found myself in the situation that I wanted to learn more about computers but found that the existing texts were either too academic or too trivial to warrant in-depth reading. I also found that I was not alone: both my students and clients shared the same problem. Basically, a need existed for a book that could explain computers in reasonable depth to caterers like myself.

The next step was to define what is meant by 'reasonable depth'. It soon became apparent that the average caterer was not particularly interested in how a computer worked but much more in what a computer could do for the business. A deliberate policy was therefore adopted to concentrate on what a computer could do rather than how it did it. Then arose the problem of the deluge of computer jargon that surrounds the computer industry and here a policy was followed to try and minimize the use of obscure terminology. Inevitably, I have been sucked into the black hole of 'computerspeak' in places, but I have tried to keep this to a minimum.

As already mentioned, the people who prompted this book were of two distinct types. Firstly, my clients as a consultant needed some background reading to help them to adjust to the world of computers. They were largely busy industrialists who needed to know where a computer application might be of use to them, and also needed to feel informed and therefore reassured about the decisions that they were making. Secondly, my students made me aware of the gap that needed to be filled for them. There they were, writing letter after letter requesting information from harassed computer suppliers who were sinking under a never-ending tidal wave and who, therefore, could hardly be blamed for ignoring my students. At major exhibitions computer suppliers wanted to sell computers and not, as it appeared to them, waste time giving away brochures to an army of information-hungry overgrown schoolchildren.

Both groups of potential computer users had certain requirements in common. They wanted to have some knowledge of the history and evolution of computers in the catering industry. They needed to know how computers could fit into business situations and what applications were readily available. Lastly, but most importantly, they needed information on how to select an appropriate system, whether this be for real or in a hypothetical academic situation. In short, they wanted to be able to contribute to purchasing decisions, while being thoroughly aware of the advantages and pitfalls that computerization can bring.

The technological advances that are continually being made mean that any book about computerization inevitably starts to be outdated before it even reaches the bookshelves. As far as computer applications are concerned, however, there is some evidence that, apart from a speeding up of processes and a higher level of integration of systems, a plateau has been reached (no doubt of a temporary nature) and in the short-term any major advances are unlikely. The time is right, therefore, to take a look at computerization but, like any book of this type, having as its subject a rapidly evolving technology, this must be regarded as a snapshot of the situation as it existed in the mid 1980s.

Making people feel welcome and looked after as individuals is a unique skill possessed only by human beings and not by machines. Penny Cheshire, runner-up in the 1987 Hotel Receptionist of the Year contest and an ex-student of Bruce Braham's
Photograph: Bruce Grant-Braham

In concluding, there is one major philosophical point that I would like to make. Having now seen computers in operation in a vast variety of hotel and catering situations I cannot emphasize strongly enough the need to view them in perspective. The hotel and catering industry provides hospitality and only people can do that. Machines cannot replace people when it comes to creating that all-important feeling of being made welcome and being looked after as an individual, which is a unique skill possessed only by human beings and not machines. Computers are not gods and should be kept firmly in their place as management tools that are there to assist the staff in providing hospitality.

BRUCE BRAHAM
August 1987

1 Catering Computers Then, Now and in the Future

WHAT ARE COMPUTERS?

> A computer is an 'automatic electronic apparatus for making calculations or controlling operations that are expressible in numerical or logical terms, i.e., a calculator' (Concise Oxford Dictionary, 1982)

A large number of caterers find the many different types of computer that are available a source of great confusion. Whichever magazine one reads or whichever trade exhibition one visits there is invariably a baffling selection on offer. There are not only mainframes, minis, and micros, but also desk tops, PCs, and computers ideally suited to the small business, and all of them boast apparently irresistible advantages for a catering business.

Many of these machines appear identical to the outsider, with television screens attached to typewriter keyboards, and printing machinery very similar to the electric typewriters which caterers have become accustomed to in their administration offices. It is necessary for caterers to have a basic knowledge of these various types of computer so that they can appreciate where the different machines might fit into the multitude of potential catering locations.

There are three basic types of computer that might be considered in a business situation and in attempting to categorize these we shall use a novel approach. Rather than describing the machines on offer by their technology, which would be the way that a computer scientist might prefer to operate, we shall look at the usefulness of computers as far as the caterer is concerned. In other words, we will categorize computers by their relevance to business surroundings which is, after all, the reason that the average caterer becomes involved with new technology.

Three categories of computer

We are now going to look at the *three basic types* of computer, which are:

- mainframe computer
- minicomputer
- microcomputer

Mainframe computer

A mainframe is a large beast, covering a huge floor area, with many cabinets containing spinning tapes and disks, that is kept in a sterile and possibly top security environment. Until comparatively recently it tended to be the type of computer that would immediately spring to people's minds when the word 'computer' was mentioned. It is something that many people have been exposed to only rarely, such as when television programmes have concentrated on mission control at Houston during a space shot.

In truth very few catering organizations require such beasts but the typical location for a mainframe would be the head office of a major hotel group or the administration of an international tour operator, where such large capacity machines handle the company payroll, for example, or holiday bookings.

However, mainframe computers are found in many of the larger hotel and catering companies. Until quite recently they were the only type of computer available to the business market. This has tended to give potential computer users the false impression that massive investment is needed to utilize computer facilities. Mainframes are of necessity very large and expensive, but this reflects the huge capacity of such machines to process large amounts of data.

Mainframe computers are produced by many of the internationally known computer companies such as IBM and ICL. The processing work they undertake can be input in a centralized location such as a head office, or via remote terminals situated in many individual units. They are commonly used by a large number of operators simultaneously.

It is quite possible for the mainframe operators to be programming the computer via the terminals actually alongside the machine itself whilst the payroll is being run from the wages office in the same building. At the same time the ordering department may be recording purchases made centrally for the company, even as a large number of reservations are being handled from the various hotels around the country. All the while the financial directors are displaying revenue statistics on the screens in their offices.

The great advantage of mainframe computers is that they have the capacity for a vast amount of processing. There is virtually no possibility of a catering problem being impossible to handle provided there is the finance available to run a suitably sized mainframe. Another benefit is that a mainframe is usually very secure, offering a high degree of hardware and software reliability, customer service and support.

Minicomputer

Minicomputers first came onto the market in about 1978 and have become firmly established in many businesses. They are most commonly found in accounting and financial applications and are most often used to monitor the operation of a single unit, whether this be a hotel or an industrial catering outlet.

Physically minicomputers are much smaller than mainframes, often fitting into a space no larger than a filing cabinet. They can be capable of handling just a small number of users or up to hundreds, depending on the application.

A normal arrangement of minicomputer hardware in a hotel would involve a processor linked to, say, four terminals. One terminal would be in reception handling room status and reservations, whilst a second would be in housekeeping to enable room status information to be communicated. The financial controller, who might well be the manager, would have a terminal, as would the restaurant to allow posting of guest meal bills direct to their accounts. It could well be that business software is also run to cope with the payroll, the general ledger, and stocktaking.

As they are usually developments of machines used widely in other industries, minicomputers are really only small capacity mainframes. They cannot be used by as many people at the same time and tend also not to be as secure as mainframes.

Microcomputer

Microcomputers are the most recent addition to the range of computers on offer to the business user. They evolved from the home computers that originally were used almost exclusively for playing games such as Space Invaders. Gradually microcomputers, particularly the ubiquitous BBC Micro, were introduced into schools. Today most school leavers have been exposed to microcomputers to some degree during their education and whilst they have used educational software at school they may well have fun software at home.

It soon became evident through the educational usage of microcomputers that there could be important business applications for these small capacity, but thoroughly justifiable machines. Gradually manufacturers realized the importance of this sector of the market. More and more business software has become available as the capacity of the machines has been increased.

Microcomputers are the breed that may also be referred to as 'desk top' or 'personal' computers. They are usually used by one person at a time, hence their 'personal' nickname, and consequently they only tackle a single problem at a time. They are commonly found in the form of word processors or, for example, being used for departmental problem solving such as menu costing or dietetics. Generally micros are used by managers who have specific routine problems that need solving.

The most recent trend in microcomputers is to link several together on a network so that their users may have access to the applications on not only their own micro but also the others in the system.

Compared with mainframes and minicomputers, the microcomputer and its software is very inexpensive. Ready-made software packages to suit the various formats of micro are usually available off the shelf.

Their comparative lack of storage capacity places micros at a disadvantage against the opposition, especially as they usually can only cope with a single application at a time. Micros are not as reliable as their larger relatives – sometimes the disk drives prove to be the fragile weak link.

Research recently undertaken reveals that of our three types of computer, microcomputers have made the highest penetration in the catering industry.

Types of Information Technology Installed (Whitaker, 1986)

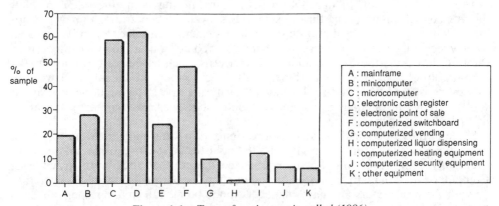

A : mainframe
B : minicomputer
C : microcomputer
D : electronic cash register
E : electronic point of sale
F : computerized switchboard
G : computerized vending
H : computerized liquor dispensing
I : computerized heating equipment
J : computerized security equipment
K : other equipment

Figure 1.1 *Type of equipment installed (1986)*

THE EVOLUTION OF CATERING COMPUTERS

Caterers were slow to adopt computerization

Whilst the application of new technology within industry in general has moved very rapidly during the various 'generations' of computers since the early 1950s, the catering and hospitality industry has frequently been criticized for lagging behind. Caterers themselves have often been unkindly regarded as technological dinosaurs by those unfamiliar with the intricacies of an industry which is primarily people and service orientated. With the benefit of hindsight, many of the early users of computers in catering might well now agree with the old adage that 'only fools rush in'.

In fact the apparently slow take-up of new technology within the catering and hospitality industry may not have been such a bad thing in the long term. The catering industry has been able to benefit from the experiences and mistakes of other industries and there have been relatively few failures on the grand scale, like that at the New York Hilton (see page 123). It is worth noting that in more recent years the take-up of new technology has speeded up:

> Already almost 50 per cent of the hotels and restaurants in this country have new technology in some form or another. (Which Computer, 1985)

However, it is still not universally accepted. It is interesting that even in America, long regarded as the centre of innovation in computers, the take-up of new technology in hotels was not as swift or as comprehensive as one might have expected:

> Although automation is becoming more prevalent in the hotel industry, fewer than 1,000 of the more than 40,000 hotels in America have automated their front offices to any extent. (Alvarez *et al.*, 1983)

Compared with many industries catering presented a complex computing problem and it is therefore hardly surprising that it adopted new technology less readily than other industries with relatively simple requirements.

Much of the very necessary research and development of computerized systems had already been undertaken by the time computer manufacturers' sales staff targeted catering as a profitable outlet for their wares. Those catering companies that did jump onto the technology bandwagon at the outset were soon to be overtaken by developments and were not to have the 'user-friendly' benefits that were commonplace in systems and software a matter of a decade later.

There is little doubt, though, that managers in catering as in other industries felt threatened by computers and this considerably slowed the penetration of new technology. There was the worry that both staff and managers themselves might be replaced by new technology and that the skills of a manager could be usurped by a computer. In catering, however, there were additional concerns, such as the perception that the relationship of a catering establishment with its customers would suffer. It was felt that the 'host' and 'hospitality' elements of a catering operation might be lost, and it was feared by some managers that guests would not have as much contact with staff as had previously been possible.

Some of these fears had already been recognized in other industries and they took some time in the catering and hospitality industry to be overcome. Many were eventually conquered only when experience showed that they were groundless. Computerization in many instances started to allow more time for members of staff to be with their customers and gave managers much better information upon which to base their decisions.

Whilst computer technology advanced at a rapid rate throughout the 1970s and 1980s the attendant publicity led to problems. The caterer was often led to expect something miraculous from the computer and despite the fact that systems had become much cheaper, in reality disappointment was often the eventual outcome. The major reasons for disappointments were:

- Potential users had insufficient knowledge of how the new technology could be applied.
- There was a severe shortage of experienced and skilled personnel, who could build reliable computer systems.
- There had been too little collaboration between system suppliers and potential users of sophisticated technology; such collaboration is vital if there is to be a smooth transition from existing methods to automated computerized systems. (Hodge, 1980)

History and significant developments

Catering computer evolution in the United Kingdom closely mirrors the emergence of similar machines in North America. It is therefore imperative when examining the history of catering computers to identify initially what happened in the United States where most breakthroughs occurred.

In the 1950s in North America computerization was the province of the large multinational firms who took up the challenge of new technology purely because it was the fashion and not because cost-effectiveness could be demonstrated. In common with most American businesses the few catering companies to make use of computers did so largely in accounting orientated applications such as the processing of the staff payroll. Applications such as this had already been developed in other industries and were therefore easily transferable to a large catering company. Such were the applications utilized that as far as the general staff and the customer were concerned these large computers, often situated at a head office, had little if any practical impact on the service given to the guest.

Strand Hotels

One very large catering company involved in computing in the United Kingdom was J. Lyons Ltd which produced a commercial computer in 1951 called LEO (Lyons Electronic Office). When Lyons first used this system on Christmas Eve 1953, it became the first company in the world to use a computer for regular commercial work.

In addition to its food production business Lyons was, of course, heavily involved in catering. The spin-off from their general computing interest was that through its hotel subsidiary, Strand Hotels, the company led the way in computerized hotel systems during the 1960s. The Strand Palace and Cumberland hotels utilized DEC PDP8 computers for reservations and other administrative functions well before other hotels became involved to any extent with the technology.

The reason for this enthusiasm was that Lyons had always been a far-sighted company and from the Board downwards there was a computer awareness within the company. Even though Lyons were to sell their computer manufacturing interests in 1963 to English Electric, which was later incorporated into ICL, the company retained a keen appreciation of the relevance of computing.

As the 1960s replaced the 1950s a realization took place that computers might actually be useful management tools in the operation of a catering business. Major investment took place as a consequence in the large catering companies.

New York failure

In 1963 the New York Hilton, then the largest hotel in the United States, became the first to use computers in its front office function. The Hilton boasted what was called a property management system (PMS) that allowed the posting of charges on to guest accounts as well as processing the check-in and check-out of guests.

Unfortunately the system was a complete failure and by the end of 1964 the original PMS was abandoned. Far from improving the hotel's operation, its 'batch' method of processing had effectively slowed down many guest transactions and sent front office costs soaring. The failure was widely publicized and it shook confidence in computerization, giving ammunition to the cynics whilst also fuelling the fears of those caterers still happier to run their businesses along well proven traditional lines. More information about the problems of the PMS may be found later in the book (see p. 123).

The New York Hilton experience illustrated to future purchasers some of the initial problems of becoming involved with new technology. It also frightened off some prospective purchasers and it took time for their confidence to be restored.

In January 1970 a top executive of IBM commented:

> Computers in the catering industry are few and far between. Many organisations, particularly in the industrial sector, are using them and the catering sections are benefiting from their use. (Brown, 1970)

From this extract it can be seen that a representative of one of the leading computer manufacturers saw the company's customers in non-catering industries making use of computers and almost by accident allowing their catering departments to benefit from the technology already to be found in-house. At the time it was suggested by IBM that British hoteliers might consider their businesses too small to benefit from computers but that in reality this was far from the truth. It was felt that there was considerable scope for handling staff wages, administration, analysing different aspects of sales and merchandising, and in forward planning in many British hotels.

Sun Valley in-house computer

In 1970 it was relatively rare to find a hotel possessing computer facilities on its own premises but one notable exception was the Sun Valley Hotel in the United States. It was looked upon as a pathfinder in computerization, having spent £25,000 (1970 value) on an in-house computer system. The computer recorded the movement of all hotel business. As well as holding the information concerning reservations the system gave each guest a punched card. Wherever the guests went throughout the hotel they produced their cards when they wanted to make use of any service. The card was punched so that the calculation of a final bill could be achieved by feeding the card back into the computer.

In addition to compiling the guest's bill the computer then analysed the room occupancy rate, the profitability of all entertainments, the food consumed, and all aspects of profit. Peaks and lows of business were detailed and the hotel's accounts were handled, as well as the issuing of daily reports.

Britain's proposed national reservations network

The early 1970s was the era in which new technology started to become a feasible proposition in catering operations with the evolution of centralized computers capable of handling a number of satellite terminals simultaneously.

In Britain a study undertaken by the government body 'Little Neddy' (National Economic Development Council) into the requirements of overseas visitors to this country, as expressed by travel agents, identified the need for a national hotel reservations system based on a computer. It was hoped that such a system would be able to effect instantaneous reservations at any hotel in Great Britain and, if interfaced with corresponding systems in other countries, throughout the world. The intention was that such a system would be run privately along the lines of similar systems then being considered in France, Germany and Switzerland.

The feasibility study left the implementation of the national hotel reservations system to private enterprise and it was a company called International Reservations Ltd who came nearest to the original study aims. Their system opened in Britain on 7 May 1970 with a membership of 450 hotels and 25,000 rooms in total. The same company had already been operating a similar system in the United States with 1,300 hotels and some 130,000 rooms. Unfortunately, heavy financial losses forced IRL to sell the system in 1972.

L'Hôtel St Jacques

On 1 March 1972 the 812 bedroom L'Hôtel St Jacques in Paris put into operation a fully integrated computer system based on an IBM 1800 processor. It attracted wide publicity as the first hotel in the world to operate such a comprehensive configuration, boasting in excess of 1,600 data capture points. Not only was the system heralded as a great step forward in the management of such a hotel but it was also recognized as giving a much improved service to customers.

Reservations, management control, and data capture for billing were handled by the system through a mixture of 'real-time' and 'batch' operation. Punched cards were issued to every individual or group guest allowing them to prove their identity and have charges sent directly to their 'electronic' bill. All the telephones and mini-bars in each of the 812 bedrooms were directly linked to the main processor. It was claimed that on arrival a customer could be checked-in in a time of one to two minutes if they did not have a reservation and in as little as 15 to 30 seconds if they had an existing booking.

In the mid 1970s hoteliers worldwide were facing unprecedented turmoil in running their businesses. Payroll costs were rising rapidly at a time when money was very difficult to borrow from banks against the background of the fuel shortage. Whilst marketing was a new concept to hoteliers who had previously relied on business just arriving in their foyers, the check-in and check-out procedures in most hotels were truly antiquated.

The number of hotels actually making use of computers at this time was negligible. Of those that were many had walked into computerization almost by accident, and many others without any meaningful expertise. Certainly few had analysed their requirements in advance and even fewer had contemplated their short- and long-term objectives. The computer industry itself had provided a bad service, mainly because of its lack of understanding of the hospitality industry.

The whole atmosphere, however, was to change in the mid 1970s with the emergence of business orientated minicomputers capable of handling back-office accounting functions. In addition, software companies began to devote more time to the hospitality industry, producing for the first time some really useful programs for the minicomputers.

St John's Hotel, Solihull – first independent in-house computer

At the end of 1977 the St John's Hotel in Solihull, with its 218 bedrooms and banqueting facilities for 1,000, became well known as the first independent hotel in the United Kingdom to invest in an in-house computer system (Barnes, 1978).

Prompted by its financial director the hotel installed a DIGICO M16E computer with a single VDU, a 150 character-per-second (cps) printer and an 11.6 megabyte disk storage facility. A software company was commissioned to convert the hotel's order processing, invoicing and credit control functions to the electronic information system as the first stage in computerizing the entire hotel. Later, bar control and reservations were to be added on to the existing system, which was primarily intended to handle the financial management of the hotel.

Hoskyns

It was in the late 1970s, with the emergence of microcomputers, that new technology really began to make its mark in catering and the snowball effect is still continuing. In 1978 the British Company Hoskyns pioneered the first microcomputer-based front office system. The system was a success.

> Today more than 10 per cent of all UK hotels with more than 50 bedrooms have a Hoskyns computer system. Trust House Forte alone now has 45 systems. Other main users include Grand Metropolitan, British Transport Hotels, Cunard International Hotels and Centre Hotels. (*Accountancy*, 1981)

By February 1981 Hoskyns had sold 160 systems in the United Kingdom and new markets were being explored overseas. The three systems offered by Hoskyns at this time were a main system based on floppy disks (twin ½Mb), 'Basic Tuffy' which used 16K core store and the 'Super Tuffy' which used a 32K core.

Back in 1967 there had been only five front desk computer systems in the whole of the UK and each of these had cost well over £100,000, so in the space of 14 years computerized accounting in hotels had come a long way. Hoskyns were wise enough to spot and seize on an ideal market as there were somewhere in the region of 800 hotels in the UK with 50 to 100 bedrooms. The marketing and sales people from Hoskyns talked to most of the major hotel groups in the UK and by getting into the hotel market early and by selling a large number of systems to this single section they managed to keep their unit costs down.

Hoskyns launched its first hotel accounting system in June 1978 and by 1981 more than half of all London hotels with 100 to 200 bedrooms and a third of those with 200 to 500 bedrooms had installed a Hoskyns system (*Accountancy*, 1981). As an important consequence a generation of hotel managers were to learn about computers from Hoskyns systems, so common were they in British hotels.

Las Vegas hotel fires prompt research

On 21 November 1980 fire swept through the MGM Grand Hotel in Las Vegas ravaging the 2,000-room, 26-storey modern hotel. Of the 3,500 guests in residence nearly 100 were killed and 400 injured. Many had to be rescued by helicopter from the roof because fire brigade ladders could not reach them and because the seat of the fire was in the hotel's casino on the ground floor, which effectively cut off the main escape routes.

*The Casino at the MGM Grand Hotel in Las Vegas burns fiercely – the manual fire
alarm allegedly proved ineffective*
Photograph: The Associated Press Ltd

Only a matter of weeks later, on 11 February 1981, a neighbouring hotel, the Las
Vegas Hilton, experienced a similar severe fire. This time eight guests died and 242
were injured. The fire was found to have been started deliberately.

That two such shocking fires could occur in such a short time was frightening enough, but that they occurred in two neighbouring modern hotels shocked many Americans. The confidence of American domestic travellers in the safety of sky-scraper-type hotels was profoundly shaken. When it was revealed that the MGM Grand's manual fire alarm had not been activated, having been quickly immobilized by the fire, the hotel industry turned swiftly towards new technology to provide automatic systems in order to restore public confidence.

The two Las Vegas hotel fires may therefore be seen as the catalyst that started off much of the subsequent research that led to the creation of the automatic computerized security systems that we take for granted in many hotels today.

Telecommunications deregulation

January 1984 saw the deregulation of the telecommunications industry in the United States and for some time in preparation for this event a myriad of communications specialists had been exploring potential applications for their wares. In many cases this was the first time that hoteliers were to be exposed to equipment that would allow them to turn their telephones into profit centres rather than a drain on resources, which many had been previously.

In addition, a complete new generation of equipment spawned a vastly different world as far as telecommunications was concerned. New concepts such as satellite connected computer networks came on to the scene, as well as microwave links. These allowed hotels to realistically contemplate such innovations as teleconferencing in order to make their businesses more attractive to corporate customers.

Satellite television reaches UK hotels

On 18 April 1985 the May Fair Hotel in London became the first hotel in the United Kingdom to install a satellite television system linked to the hotel bedrooms. Provided by IVS the system allowed guests to view TV programmes available from two satellites situated over the equator which served the European market.

North Americans had been used to satellite television for some time and the installation at the May Fair had been undertaken because of the findings of research in the United States. This research had confirmed that the wider programme choice offered to hotel guests by satellite television encouraged them to stay in the hotel and to make use of the hotel's facilities, such as room service, rather than looking for entertainment off the premises.

IBM Compatibles

The real penetration of the UK catering industry by new technology came with the increased computer awareness of the mid 1980s. Both at work and in the home there was a much greater acceptance of microcomputers, which demonstrated to a much wider audience than had previously been possible the abilities that computers possessed. By the mid 1980s new technology was widely available and research was appearing that demonstrated the penetration that it had made into the various sectors of the catering and hospitality industry.

A significant milestone was passed when the much respected IBM put concentrated effort into selling systems to the hotel and catering industry in the mid 1980s. Acting through their *accredited industry centres* IBM gave hotel and catering credibility in the eyes of computer manufacturers and suppliers in general. If IBM were interested, it was perceived, then the hospitality industry must be ripe for and able to benefit from computerization.

Northampton's EFTPOS 'Paypoint' trial

October 1985 saw the start of a trial of an EFTPOS (Electronic Funds Transfer at Point-of-Sale) experiment in Northampton. Backed by the Anglia Building Society and ICL, the intention of the trial was to speed up progress towards a national EFTPOS network.

Cashless shopping schemes had been around in the United States since 1975 but Britain had been a long way behind due to wranglings and disagreements over a uniform system. In the Northampton experiment 40,000 people were issued with special cards and 170 EFTPOS terminals were issued to retail outlets, including catering establishments. In using the system the customer's plastic card was 'wiped' through the establishment's terminal, a personal identification number (PIN) was entered and if everything tallied the money was automatically debited from the customer's account.

The pilot scheme was treated cautiously by both the retailers and customers at first but was an important indication of the way that cashless payments would be going in the future.

Automated guest registration systems

On 29 July 1986 the first electronic check-in machine was installed in the Fenwick Islander Motel in Maryland heralding a new step in the application of computers in hotels.

The machine, called the 'Night Clerk', allowed customers to insert a major credit card then punch in the number of guests in the party and the type of accommodation required. The Night Clerk then displayed prices, ran a quick credit check and, if the card was acceptable, dispensed a room key. Lastly, the machine displayed a personalized 'thank you' using the name on the credit card.

The concept of the Night Clerk caught on and the machine sold in large numbers, especially to American Motels where the advantages of the consequent saving in staff and reduction in robberies were major considerations.

Guest service centres and handheld terminals reach the UK

At the Hotech exhibition in London in late 1986 EECO Computers revealed for the first time in the United Kingdom their 'Self-Chek' Guest Service Centre. With the growing concept of self-service for guests the machine not only allowed them to check-in and check-out automatically, but also provided interactive videodisc displays about the hotel's services when not in use for other operations. A unique blend of touchscreen, interactive videodisc and integrated computer technology had been introduced to the European hotel industry for the first time.

At the same exhibition Remanco revealed the first handheld terminals utilizing radio communication to be seen in this country. The terminals were intended to allow restaurant staff to transmit details of guests' orders direct from the tableside to a receiver linked to a restaurant management and point-of-sale system. This was another application already successfully used in the United States.

The EECO 'Self-Chek' Guest Service Centre. Guests could automatically check-in, check-out and receive information for the first time in a European hotel.
Photograph: Bruce Grant-Braham

Hotels

Hotels cover a very wide spectrum. They vary tremendously in size, market and location, and it is not easy to define a typical establishment. Table 1.1 shows an analysis of UK Hotels by the Hotel and Catering Research Centre at Huddersfield.

In the early 1980s a survey into the use of computers in hotels, carried out by the British Association of Hotel Accountants (BAHA), revealed that most people using computers in the hotel industry did not feel they were making adequate use of the new technology. The reasons given were (BAHA, 1981):

- lack of awareness of the available technology
- lack of communication/cooperation within the industry
- lack of involvement in the specification of industry related software
- lack of specialist expertise within the hotel

Table 1.1 *Analysis of UK hotels (1986)*

No. of rooms	No. of hotels	% of total hotels	% PLC and group owned and operated
1,000 +	2	-	100
500–999	19	0.1	100
200–499	169	1.0	67.5
100–199	458	2.3	61.2
50–99	1,203	6.0	42.0
25–49	2,968	15.0	17.4
10–24	11,757	59.4	4.6
9 fewer	3,203	16.2	10.7

As can be seen, units of 49 rooms or fewer account for almost 91 per cent of the industry's total number of hotels.

Around the same time a BHRCA poll of their members found that the most popular applications in use at that time in hotels were (BHRCA, 1980):

- guest billing
- reservations
- business accounting
- stock control
- payroll

In 1986 the applications most commonly used were (Whitaker, 1986):

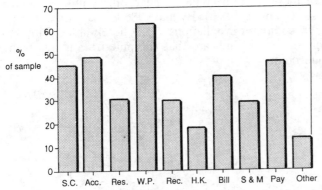

S.C. : stock control
Acc. : accounts
Res. : reservations
W.P. : word processing
Rec. : reception
H.K. : housekeeping
Bill : billing
S&M : sales and marketing
Pay : Payroll

Figure 1.2 *Most popular hotel computer applications*

Computers were being used in a wider range of functions and overall there was much more involvement, expertise, communication and awareness of new technology within the hotel industry.

By 1986 computer systems were approaching a usage rate of 100 per cent in hotels of 400 rooms or over. The typical installation was a dual minicomputer supporting a large number of terminals, with the system costing £200,000 plus. In the medium range of hotels of 100 to 400 rooms, computer usage was still high with usually a pair of microcomputers and a large capacity Winchester disk linked to about 20 terminals.

This type of system would cost between £10,000 and £60,000. In small hotels of 25 rooms plus, however, computer penetration was still negligible. A typical installation would be a single stand-alone microcomputer, costing about £2,500 (Gamble, 1986).

The pattern and extent of computer adoption by the mid 1980s can be illustrated as follows (Whitaker, 1986):

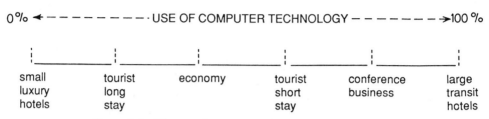

Figure 1.3   *The use of computer technology in hotels in 1986*

From the diagram it may be seen that new technology had hardly had any influence at all on the small hotel of, say, less than 12 rooms, whilst the large city centre or airport transit hotels were well equipped – indeed, they could hardly conceive operating without a computerized system. It is perhaps worth noting that even though the small establishments could have made use of new technology in one form or another, the arguments put forward for reducing costs and improving profitability through computerization were largely irrelevant to this size of hotel.

To put some numbers to the percentage figures already given, in 1978 an investigation revealed that there were just under 41 computers in use in the British hotel and catering industry, and some of these were machines at head offices utilized almost entirely for accounting purposes (Gamble, 1986). By late 1986 it was estimated that this had increased to about 1,000 computer installations in UK hotels alone. This was by no means a large number, but it did indicate that computerization was being accepted on a wider scale than before.

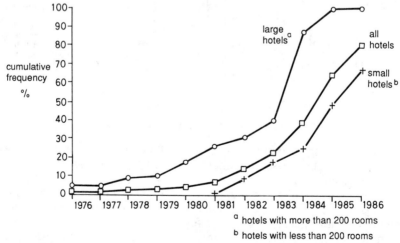

Figure 1.4   *The diffusion of information technology in hotels (Whitaker, 1986)*

In 1985 it was the large hotels of the higher star ratings in the United Kingdom that were making the greatest use of computerization in accommodation management applications. It is also of interest to note that it was primarily hotels that were part of a group or a chain that made use of computers in their front offices. At that time the microcomputer had not made its great impact on the industry and it would appear that the expense of minicomputers largely precluded their use in independent hotels. Figures 1.5 and 1.6 give breakdowns of hotels by number of rooms and by star rating between those that possessed computers in their front office by 1985 and those that did not (Braham, 1985).

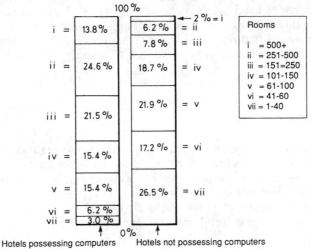

Figure 1.5 *Computers in hotel front offices, by number of rooms*

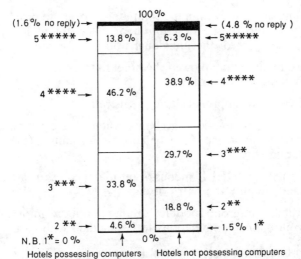

Figure 1.6 *Computers in hotel front offices, by star rating (AA classification)*

By 1985 the capital cost of computers was dropping by as much as 10 per cent per year, while the spend on computer systems was rising by as much as 40 per cent. This was due in part to a demand for extra terminals, perhaps indicating a move towards more integrated systems than had previously been the case.

Perhaps the greatest revolution in hotel computerization recently has been the change in attitude of the suppliers, who are now paying attention to smaller hotels that require small microcomputer systems. The early investment of the large hotels has been crucial to this revolution as they could be said to have paid for the evolution of the microsystems which were largely developed from their mainframe and minicomputer systems.

One statistic that should be borne in mind is that Britain has the highest ownership of microcomputers per head of population in the world. Unfortunately there is very little evidence in this country of innovation with microcomputers in an office situation and it has been argued that our basic home computers may have hindered instead of helping the development of positive attitudes to computer-based business systems (Gamble, 1986).

The situation in the United States

By 1987 there were more than 50 separate property management systems on offer to hoteliers in the United States thereby giving a huge choice for potential purchasers to examine. At the International Hotel/Motel & Restaurant Show in November 1986 it was apparent that a number of trends were appearing which centred specifically on enhancements. As the European market closely follows that in the United States it is of interest to examine these trends which were to affect European systems shortly afterwards:

- property management systems that interfaced with televisions in guest bedrooms to provide in-room check-out and electronic display of messages via the guest room television

- 'Lost and Found' modules within the computer software to provide the hotel with the capability to record the description of a lost/found item, the date, the location, and the name of the individual who lost (or found) the item

- a maintenance module that allowed the hotel to track the maintenance schedule of rooms, equipment and furniture

- automated credit-card approval during registration

- automatic checking of previous accounts when a reservation is made by an individual or company to see if any balance is outstanding (the same process to take place during check-in)

- increased emphasis on 'HELP' menus or tutorial screens to ease the operation of a computer and simplify the entry of data

- increased flexibility in group modules to maintain more information on groups and to allow all billing combinations to be handled with ease

Future work by systems manufacturers also seemed to be concentrating on marketing information, electronic mail facilities and employee timekeeping (Mable, 1987).

Fast-food outlets

The vast majority of fast-food outlets are small, private businesses such as the corner fish and chip shop or high street Chinese take-away, and though they have sufficient money to invest in electronic cash registers they can rarely afford, or need to contemplate, complete computerization. Where computers were accepted from the outset in fast-food was amongst the national chains, such as the American-style hamburger restaurants.

This section of the fast-food industry is, like computers, a new industry and it has grown up alongside computerization. It exists in an atmosphere of stiff competition and makes use of uninhibited management who are not specialist caterers but hard-headed business people needing swift access to information for control as well as marketing. The standardization of the products provided meant that computerization techniques could be readily adapted from other industries.

Certainly the few statistics available make it quite plain that it is in the fast-food chains that computerization is most common. With America being the leader in the adoption of such technology it was estimated that most of the 80,000 fast-food outlets in the United States were using computer systems by the mid 1980s.

Interestingly, in America computerization in fast-food has centred largely on point-of-sale systems to date with little emphasis being placed on management back office functions. Indeed companies such as McDonald's have deliberately avoided managers undertaking management control and prefer them to be working with their staff and customers. Some organizations have moved management control away from individual units into regional or head offices whilst in others, like Burger King, managers are in control of their units utilizing computer generated information.

It is apparent from research undertaken in the United States in 1986 by Restaurants & Institutions magazine that the chain restaurant and fast-food sectors intended to invest further in computer systems (Tougas, 1986).

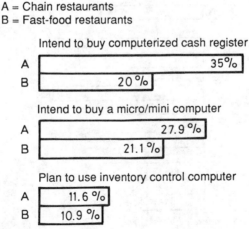

A = Chain restaurants
B = Fast-food restaurants

Intend to buy computerized cash register

A 35%
B 20%

Intend to buy a micro/mini computer

A 27.9%
B 21.1%

Plan to use inventory control computer

A 11.6%
B 10.9%

Figure 1.7 *Computer purchasing intentions of chain restaurant and fast-food restaurants in 1986*

Restaurants

The vast majority of restaurants are privately and independently run and therefore computerization has made little penetration. Similar to the fast-food sector, it is the steak, pizza and spaghetti houses grouped together into chains that have reaped the benefits of computerization.

In the early 1980s the BHRCA polled its members to see what the most popular restaurant applications of computers were at that time and they turned out to be (BHRCA, 1980):

- guest billing
- dish costing
- sales analysis
- business accounting
- stock control
- payroll

Restaurants & Institutions magazine took the examination of restaurant computer systems a stage further in the United States by undertaking a survey into what computers were actually used for. In looking at both hotel and institutional users who possessed computer systems they established the following information:

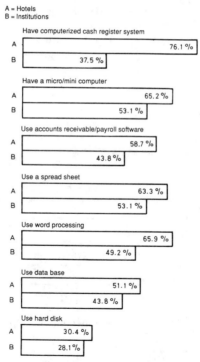

Figure 1.8   *Computer use by restaurants and institutions (Tougas, 1986)*

It was apparent from the Restaurants & Institutions survey that restaurateurs of the hotel and institutional variety were the most widespread and versatile of computer users. From the graphs it is interesting to note that the most popular computing tool in hotels was the computerized cash register which was used by 76.1 per cent of respondents. In the institutional sector a micro or minicomputer was the most common hardware and the spreadsheet the most commonly used application.

Industrial catering

Whilst computers have been used at the head offices of industrial catering firms, they tend not to have been utilized by the large number of scattered operational units. There is obviously the potential to install computers at each location and to network these together, thereby reducing bureaucracy and the need for regional administration which is common in industrial catering companies. It is particularly interesting to see that large scale caterers have explored information technology more than any other type of caterer.

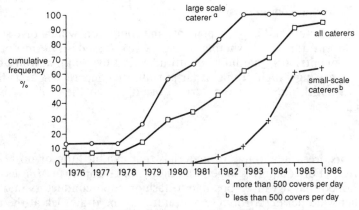

Figure 1.9 *Diffusion of information technology in catering (Whitaker, 1986)*

Welfare catering

Whilst the National Health Service has a policy of encouraging computerization, the practicalities and bureaucracy involved in implementing this have led to relatively few catering departments actually taking up the technology that is available. This is a problem when one considers that as long ago as 1970 the catering department of a new Swedish university hospital had, like all the other hospital departments, a computer link which provided information about each patient.

> Information technology is a very recent development in welfare catering; only 10 per cent of NHS hospital catering departments have adopted the technology to date [December 1984] (Whitaker, 1984)

Where they do exist in hospital catering computers are generally employed to assist in the reduction of costs and particularly to help cut down food wastage. There is, however, a massive potential market for microcomputer systems, as illustrated by the following extract:

> There are currently an estimated 200 microcomputer based catering systems in use in the NHS representing 10% of all hospitals or 16% of the potential market of 1,250 hospitals where systems could be justified. Put another way, 80% plus of the market remains untapped. (Chambers, 1985)

Pubs

Whilst all pubs have been used to the managerial aspects of tills for many years, the change to computerized electronic systems has taken some time to occur. Programmable cash registers have started to become common but systems possessing stock control facilities are by no means common and manufacturers of automatic drink dispensing systems have found the UK market very difficult. The lack of penetration of computers can be seen in a 1985 estimate that only 2.5 per cent of UK pubs and restaurants possessed an EPOS system. This figure was likely to treble by 1988 (Whitehall, 1985).

The future of catering computers

The future of computers and in particular catering computers will involve some major changes in current thinking, whether these be expressed in terms of different computer components, work methods, or attitudes. It is evident that whilst computers will have an increasingly high profile as far as staff are concerned, guests themselves will be exposed much more to computerized facilities that they will be expected to operate themselves.

Superconductors

Superconductors are a new range of materials that exhibit little or no resistance to electrical current. For computers in general, they could mean an enormous increase in speed. It is hoped that it will be possible to fashion superconductors into wires and then chips that will operate at room temperature, as the drawback at the moment is that they only operate in very cold conditions (−180 degrees Centigrade). Research continues to develop superconductors that will work effectively at room temperature.

Integrated microcomputers

The future of the catering computer revolves primarily around the increasing use of microcomputers, thanks to their reducing cost, and on the improvements in communication between micros that have already come and are coming. No longer will there be a large number of separate devices operating independently within the same establishment and relying on manual communication, but all the caterer's systems will be fully integrated.

The microcomputer will be allowed much more freedom within the catering business being left operational at night collecting information from remote terminals and creating reports, much as a night auditor might do now, ready for assimilation by staff when they arrive on duty the next morning.

Cards and guest activated technology

The credit card is already playing a large part in the new technological systems that operate in hotels, whether these involve EFTPOS terminals or automatic check-in systems. In the future it is certain that guests will use their own credit cards or 'smart cards' as keys to their rooms, thereby removing the current necessity to produce a 'key', whether this be a card or not, for a guest.

Cards will become increasingly commonplace in catering applications such as cashless vending
Photograph: GiroVend Cashless Systems

Automatic guest check-in systems will become accepted more when credit cards and smart cards are the main method of payment.
Photograph: ERS Technologies inc.

Systems such as the automatic guest check-in will become familiar features as an alternative to full-service facilities in some hotels as the next step toward the 'electronic hotel' of the future. Systems like this become more feasible once credit and smart cards are accepted as the main method of payment but until that happens the existing members of staff will be quite safe in their employment.

In-room facilities

It is by no means certain that a computer will sprout in every hotel bedroom in the short term. There has already been a move away from this trend in the United States but at that time computers were not as common in the home and office as they are now.

In the longer term computers will become a commonplace hotel room facility and research by *Hotel & Motel Management* magazine in the United States has already given an indication of the most popular uses to which they will be put by business travellers.

Table 1.2   *The in-room guest computer*

What the business traveller wants it to have	
FEATURE	CITEDBY
Word processing	71.1%
Self check-out	66.7%
Listing of nearby restaurants	64.4%
Ability to make hotel reservations	55.6%
Room service menu	53.3%
Ability to make airline reservations	35.6%
Video games	33.3%

Source: H&MM Survey (Romeo, 1984)

Networks

It will become commonplace for cash registers to be linked directly to a microcomputer that collates the customer's bill, whilst also allowing the consequent compilation of such information as stock control and sales analysis. It will also be possible for this information to be sent direct along a network to head office to facilitate total corporate management.

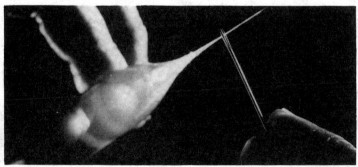

Up to a dozen fibre optic cables can fit through the eye of a needle
Photograph: Westminster Cable TV

Networks will be linked by many more optical fibre cables which provide the most compact and also the best current medium for transmitting data.

Networks themselves will expand as services such as British Telecom's Packet Switched System (PSS) are used much more heavily as well as the X-stream network which is specifically designed to carry computer data cheaply.

Televisions

The next few years will see a great expansion of the use of television sets in the home for placing reservations. The potential customer will be able to use their television set to communicate directly with central reservations facilities, whether corporate or run by a marketing consortium, in addition to the more common media of telephone and telex.

There is nothing particularly new about the potential guest using the home television as services such as Prestel have utilized this communication medium for some time, but what will be new is the sophistication of the computerized service that is offered. A customer will be able to identify themselves by a personal identification number (PIN) which will tell the computer system what type of customer they are and what tariff structure is applicable to them. From the PIN number the system can identify whether the full rack rate for rooms applies, or whether a discount is allowed to that customer individually or to their organization.

The customer will then be able to either select a specific hotel from the available list, or to input criteria for their stay and ask the computer to suggest suitable hotels. Such criteria as price bands, standard of hotel, geographical location and amenities might be included. The computer will then display a selection of hotels and back up this information with video guides to help the customer make their choice.

If specific types of room have been requested then video pictures of the actual room being reserved will be available along with similar illustrations of facilities, view from the room, etc. The display will include rates for the dates concerned and information on such details as bargain breaks that might be applicable. Finally, the customer will be able to confirm the reservation and pay a deposit, if required, by using their credit card number.

All this will be possible from the seclusion of the guest's lounge in their home or wherever they keep their television. It could even be that business travellers will book their next hotel from the hotel room they are about to vacate.

Continued improvements

Catering establishments will continue to enhance the computerized facilities they already possess to the benefit of both staff and guests. Indeed the increased competitiveness of the business world in which they find themselves will force a continued updating of computer facilities.

References

Accountancy, January 1981. Hotel accounting: here's a 'maid-of-all-work'.

Alvarez, R., Ferguson, D. H. F. and Dunn, J., November 1983. How not to automate your front office. *Cornell Hotel and Restaurant Administration Quarterly*.

BAHA, March 1981. BHRCA/Scicon computer system tailored to smaller hotel. *British Hotelier and Restaurateur*.

Barnes, P., January 1978. Solihull's St John's Hotel leaps into the computer age. *British Hotelier and Restaurateur*.

BHRCA, July/August 1980. Microprocessors and the small business. *British Hotelier and Restaurateur*.

Braham, Bruce, December 1985. New technology and hotel accommodation management. Thesis, Bristol Polytechnic.

Brown, N., 1970. Presentation by IBM to Hotel and Catering Institute.

Chambers, J. R., August 1985. *Computer Technology in Hospital Catering* (booklet).

Concise Oxford Dictionary, 1982. Seventh edition.

Gamble, P., October 1986. Technology: host to the future. In *Computer Solutions for Hotel & Catering*.

Hodge, E., March 1980. Microprocessors. *British Hotelier and Restaurateur*.

Mable, Cynthia A., 12 January 1987. New property management systems offer many features. *Hotel & Motel Management*.

Romeo, Peter, November 1984. Whatever happened to in-room computers? *Hotel & Motel Management*.

Tougas, Jane Grant, 25 June 1986. Why computers make dollars and sense. *Restaurants & Institutions*.

Whitaker, Marian, 1984. *The Impact of Information Technology on the Hotel and Catering Industry*. Brighton Polytechnic.

Whitaker, Marian, December 1986. *Survey into the use of Information Technology in the Hotel and Catering Industry*. Brighton Polytechnic.

Whitehall, Bruce, September 1985. Bar management on the brink. *Caterer and Hotelkeeper*.

2 Computer Applications in Food and Beverage

COMPUTERS AND FOOD AND BEVERAGE

One of the major problems of the hotel and catering industry is that food and beverages are extremely difficult commodities to control, both physically and economically, and are also difficult to market precisely. The main constituents of the catering business, food and drink, provide complex consumption problems with varying shelf lives and perishability, and furthermore they 'disappear' once consumed. Most stock managers in other industries would recoil in horror at the problems of controlling the myriad of widely differing commodities one finds in catering.

Whilst there are no systems as yet that can accurately count the number of beans, say, being dispensed on to a guest's plate in a restaurant, there are a wide variety of computerized food and beverage systems to assist mainly in the production of statistics and results once detailed stocktaking has taken place. Their main contribution is really with the paperwork involved in food and beverage operations which in the past has been time consuming and labour-intensive.

General features of food and beverage computer systems

Stock control

The central part of any food and beverage system is stock control. A typical system will require information on every single ingredient and unit of food and beverage sold by the establishment, as well as the quantities being used. In addition, the exact costs and values of stock must be held, and full details of all suppliers. The information held will enable precise calculations to be made of the daily usage of each stock item, which can be used to provide sales comparisons and analyses of transfers, requisitions and returns.

With details of suppliers held centrally the accuracy of deliveries against orders may be checked as well as the prices charged so that problems can be identified rapidly. Minimum stock levels can be set so that the system warns automatically when re-ordering needs to take place.

The system may be set up to produce stock sheets automatically, including the opening balance taken from previous stocktaking reports, thereby reducing the opportunities for copying errors.

Control of revenue

Stock control in itself goes a long way towards controlling revenue but there are other problems to consider such as breakages, losses and 'Happy Hours'. All of these present difficulties in calculation, but may easily be identified or catered for by a computerized system.

Returned containers

If catering managers actually examined how much money they lose by writing-off or ignoring returnable containers like bottles, for example, they would frighten themselves. Some computerized food and beverage systems have recognized this and allow for the recording of such containers and the charge which needs to be recovered.

Price changes

Price changes occur for several reasons, such as changes in government duties, revisions of VAT rates, suppliers' increases – possibly due to the seasonality of some stock items. Whatever the cause, price changes are a major headache to catering managers. A computerized system can considerably ease the problems associated with price changes. The stock, for example, that was bought at the old price can be identified by the computer and revisions costed in swiftly to the stock sheets and price lists.

The main benefit of a computerized food and beverage system is that it can greatly improve the mathematical accuracy of food and beverage control. With most systems the information needed to compile statistics only has to be entered once, so duplication of work is largely eliminated, as are the often untidy handwritten records. The computer system will undoubtedly hold a greater quantity of information in accessible form than the corresponding manual system, thus enabling the catering manager to make fast decisions. A computer will be capable of producing word processed forms for operations such as stocktaking, and will also retain details of recipes, ingredients and prices for a large number, perhaps hundreds, of dishes and cocktails. The major benefit, however, is in the time saved when maintaining and calculating stock details and accounting for price increases. The complete system will provide precision information for sales use and future forecasting.

Catering Information Systems

Computerized Catering Information Systems (CIS) allow management fast access to accurate costings where food is concerned. Such a level of control was not possible with a manual system because so much information is involved that any conclusions drawn manually were out of date by the time they were actually produced. Indeed, in pre-computer days food and beverage managers sweated for hours over paperwork, often producing very limited and meaningless statistics that had been overtaken by events. The benefits of a CIS system include:

- more accurate information
- quicker access to that information
- improved control of costs

A typical CIS utilized in a hospital is described on page 71. Similar systems are found in many other catering outlets and they are all generally based on the same principles.

A Catering Information System typically has a database that contains all the recipes used in the catering outlet together with the individual ingredients costed up-to-date. The CIS calculates all the necessary menu costings and summarizes the requisitions needed from the stores having taken into account production forecasts. The planning of menus can be undertaken, as can stock control for both the central stores and any 'satellite' kitchens. Current and historical analyses of sales can be produced and eventually used for sales forecasting while variances in production costs can be identified.

One of the main problems of introducing a CIS is that the database can take an enormous length of time to establish: a period of several months is not uncommon. In addition, there may have to be changes to existing working methods to enable standard recipes to be established. It can be quite a problem to compare amounts of goods issued by central stores with the measuring of ingredients that a chef undertakes instinctively. How large, for example, is 'a pinch' or 'a handful' as far as the computer is concerned?

It is recognized that a CIS is more suited to a large, institutional and standardized catering operation than to an à la carte restaurant where dishes and policies change much more frequently. Caterers operating the latter type of restaurant have argued that a CIS would be far too constraining.

HOW CAN COMPUTERS HELP THE OPERATION OF A RESTAURANT?

In recent years computers have become much more common in restaurants whether they be the fast-food variety or the fine dining room. Systems vary in configuration from single microcomputers to intelligent point-of-sale terminals integrated into extensive networks.

Research has been undertaken in the United States by *Restaurants and Institutions* magazine to quantify the uses to which restaurateurs put their computers in various categories of establishment. The results are summarized in the following graphs (Tougas, 1986).

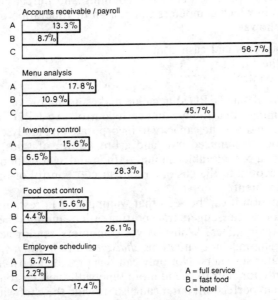

Figure 2.1   *What does software do for the restaurateur?*

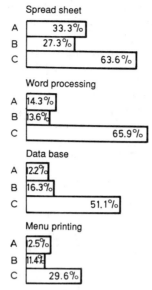

Figure 2.2 *What computer features do restaurateurs use most?*

Point-of-sale (POS) terminals have replaced the mechanical cash registers that were commonplace a decade ago for cash control within a restaurant. Cash control itself is only one of the functions of the new sophisticated POS system that will also monitor exact details of dishes sold, ingredients used, and efficiency of individual members of staff, and even calculate their wages and tips. Back office systems can be integrated with POS terminals to provide detailed accounting and purchasing information.

The major areas in which computers can help in the operation of a restaurant may be identified as follows:

- billing of customers and cash control
- liaison with the kitchen
- management control

An electronic point-of-sale (EPOS) machine makes its major contribution in the first of these areas – billing of customers and cash control. An EPOS machine is quite a powerful computer that has the capacity to incorporate and analyse a large amount of sales data and produce itemized bills and a breakdown of sales, either by dish or payment. This saves a considerable amount of time and aggravation for staff, allowing more time to be devoted to the customer and stricter control of the restaurant to be achieved by management.

On close examination it can be seen that waiting staff in restaurants spend a large amount of their time as messengers transporting orders and food between the kitchen and customers at their tables. Whilst as yet computers cannot actually serve food, other than in vending-machine situations, *liaison with the kitchen* has attracted the attention of computer suppliers. Not only can this provide a cost-effective and time-effective opportunity for staff to spend more time with their customers, serving them with dishes cooked to perfection, but it can also provide the chef with legible orders in the first place.

In a modern computerized restaurant the waiter receives a customer's order and keys this into a terminal. The terminal may be near at hand or may actually be handheld so that the waiter can communicate with the system without even leaving the table. The computer sends the order to the chef and records the financial details on the guest's bill. The waiter can be called through to the kitchen when a course is ready to be served and he can also alert the chef when the next course is required. Throughout the meal drinks and additional items are added to the bill so that a complete account is instantly ready for the guest on departure.

The third main area where a computer can help is in analysing the sales information fed into the system by waiting staff, thus facilitating strict *management control*. Total payments can be shown by different methods so that an exact breakdown of the turnover achieved during a particular meal can be readily available for management within minutes of the close of business. The system will show exactly how many sales each member of staff achieved and which dishes were the most popular during the meal. Furthermore, the system can be further developed to use the sales information for stock control, alerting management to the need to replace stock used and even printing out the order if required.

In the back office management may have the benefit of a wide variety of reports which may include the following (McDermid, 1986):

- revenue statistics
- sales analysis
- inventory usage
- labour costs
- server's productivity
- profitability

In a hotel the restaurant system may be linked to the front office systems so that meals are automatically added on to guest's room accounts, thus obviating such problems as guests checking-out before their breakfast charges have been added to their bills.

Trends

As far as configurations of equipment are concerned, the latest and most effective systems demonstrate the linking of microcomputers to point-of-sale terminals thereby giving a network all the potential of the microcomputer.

The microcomputer may be harnessed in a variety of ways depending on the requirement of the restaurateur concerned. In a single-site operation the microcomputer may be needed to undertake the traditional back office tasks including payroll, accounting, ledger work and menu preparation, as well as monitoring the point-of-sale terminals. On some PCs it is possible to convert food bought into a restaurant into portions sold so that exact calculations of ingredients may be analysed, thereby very closely controlling wastage. Where the profitability of a restaurant may depend on reducing costs by very small amounts, this ability to identify potential waste may be vital to the continued existence of the business.

Where the installation is in a chain of restaurants, the unit manager may only need to undertake limited functions with the PC, such as the immediate handling of cash, whilst detailed accounting takes place via the microcomputer at the regional or head office.

Whatever the system configuration it is notable that software is all the time becoming more user-friendly. This is an increasingly important consideration when purchasing a computer system of this type, especially for establishments where staff turnover is high and training is therefore a constant process.

Essential features

In selecting a system suitable for a restaurant there are a number of essential features that must be borne in mind. Whilst it is obvious that a point-of-sale system will improve control over order entry, cash, productivity, stock and management reporting, there are also some other important features to watch out for:

- The system must be totally reliable and whilst a system conforming to this description probably does not exist it is essential that the restaurant is not brought to a halt by the computer 'going down' regularly. It is wise to buy from a recognized supplier who can provide prompt back-up and maintenance.
- The system must be expandable and thereby capable of growing with the business both in size and functionality so that it does not become obsolete.
- The system must possess software that can be readily updated to allow for changes in price structures and menus.
- Preferably, the system should be compatible with existing equipment used for data processing so that investment in equipment is protected.
- If the restaurant is part of a group there must be the ability to transmit information to head office so that a total picture of the business may be drawn.

It should be remembered that a restaurant computer system will be expected to function in a hostile environment. There will undoubtedly be electrical interference, erratic power, humidity, grease and dust, all of which can cause problems in themselves but when mixed together can add up to a distinctly hostile environment for the computer. Specialist restaurant computer suppliers have long since recognized this and have built their hardware with these problems in mind. Some insist on using fibre optic cabling as opposed to electrical cables as the light they transmit is not subject to power fluctuations or interference from fans, compressors or electrical signals.

CASE STUDY NUMBER 1

RESTAURANTS BENEFIT FROM IN-HOUSE COMPUTER

A small American 17-restaurant franchise operation has definitely found the benefit of computerization and the company controller is also able to give firm advice to anyone contemplating computerization. "Don't take short-cuts," he says. "Take the time to do a detailed feasibility study. Talk to users. And make sure to check out maintenance and system support costs."

The company is certain that the computer arrangement has added $100,000 to their profits and it is therefore there to stay. In achieving these substantially improved profit figures the customer has not been forgotten. "We want our managers to devote their time to guests," says the company controller. "We believe that extra attention to the customer will increase sales. Because of this, we need information from the field that doesn't require a lot of manager time."

"It's virtually impossible for a manager with pencil and paper to follow raw materials and staff through his operation and still manage his restaurant," says the computer consultant attached to the company. He argues that many restaurant operators make most of their decisions on the basis of too little information and that is why restaurants have one of the highest business failure rates in America.

Originally the company utilized a computer service bureau but the arrangement did not work as it was felt that the company were paying "a tremendous amount of money for very little information." A year was then spent researching in-house systems applicable to restaurants. Some suppliers offered to re-write software from other business sectors but the company realized that this was not the answer. "Food service is totally different from other manufacturing environments," states the company controller. "We needed software written by someone who knew about restaurants."

The user-friendly system eventually selected has the capability to undertake payroll, general ledger, sales analysis, recipe costing and inventory management.

The recipe costing program has proved a great benefit. "We used to know only how much we had spent on bakery products in the course of a month," says the controller. "Now we have been able to refine our controls to the point where we spend 2.5 per cent on bakery products. If a statement says we spent 2.7 per cent or 2.8 per cent then we look into it."

The sales analysis program allows the company management to see restaurant by restaurant or shift by shift which menu items contribute the highest financial amount to a given day's sales. It also compiles sales histories on individual menu items and calculates how the menu mix at a given restaurant affects its sales and profits.

"The inventory control program shows us exactly how much of an ingredient we should be using compared to how much we are using," says the controller. "This gives us an extremely fine edge on inventory control. We used to spend a couple of weeks going through more than 160 single menu items, breaking down every single recipe. By the time we finished, all the prices would have changed." The computer now runs a recipe cost report in half an hour. (*Restaurants & Institutions*, 1982)

Kitchen liaison

The fact that restaurant staff need to communicate table orders to and eventually fetch those orders from a kitchen has been of primary interest to new technology suppliers from the outset of computerized restaurant systems. It is a simple fact that this aspect of the job wastes a lot of time, even when all runs smoothly. At other times waiting staff make that often long and tortuous walk out to the servery to pick up their tray full of dishes only to find that the order is not ready. The waiter or waitress then has to decide whether to loiter until everything is prepared or to go back to look after other tables and return to the kitchen for a second attempt later on.

Ideally management want their staff to be at the guest's side for as long as possible as this generates more business: time spent walking to and from kitchens is 'dead time' that could be better utilised. In the ideal restaurant the waiting staff will be readily available to deal with the whims of customers rather than disappearing behind the scenes into the kitchen leaving their customers temporarily stranded. Any system, therefore, whether computerized or not that can make the restaurant ordering process more efficient will attract the attention of caterers.

It should be recognized too that chefs, who cannot see the restaurant, have a difficult task in providing the dishes that they have been asked for at the ideal moment. The only guide they have to help them may be a pile of individual orders and it is largely down to their intuition as to when they serve them. They will invariably receive a complete listing of each particular table's requirements but they have to choose when to present these at the servery. They are faced with the decision as to whether they serve the food up when the waiter actually comes and asks for the dish, which will invariably keep the waiter hanging about for a period of 'dead time' but at least guarantees that the food is freshly prepared. Or alternatively chefs can guess how long the guests will take to eat their meals and anticipate orders by having them ready at the servery in advance of the arrival of the waiter, which risks spoiling the food if the estimate was incorrect.

In the ideal restaurant the whole system will run at the speed at which the customer wants to eat. In reality it is too often the chef or the waiter, who are frequently totally out of touch with each other, who decide how fast a meal will be eaten. No two customers are the same: some want to linger over their meal, whilst others eat quickly perhaps because they have an appointment to keep: some guests are called away to the phone during their meal, and at times it seems that all the customers want to select from the sweet trolley at the same moment. A restaurant system is therefore often a perfect example of *management by crisis* and anything that can improve communication between the waiting staff and that invisible chef will be well received.

The computerized answers that are on offer include linking cash registers to the kitchen whereby the chef can be prompted to have the next course ready, or alternatively a waiter may be called to the kitchen by the use of a radio-pager.

Auto-call systems

The Auto-call system involves visual display communication between staff in the restaurant and kitchen. The paged prompts that are displayed by the system either alert waiters that their table's next dish is ready, or tell the chef that the next course for a particular table is required.

An Auto-call may be supplied as part of an overall computerized restaurant system or as a stand-alone operation. They rely on display stations being placed strategically around the restaurant and kitchen: messages are input through a call station. The display station may refer to a particular area of the restaurant or may display information on food orders for the whole restaurant. There are sometimes chimes attached to the display to draw attention to it and/or the message will flash after a period of time if the order has not been collected.

Whilst the Auto-call system described above was originally intended for two-way communication between chefs and waiting staff, it can be used to facilitate communication elsewhere in an establishment, for example between reception and housekeeping. The next development of the system is to connect it into a radio network thereby dispensing with the wiring.

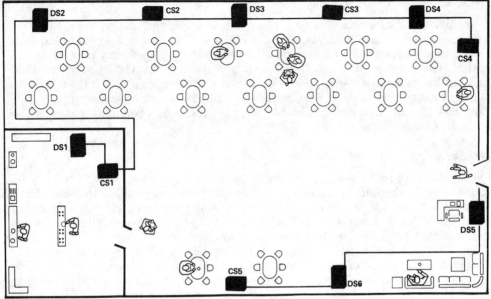

Figure 2.3 *Multi location configuration for an automated call system*
Source: Monitor Auto-call
DS = display station
CS = call station

The chef's call station on the right has just displayed the fact that a meal is ready for table 36 on the restaurant display station on the left
Photograph: Monitor Auto-call

Assisting customer/staff communication

A further modification of this type of system can facilitate better communication between customers and the restaurant staff. A small call station can be fitted to each table so that when customers require additional service they simply press their call button. This displays their table number on a display station. If the customers wish, they can key in a particular request, such as ordering more wine or asking for the bill. It is claimed by the supplier, who conducted a survey of such a system with a major catering company, that this idea could boost that company's liquor sales alone by an extra 10 per cent (Hughes, 1986/87).

Handheld restaurant terminals

One of the more recent additions to the array of computer equipment on offer to the restaurateur is the handheld terminal which takes the computer to the side of the customer's table. The idea is that the whole existing paperwork ordering system can be replaced by a remote computer link thereby speeding up service whilst at the same time maintaining a constant link with the computer.

In some people's minds the idea of a computer beside each customer's table conjured up the image of a VDU and associated wiring sitting on a trolley alongside the host, but nothing could be further from the truth. The handheld terminals are little bigger than a calculator and are capable of communicating with the computer by one of three methods:

- by plugging into a nearby order point
- by radio control
- by infra-red technology

All of these systems have an outwardly similar palm-of-the-hand battery-operated terminal. The first type operate by being plugged into a Rapid Order System Point Of Delivery (ROSPOD), several of which would be strategically placed around the restaurant. The ROSPOD is in effect a 'socket' providing a direct link to the computer. When the waiter takes an order at a table, it is recorded within the memory of the handheld terminal. At completion of the order the terminal is plugged into a ROSPOD and interrogated by the main computer. The computer then sends details to the chef of dishes that need to be cooked and also starts to compile the bill.

The radio-controlled handheld systems have the advantage that communication can take place with the host computer from immediately alongside the customer's table. The systems depend upon uncluttered radio reception and prove particularly useful in remote food service areas some distance from the kitchen. Such areas might include terraces and swimming pool areas. The concept has been readily received in America, and also some Swiss and Italian hotels, where garden lakeside restaurants are on the opposite side of the road to the hotel itself, have shown great interest in the radio-controlled handheld systems.

Radio transmission is not easy or even possible in every situation. An alternative is infra-red transmission which has been developed by Sanyo in Japan. This system works through a series of sensors fitted throughout the restaurant so that waiting staff are never more than seven metres away – the current range of the sensors. The waiting staff are equipped with handheld infra-red terminals with liquid crystal displays, that are backlit for situations such as candlelit restaurants where they must be read in semi-darkness, and an infra-red light emitting unit. The data is transmitted and picked up by any of the ceiling-mounted sensors which send it direct to the microprocessor.

*Remanco's handheld restaurant terminal providing radio contact
with the restaurant's computer*
Photograph: Bruce Grant-Braham

Restaurant management control

The application of computerization in a restaurant as far as the management is concerned surrounds the possibility of data capture at the point-of-sale. Whilst some restaurant systems have been offered with the principal Central Processing Unit (CPU) linked to non-intelligent terminals, the CPU has invariably only acted as a system driver. There have sometimes been reliability problems and costs have been high where systems have incorporated system specific CPUs. We are therefore going to look at the solutions offered by networked cash registers either linked to a microcomputer or not. We shall then look at restaurant computer systems using non-intelligent terminals.

Point-of-sale cash register network linked to a microcomputer

Modern cash registers are much more sophisticated than just cash tills, having in many cases a memory similar to a microcomputer and a programming facility. It is the keys themselves that are programmable: they may be 'preset' to remember information about a particular item in addition to its price. If an item is not included in the preset keys it may be accessed by referring to a 'price look up' (PLU) number. This is a reference number or code assigned to each individual item which is entered on the cash register for data retrieval. Many cash registers have sufficient memory to retain in excess of 2,000 PLUs.

Point-of-sale cash registers possess the facility to be networked: the usual configuration would be a 'master' till coordinating a number of 'slave' tills which may be widely dispersed throughout a large establishment. The information collected during a service period is collated by the master till which analyses the number of items sold, the number of customers, and the average spend, and thereby provides all the data necessary for efficient stock production and cash control, which allows a rapid response to customer requirements.

A problem of using networked tills in this way, however, is that with some systems whilst the master till is operating as a cash collecting machine it cannot always be operated as a generator of reports. Consolidated reports from all tills may be slow to produce, and may only be accessible from the master till's internal audit. In many cases, the data then has to be entered by hand on to a recording system which may be either manual or computerized.

Slow feedback from the tills in the various restaurant outlets has the knock-on effect of slowing down the efficiency of any centralized stock control and production planning system. Exact consumption figures can become tedious to determine, leading to production schedules falling behind and discrepancies being overlooked.

A microcomputer linked to a cash register for stock control purposes
Photograph: *Caterer & Hotelkeeper*

It has therefore been found beneficial to insert a microcomputer into the network of tills, linking it directly with the master till. The advantages are threefold bringing improvements in:

- operational control
- financial control
- catering control

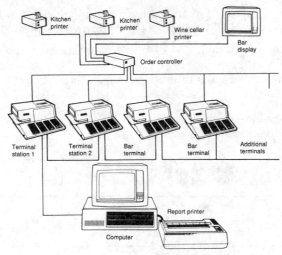

Figure 2.4 *Microcomputer-monitored restaurant system capable of expansion*
Source: *Micros Systems Inc.*

Operational Control is fully achieved from the computer terminal providing the following facilities:

- All dishes on the cash register may be priced from the central computer terminal.
- PLU number and caption updates may be carried out whenever necessary.
- 'Floating' preset keys (Main Course 1, etc.) may be reset before each meal to accommodate a large changing menu cycle, making for ease of operation during pressure periods.
- All till transactions are accessible from the central computer, so that activity and cash reports for individual tills, with cash in drawer as required, may be obtained without the need to visit each till.
- Cashing up and zeroing may be carried out from a central point.

Table 2.1 shows a sample daily sales analysis of a five-till network:

Table 2.1 *Sample daily sales analysis*

| | The University of Newtown | | | 04/04 | | | |
| | Daily sales analysis by till | | | | | | |
Till No.	Gross Receipts	Cash Receipts	Cash in Drawer	Voids Credits	No. of Sales	No. of Customers	Average spend Per Customer
1	274.40	268.54	268.54	0.00	3	220	1.24
2	197.40	178.90	172.25	6.65	2	204	0.97
3	223.60	207.43	202.43	5.00	0	127	1.71
4	454.67	433.22	433.22	0.00	1	372	1.22
5	103.94	100.46	97.96	2.50	0	164	0.63
Total:	1,254.01	1,188.55	1,174.40	14.15	6	1,087	1.05

Source: Fretwell-Downing Computer Group

Financial control is improved as transactions are immediately recorded and easily accessible, giving the financial manager all the information needed such as:

- gross profit percentages taking VAT into account for each and every menu item and each cash register
- consolidated reports of gross profit percentage achieved overall for each trading period

Table 2.2 shows a sample financial breakdown of one serving session:

Table 2.2 *Sample activity report*

<table>
<tr><td colspan="8" align="center">**The University of Newtown**   04/04
Activity report for tills – total sales this meal-time</td></tr>
<tr><th>PLU</th><th>Ingredient/
Recipe Code</th><th>Description</th><th>Selling
Price</th><th>Number
Sold</th><th>Total
Income</th><th>Cost
Price</th><th>Gross
Profit
%</th></tr>
<tr><td>1</td><td>a02</td><td>Steak Pie</td><td>0.75</td><td>40</td><td>30.00</td><td>16.00</td><td>38.67</td></tr>
<tr><td>3</td><td>b05</td><td>Chips</td><td>0.25</td><td>50</td><td>12.50</td><td>7.50</td><td>31.00</td></tr>
<tr><td>4</td><td>d11</td><td>Beef Salad</td><td>0.75</td><td>55</td><td>41.25</td><td>19.25</td><td>46.33</td></tr>
<tr><td>6</td><td>d13</td><td>Moussaka</td><td>0.90</td><td>32</td><td>28.80</td><td>17.60</td><td>29.71</td></tr>
<tr><td>7</td><td>e12</td><td>Coffee</td><td>0.30</td><td>75</td><td>22.50</td><td>9.00</td><td>53.99</td></tr>
<tr><td>11</td><td>e21</td><td>Tea</td><td>0.20</td><td>40</td><td>8.00</td><td>4.00</td><td>42.53</td></tr>
</table>

Source: Fretwell-Downing Computer Group

Catering control is achieved as, after each service period, data is downloaded for immediate analysis and update of the catering management goods control system. In addition:

- menu items are 'exploded' by an automatic process to produce a comparison of theoretical with actual consumption at ingredient level
- individual menu uptake analysis enables ongoing production planning, thus increasing the cost-effectiveness of any computerized catering operation

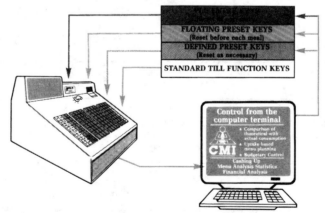

Figure 2.5 *Point-of-sale data capture using a microcomputer linked to a 'master' cash register*
Source: Fretwell-Downing Computer Group

Networked cash registers

Many restaurant systems involve purely networked cash registers which are in effect terminals possessing their own memory and 'intelligence'.

A typical terminal/register will have over 80 programmable keys capable of handling complex menus with many hundreds of PLU numbers, as well as at least a 12-character menu item descriptor that provides a detailed bill for customers and for staff reference. The built-in memory in each terminal/register will retain all the server and sales data for the entire operation so if one terminal is removed from the operation vital information will not be lost.

Where these terminal/registers are useful is that they are quite capable of bridging the gap between systems using a microcomputer and the old-fashioned cash register. When networked they allow the opportunity to send information to kitchen printers thereby handling the important feature of kitchen liaison. They have the flexibility to handle unusual situations such as special food preparation requests, no-charges or cancelled orders, and provide comprehensive reports that reveal the efficiency of each server. Where control is concerned discrepancies between meals prepared and charged may be spotted and for market analysis the numbers of customers served during specific time periods as well as specific menu items and categories sold can be analysed. This information, as already appreciated, allows management to control labour costs, manage the stock more effectively and increase the average spend per head.

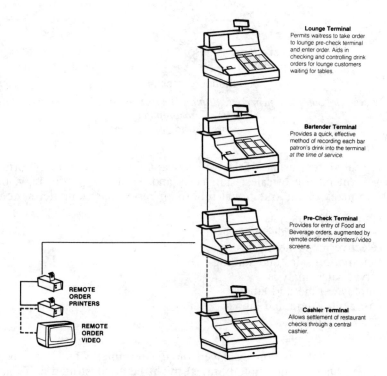

Figure 2.6   *A typical terminal/register network*
Source: Micros Systems Inc.

Restaurant computer systems using non-intelligent terminals

The main difference in these systems is in whether the non-intelligent terminals possess VDUs or not.

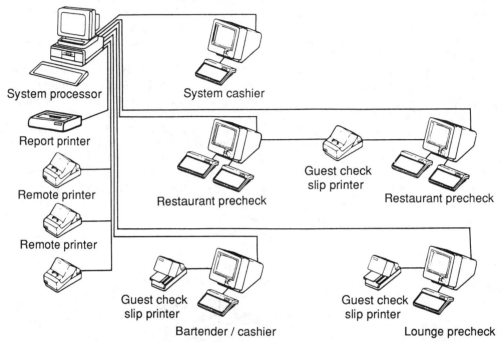

Figure 2.7   *Sample system configuration of a system using VDU terminals linked to a microcomputer*
Source: Micros Systems Inc.

A typical system using VDUs will be capable of generating reports to keep the management on top of sales, staff costs and employee productivity, and also give access to many of the traditional reports of restaurant computer systems such as:

- system sales analysis
- revenue centre sales analysis
- selective menu item sales
- time period sales and staffing
- server sales analysis
- employee time and labour
- cost centre time and labour
- open bills listing
- cashier balancing

The sort of information displayed on the terminal VDU (or precheck as it is sometimes called in the United States) might be as illustrated in Table 2.3.

On this sample VDU screen the server (Kathleen Jones) has just entered a new item (1 Fresh Fruit) which appears both on the 'electronic' guest bill on the left of the

Table 2.3 *Sample display whilst a transaction is in progress*

11 Garden Room Prechecker #2			Transaction	Jones
1 Dewars	2.75	*	Enter Item	
Water		*		
1 Glass Rose	2.25	*		
1 Shrimp Cocktail	4.75	*	1 Fresh Fruit	1.95
1 Escargot	5.50	*		15 Kathleen
1 Filet Mignon	12.95	*		
Medium Rare		*	Chk 1234 Tbl 125	Grp 1 Cov 2
Baked Potato		*	01/15/	07:35pm
1 Chicken Kiev	9.95	*		
Rice Pilaf		*	Subtotal	43.60
1 Cheese Cake	2.50		Tax	2.18
Strawberries	1.00		Charge Tip	.00
1 Fresh Fruit	1.95		Payment	.00
			Total Due	45.78

Source: Micros Systems Inc.

screen and in the 'latest entry' section on the right of the screen. Asterisks identify items previously entered. The great advantage of this type of system is that at any point the server may obtain a complete and accurate transaction picture in detail.

The manager has access to a tremendous amount of detail via the system processor both during a service and at the completion. Amongst the many reports produced would be the Serving Period Sales Report which accurately records the success or otherwise of the particular service period.

In selecting a system with non-intelligent terminals it is wise to examine closely the microcomputer that is being used as the basis of the entire network as there are certain practicalities of today's micro marketplace that need to be borne in mind. It will be a great benefit if the microcomputer is a standard, mass produced off-the-shelf machine as this will give the user access to a vast library of standard software that will be able to help with other tasks within the business. The system will not then be lying idle in the back of the restaurant between service periods: it will be possible to use it for a large number of non-restaurant tasks.

The great advantage of systems with non-intelligent terminals that do not have VDU screens is that the terminals can fit unobtrusively into the restaurant operation so that service staff are never more than a few feet away from access to the computer which is their means of communication with the kitchen and bar. The terminals themselves will be compact, quiet, and resistant to spills, static and heat.

CASE STUDY NUMBER 2

MANAGERS ARE GIVEN TIME TO MANAGE BY THE RESTAURANT COMPUTER IN A LARGE LONDON HOTEL

A large London Hotel was looking for a computerized restaurant system to coincide with the opening of its new Brasserie restaurant to cover all the food and beverage areas of the hotel, ranging from banqueting and room service to the cocktail bar and lounge. The restaurant computer system, which is the largest ever installed by the UK's market leader in such systems, is interfaced directly with the hotel's existing mainframe computer.

The hotel's accountant wanted the system to enable streamlined control throughout the hotel. "Our immediate area of concern was the Brasserie," he recalls, "but it was more cost-effective to do the whole place in one go."

The supplier's systems consultant produced a custom-configured package for the Brasserie and subsequently for the whole hotel arguing that his company does not just put the same package in everywhere but that systems are unique to individual establishments. The Brasserie's system is configured around a 60-cover restaurant with one bar and one kitchen and although the hardware is similar to that in many other establishments the software is the unique part of the restaurant computer. The system is capable of generating more than 20 standard reports but a minimum of three are supplied with each system always including revenue analysis and sales mix.

In April 1986 the Hotel paid £70,000 for the system which boasts a total of 16 printers and 10 terminals in 15 different locations. One special feature is that in the hotel's up-market restaurant use is made of a 'guest check presentation' option that allows the printer to produce a more sophisticated and personalized bill than normal after manual insertion.

The system can cope with as many as 1,400 menu items and one of the major advantages managerially that the hotel has identified is that "the Food and Beverage manager isn't spending 80 per cent of his time finding information, he's spending 80 per cent of his time analysing it." (McDermid, 1986)

To have a terminal close at hand is a great advantage to the service staff as well as to the customer, although the latter may not realize it. In a traditional restaurant the server walks several miles during a shift and spends as much as 60 to 70 per cent of their time away from the guests. With a server terminal nearby this distance and time are cut dramatically as it is possible to communicate directly with the other areas of the operation without losing sight of the guests. All the server has to do is to punch in details of the order which is then transmitted to the kitchen and bars or up to fifteen other preparation areas and does not have to leave the restaurant area until informed by the system that the dishes are ready to collect. As a result either fewer servers can serve the same number of tables, or the same number of servers may handle the same number of tables more comprehensively. Whichever the scenario, the computer may have helped in providing not only improved service but also more satisfaction to guests and happier staff.

First class restaurants, which for some reason are not yet identified with computerization, can benefit as much as any other restaurant as their staff may spend more time on station assessing customer needs and helping with menu choices. Higher sales could be encouraged as a result and also more return visits from customers. In fast-food establishments the turnover of tables may be increased as the throughput of customers speeds up due to the extra efficiency provided by a computerized system.

Mistakes or carelessness by staff, such as forgetting to charge for extra items or charging incorrect amounts, may cost a restaurant a large amount of money. Untidy handwriting and orders given verbally can be confusing and all of these problems may be tackled directly by the use of a computer. Systems are flexible enough to allow for the individual approach of a restaurant operation: they are capable, for example, of communicating the exact method by which a customer wants their steak cooked.

As far as the managers are concerned, whilst coping with a smooth service operation in the restaurant they can feel safe in the knowledge that the computer system is recording every drink and bill by time of day, by table, and by whom served, so that the eventual analysis of the service can be produced easily even if not automatically. The manager is therefore free to satisfy the requests of customers and may not have the old problem of a mountain of paperwork to face at the end of the service period. In a quiet period, however, it may be possible for the manager not only to monitor what is going on in the restaurant but also to complete the daily or weekly reports while the restaurant is operational.

CASE STUDY NUMBER 3

COMPUTER RULES ROUX RESTAURANTS

Rouxl Britannia is a split level 200-table restaurant complex run by Master Chefs Albert and Michel Roux in the centre of a plush office development in the City of London. Having been opened for a short period of time the whole operation was planned around the integral use of a computer system to assist the restaurant, kitchen and bar staff with service as well as to facilitate easier management control.

On the ground floor at pavement level is the popular 'La Restaurant', whilst on a lower level and facing onto a piazza where fountains play is 'Le Café'. Both restaurants and their respective kitchens and bars are serviced by the same computer system. This system allows for eight point-of-sale terminals incorporating bill printers for the use of the waiting staff in each service area, as well as order printers in the bars and kitchen. All are linked to the managerial terminal and processor in the back office.

Being French-inspired the service offered to customers is a modern version of the traditional continental 'Brasserie service' where waiting staff carry their own float and settle the bills. They are subsequently responsible for paying the restaurant the total of their sales, as calculated by the computer, on individual cashing-up sheets. Each member of the waiting staff is therefore responsible for their own money until the completion of service and they have their own cash drawer for security reasons.

Each member of staff is issued with their own key which identifies them and which has to be inserted into a point-of-sale terminal before any orders can be activated. The point-of-sale terminal records their individual transactions in the computer's memory. Staff are therefore free to use the most convenient terminal, but are only able to access the tables that have been 'opened' by their key, and are responsible for 'closing' those tables for cashing-up. Waiting staff are not able to access the table of another member of staff. There is a Management Key which will access all tables, but is obviously only used by the Manager.

When the restaurant managers went for initial training at the supplier's training facility they took a special interest in the layout of keys on the keyboard. "We felt it important to update the layout of the keys when changing our menus," states the manager, "and we feel we have reached an easy-to-use arrangement for our staff. Certainly the dishes and drinks system is picked up very quickly by staff thanks to the layout and colour coding we agreed."

Some customers take a drink at the bar before being allocated a table. The barman records this information into the bar terminal and later, when a table number has been agreed, the waiting staff marry up the drinks information already held in the computer to the new meal bill.

Orders taken from tables are entered sequentially into the nearest terminal. The computer's identification basis for the whole system is the individual table number. To avoid confusion tables in 'Le Restaurant' are coded 0 to 99 and in 'Le Café' 100 to 199. The processor receives the order and automatically sends relevant information to the printers in the bar and kitchen. For the kitchen the processor differentiates between cold and hot food as each have a different preparation area with separate printers. The computer automatically routes orders to the correct printer.

At the conclusion of the meal the waiting staff are able to print a 'customer bill' which records fully each item sold. Upon payment of the bill the waiting staff are able to close the table by identifying the payment method and producing a 'customer receipt' which records date, time, identity of waiting staff, payment method, VAT number, restaurant address, etc.

When a particular printer runs low on paper or if the system at the peak time of service directs too much through it, then that printer will lock. The system then immediately diverts the order to come through the bill printer next to the point-of-sale terminal, thus alerting the waiting staff who will take orders to the preparation area whilst the fault is remedied.

With so many nationalities on the staff it is a benefit that everyone can read the clear print-out and display layout easily. One of the important gains is that the computer removes the need for restaurant cashiers.

For the benefit of management the system will produce a detailed Analysis Report for each service area after each meal, day and week. As far as the management are concerned they often finish late at night and rather than them having to sit through to the early hours compiling manual cashing-up reports the computer will produce a full report by the time they arrive the following morning. A useful facility is the 'Voided Product Report' which shows who made any mistakes, such as the waitress who accidentally ordered 41 bottles of Beaujolais for a table with two covers! The management can monitor the progress of the staff through this facility. The daily reports will also show how much each member of staff has made that day.

The restaurant management feel they have a first-hand knowledge of what is going on in their area but agree that where the computer's reports are particularly useful is in the hands of the boss and the company financial controller at head office. At the moment the system only records sales and income but shortly a stock control program will be added.

As far as problems are concerned the management admit that the computer system has had its teething problems as with any new idea being installed in such a large service area, but apart from being 'overwhelmed' by computer paper and computer jargon the management are pleased with the consequent benefits.

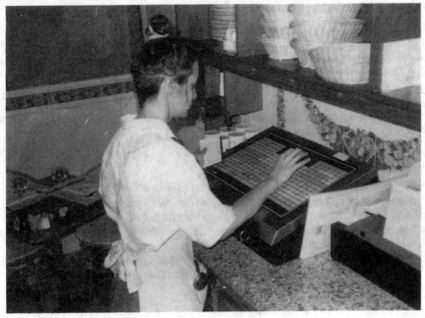

The server's identification key can be clearly
seen inserted into the right-hand side of the terminal
Photograph: Bruce Grant-Braham

COMPUTERS AND KITCHENS

The main uses to which computers are put in kitchens are to help with liaison with the restaurant, to facilitate nutritional analysis and to assist with stock control.

Restaurant liaison

Where many restaurants are concerned there are times when there seem to be as many waiters and waitresses in the kitchen as there should be in the restaurant and in many cases the customers have been totally deserted.

These staff are delivering orders, collecting orders, checking on whether their order is completed, as well as complaining at the kitchen staff that they have received, for example, soup and not grapefruit cocktail as ordered. In some cases they have just come out for a chat whilst their customers wait to be served. A computerized restaurant and kitchen system will eliminate this convergence on the kitchen as the only time that a server needs to be in the kitchen is when an order is actually ready for collection.

The computer will print out a record of the time that each order was placed via the terminals in the restaurant so that a first-come-first-served basis is used fairly. Service staff can then be called in order by the chefs to come and collect their dishes.

Whilst this all sounds simple in a small kitchen even in the larger operations the system will be capable of sending orders for dishes to up to fifteen different preparation areas so the kitchen, larder, pastry and many more areas, if necessary, may be kept constantly informed of customer orders.

Nutritional analysis and computerized dietary control

Healthy eating has become an important way of life for many customers of hotel and catering establishments, as witnessed by the increased volume sales of 'health' foods. Whilst nutrition is important to all of us, nowhere is it more important than in a hospital. Here computers have been harnessed to aid the work of dietitians.

There is a danger when looking at the nutritional work of a hospital of thinking that the software is only of use there, but in reality nutritional analysis may be used in many other catering applications whether in hotels, restaurants, health farms or food manufacture.

Menu choice and diet histories

An efficient catering management computer system in a hospital will possess a digitizer and an optical card reader interface which are the means by which details of a patient's menu choices are entered into the computer for meal preparation purposes. These applications themselves enable some degree of dietary validation as a patient on a low-fat diet, for example, would be prevented from making a high-fat selection.

The diet history may be recorded over any period, from one meal to several days' food consumption, and it will be processed in conjunction with a recipe database to produce a variety of report facilities:

- A detailed nutritional analysis of the food consumed during the diet history period specified – any or all of the nutrient groups contained within the database may be selected to appear in the report. The constituent values for each food consumed and the total amounts consumed over the period chosen are given.
- The facility to analyse preset groups of nutrients – where there is a particular group of critical nutrients, specific report formats may be stored and selected. For example, in a diabetic diet, the carbohydrate content is critical.
- Comparison of the diet history compiled with the patient's recommended daily intake (RDI) to show percentage difference – a file giving RDI data (determined by age and physical fitness) will be provided with a good system, but may be edited.
- Accumulation of individual patient diet histories to produce statistical reports, for research and archive purposes.

Augmenting and updating the database

McCance and Widdowson's *The Composition of Foods* provides the standard detail of food composition in the United Kingdom. Their table of nutrients, and the supplementary files containing tables of amino acid, fatty acid and cholesterol content, remain largely static. Any new ingredients or recipes are assigned code numbers and added to the database, but details may be edited because:

- Data supplied by food manufacturing companies may be added, so that the nutritional content of proprietary foodstuffs (e.g. babyfood) is accessible which is an important factor in the real situation of institutional catering.
- If experimental evaluation of nutrient content is undertaken, water and vitamin loss in cooking will be taken into account during data input.
- When entering a new recipe, if the exact value for a particular nutrient is unknown, the McCance and Widdowson code for a similar food may be entered for automatic transfer of that nutrient's value to the new recipe.

Table 2.4 *Sample diet analysis*

Patient	J. Smith	Date 05/04	Page: 1
Date of Birth	25/10/55		
Ward	Chatsworth		

Breakfast

Amount (g)	Code	Description	KCAL	Protein	Fat	Carbohyd	Calcium	Iron	Vit D	Vit C
30.00	48	Cornflakes	110.40	2.58	0.48	25.53	0.98	0.18	0.00	0.00
30.00	30	Bread (whole)	64.80	2.64	0.81	12.54	6.90	0.75	0.00	0.00
10.00	140	Butter (salt)	74.00	0.04	8.20	0.00	1.50	0.01	0.07	0.00
15.00	853	Marmalade	39.15	0.01	0.00	10.42	5.25	0.09	0.00	1.50
120.00	124	Milk (cows')	78.00	3.96	4.56	5.64	144.00	0.06	0.03	1.80
10.00	843	Sugar (white)	39.40	0.00	0.00	10.50	0.20	0.00	0.00	0.00
Totals			405.75	9.23	14.05	64.63	158.75	1.09	0.11	3.30

Source: Fretwell-Downing Computer Group

- Comparison of newly added recipe data with a relevant recipe from the database produces a report of the mean percentage difference and the variance of percentage difference between the values.

This application is especially designed for dietary control in hospitals although it may also be useful as an aid to general meal planning in schools and restaurant chains. (See Figure 2.8 overleaf.)

Stocktaking and computers

Carrying too much stock and pilferage are two of the largest stock control problems facing any caterer.

Overstocking is often the result of staff, who are not spending their own money, not knowing exact consumption figures and simply guessing how much of a commodity will be needed. The caterer will therefore need to work out stock level and buying policies. Where pilferage is concerned, too many of the raw materials in catering can be consumed and may leave the premises literally inside staff. Shrinkage will never totally be combated but at least losses will be minimized if accurate figures are kept. Losses may also stem from wastage caused by bad menu planning and unexpectedly low volume sales. Before examining stocktaking in detail the overall philosophy behind stock control of liquor and food should firstly be outlined.

Liquor stock control

Using beverages as an example the following sequence may be followed by a typical stock control system:

Goods arrive details keyed into computer and cost and selling prices analysed
Price changes keyed into computer which updates all prices as they occur

MODULE STRUCTURE

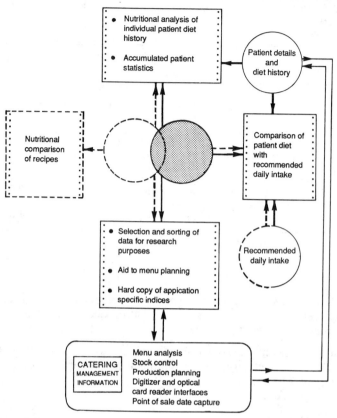

Figure 2.8   *Nutritional analysis and dietary control module structure*
Source: Fretwell-Downing Computer Group

Transfers   all movements of stock, for example between bars, is recorded into the computer

Revenue   cash received in various bars is recorded and compared with consumption

The computer will therefore be able to calculate:

- consumption
- cost price
- selling price
- VAT rate applicable
- gross margins
- comparisons between bars
- the correct selling price to achieve a specified gross margin

Food stock control

The same sequence applies here although there is one further complication in that the same ingredients may be referred to in three different ways. These are as:
- ingredients
- recipes
- menus

The computer will therefore be able to:

- calculate the effect on all menus and recipes of an alteration in price of one ingredient
- alter ingredients to make a dish more cost-effective
- predict a recipe explosion or calculate what quantity of ingredients are required for a particular number of covers
- identify steep commodity price increases of say more than 10 per cent from suppliers. The decision may be taken then to change supplier

Benefits of computerized stock control

A computerized stock control system:

- provides accurate stock information
- reduces overstocking or out of stock situations
- controls till receipts
- provides considerable management information
- saves clerical time in preparing:
  - recipe costs
  - buying lists
  - stock sheets
- discourages pilferage
- improves productivity

Data capture

The whole stock control process depends on accurate knowledge of the stocks, i.e. on knowing exactly how many bottles are on the shelves and how many tins are in the stores. There is no replacement for a physical examination of the stocks: although automatic dispensing systems go some way towards assisting with the 'count' they still have to be checked.

Computers can help considerably with the physical counting of stock items by, firstly, replacing the need to carry immense stock sheets and the attendant pencils and erasers. Portable computers will allow the stocktaker to be mobile while holding a permanent record of what is being counted. The stock information may be either downloaded to a host computer for analysis or calculated whilst the 'count' is taking place so that it only requires downloading to a printer at the completion of the stocktake.

The process followed using an intelligent handheld computer revolves around two files of information. These are the files for products and prices. To carry out a stocktake the manager, working from the last agreed stock figures, feeds in purchases and existing stock figures and arrives at consumption and overall sales figures. When product quantities and cash receipts are entered into the computer a print-out is produced of the overall result. The end result is a quicker stocktake, more accurate information and greater management control.

Data capture taking place during a bar stocktake utilising a portable computer
Photograph: Inn-Ventory Computers Ltd

Many data terminals just record the 'count' information during the stocktake and then their contents are downloaded for analysis by a second computer. Some have the advantage of laser scanners, often in pen form, which enable them to read computerized bar codes and this facility can obviate the accidental input of incorrect stock identifications.

Bar codes

From early beginnings where they were a novelty, we are now all familiar with bar codes as they appear on virtually all consumer goods ranging from tins of baked beans to books. They exist now as a reliable method of automated data collection.

The way they work is quite simple. Bar codes rely on the fact that light is reflected in different amounts by surfaces of different colours. The bar code scanner recognizes reflective differences between black and white lines of varying widths and translates these into signals. Large quantities of light are reflected by the white spaces but very little from the black bars. The scanner translates the reflections, which it receives as binary signals, into numerical reference numbers corresponding to the item the bar code is carried on.

The examples in Figure 2.9 correspond to the Universal Product Code (UPC) used by the retail grocery industry. The first sequence of digits refers to the product's manufacturer and the remaining digits to the product itself and its size. In a catering

Figure 2.9   *Bar codes as they appear on Corn Flakes, Frosties and Weetabix cereal packets*

situation this information may be read by a scanner and then subsequently analysed by a stocktaking computer so that the cost and selling prices are worked out and a note is made that the packet of cereal should be deducted from stock. If the stock has fallen to near the re-order level then the computer will prompt the management, warning them that there may not be sufficient cornflakes for tomorrow's breakfast service.

Generally where data collection is required bar codes and scanners speed up the process (up to three times faster than a typist), and are more accurate and reliable than the traditional manual method.

Single or integrated systems?

A single stocktaking system is suitable for caterers who just want to know what stock is held in the sales outlets and stores. For comprehensive analysis, an integrated system is needed which will allow order processing, accounting and other functions to take place.

Controlling food production by computer

Catering Information System (CIS) computers have particularly caught on in centralized food production operations of the type familiar in industrial catering situations such as schools, hospitals and food manufacturing businesses. They are rarely found in the hotel sector.

Those businesses that have decided to produce food on a system basis have found that they readily lend themselves to computer usage as all the facets of production have to be tied together into a unified system that in effect is a production line. The computer helps in the coordination of the various elements involved in the creation of the eventual food product. (Plumb, 19867/87)

Whatever the product the aim is to produce as many portions as possible as cost-effectively as possible, and the computer acts as a progress chaser. It can help management ensure that the various pieces of equipment are utilized systematically, that staff are fully employed, and that the various dishes being created are channelled through the available equipment sequentially.

'Cook-chill' and 'cook-freeze' methods have become firm favourites with caterers dealing with this type of catering for large numbers. Using these methods it is possible for a central production unit to produce food for distribution in a chilled/frozen state to many outlets. This offers vital economies of scale and production scheduling to group operations. Furthermore, food surplus to requirements at the central catering outlet can be preserved for distribution, cutting down on waste.

In utilizing cook-chill and cook-freeze methods, temperature and shelf life are highly critical: both must be very tightly controlled if bacteriological hazards are to be avoided and batches of 'at risk' foods not wasted. Control of despatch to other outlets and payment for foods supplied add further complexities.

A typical computer system for a cook-chill/cook-freeze production kitchen would link an integrated finished goods stock and production control system with sales order processing, to give full and flexible control of operations.

A centralized food production process supplying several units might be regulated by computer as outlined in Table 2.5.

RECEIPT OF ORDERS
|
PLANNING
|
PURCHASING
|
STOCK CONTROL
|
RECIPES
|
PRODUCTION MONITORING
|
PACKING
|
LABELLING
|
STOCK STORAGE
|
ACCOUNTING

Table 2.5 *Computerized cook-chill/freeze production process*

Receipt of orders

Take an example of an industrial caterer supplying 10 schools with lunches over a five-day week, where there will be a large number of alternative dishes progressing through the centralized kitchen. If, say, there are 12 choices for each lunch then this will involve a possible 600 alternative dishes that have to be catered for over the period of the week. When one realizes the quantities of dishes that might be needed for 10 schools one can see that there is a considerable requirement for a controlled system approach to the food production. This can be greatly assisted by a computer system.

The ordering system must be set up so that it gives the maximum warning possible to the centralized kitchen. Whilst it would be ideal for remote terminals to be used in each school to feed information directly into the computer at the kitchen itself, it is more than likely that this facility will not be available. If the latter is the case then data preparation facilities would have to be available at the kitchen where both written orders, received by mail, and telephoned orders would be recorded into the computer.

The computer should automatically check whether there is sufficient finished goods stock to meet the orders received. In the case of cook-chill meals, if the order is to be delivered the following week, it will be incorporated into the week's production schedule because any finished stock held will no longer be fresh by the time the order is needed.

Planning

Having received the orders the computer can assist in drawing up a production schedule for the required meals, combining similar orders from schools so that use of cooking and chilling equipment can be maximized.

The point should be made that in a school situation there is likely to be much more standardization of dishes. The whole menu cycle might be tailored to make the production process easier by, for example, operating a standard menu in every school on particular days.

Purchasing

Sufficient warning of the menu requirements will give the caterer valuable information to enable purchasing to be undertaken accurately. If there is not sufficient finished stock to meet requirements, a list of required stock is generated by 'exploding' the recipes. Stocks at ingredient level are then checked and re-ordered if necessary, and the production schedule currently in hand is amended. This is one of the main areas in which a computer can be of assistance.

Taking into account the shelf life of foodstuffs, and many catering items have a short shelf life, the computer can assimilate what foodstuffs are already in stock and produce purchase orders for the necessary replacements to satisfy the meal orders received from the schools. If the purchase orders are produced separately for each individual supplier this leaves very little room for error.

Stock control

It is important to keep sufficient food raw materials in the stores to cope with the orders from schools whilst not tying up too much finance in stock that is not going to be used for some time. A fine balance has to be maintained which can be achieved if the computer program is applied correctly and stocktaking is accurate.

In some systems an ingredient picking list is set up that gives a summary of stock required for a complete day's production. This can either be used as a checklist in advance to make sure that all that will be required for production is actually in stock, or as an actual requisition from the stores at the time the foods are needed in the kitchen.

Up to this point the computer has dealt solely with theoretical stock holding of ingredients, but there is similarly a need to keep control of those dishes already completed. As a guard against discrepancies between theoretical stock and actual stock held, it is useful if the computer produces a *finished stock picking note* against which actual stock held can be physically checked. (See Figure 2.10 overleaf.)

Whilst the orders from the schools will give information regarding what has to be taken out of existing stock there will also be items, such as vegetables and dairy produce, that have to be bought in on a daily basis. The computer will indicate those items that have to be bought in as well as those that are needed to replenish stock used. The computer should be able to set up the stock required for the following day's production rota.

Recipes

The accuracy of the whole computerized production programme depends on the creation of standard recipes for the dishes that the kitchen produces. The detail

```
**********  PICKING NOTE  **********

Picking note ref :   0000003
Today's date :       03/04/        Picking date  :   03/04/
Week    :      1
Day     :      6
Van no. :      1

Line   Stock code    Quantity    Description                Case size/Pack type
  7      3104           5        Quiche Lorraine Large        6  x      1  'S
 11      3201          10        Moussaka                    24  x     14 oz
 13      3222           2        Pollo Paesana               12  x      1  'S
 16      5503           6        Apple Crumble                4  x      1 tray
 19      5013          10        Fresh Cream Choc.  Dessert  24  x      1  'S
```

Figure 2.10 *Finished stock picking note (Fretwell-Downing, A)*

entered into the computer will depend on obtaining accurate information from the chefs and catering advisers as to the exact quantities of raw materials, including allowances for cooking loss, that will go into particular portions of individual dishes. Allowance will also have to be made for the recommended method of cooking used in the production kitchen. The recipes will be multiplied out to enable exact quantities of ingredients required to be allocated to the chefs for cooking.

Production monitoring

Invariably a centralized production kitchen will be aiming to either cook-chill or cook-freeze the food once prepared. The organization of the cooking process should maximize the use of all equipment and therefore a schedule should be drawn up to take into account the following criteria, which are not always applicable to a traditio-nal kitchen:

- preparation time
- cooking time
- total weight and volume of each recipe
- blast chiller/freezer capacity
- chilling/freezing time
- available staffing

Once researched and established this detail will be recorded for each dish commonly prepared by the production kitchen and is essential to the computer to allow accurate production scheduling to be established.

The point should be made that all the arrangements for production assume every member of staff and every piece of equipment working perfectly. As this is not always the case, for numerous reasons, the option must be available to alter the schedule. Close monitoring of what is actually occurring during production should therefore be maintained and any alterations fed into the computer so that contingency arrange-ments can be employed.

Packing

With a large variety of dishes to be distributed to the various schools attention to packing is important to ensure that the correct number of dishes arrive at the right location. Such constraints as the size of packs must be recorded within the computer. The computer should be able to produce a packing summary showing exactly how many portions of a particular dish are destined for a particular school.

Labelling

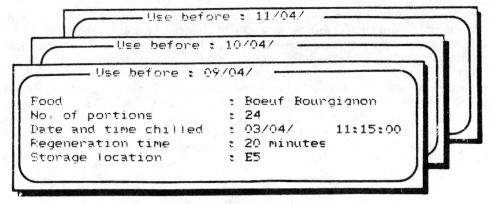

Figure 2.11   *Labelling (Fretwell-Downing, A)*

The packing summary will be of use in identifying packs by labels. Each pack should have an individual label, that may be produced automatically by the computer showing such items as:

- product name
- number of portions in pack
- use by date
- satellite unit name
- storage details
- cooking instructions

It should be noted that as the computer is producing the exact number of labels for the orders received this gives a useful second check of the production. If there are too many labels or too many packs then something has gone wrong in the production system somewhere and should be investigated.

The labels help to locate chilled and frozen dishes, and to avoid waste by ensuring that the oldest goods are always consumed first. The computer is also able to maintain information about the location of goods, a factor of particular importance to the cook-freeze process in which it is easy to lose track of goods which may be held in stock in large freezers for up to three months.

Stock storage

Whilst cook-chill food will be sent immediately to its destination cook-freeze products will, by definition, be kept in storage until required. Indeed the latter type of production kitchen is much easier to coordinate than the former. Where food is being stored in a freezer the computer can be programmed to control the stock, alerting management particularly to foodstuffs that are nearing or have reached their maximum storage time. Rotation of stock can thus be controlled accurately.

When the finished goods have been selected for despatch to the schools a despatch note is raised and the goods are distributed. Stock levels are adjusted automatically, registering that stock is allocated when orders are received and deducting the completed order when it is despatched and the invoice sent out.

Accounting

In a local authority school situation payment for food sent to each location will be in the form of a 'paper entry' with no cash actually changing hands, but there will still be a need to record production to the satisfaction of the appointed auditor. Both invoices and delivery notes will be produced for each school so that an accurate record can be kept of the consumption at each satellite.

In the case of a privatized school meal system cash will eventually change hands and again a strict record must be kept so that cash-flow can be controlled.

Invoices are produced by the computer according to a pricing structure which can be variable as some outlets might be invoiced at one level and other commercial outlets at another. Appropriate prices may be calculated with the help of the computer which enables costing at both ingredient and finished stages.

The Cook-chill/Cook-freeze System

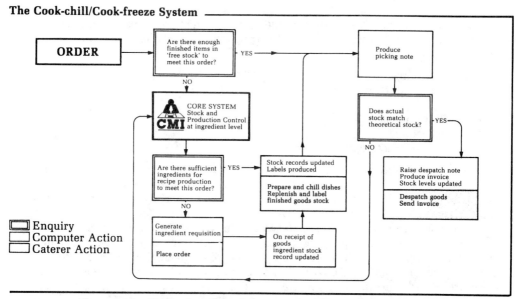

Figure 2.12 *The cook-chill/cook-freeze system (Fretwell-Downing, A)*

COMPUTERS AND HOSPITAL CATERING

In catering terms, hospitals are often seen as places providing only a basic catering function, but in reality they often have far more complex expertise in this field than most people would imagine. They serve a constantly changing clientele, many of whom have quite specific and exact dietary requirements and these 'customers', who might easily run into thousands in number, may be widely dispersed over a large physical area. Furthermore, in a hospital the caterer is not only satisfying the needs of the patients but also the requirements of the staff.

If a catering information computer system (CIS) is to help the hospital caterer then it needs a powerful integrated management information system to bring together the many day-to-day activities of the management, clerical and production staff with the eventual aim of providing a comprehensive catering service to the widely dispersed patients and staff of the hospital.

The main purpose behind a computer system in a hospital catering operation is to control meal production and stock. The software requirements are complex and a typical system might be outlined as follows:

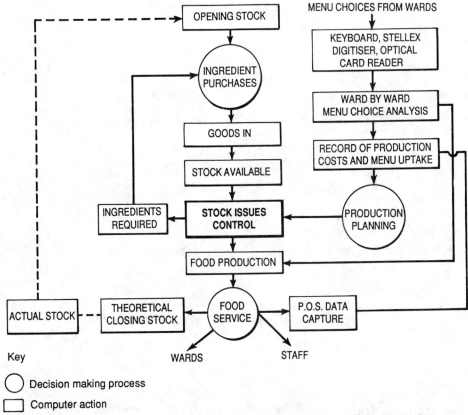

Figure 2.13 *Hospital catering production and stock control (Fretwell-Downing, B)*

A computerized system might be single, multi-user or networked and will need a minimum of 10 Mb hard disk storage with a capacity for expansion.

Computerization might well be built into a health authority district by installing systems in principal hospitals only and incorporating smaller hospitals and annexes as separate sites or satellites within these systems.

Setting up a hospital system – key information files

A comprehensive computer system in a hospital will of necessity take some time to set up. At the heart of the operation is the need to create and store certain key information files upon which the whole computer system relies. Without the information in these key files the system cannot achieve full operational use. The key information files in a typical system might be as follows:

- supplier
- stock
- recipe
- ward
- menu

Supplier details

```
Screen No. 1          *** SUPPLIER CREATE AMEND ***

Supplier Number :              Contact      :

Name             :

Address Line 1   :

Address Line 2   :

Address Line 3   :

Telephone No.    :             Credit Limit :

Telex No.        :             Discount     :

Comments         :
```

Figure 2.14 *Supplier details (Fretwell-Downing, B)*

The creation of a filing system within the computer containing details of each individual supplier that the hospital makes use of is essential to enable the computer to produce supplier orders from the production planning module. Supplier details will be validated on the stock screen.

Stock details

```
O    Screen No. 1              *** STOCK CREATE/AMEND ***              O
O                                                                     O
O                                                                     O
O       Stock Code :    Description:                                  O
O                       NSV Code   :                                  O
O                       Location   :                                  O
O                       Group      :                                  O
O                       Comments   :                                  O
O                                                                     O
O    Supplier 1 :                     Lead time 1 :    days           O
O    Supplier 2 :                     Lead time 2 :    days           O
O                    Purchase unit    :  (              )             O
O                    Recipe unit      :                               O
O                    Minimum Stock Level:                             O
O                    Maximum Stock Level:                             O
```

Figure 2.15   *Stock details (Fretwell-Downing, B)*

The stock screen, as in the example in Figure 2.15, is fully integrated with the supplier file. It shows stock items both by purchase units and by recipe units, with automatic quantity and value calculations in either metric or imperial or sometimes both.

The stock screen permits the setting of maximum and minimum stock levels for stores items and a report can be obtained at any time detailing those items requiring re-order.

Recipe details

The computer allows recipes to be tailored around portion sizes for patients, whose eating requirements may be described as either small or large, as well as staff portion sizes. The computer should be able to specify the wastage factor as a percentage of cost against any or all of the recipes.

Where selling price is concerned, a typical system would allow an automatic calculation of three selling prices based on the hospital's experience and requirements of gross margins, with or without VAT. The normal equations would be 75:25, 60:40 and one variable for the costing of special functions. The specified final selling price would be handled by the computer which would also produce an automatic gross margin calculation.

The system should include diet validation in the menu card analysis and it should be possible for recipes themselves to be used as ingredients within other recipes; for example, the Chaudfroid Sauce recipe will be an ingredient in the Chicken Chaud-froid recipe. The software should allow all ingredients to have comments made about them concerning such details as the exact specification.

```
 B/A)                      *** RECIPE CREATE AMEND ***

 Recipe Code       :          Description    :
 Portion Size      :          Group          :

 Yield (Portions)  :
 Weight/Volume     :
 Staff Portion     :
 Portion Cost      :          pence


 SELLING PRICES
 Wastage factor    :
 Gross Margin      :          Gross Margin   :          Gross Margin
 V.A.T.            :          V.A.T.         :          V.A.T.
 Selling Price     :          Selling Price  :          Selling Price

                        Final Selling Price   :
                        With V.A.T.           :
                        Gross Margin          :
```

Figure 2.16 *Recipe details (Fretwell-Downing, B)*

Ward details

The ward name is validated by the computer in the menu analysis whilst individual ward accumulations of direct stock issues, meal issues and bed occupancy (state) figures are calculated by the computer.

Menus

Menu cycles are stored by the computer for both patients and staff, as well as for different diet types if a multi-menu patient system is used by the hospital. Any 'fixed list' of staff items to be available at all times is recorded separately.

Running the system

A typical hospital CIS is set up to produce regular consolidated management reports by week, by period and by year-to-date, summarising the following:

- stock movements
- recipe finished goods movements
- staff income and gross margins
- patient and staff feeding costs

To support these consolidated management reports a wealth of more detailed reports and audit trails are available showing the movement of individual stock items and recipes through the system, daily production schedules, menu uptake figures, sales analysis and wastage. In addition user-defined interrogation and reports should be possible.

Consolidated stock report

```
CONSOLIDATED STOCK REPORT                            PERIOD 1

                                          PERIOD         YEAR

OPENING STOCK                             1694,78       1694,78
DELIVERIES                                5315,80       5315,80
CLOSING STOCK                             2115,88       2115,88
ACTUAL COST OF PROVISIONS                 4894,69       4894,69
RECORDED COST OF PROVISIONS

         General  Kitchen                 1096,00       1096,00
                  Diet Kitchen             114,20        114,20

         Patient  Wards Milk               429,20        429,20
                  Wards Misc               405,80        405,80

         Staff    Restaurant 1             249,20        249,20
                  Restaurant 2             303,80        303,80
                  Doctors D/R              422,60        422,60
                  Vending                  233,00        233,00
                  Credits                  284,60        284,60

         Direct   Day Care Unit            998,00        998,00
                  Regional off             123,80        123,80
                  Pond Hospital            114,20        114,20
                  Fulwood Annex             33,80         33,80


         Total                            4808,20       4808,20
```

Figure 2.17 *Consolidated stock report (Fretwell-Downing, B)*

This report shows the financial value of the provisions utilized by the various cost centres in the hospital for a specific period and for the year-to-date.

Further reports might outline:

- physical consumption against *recorded usage*
- *recorded usage* against *theoretical requirements*
- *physical consumption* against *theoretical requirements*

Management report

Staff. Where staff are concerned, the management report will outline a number of areas of income along with automatic VAT calculations, whilst individual gross margin calculations may be computed for specified cost centres.
Patients. In this section of the management report a separation is made between direct stores issues and recipe issues to the wards and in addition there is a comparison with budget.

```
                    MANAGEMENT REPORT              PERIOD 1

                    *** STAFF ***
                                            PERIOD              YEAR
      REVENUE
          Restaurant 1                     2512,36           2512,36
          Restaurant 2                         56                56
          Doctors D/R                        452               452
          Vending                          253,98            253,98
          Credits                           25,63             25,63
          Functions                         89,00             89,00
          Coffee Lounge                     78,00             78,00
          Night Service                     85,00             85,00
          Miscellaneous                     12,63             12,63

          Total Gross                      3564,33           3564,33
          Total Net                        3447,12           3447,12

      COST OF PROVISIONS
          Actual                           1396,30           1396,30
          Recorded                         1362,70           1362,70

      PERFORMANCE                            40,51             40,51
      GROSS MARGIN%                         59,49%            59,49%

                    *** PATIENTS ***
      COST OF PROVISIONS
          Actual
              Meals                        1393,58           1393,58
              Wards Milk                    429,20            429,20
              Wards Misc                    405,80            405,80
              Total                        2228,58           2228,58
          Recorded
              Meals                        1393,58           1393,58
              Wards Milk                    429,20            429,20
              Wards Misc                    405,80            405,80
              Total                        2175,69           2175,69

      PATIENT MEAL WEEKS                       120               120

      COSTS PER MEAL WEEK
          Ward Issues                        6,95              6,95
          Meals                             11,61             11,61
          Total                             18,57             18,57

          Budget Cost                       10,00             10,00
          Variance                          -8,57             -8,57
      UNALLOCATED                          -338,77           -338,77
```

Figure 2.18 *Management report (Fretwell-Downing, B)*

Stock control

A computer program concerning stock control in a hospital will possess fully integrated routines covering the following:

- opening and closing stock (automatic carry forward)
- deliveries and return deliveries
- direct issue of deliveries (for non-stores items)
- issues and return issues (in whole or 'broken' stock)
- recipe issues (to other units such as cook-chill operations)

At ingredient level the following information might be maintained:

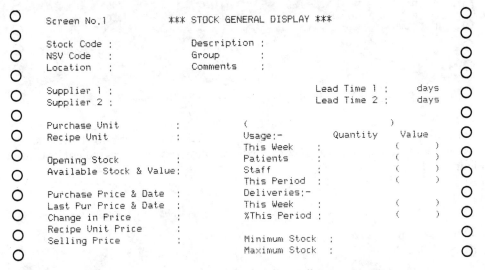

```
    Screen No.1            *** STOCK GENERAL DISPLAY ***

    Stock Code :           Description :
    NSV Code   :           Group       :
    Location   :           Comments    :

    Supplier 1 :                              Lead Time 1 :    days
    Supplier 2 :                              Lead Time 2 :    days

    Purchase Unit          :        (                    )
    Recipe Unit            :        Usage:-      Quantity   Value
                                    This Week    :          (      )
    Opening Stock          :        Patients     :          (      )
    Available Stock & Value:        Staff        :          (      )
                                    This Period  :          (      )
    Purchase Price & Date  :        Deliveries:-
    Last Pur Price & Date  :        This Week    :          (      )
    Change in Price        :        %This Period :          (      )
    Recipe Unit Price      :
    Selling Price          :        Minimum Stock :
                                    Maximum Stock :
```

Figure 2.19 *Stock control display (Fretwell-Downing, B)*

In addition, a Purchase Day Book is produced by the computer on both the
deliveries and direct issue of deliveries routines.

```
    GOODS INWARDS               Week Number   2              Date: 27.09.

    Del No   Del Date  Order No    Invoice    Supplier
    36       25.09     A0123                  1 HARDYS BAKERIES

    Item Code     Description           Unit     Price   Quantity    Cost

     1   BR01     Breadcrummbs           LB      0.0600   12.00     0.7200
     2   BR02     Loaf Medium Slice Bread LOAF   0.2800  144.00    40.3200
                                                                   41.0400

    Del No   Del Date  Order No    Invoice    Supplier
     1       25.09     A0124                  2 ROY'S VEGETABLES
```

Item Code		Description	Unit	Price	Quantity	Cost
3	FR06	Lemons	1x12	2.0000	12.00	24.0000
4	FR02	Bananas	LB	0.7500	25.00	18.7500
5	VE02	Parsley	LB	0.4500	2.00	0.9000
6	VE11	Turnips	30LB	37.0000	1.00	37.0000
7	VE07	Peas	12.5KG	25.0000	2.00	130.6500

Del No	Del Date	Order No	Invoice	Supplier
20	24.09	A0125	2211T	3 DRY STORES SUPPLIES

Item Code		Description	Unit	Price	Quantity	Cost
8	DR02	Sugar Caster	500GM	0.5000	2.00	1.0000
9	BA01	Trifle Sponges Cake	48xP	3.0000	5.00	15.0000
10	BA06	Gelatine	4OZ	0.4800	10.00	4.8000
11	DR05	Sugar Granulated	5KG	1.9000	5.00	9.5000

						30.0000
				CUMULATIVE TOTAL		201.9900

Figure 2.20   *Purchase day book (Fretwell-Downing, B)*

At each period end the physical consumption (opening stock plus deliveries, less closing stock) is compared with recorded consumption (issues) at ingredient level as in Figure 2.21:

*** PERIOD 1 STOCK REPORT ***

CODE	DESCRIPTION	UNIT	OPENING STOCK	GOODS INWARD	CLOSING STOCK
AL01	Sherry	1LT	12.00	10.00	10.00
BA01	Trifle Sponges	48 PKTS	10.00	0.00	2.00
BA02	Angelica	PKT 4OZ	25.00	0.00	13.00
BA03	Cherries Glace	PKT 20	10.00	12.00	2.00
BA04	Cloves	PKT 100	3.00	5.00	2.00
BA05	Gelatine	PKT 4OZ	25.00	0.00	0.00
BA06	Custard Powder	24LB	2.00	0.00	3.00
BA07	Yellow Colouring	BTL 10ML	2.00	2.00	3.00
BA08	Yeast	PKT 4OZ	3.00	5.00	1.00
BA09	Breadcrumbs	1LB	5.00	3.00	1.00
BR01	Cream	1LT	13.00	15.00	1.00
DA01	Eggs (Size 2)	1x12	3.00	56.00	2.50
DA02	Cheese (Cheddar)	500G	6.00	12.00	6.00
DA03	Milk	1PT	26.00	100.00	1.00
DA05	Egg Yolks	1LB	5.00	0.00	2.00
DR01	Flour	12.5KG	2.00	3.00	1.00
DR02	Caster Sugar	500G	3.00	2.00	0.50
DR03	Cornflour	500G	1.00	2.00	0.50
DR04	Bovril	500G	2.50	3.50	1.50
DR05	Sugar Granulated	5KG	2.50	5.00	1.75

PAGE TOTAL				Consumption	420.79
CUMULATIVE TOTALS				Consumption	420.79

Figure 2.21   *Stock report (Fretwell-Downing, B)*

Menu analysis

The stock control analysis will have established the total value of goods issued to the kitchen during a particular time and a comparison can now be made with the kitchen's recorded production. This will highlight such problems as:

- wastage
- non-adherence to standard recipes

Where menu analysis is concerned the two types of customers – patients and staff – must be treated separately.

Patient menu analysis

The collation of menu requirements for every patient in the hospital is in itself one of the major problems faced by the hospital caterer and was one of the original reasons that computers were considered.

The control of completed meals presents a great challenge for the hospital caterer as there are not only changing menu cycles but also a constant changeover of patients. Hospitals deal with a constantly fluctuating number of patients, a large percentage of whom have critical dietary requirements catered for by special menus. Speed and

CONSUMPTION		ISSUES		VARIANCES		
QTY	VALUE	QTY	VALUE	QTY	VALUE	%
12.00	51.00	12.00	51.00	0.00	0.00	0.00
8.00	22.80	8.00	22.80	0.00	0.00	0.00
12.00	3.84	11.00	3.52	1.00	0.32	9.09
20.00	136.00	19.00	129.20	1.00	6.80	5.26
6.00	3.24	7.00	3.78	-1.00	-0.54	-14.28
25.00	17.50	25.00	17.50	0.00	0.00	0.00
-1.00	-4.75	1.00	4.75	-2.00	-9.50	-200.00
1.00	0.75	1.00	0.75	0.00	0.00	0.00
7.00	5.53	7.00	5.53	0.00	0.00	0.00
7.00	3.15	6.00	2.70	1.00	0.45	16.66
27.00	31.25	27.00	31.25	0.00	0.00	0.00
56.50	51.98	56.00	51.52	0.50	0.46	0.89
12.00	28.32	12.00	28.32	0.00	0.00	0.00
125.00	27.50	125.00	27.50	0.00	0.00	0.00
3.00	5.28	2.00	3.52	1.00	1.76	50.00
4.00	19.20	5.00	24.00	-1.00	-4.80	-20.00
4.50	2.25	5.00	2.50	-0.50	-0.25	-10.00
2.50	0.62	2.50	0.62	0.00	0.00	0.00
4.50	4.41	4.50	4.41	0.00	0.00	0.00
5.75	10.92	5.75	10.92	0.00	0.00	0.00

Issues   426.09   Variance -5.30

Issues   426.09   Variance -5.30

Figure 2.21   *Stock report (Fretwell-Downing, B)*

efficiency of menu choice is essential for accurate meal production, cutting down on wastage and improving patient satisfaction and morale.

The first task is to obtain information from patients and of necessity this is usually carried out on the day before the meals are actually to be consumed. This gives time for the preparation of meals in exact quantities and to exact specifications as required by the medical conditions of patients.

In order to take full advantage of the patient menu analysis made possible by a typical hospital CIS, an effective method of entering the details of the patient menu requests must be found. Whilst the obvious method is to use a standard computer terminal, the mere quantity of information found in a large hospital makes this an extremely onerous job. In addition, in a large hospital the scale of data to be entered makes keyboard entry both labour-intensive and prone to error.

There are two practical alternatives to keyboard entry. These are by the use of:

- a digitizer
- an optical mark reader

In most cases a digitizer will be the best solution, but in large institutions of say 800-plus beds the optical mark reader may be more appropriate.

Digitizer

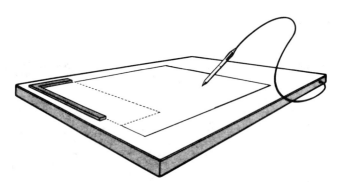

Figure 2.22   *Digitizer (Fretwell-Downing, C)*

The great advantage of a digitizer is that it is accurate, flexible, simple to use, facilitates menu choice meal-by-meal and allows dietary validation.

The 'active pad' of the digitizer is clearly divided into sections denoting ward, portion size, diet type and other appropriate details. Data entry is achieved simply by 'touching' the particular menu choice of the patient with the special pen. Entry and accuracy are controlled by a variety of audible 'bleeps' from the digitizer: one bleep signals correct data input, a second tells the operator that the correct place on the digitizer has not been pressed, and a third denotes 'invalid entry' when a choice has been made which is disallowed by the patient's dietary restriction.

Time and money are not wasted in the preparation of unsuitable meals, and more importantly patients cannot be served with meals which are inappropriate or even dangerous.

The digitizer demonstrates its flexibility in that it can be programmed to accept whatever types of data the hospital caterer requires. It is thus possible to produce a tailor-made system for individual or specialist requirements.

The digitizer is simple to use as it gives the user clear visual guides and audible signals which make it 'user-friendly'. Unlike keyboard entry which relies on the skill of the operator, no specialist training is needed to enter data accurately and quickly, so less staff time is taken up with the routine aspects of patient menu analysis.

Whereas optical mark readers only accept menu cards of a particular quality, which in themselves are expensive to produce, the digitizer needs no special supplies which gives a considerable saving in costs.

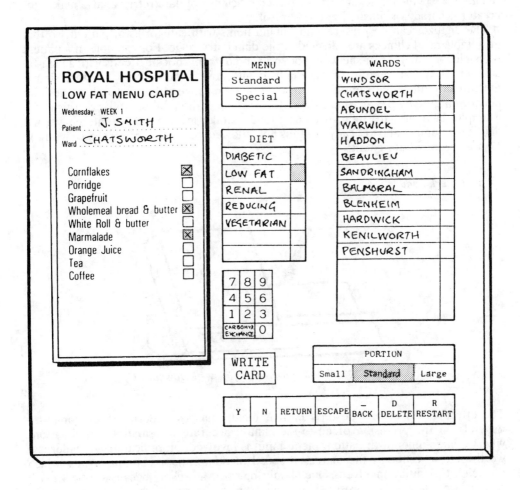

Figure 2.23   *Typical Digitizer 'Active Pad' (Fretwell-Downing, C)*

A DHSS survey in 1977 showed that in long stay and mental handicap hospitals 36 per cent of the food was wasted, while in acute hospitals it amounted to over 40 per cent. (Fretwell-Downing, C)

Most of the waste outlined above is plate waste or, in other words, food that has been cooked and served which for one reason or another has not been consumed by the patients. Plate waste is in fact the costliest type of waste, since it includes the labour costs of preparation and serving and the energy costs of cooking.

Traditionally, hospital ward staff have asked patients to complete a menu choice card a day in advance. This makes for food waste through patients being transferred to other wards or discharged, or simply because the patient may no longer relish the meal ordered when it eventually arrives. Using the digitizer cuts down on plate waste by enabling menu choice on a meal-by-meal basis: as one meal is served, patients select the next one. This is possible with a digitizer simply because collation of requests is so much quicker. The increased efficiency of data retrieval also makes for greater accuracy of finished goods control.

The digitizer can be preset to link menu items with categories of patient, so that unsuitable meal choices are rejected at the data entry stage. For example, if a patient is on a low-fat diet, he or she would be 'prevented' from choosing foods with a high-fat content. A special feature of the digitizer interface is the capacity to store simple nutritional data. For example, a carbohydrate exchange value for each menu item may be entered by the dietitian. Patients for whom carbohydrate intake is critical, for example diabetics, are then assigned a daily intake level which is entered via the digitizer's numerical pad. They are thus not 'allowed' to make a menu choice with too high a carbohydrate count.

Optical mark reader

Figure 2.24   *Optical mark reader (Fretwell-Downing, C)*

The effectiveness of any hospital patient menu analysis undertaken by computer depends on the provision of up-to-the-minute accurate information. In situations where a large amount of patient menu input is involved, an optical mark reader is a worthwhile investment: the increased speed of data entry results in savings which outweigh the outlay involved. One should beware, however, because optical mark readers are notoriously sensitive, although problems of sensitivity can be overcome.

Once the patient's choices have been entered the total analysis will be provided by the computer either by wards or in bulk.

```
                        *** PATIENT MENU ANALYSIS ***              25/09/

        WED1L     Wednesday Week One Lunch

   Ward Code                    1       2       3       4       5    TOTAL

   DUCHESSE POTATOES           24      30      29      21      29     127
   GARDEN PEAS                 25      25      29      21      20     120
   GLAZED CARROTS              27      24      25      20      25     121
   ORANGE JUICE                16      28      12      10      13      79
   CREAM OF TOMATO             11       0      16      11       2      40
   BRAISED STEAK               12      24      16      19      13      84
   CHICKEN CHAUFROID           15       5      13       2      10      45
   SHERRY TRIFLE               20      25      30      18      10     103

   Number of cards             27      28      29      21      23     128
   Cost  (in pence)          3132    2856    3741    2625    2254   24929
   Cost per patient           116     102     129     125      98     194
```

Figure 2.25   *Patient menu analysis (Fretwell-Downing, B)*

In producing the patient menu analysis, diet and other validations such as diabetic carbohydrate counts are available. The total cost of patient feeding can be posted to the management reports.

Recipes 'consumed' may be automatically exploded to produce the theoretical ingredient quantities required for production. At the week-end the theoretical ingredient quantities are compared with the total usage of each ingredient.

As a means of forecasting, patient uptake figures can be maintained on a rolling average basis for future production planning.

```
                        *** PATIENT UPTAKE FIGURES ***

      Menu Code    :   WED1L     Wednesday Week One Lunch

                                        Service Dates

      Code     Description        Last   Last -1   last-2   Average

      RF01     DUCHESSE POTATOES   211     420      438       356
      RF02     GARDEN PEAS         238     284      269       263
      RF03     GLAZED CARROTS      290     175      153       206
      RG01     ORANGE JUICE        150      90      102       114
      RG02     CREAM OF TOMATO     177      75       68       106
      RJ01     BRAISED STEAK       157     103       94       118
      RN01     CHICKEN CHAUFROID    96      89       85        90
      RP01     SHERRY TRIFLE       315     215      212       247
```

Figure 2.26   *Patient uptake figures (Fretwell-Downing, B)*

Staff menu analysis

In addition to the patients, there will be a need within the hospital to analyse the menu details of staff. In this case data entry to the computer system is available manually via a terminal or automatically via point-of-sale by linking with electronic cash registers.

Output is similar to that for patient menu analysis with the total cost of staff feeding being posted to the management reports. Recipes consumed will also be exploded automatically to produce the theoretical quantities required for production, and at the week-end the theoretical list is compared with the total usage of each stock item. Uptake figures of the variable menu cycle items are maintained for future production planning.

Production planning

With the information received from the uptake summaries of both patients and staff, more accurate forecasting of requirements is possible. Within its production planning module the computer will permit the translation of these forecasts into:

- costed production schedule
- stores requisition list (picking list)
- individual recipes
- purchase orders

Costed production schedule

```
              *** PRODUCTION PLAN FOR 03/10/   ***

Recipe   Code    Description                       Portions      Cost

  1      RG01    ORANGE JUICE                        225         13.50
  2      RG02    CREAM OF TOMATO                     300         22.08
  3      R101    FRIED SCAMPI                        321        242.90
  4      RL01    ROAST PORK AND APPLE SAUCE          235        115.73
  5      RN01    CHICKEN CHAUFROID                   250        187.77
  6      RF01    DUCHESSE POTATOES                   500         15.80
  7      RF02    GARDEN PEAS                         550         63.63
  8      RF03    GLAZED CARROTS                      500         19.85
  9      R001    APPLE PIE                           225         28.32
 10      R002    RHUBARB CRUMBLE                     300         32.10
 11      RP01    SHERRY TRIFLE                       125         83.40


                            TOTAL PRODUCTION COST             825.10
```

Figure 2.27 *Production plan (Fretwell-Downing, B)*

The production plan in Figure 2.27 allows any number of recipes for any quantities to be included. Full edit facilities should be incorporated.

Stores requisition list

The stores requisition list (order list) outlined above is produced in code order of ingredients and in recipe units so that issues of broken stock may be facilitated.

```
                    *** STORES ORDER LIST ***   03/10/

    Number   Code     Description           Quantity   Unit
    1        AL01     Sherry                    2.50   pt
    2        BA01     Trifle Sponges           10.00   pkt
    3        BA02     Angelica                  3.75   oz
    4        BA03     Cherry Glace              2.50   pkt
    5        BA05     Cloves                    4.50   oz
    6        BA06     Gelatine                  1.05   oz
    7        BA07     Custard Powder            0.00   lb
    8        BR01     Breadcrumbs             410.88   oz
    9        DA01     Cream                    13.50   pt
    10       DA02     Eggs   (size 2)         128.40   unit
    11       DA04     Milk                     13.14   pt
    12       DA05     Egg Whites dried          0.40   oz
    13       DA06     Egg Yolks                63.02   unit
    14       DR01     Flour                    21.03   lb
    15       DR02     Sugar Caster              5.25   500GM
    16       DR04     Bovril 3                  0.10   oz
    17       DR05     Sugar Granulated         57.06   kg
    18       DR06     Red Jelly                12.50   pkt
    19       FA01     Frying Fat                6.25   kg
    20       FA02     Margarine                36.02   lb
    21       FA03     Cooking Oil               6.42   pt
    22       FA04     Dripping                881.25   gm
    23       FA06     Salad Oil                 0.94   lt
    24       F101     Scampi                   44.94   kg
    25       FR01     Apples Cooking           13.89   lb
    26       FR03     Rhubarb                  15.00   A10
    27       FR04     Peaches Tinned            6.25   A3
    28       FR06     Lemons                   77.04   unit
    29       FR07     Fruit Juice              13.50   A10
    30       ME01     Chicken Portions        250.00   unit
    31       ME05     Pork Leg                 58.16   lb
    32       ME06     Meat Bones               11.52   lb
    33       PR01     Jam Raspberry             3.75   500GM
    34       PR02     Gherkins                  2.56   oz
    35       SE01     Salt                     26.87   oz
    36       SE02     Pepper                   13.41   oz
    37       SE05     Mustard                   0.18   oz
    38       SE06     Vinegar                   0.06   lt
    39       SE07     Cayenne Pepper            0.32   oz
    40       SE08     Gravy Granules         1175.00   gm
    41       S001     Soup Tomato              18.00   A10
    42       VE01     Onions                    0.98   lb
    43       VE02     Parsley                   0.64   lb
    44       VE03     Onions Button             5.75   gm
    45       VE05     Potatoes                175.00   lb
    46       VE06     Carrots                 175.96   lb
    47       VE07     Peas                     68.75   lb
    48       VE08     Leeks                     0.48   lb
    49       WA01     Water                     6.90   GALLON
```

Figure 2.28   *Stores order list (Fretwell-Downing, B)*

Individual recipes

```
                    *** PRODUCTION PLANNING RECIPE LIST ***        3/10

    RA01   WHITE STOCK
    Yield        :           48 Portions  (   4.80  PT  )
    Portion Cost :      5.26 pence

    INGREDIENTS

    CODE      DESCRIPTION                  QUANTITY    UNIT    COMMENT
    ME06      Meat Bones                     11.52     lb
    VE06      Carrots                         0.96     lb
    VE01      Onions                          0.96     lb
    VE08      Leeks                           0.48     lb
    WA01      Water                           4.80     Gallon
    SE01      Salt                            0.48     oz
    SE02      Pepper                          0.48     oz

    --------------------------------------------------------------

    RB01   WHITE SAUCE
    Yield        :            2 Portions  (   0.25  PT  )
    Portion Cost :      3.37 pence

    INGREDIENTS

    CODE      DESCRIPTION                  QUANTITY    UNIT    COMMENT
    FA02      Margarine                       0.02     lb
    DR01      Flour                           0.03     lb
    VE01      Onions                          0.02     lb
    DA04      Milk                            0.30     PT
    SE01      Salt                            0.02     oz

    --------------------------------------------------------------

    RA04   ASPIC JELLY
    Yield        :           20 Portions  (   1.00  PT  )
    Portion Cost :      2.72 pence

    INGREDIENTS

    CODE      DESCRIPTION                  QUANTITY    UNIT    COMMENT
    RA01      WHITE STOCK                     0.80     PT
    BA06      Gelatine                        0.80     oz
    DR04      Bovril 3                        0.10     oz
    DA05      Egg Whites Dried                0.40     oz
    SE01      Salt                            0.20     oz

    --------------------------------------------------------------

    RB09   CHAUDFROID SAUCE
    Yield        :           25 Portions  (   2.50  PT  )
    Portion Cost :      1.82 pence

    INGREDIENTS

    CODE      DESCRIPTION                  QUANTITY    UNIT    COMMENT
    RB01      WHITE SAUCE                     0.75     PT
    RA04      ASPIC JELLY                     0.25     PT
    BA06      Gelatine                        0.25     oz
    SE01      Salt                            0.25     oz
    SE02      Pepper                          0.25     oz

    --------------------------------------------------------------
```

```
RN01   CHICKEN CHAUDFROID
Yield          :              250 Portions  (  112.50 LB  )
Portion Cost   :        69.54 pence

INGREDIENTS

CODE       DESCRIPTION                    QUANTITY     UNIT    COMMENT
ME01       Chicken Portions                 250.00     unit    frozen
SE01       Salt                               5.00     oz      to taste
SE02       Pepper                             2.50     oz      to taste
FA01       Frying Fat                         6.25     kg
RB01       CHAUDFROID SAUCE                  10.00     PT
VE03       Onions Button                      5.75     gm      chopped

----------------------------------------------------------------------
```

Figure 2.29   *Individual recipes (Fretwell-Downing, B)*

The details of individual standard recipes may be produced by the computer system in the form above so that there is little room for error in the production of meals.

Purchase orders

```
              *** PRODUCTION PLANNING SUPPLIER LIST ***        3/10/

Supplier    :   1 HARDYS BAKERIES

Contact     :   Jim Knight
                256 Bakers Row
                Sheffield
                S31 55E
Telephone   :   26589              Telex   :

Item   Code   Description           Quantity   Unit
1      BA01   Trifle Sponges            0.83   48xPKT
2      BR01   Breadcrumbs              40.00   LB

----------------------------------------------------------------------

Supplier    :   2 ROY'S VEGETABLES

Contact     :   Royston Darley
                Green Acre Arcade
                Wilmslow
                Greater Manchester
Telephone   :   061 223 55478      Telex   :

Item   Code   Description           Quantity   Unit
1      FR01   Apples Cooking            0.99   30LB
2      FR03   Rhubarb                  25.00   A10
3      FR06   Lemons                   10.00   1x12
4      VE01   Onions                    0.06   30LB
5      VE02   Parsley                   1.00   LB
6      VE03   Onions Button             0.00   5KG
7      VE05   Potatoes                  3.12   56LB
8      VE06   Carrots                 176.92   LB
9      VE07   Peas                      2.26   12.5KG
10     VE08   Leeks                     0.96   LB

----------------------------------------------------------------------
```

```
Supplier    :   3 DRY STORES SUPPLIES

Contact     :   Mr Smith
                25, DrymaceLane
                Sunny Bank
                Rotheram
Telephone   :   22564                Telex  :

Item    Code    Description          Quantity    Unit
1       AL01    Sherry                   5.68    LT
2       BA02    Angelica                 3.75    4OZ
3       BA03    Cherry Glace             0.83    12xPKT
4       BA05    Cloves                   2.50    4OZ
5       BA06    Gelatine                 0.52    4OZ
6       BA07    Custard Powder           0.00    12.5KG
7       DA05    Egg Whites Dried         0.05    LB
8       DA06    Egg Yolks                5.39    1x12
9       DR01    Flour                    1.45    12.5KG
10      DR02    Sugar Caster            10.00    500GM
11      DR04    Bovril 3                 0.01    500GM
12      DR05    Sugar Granulated        25.16    5kg
13      DR06    Red Jelly               50.00    48xpkt
14      FA01    Frying Fat               2.50    5KG
15      FA02    Margarine                1.63    12.5KG
16      FA03    Cooking Oil              5.68    LT
17      FA06    Salad Oil                0.32    GALLON
18      FR04    Peaches Tinned          25.00    A3
19      FR07    Fruit Juice             30.00    A10
20      PR01    Jam Raspberry           15.00    500GM
21      PR02    Gherkins                 0.02    5KG
22      SE01    Salt                     2.44    500GM
23      SE02    Pepper                   4.18    4OZ
24      SE05    Mustard                  0.01    LB
25      SE06    Vinegar                  0.02    GALLON
26      SE07    Cayenne Pepper           0.12    4OZ
27      SE08    Gravy Granules           5.00    500GM
28      S001    Soup Tomato             30.00    A10


Supplier    :

Contact     :


Telephone   :                        Telex  :

Item    Code    Description
-----------------------------------------------------------------
```

Figure 2.30   *Purchase order (Fretwell-Downing, B)*

Purchase orders may be produced on demand or automatically by the computer system when required. The orders are produced in code order of suppliers, items and purchase units.

COMPUTERS AND BARS

Computers can be successfully utilized in a variety of ways within bar operations, whether the bar is in a pub, hotel, club, restaurant, or mass catering establishment. Bars themselves will, of course, vary immensely ranging from the sleepy village inn where the pace of service is slow, to the theatre complex where several hundred drinks are dispensed within a matter of a few minutes.

The main areas in which a computerized system may contribute to a bar operation are:

- point-of-sale accounting
- stock control
- stocktaking

Compared to their labour-intensive sister, restaurants, computerizing bar and pub operations is relatively simple as they do not involve the problems of linking a large number of floor waiting staff with a behind-the-scenes chef. In addition the installation of a computerized bar system is simplified by the good shelf life of most drinks that largely removes the problem of high wastage that can be found in food operations. The only substantial cause of wastage is through pilfering and bar operations are renowned for this problem. Whilst there are a great variety of fraudulent practices that staff can utilize in a bar, most may be detected or prevented by a tight control and stocktaking system. A computerized system will help greatly towards achieving this.

In pubs the control of liquor is frequently the responsibility of one person – usually the manager or owner. In most cases this person has had other immediate priorities that have pushed computerization into the background, but recently it has become more apparent that manual systems of controlling the business can be satisfactorily replaced by a computerized system. Bar owners and managers are realizing that there are a number of advantages in computerization, such as saving time in compiling stock calculations.

The typical areas in which a computerized system might help the control of liquor in a bar operation might be:

- cash control
- ordering
- payment of accounts
- VAT returns
- reconciliation of stock with revenue
- highlighting of discrepancies

There are four basic methods by which computerization may penetrate a bar and they are:

- electronic cash register terminals arranged as master and slaves to allow central collation of data
- electronic cash register terminals linked to a microcomputer
- a microcomputer controlling a number of sales input terminals
- automatic drink dispensing systems that automatically record amounts of stock dispensed and allow processing of figures

CASE STUDY NUMBER 4

OLD PUB BENEFITS FROM NEW TECHNOLOGY

A 200-year-old, three-bar pub in the Home Counties moved into the hi-tech age in the summer of 1986 with the installation of a sophisticated computer system.

The landlord admits that he had had no previous experience of computers but took the attitude that if he had not gone for new technology he would have been left standing still. "It's like driving a horse and cart instead of a car," he says. "We now have complete control of the business."

All the bar staff have to do is to enter their personal identification code on to the keyboard followed by the code number of the meal and the order is then printed out in the kitchen. "Every cigar, bag of crisps and pork scratching is entered, charged for and deducted from stock", says the landlord. "Up-to-the-minute facts and figures are transmitted to the office control system and information – number of meals served, stock in hand and staff performance, for example – is available at the touch of a button either on screen or as a print-out."

The system has four main terminals with waterproof touch-sensitive keyboards, each with 128 or 256 keys. In addition, reports produced can be inspected remotely at the head office of the brewery if necessary. The system can in effect allow brewery monitoring of the operation in not only this pub but all pubs in the group so equipped.
(McDermid, 1986)

Bar point-of-sale accounting

One of the benefits of a computerized system to a bar operation or pub is that it can be of major assistance in settling disputes. Most arguments that occur in a pub situation concern the pricing of food and drinks and many of these simply evaporate when a properly itemized and exact breakdown of the liquor purchased by a customer can be placed in front of them. Such an analysis is easily produced by a computerized point-of-sale system.

The pricing itself should be more accurate because if the system uses code numbers for drinks and tobacco the computer can calculate the pricing automatically thereby freeing the member of staff totally from arithmetic.

Point-of-sale systems (Yeadon, 1987)

Typical point-of-sale systems have terminals in all the service areas, each of which may only be activated by a 'server key'. Each time servers use the terminal they must press their own numeric code and server key before commencing a transaction. Failure to do this will lead to an 'error' message appearing on the screen.

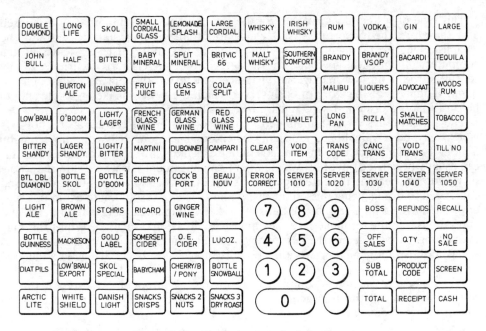

Figure 2.31 *Typical point-of-sale keyboard*

The terminal keyboard in Figure 2.31 has 'preset' keys for more than 80 of the most popular lines sold in the bar. The pressing of each of these keys produces an automatic costing of the drink concerned thereby removing a major possible source of error.

Keyboards are not necessarily situated in the same place as the cash drawers and should ideally be where drinks are actually being dispensed which would speed up the whole operation. It is also useful for the keys to be colour coded so that there is an obvious difference, say, between beers and wines. Amongst other advantages, colour coding helps new staff to pick up the operation of the system more quickly. On the keyboard illustrated the following colours might apply:

Orange: fortified wines, wines and flavoured wines, spirits
Green: draught beers
Yellow: bottled beers
Blue: mixers

With rigid preset keyboards drinks such as draught beer are usually costed into the memory in pints, so a half pint has to be indicated by pressing the 'half' key before the product key. Similarly, single spirit measures are usually costed into the memory and a double is indicated either by using the 'large' key or by pressing the product key for each separate measure that has been dispensed.

When making a sale the barperson completes the following routine:

Step 1 press personal code and server key
Step 2 key in the items dispensed

On completion of the details of the round of drinks the 'total' key is pressed whereupon the till drawer opens and change may be given. In addition a highly itemized receipt can be given to the customer showing complete details of the round.

This type of system does not control the actual amounts of liquor being dispensed and therefore the opportunity still exists for a member of staff to defraud the establishment by taking drinks or by giving drinks away. The existence of the computer, though, will go some way to deter this relatively rare occurrence. Only careful stocktaking and managerial vigilance can reveal this practice, although the detailed analysis of the work of each server which the system makes possible should help to identify dishonest staff much more easily.

The system relies on customers getting their drinks orders correct at the outset – which may be a vain hope, especially when some customers become affected by liquor. If customers change their minds then items may have to be voided and as this can usually be carried out only by a member of management this would slow the whole service down. Leaving the entering of items until the whole order has been dispensed could lead to drinks being missed off by accident. The best solution to avoid this type of problem would appear to be for bar staff to keep complete orders in their heads and enter items into the terminal once they have actually been dispensed. Whilst this may take a longer time it seems the best policy in order to minimize potential errors and is a classic illustration of how working practice may have to be changed to suit the computer.

When a service session is completed the manager can obtain a full report on the session showing all the transactions completed at each terminal. The information shown will include:

- date
- terminal number
- number of transactions
- start time of session
- finishing time of session
- quantity of each item sold
- total cash taken
- amount of money that should be in till drawer

Once the manager has cashed up the tills the 'end-of-day procedure' may be followed. This procedure gives the manager the following reports:

Activity Report.
An analysis of daily sales in hourly periods through the day. This is valuable for setting staffing levels or for identifying low periods where promotions or marketing may need to be employed.

Daily House Cash Report. This shows:

- total sales
- void items
- nett sales
- refunds
- discrepancies (between amount recorded and cash received)

Daily Server Report. This lists:
- staff using their keys during each session
- nett sales by each server
- number of transactions by each server
- average amount per sale
- use of 'no sale' key
- number of items voided by management

Once the information has been produced as a print-out it can be automatically transferred on to a cassette tape. The cassette tape can then be used to transmit the information to the head office of the brewery via a telephone link. The information can be collected during the night to facilitate the production of daily statistics for the entire company.

Dispense bars

Frequently the bar in the corner of the restaurant is also where drinks are dispensed for customers sitting at table. If a point-of-sale system is in operation for the restaurant staff then they should be able to transmit their orders for drinks through the system to a printer at the bar. This can greatly assist the bartender because it removes the queue of servers hassling each other and the bartender for their table drinks. The servers need only be called over, via the system, once their drinks are ready allowing the bartender more time and space to give attention to customers at the bar.

Bar stock control by electronic bar management system

The control of stock in a bar is fraught with difficulty and has numerous hidden traps for the unwary manager. Bearing these potential problems in mind, computer manufacturers have produced several types of electronic bar management systems (EBMS) to assist the bar manager.

The installation of an EBMS is claimed to produce startling results. It is said that a club owner was able to reduce the establishment's stock shortages within 24 hours of installation, bringing control to what had been described as an uncontrollable business. In some cases manufacturers claim to have eradicated stock shortages completely, whilst in others the manual stocktaking has been shown to be wildly inaccurate when the same figures have been analysed by computer. As much as 7 per cent difference has been found in the calculation of consumption.

The basis of most EBMS systems is that sensors are fitted to every optic and beer pump so that most drinks, whether by measure or flow, can be accurately monitored. Every bottle change on the optics is recorded so that a complete picture of sales is always to hand. The sensors require modified spirit dispensers but are similar in appearance and are just the same to operate as standard optics. Therefore staff need no special training to operate the system.

It is evident, though, that most establishments would need some rationalization of the way in which the drinks are dispensed. Spirits and fortified wines can easily be dispensed through optics in units of one sixth of a gill, but some less popular lines might not warrant the cost of an optic connected to sensors and then the usual thimble-type measure would still be utilized. Both light wines and draught beers can be served through free-flow dispensers. It is common for cola and lemonade to be served through post-mix dispensers, whilst most other mixers would probably be sold in baby and split bottles. Cordials from litre bottles will often be guess measured.

The sequence is that when a measure is emptied out of the optic an electronic pulse is sent along a wire to the computer which records the information by dispense point. The information is then added to the total for the dispense point and recorded in the computer's memory. A similar sequence occurs with the beer pumps.

The standard EBMS can monitor up to 128 dispense points in one or more bars and can provide consumption information on a print-out for periods of a single session, a day, a week and a month.

An EBMS has to be designed and built to withstand interference from bar staff and ideally the compact monitoring unit should be housed out of reach so that it cannot be turned off by unauthorized staff. Should this prove impossible, the unit will record the number of times that attempts to interfere with it are made. Beer monitoring sensors can be fitted in the cellar and in addition to pints pulled they will also record the number and time of keg changes.

An EBMS cannot relieve the manager of physical stocktaking of liquor at various times. This involves counting all the existing stock left in the cellar and on the shelves fortnightly, weekly or even daily if a specific problem is being investigated. It has been known for managers to stocktake a bar after each session if a member of staff is under suspicion of fraud. The system itself will calculate the sales and then this must be compared against the physical stocktake to show up any discrepancies.

The EBMS and cash control (Yeadon, 1987)

Some, but by no means all, EBMS computers can interface with cash control terminals which would allow staff to cash-up against the amount that the computer has calculated was taken during a service period. With this arrangement the terminals are in effect electronic cash registers, linked to a central processor, possessing a facility by which drinks dispensed can be displayed. As each of the optics, beer and mineral dispensers with electronic sensors record a drink being served then this is displayed on the VDU on the cash register. Each member of staff possesses their own button on the keyboard and may obtain the total amount of money due for a round by 'claiming' the drinks served that already appear on the screen. Change will be calculated and whilst drinks being dispensed by other staff will still appear on the screen no other member of staff may use the terminal until the initial transaction has been completed.

The system's apparent lack of concern for items not recorded by sensors, such as bottled beers and minerals, can be overcome by the use of preset keys on the terminals that will record and display the item. As an alternative, touch pads may also be used.

One distinct advantage of an EBMS is that different price structures can be built in for each terminal to reflect the various 'qualities' of each bar. Each terminal may also carry a number of different price structures to cater, for example, for 'Off-Sales' or 'Happy Hour'.

Problems

A common problem with EBMS systems is the dispensing of beer. Quite often an EBMS will show up theoretical losses because the cellar-situated beer flow-meters utilized by some systems cannot tell the difference between 'fob' and beer. Units of fluid are therefore recorded rather than just the liquid and at the end of a session there may be many units of beer recorded that have not been dispensed. One solution is to install much more sensitive flow-meters, which naturally are much more expensive, or alternatively to mount the meters in the bar itself to measure the beer after it has been cooled and is therefore less lively.

Electronic drink dispensers (EDD)

An electronic drink dispenser is a means of accurately controlling the exact quantities of drinks dispensed from a bar. A typical EDD will be installed with the intention of allowing the bar manager to keep a record of sales to check against takings. They monitor every measure sold through their optics, record operator errors and alert staff to the need to replace bottles.

This is achieved through a self-contained microcomputer which automatically monitors each drink dispensed and can print results by means of the printer linked to the system. An EDD can be interfaced with an external computer as part of a total electronic bar management system, allowing a complete analysis of sales without interfering with the traditional atmosphere of the bar.

An electronic drink dispenser has a microprocessor controlled delivery and refill system which helps to eliminate manual slips, stock shrinkage and the effect of overnight volumetric changes and evaporation. It not only satisfies the legal requirements of drink dispensing but also provides a reassurance to customers that they are not getting short measures. The Optronic EDD system is illustrated in Figure 2.32.

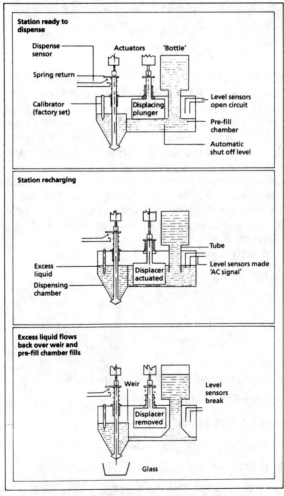

Figure 2.32 *Detail of electronic drink dispenser*
Source: Anglo Manufacturing Ltd

EDD constituent parts

The typical EDD possesses easy fitting bottle adaptors at the top which will take both 75 cl and 1.5 litre bottles. A built-in one-way valve prevents spillage and the bottle is held in place by a locking ring which is strong, hygienic and secure.

The dispense outlet is 'contact-free' thereby removing a problem of standard optics where the press bar can harbour and transmit contamination. An important consideration is that the dispense outlet can be easily cleaned.

The sensor pad under the glass prevents delivery of a measure of liquor until the glass is positioned underneath the outlet. As a safeguard an indicator lamp lights when the system is set up to dispense the required measure.

One of the advantages of this type of system is that six drinks may be dispensed simultaneously which is a distinct benefit to the busy bar where a large number of customers may be waiting at the same time. Another important advantage is that an EDD system allows tighter control of stock and, if applied properly, this should allow the bar operation to carry lower stocks thereby releasing capital that would otherwise be tied up.

Cocktail bars

In America computerized electronic drink dispensing systems have been employed with success in cocktail bars. Cocktails made traditionally can lead to a large number of problems, especially where exact monitoring of ingredients is concerned. A typical EDD system can be set up to an accuracy of one thousandth of a measure and can be capable of pouring 1,200 different cocktails at the press of a button. All the cocktail bar staff have to do is to select the desired drink on the keyboard and hold the glass under the pouring head and the system does the rest.

The system draws ingredients from a central rack of up to 120 bottles. An alarm indicator warns when a bottle on the rack is about to run out when there are still three measures to go. In addition the computer memory retains information on prices, records every drink, prints bills and receipts, and provides management with complete sales, book-keeping and stock records.

The advantages of such a system are:

'Lost' revenues are recovered by the elimination of:

- employee theft
- giveaways
- human errors in ringing a sale

New revenues are generated by:
- the service of a greater number of drinks per hour
- more effective merchandising
- pouring to exact recipes for drink consistency

Pour costs are lowered by:

- elimination of overpours
- reduction of waste, spillage and breakage
- the use of larger, less expensive liquor bottles

Labour costs are lessened by:
- reduction of the number of employees
- generation of complete sales records
- automatic inventory control

A bar stock package (Yeadon, 1987)

A typical bar stock package would run on a microcomputer system of between 20 and 40 megabytes and should be easily capable of handling 10 cellar, 10 cash and 10 sundry points. The system might be capable of receiving stocktaking information either from manually collated data, or directly when downloaded from handheld devices that in some cases plug into the computer. The system should therefore be able to undertake the following:

- control of transfers
- control of deliveries
- calculation of stock position
- detail losses
- calculation of re-order levels
- production of stocktaking results

In setting up a package from scratch one of the lengthiest parts of the operation is entering the historical information. Wherever possible it is best to initiate a new package at the commencement of the financial year so that a large amount of time is not wasted in entering past data that would otherwise be needed to calculate cumulative results.

Typical stock records may be set up using the following headings:

- *Stock number*   Usually cellar bin numbers are used but not always in all establishments
- *Description*
- *Supplier*
- *Base unit*   The unit by which the commodity is received into stock, for example, keg
- *Sub unit*   The unit by which the commodity is sold, for example, pint.
- *Yield/conversion factor*   The number of sub units in a base unit
- *Cost price*   Per base unit
- *Retail price*   Per sub unit
- *Minimum stock*
- *Maximum stock*
- *Current stock*
- *Year-to-date quantity*
- *Year-to-date cost*

The typical reports that might be obtained include:

Details of stock items

This report will give the manager an overview of the complete stock position. Amongst other details it will show which commodities are nearing their minimum stock level, as well as those where too much stock is held.

Table 2.6   *Sample stock item details*

Description	Base Unit	Sub Unit	Minimum Stock	Maximum Stock	Current Stock	Status
Export Lager	Barrel	Pint	4.00	10.00	2.05	gLOW*
Guinness	Bottle		25.00	50.00	17.00	gLOW*
Guinness	Keg	Pint	5.00	15.00	0.52	gLOW*
House Claret	Bottle	Glass	2.00	5.00	7.00	gHIGH*
Champagne	Bottle		3.00	10.00	5.00	

Supplier details

This part of the package will contain the names and addresses of all suppliers as well as a listing of items purchased by price and quantity. The total amount will be shown as a percentage of the total liquor purchased. Such statistics might help to negotiate better terms or services from a supplier.

Table 2.7   *Sample supplier details*

Stirlings Brewery,   Contact: James Stirling, Snr.
34 Cellar Street,   Phone : 779543 (24 hr answer)
Southby, Devon.

Amount spent year-to-date with this supplier: 7,343.21
Supplier's percentage of total cost   :76.49%

Description	Base Unit	Cost Price	Year-to-Date Quantity	Year-to-Date Cost
Guinness	Keg	36.50	6.000	219.00
Export Lager	Bottle	0.35	5.000	1.75
Pils	Bottle	0.27	6.000	1.62
Pale Ale	Bottle	0.27	8.000	2.16
Cider	Keg	36.45	7.000	255.15
Gin	Bottle	3.21	14.000	44.94
Total				524.62

Re-ordering report

A re-ordering report will pick out all those items of stock which are below the desired maximum stock level. In many cases a calculation will be carried out to show the quantities required to restore stock to the desired level. In addition information can be produced in relation to each supplier, including the cost of required replacement stock based on the last purchase price from that supplier. One of the great benefits of this report is that items that need analysis will not be overlooked as may easily happen when some are physically hidden away in the corner of the cellar.

Whilst the computer will produce the necessary information it will be down to the manager to actually make the decisions regarding purchasing, but these decisions will be based on much more accurate information than previously available. A decision may not be as straightforward as just ordering what is indicated on the report, as external influences such as the cash-flow of the business must also be taken into account. The vagaries of demand for drinks will also be analysed by the manager, being a difficult factor for a computer to anticipate.

Table 2.8 *Sample re-order report*

Supplier: Stirlings Brewery

Description	Base Unit	Cost Price	Current Stock	Maximum Stock	Re-order Quantity	Re-order Cost (£)
Spirits & Liqueurs						
Grenadine	Bottle	1.49	3.100	10.00	6	8.94
Vodka	Bottle	2.75	4.500	25.00	20	55.00
Gin	Bottle	3.21	2.250	25.00	22	70.62
Bacardi	Bottle	2.15	3.200	10.00	6	12.90
Brandy	Bottle	3.15	3.050	20.00	16	50.40
Malt Whisky	Bottle	5.15	2.000	5.00	3	15.45
Tia Maria	Bottle	3.35	3.667	5.00	1	3.35
Cointreau	Bottle	3.25	3.100	10.00	6	19.50
Baileys IC	Bottle	1.95	3.500	25.00	21	40.95
Drambuie	Bottle	5.15	2.034	5.00	2	10.30
Pernod	Bottle	2.95	4.000	20.00	16	47.20
Total						334.61

Stock usage report

The information for this report will have to be downloaded from cash registers connected to the computer, or in some systems may be entered manually. The report shows the anticipated revenue and the gross profit percentage on sales and can be calculated on individual bars or over a complete liquor operation.

Table 2.9 *Sample stock usage report*

Stock Point: Devon Room Lounge Bar

Description	Base Unit	Opening Stock	Goods In	Total Transfers	Till Sales	Usage	Usage at Cost	Usage at Retail	GP%
Sherry	Bt	5.00	0.00	0.00	4.600	4.600	6.67	66.70	88.50
Whisky	Bt	3.00	0.00	0.00	1.333	1.333	4.33	31.99	84.43
Brandy	Bt	2.00	0.00	0.00	0.766	0.766	2.11	18.38	86.79
Campari	Bt	5.00	0.00	0.00	1.050	1.050	2.23	10.50	75.57
Lowenbrau	Barl	2.00	0.00	0.00	0.209	0.209	7.80	15.36	41.60
Guinness	Bt	50.00	0.00	0.00	13.000	13.000	5.20	8.45	29.23
Fleur de Lys	Bt	6.00	0.00	0.00	2.900	2.900	3.25	0.00	0.00
Champagne	Bt	20.00	0.00	0.00	12.000	12.000	71.40	150.60	45.57
Mateus R	Bt	10.00	0.00	0.00	11.000	11.000	18.15	38.50	45.78
F. Spumante	Bt	25.00	0.00	0.00	16.000	16.000	31.20	72.00	50.16
Totals							152.34	412.48	57.52

Period-end stock report

This report gives the manager a quick reference as to whether margins are being achieved or not and is arrived at from the information accumulated during a physical stocktake.

Period-end reconciliation at retail

This report highlights differences between actual and anticipated revenue thus indicating to the manager which areas need attention and explanation.

Bar stocktaking

Computers can greatly ease the onerous task of stocktaking by undertaking the lengthy arithmetic involved in the calculation of the eventual results. This is a classic computer task as it is an obvious 'number-crunching' application.

The main problem with stocktaking of bars is the time that it takes. Many managers simply do not have the sort of time needed on a regular basis so in many cases they have to rely on external stocktakers who could take anything up to a week to produce results. Furthermore, external stocktakers may not be available exactly when required if they have already been booked by other customers. If the stocktaking is undertaken in-house then one member of management, probably the food and beverage manager, will have to devote a considerable amount of time to undertaking calculations before a result is achieved. Whichever method is used the results take time to produce and the process is labour-intensive.

The point should also be made that if there is a problem with a particular bar operation, for example a member of staff suspected of dishonesty, then stocktaking of that bar may be required after each service or in other words twice a day. This could keep a member of management fully employed until a conclusion is reached, which might take several days.

As no computer can yet walk around a bar or cellar measuring exactly how many bottles are in crates or pints of beer are left in kegs the legwork for the foreseeable future will still have to be undertaken by a member of staff. The time-saving is in the calculation of results. If a computer is used for the calculations, the stocktaker will record quantities on to a stock sheet and then transfer these manually into a computer terminal once the physical tour of the bars and cellars is complete.

Portable handheld stocktaking computers

There are a number of portable handheld stocktaking computers on the market which have many features in common. For a bar operation it is best to choose one that is durable, waterproof and light. The software run on the portable should be adapted to suit the manual stocktaking system in existence in the individual bar operation, as no universal software package will cover all eventualities. To save space all the items of beverage stock should be given code numbers for identification.

Having programmed in the purchases and issues for the period being examined and re-entered the closing stock from the last examination, the stocktaker then counts the quantities of the beverages that are left in the cellar and on the shelves. The calculations themselves will be carried out very rapidly: calculations that could have taken up to three hours by the traditional manual method can be completed by a computer in less than a minute. For ease of reference and analysis it is best if the portable can be plugged into a printer to obtain a hard-copy print-out of the results.

The capacity of a portable is quite sufficient for the largest of operations with a 144K portable being quite capable, for example, of holding stocktaking information for the Inn on the Park Hotel in Park Lane where there are no less than eight bars and a cellar with a total of 893 stock items. (Bradshaw, 1983)

In some cases the information held within the portable will be downloaded into another micro or minicomputer so that stocktaking results may be added to the overall accounting results of a large operation such as a hotel or leisure centre. The down-loading could take place directly or via a modem and telephone link. Whichever route is used the results can be produced rapidly and any obvious omissions, such as missed barrels, can be added in and the figures adjusted on the spot. Trends and fashions in drinking can be spotted instantly by the bar manager or publican, which might not have been possible inside a week using the external stocktaker's system.

COMPUTERS AND VENDING

The recession in the mid 1970s caused industrial caterers to take a fresh look at how they could provide a more reasonable service to their customers. In most cases this self-analysis was forced upon them because the pressure was on from clients to reduce overall expenditure. As labour was one of the major costs, automated catering became an even more attractive proposition. The application of new technology to vending machines has led to a much greater sophistication in the vending services on offer.

Whilst payment used to be a matter of possessing exactly the correct change which had to be inserted in a specific order for the purchase of vended goods, nowadays the new coin mechanisms will accept a large number of coins in any order to make up the particular price for the goods. In many cases change may also be given which was not possible just a short time ago.

Payment is now not necessarily a matter of possessing change at all. Many vending machines accept cards that may either be purchased by or given to users depending on the philosophy of the operator. Not only do these cards allow a close control of the usage of the machines which is popular with users, but they also remove the accumu-lation of cash in a machine which was previously an attraction to vandals.

The machines themselves can now produce detailed sales figures which can either be held within the machine until extracted by the operating staff or transmitted direct to a host computer. At the same time machines can self-diagnose faults and display these for the attention of the maintenance staff.

A much more variable pricing policy is available with the ability to accept a large variety of coins. Also price changes may be catered for much more easily as these can now be set on a keyboard within the vending machine. The internal microprocessor makes it possible to offer a much wider variety of service. For example, machines can be equipped with timing devices permitting such facilities as free vending at specific times and the internal clock mechanism will revert the machine back to normal operation when the 'free-vend' session is over. Similarly, 'Happy Hours' with drinks offered at reduced prices are possible thanks to the sophistication of the internal electronics.

Cashless vending

One of the major technological moves as far as vending has been concerned in recent years has been towards cashless vending. Systems have been developed for the catering and leisure industries which are attractive to operators because they offer a fast, efficient method of payment and complete automatic account control.

Cashless vending systems first became popular with caterers for the same reasons that cashless telephone kiosks appealed to British Telecom. In the case of British Telecom the use of a phone card system immediately removed accumulations of cash which were vulnerable to vandalism. For similar security reasons caterers are keen to remove the cash element from vending machines in order to reduce the abuse of machines which is a particular problem in unattended areas.

The next reason is that there is an inherent weakness in all cash handling situations because the handling and counting of cash unavoidably exposes the system to fraud and human error. Thirdly, cashless automatic vending machines appeal to operators because a large number of faults may be attributed to the coin handling processes.

Magnetic cashless vending card about to be inserted into a drinks machine
Photograph: GiroVend Cashless Systems

The secure magnetic card is the medium by which consumers can pay for all their transactions in a cashless system. They completely eliminate the need for change-givers, tokens and cash at the point-of-sale and bring the benefits of microchip technology to the caterer utilizing cashless vending.

How does the card-holder make use of the system?

The first step with a cashless vending system is to issue all the consumers with cards. In an industrial catering unit, such as a staff canteen, these can be personalized cards which are signed by the individual consumer. In a hotel or other situation involving the general public cards can be issued by means of a dispenser which will issue cards of specific predetermined values in exchange for coins.

In issuing the cards it is possible to allow 'free-vends' and subsidies which can be allocated to individual users. There is also the facility to recall cards where necessary.

The consumers should be warned that the magnetic strip on the back of the card holds all the information regarding its value and should therefore be protected from any magnetic or mechanical influences. Until cashless vending systems are totally accepted it might be worth pointing out to consumers some of the benefits of a cashless system:

- no more searching for change
- no more coins lost in vending machines
- a faster service
- a convenient method of payment

An explanation can then be made that their card has been created for their personal use and once it has been loaded with cash it may be used to make purchases from any of the vending machines and tills operating in the cashless system.

Having supplied the cards the next step is to load a cash value on to them so that they are validated. The card-holder is then free to make purchases from the various machines working within the system. There are basically two ways to load cash onto a card and the first is to make use of a note or coin *cash loader*. Cash loaders centralize cash collection at one point and will accept a variety of coins or notes. They may be used not only to load cash but also to view the current value of the card.

One great advantage of cash loaders is that the denominations of money taken are reduced to £0.50 and £1.00 coins and £5.00 notes which greatly improves the speed of counting. The system tells the operator how much money there should be so all that has to be done is to balance it. Previously tills had to have floats left in them once the contents had been counted and this could be a lengthy business. In one unit with 1,700 staff the cash counting used to take three hours a day, but that has now been reduced to half an hour. In some all-night industrial catering units the cashless card system has allowed staff to work much fewer anti-social hours thanks to the reduction in cash counting time.

To summarize, cash loaders will:

- centralize cash collection
- give clear customer information via visual displays
- prohibit the validation of 'blocked' cards
- forbid the validation of cards over a predetermined limit
- provide a 24-hour service
- automatically provide printed turnover information for reconciliation with cash in the loader

The second method of loading cash on to the cards is by using a *direct debit loader*. This connects directly with the wages or salary department and allows card-holders to validate their cards from their wages or salary account. The unit works in a very similar way to bank automatic cash dispensers: the card-holder gains access directly to his own wages account and transfers a specified value to the card. The direct debit loader has the added benefit of allowing the card-holder to return values back to the wages account if desired. So in addition to the features outlined above for cash loaders the direct debit loader will:

- allow the transfer of value from wages to the card and vice versa
- provide a completely cashless system

Whether utilizing a vending machine or a till the procedure with a card is almost identical. The card is inserted into the appropriate reader, the value of the card is displayed, the value of the purchase is subtracted, either by the vending machine or the till operator, and the new value of the card is displayed.

Vending machines and tills

The cashless system may be incorporated into most types of vending machine, both old and new, so capital investment requirements are minimal. Indeed because cash is obtained before purchases are made there is an unusually fast cash return.

There is the benefit of being able to eliminate rigid price thresholds so that the system may be much more flexible than traditional operational methods. It is quite common for up to eight price bands to be operated by any one machine and within each price band there may be 12 different selection prices. Different price bands may therefore be assigned to specified users. Prices are easy to change with no upper limit and may be defined as closely as fractions of 1p if required.

It has been found that where a cashless till is in operation customers may pass through the till at a rate of between 15 and 20 customers a minute, whereas when change was being given in the traditional way this was usually seven a minute. A cashless system therefore can definitely speed up the whole process, cutting down aggravation in queues and allowing customers to reach their tables more quickly with hot food.

Does a cashless system increase sales?

The tangible sales benefits of a cashless vending system may be listed as follows:

- the customer is retained 'in-house'
- overall spend per head is improved
- purchase frequency is increased
- more impulse sales are made
- product and service ranges are easily increased
- rigid price structures are eliminated
- faster service is provided
- 24-hour spending facilities are available
- no more machine 'coin jams'
- less machine faults
- wide range of service offered on just one card

Improvements in cash accounting

The improvements may be listed as follows:

- errors are reduced (Automatic Accounting)
- improved cash-flow because of prepayment
- different types of user automatically monitored
- automatic price discrimination between different types of user
- automatic restricted use of machines if required
- controlled free services
- automatic collection, protection and balance of data
- numerous cash collection points eliminated
- machine vandalism reduced – no cash to steal
- no cash floats required
- direct debiting from wages/salaries
- interfaces with a wide range of equipment

Additional uses of cards

The cards themselves need not be used solely for vending and restaurant purposes but can be incorporated into other systems too. These may include:

- *Security passes.* All the necessary safeguards are built into some cards to allow them to double as security passes
- *Identification cards.* Polaroid pictures of the holders may be placed on the cards on site
- *Door entry.* The cards can act as 'keys' to allow restricted access
- *Turnstiles.* Cards can be used to operate turnstiles
- *Clocking-on.* Instead of having special cards for staff to clock-on for flexible working hours, these cards can be used for this purpose
- *Bar codes.* The cards can have bar codes printed on them so that they can double, for example, as library tickets.

References

Bradshaw, Della, January 1983. Stock answers from a Husky. *Practical Computing*.

Fretwell-Downing Computer Group, A. Computer controlled cook-chill and cook-freeze operations – CMI overview.

Fretwell-Downing Computer Group, B. Catering Management Information (CMI) System – operational overview.

Fretwell-Downing Computer Group, C. Computer controlled Patient Menu Analysis System – operational overview.

Hughes, Alwyn (Director, Monitor Auto-call). Paging for efficiency. *HCIMA Yearbook 1986/87*.

McCance, R. A. and Widdowson, E. M. 1978. *The Composition of Foods*. Paul and Southgate.

McDermid, Kate, November 1986. Better service at your fingertips. *Hospitality*.

Restaurants & Institutions, 15 November 1982. In-house computer perks up profits.

Plumb, Richard (Director, Fretwell-Downing Computer Group). Cook-chill control. *HCIMA Yearbook 1986/87*.

Tougas, Jane Grant, 25 June 1986. Why computers make dollars and sense. *Restaurants & Institutions*.

Yeadon, Cynthia, February 1987. *A Survey of Computerised Liquor Control Systems currently implemented within the Hotel and Catering Industry and their Effectiveness*. Huddersfield Polytechnic.

3 Computer Applications in Hotel and Catering Administration

COMPUTERS AND RESERVATIONS

The primary reason for making use of computers in the handling of reservations is to increase room occupancy rates. How an establishment actually goes about achieving this aim depends entirely on the level of computerization that the management settle upon.

Controlling an accurate reservations record on any scale is extremely difficult. However, by making use of a set of on-line computer files these records may be stored centrally with a great degree of accuracy and, compared with manual systems, much reduced staff effort. The on-line magnetic storage medium of disks or 'floppies' can hold thousands of reservations and find any one of them within a fraction of a second. Any system can automatically sort and update these reservations records and files. Confirmations are printed on high-speed line printers. Advance deposit requests are simplified and a good system may even generate personalized deposit requests. Control and communication of deposit information is made fast and simple by using a computerized centralized database.

A reservations system can be required to handle bookings for up to years in advance and needs to be sufficiently flexible to make it simple to operate for staff whilst allowing maximum management control. The whole operation of the system, including the screen formats, should be designed so that the computer falls naturally into daily work routines thereby assisting the staff to handle bookings both quickly and efficiently.

Amongst the many features of a reservations system, no matter what type of hardware it runs on, is an ability to view the current availability of the hotel's accommodation. This should be possible at any time for some years ahead, and in addition special requests for certain rooms should be accommodated within the system. Some hotels prefer to assign rooms in advance of check-in, but this is by no means a universal requirement. The system should be set up to offer the best available rooms for guests, thereby improving hospitality.

The computer should in effect be a practical tool complementing the work of the reception staff by eliminating much of the paperwork that is both time consuming and prone to errors. Details of individuals and groups should be readily accessible both for reference and alteration, and it should be possible for mistaken cancellations to be re-activated by the computer. Confirmation slips can be printed automatically thus saving an enormous amount of secretarial time.

Group business can be a problem for the reservations systems in many hotels. Groups are complicated affairs with a variety of arrival and departure dates, room types and rates, but a good computer system should be able to accommodate these with ease.

A good computer reservations system can provide daily availability reports both in tabular and graph form either on-screen or as a print-out, whilst statistics of a more specific nature can be obtained on such items as occupancy and room status. A good system will also ease complicated administrative tasks such as recording deposits which can be handled automatically. Details will be stored within the system along with information in diary form as to when the balance of the payment is due.

It is vital that extreme care is taken with the creation of a reservations system and that once installed the detail is closely monitored by the management concerned. In one celebrated case in the United States an error by a member of staff led to a computerized reservations system indicating there was no room available when in fact the hotel was running at a 45 per cent occupancy level. The error was only found when the hotel was in the hands of the receivers. The computer had refused 27,000 room nights of business over a period of eight months because someone on the staff had closed off a specific type of room in the reservations program. This error caused the hotel to lose over $1 million worth of business (*Hotel & Motel Management*, 1985). There are many different methods by which new technology may be deployed to handle reservations and not all have been universally successful.

The levels at which a hotel may make use of computerized reservations systems are:

- external reservations networks
- in-house reservations networks
- single-site reservations systems

External reservations networks

The idea of handling hotel reservations by the use of large networks had always been the dream of computer applications specialists. One of the great abilities of a computer is that it is able to collate large quantities of information and subsequently exchange it between workstations, and therefore large reservations networks should be ideally suited to the application of new technology. Unfortunately the practicalities in the early days did not always match up to the theory and there were some expensive failures. These failures, though, were through no fault of the hardware being used but largely because the accountants produced financial projections of profitability that were far too optimistic.

Whilst theoretically large networks seemed an ideal solution to handling hotel reservations, reality soon crept in. By the beginning of the 1970s some of the early ideas were being thought through for a second time. The problem was that several airlines had managed to make their seat reservations systems work satisfactorily but the booking of bedrooms was not perceived as a totally different kettle of fish. With the benefit of hindsight, perhaps it should have been.

Where the early hotel bedroom reservations systems were concerned the huge expense of creating a computerized operation was initially largely ignored. The ensuing charges did not take into account the differential between the average value of an airline ticket and the price of a hotel room. Furthermore, there were a large number of reservations systems competing against each other, particularly in the United States, with the effect that charges for bookings were reduced below economic levels. As a consequence several ambitious systems failed.

The first bureau reservations network in the United States was the *Telemax* system set up in 1967, but it was American Express (Amex) who were to be the pathfinders, having been prompted by IBM in November 1968 to create a worldwide reservations network with a computer facility in Memphis using IBM 360/40s. In June 1969 the *Express Reservations Space Bank*, as the Amex system was called, went into operation and by 1970 it boasted 17 reservations centres all over the world handling the bookings.

The Amex system was never budgeted to make money, but the company recognized that it picked up additional credit card business through hotels because of its involvement with computerized reservations.

The fact that Amex were interested in hotel reservations led other organizations to look at computerized booking systems that were complimentary to their businesses. Notable amongst these were the airlines who saw the benefit of booking both airline seats and hotel rooms at each end of a flight. The airlines also realized that they possessed great expertise where aircraft seat reservations were concerned and believed that as a consequence they would be well placed against opposition. Amongst the many systems that appeared at this time were the TWA-backed *DOARS* network, PanAm's *Panamac* system and *Reservations World*, which was to become part of American Airlines. In Europe the *Citel* system was backed by BOAC (now British Airways) and Air France when these two airlines took a minority shareholding.

America also boasted systems called International Reservation, Telemax, Hoteltex, SAFIR, GETS, NARS, TARS, MARS, and ATARS, amongst others. Their European counterparts were the Paris based SITA–ITT and *Telesysteme* reservations networks. The sheer number of competing computerized systems meant that any profits were dissipated amongst all these contenders. When the small margins on hotel bedroom sales were realized the true bleak economic picture became obvious and most of the systems quickly disappeared.

Interestingly most of the reservations systems mentioned so far had one major similarity. They operated by obtaining guaranteed allocations of rooms from hotels in advance that could then be sold via computer directly to travel agents and the public.

Europe became the hunting ground for Citel, Express Reservations, International Reservations Corporation and Express Reservations Space Bank. Citel outlasted the other systems, absorbing Amex's European business in 1972, and by 1973 it was handling 150,000 room allocations from 1,500 hotels and utilizing 16 reservations centres. The Citel computer network was designed in conjunction with BOAC's Boadicea team and could therefore be linked to IBM airline reservations systems. Citel soon linked up with the Avis car-hire reservations system and both the BOAC and Alitalia systems.

Unfortunately many conservative hotel managers in the early 1970s were sceptical of computerized networks such as Citel, often saying that they received only 1 to 3 per cent of their total bookings from the system.

In-house reservations networks

The first in-house reservations networks to be set up in the United States were the Sheraton and Holiday Inns systems in 1964. The Inter-Continental group also had their Panamac system thanks to their parent company PanAm airways.

Hilton International initiated their Hilton on-line reservations system in the USA and Canada in the early 1970s and were the first company to install two-way terminals in each of their hotels so that reservations could be both made and received throughout the company. It was to take until 1984 for Hilton to create its own reservations network, called Hiltonet, having previously relied on a telex and airline network called SITA for communications outside North America.

Single-site reservations systems

Two of the first hotels to install computers to handle reservations solely for their establishments were the Diplomat Hotel in Hollywood (IBM 360) and the St Jacques in Paris (IBM 1800) where the system boasted 50 on-line terminals. In London Strand Hotels, a subsidiary of Lyons, installed Olivetti computers in their economy class hotels for the same purpose.

A computerized system provides many benefits that perhaps were not possible with manual systems; for example, it should be possible to respond more swiftly to requests for accommodation. Whereas a complex system of charts might have been common-place in hotels at one time it is now possible for staff to have an instantaneous picture of the exact booking situation on any given date so that the customer may be dealt with more quickly.

Integrated reservations systems

Reservations is perhaps the starting point for the majority of hotel computer systems as it is here that some of the basic information required by an integrated system is identified.

At the time that a reservation is taken it is possible to obtain not only the name of the customer but also the price that they are going to pay. If the intention of an integrated computer system is to charge the customer the right amount for their stay then here, at the time of booking, is the opportunity to obtain information that can be used subsequently to compile accounts. As a by-product the reservation will allow such items of information as room status and market and sales analysis to be com-menced. The successful handling of reservations by computer is therefore essential to the assembly of an integrated hotel computer system.

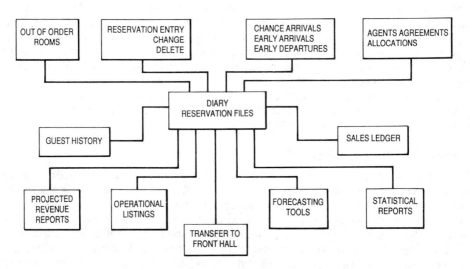

Figure 3.1   *Integrated advance reservations system*
Source: Thorn EMI CHAMPS Systems

If the reservations system is fully integrated then a number of effects are going to be felt due to input of bookings from various sources. The front desk, for example, will be booking in 'walk-in' or 'chance' customers and as a consequence altering the availability of rooms on a minute-by-minute basis. They will also be informing the computer of guests who have decided to leave early, rooms that have been taken out of service and guests who have decided to stay on longer than expected. A good system, therefore, allows access to a common file containing the relevant information thereby enabling all staff to have access to the current availability situation. In other words, a single input of reservations data into the central files in an integrated system makes that data available to all the other users needing this information.

It is a time-wasting process to have to enter guest details into the reservations system if the guests have stayed before. Therefore there should be the facility in an integrated system to enter details direct from the guest history files, or even to make the reservation from this sector of the files. Using the guest history will make sure that guest preferences are spotted and acted upon. Similarly, the sales ledger files will be checked when making reservations for account verification and control. This will warn the reservations clerk whether a particular guest or company has had its credit withdrawn.

An integrated reservations system will facilitate financial modelling; for example, to project the average room rate for any date or period in the future so that accurate forecasting may be undertaken. The forecasting may reveal many statistics under a number of classifications such as the take-up figures for tour operators with allocations of rooms, which may affect the sales policies of the establishment.

An integrated reservations system permits a number of useful lists and reports to be produced in far more detail than their manual counterparts and statistical print-outs can also be obtained from the system to show, for example, nationality and booking source information.

In summary, an integrated reservations system has at its core the central reservations files that are constantly being updated by reservations clerks, receptionists, cashiers and sales ledger clerks to provide a comprehensive profile of the mainstream business of the hotel. This database is vital to the effective operation of the system and the business and is the key to operational success.

Essential reservations facilities

The essential facilities that a well-constructed computerized reservations package should provide include the following:

- flexible inventory of at least 20 different room types
- unlimited future availability
- unlimited booking capability
- immediate availability update
- immediate rooms inventory update
- overbooking (oversell) capability
- complete and detailed reservations screen
- individual and group reservations
- individual and group blocking
- group master records, summary and detail
- company information entry
- travel agency information entry
- travel agency activity reports
- computer-assisted travel agency commission handling
- guest information enquiry
- reservations linked to city ledger
- strong guarantee parameters
- advance deposit posting and auditing

- advance deposit journal
- 'request for deposit' and deposit received
- confirmations, plus printing of confirmation forms
- modification and cancellation confirmations
- free-form comments field on all reservations
- services field on all reservations
- system-generated confirmation numbers on all reservations
- user identification entered on all transaction screens
- confirmations printed automatically or on demand
- forecast reports, current and future dates to five years historical information
- detailed inventory reports
- 'no-show' reports
- computer-assisted no-show handling (charging and billing)
- all guest information – past, present, future – retained in system

Source   Auditel Lodging Management Systems

Useful reservations features

Whilst there are many facilities that a computerized reservations system must provide, there are other useful abilities of some systems that are very helpful where both profitability and organization are concerned. One such facility is the ability to sell rooms floor-by-floor, thereby allowing not only the most economical use of the housekeeping staff but also permitting economic usage of energy for lighting, heating and hot water provision.

It is often assumed where reservations packages are concerned that only individuals book rooms, ignoring the special demands of tour operators and airlines. That a reservations system allows fast block and group bookings will be a major consideration in the selection and usage of such systems.

By the same token, by no means every reservation will be for one person or one type of room. The reservations system should allow for as many different types of room as possible so that, for example, families may be accommodated in a variety of rooms to suit the parents and children.

The actual allocation of rooms may not necessarily take place at the time the guest checks-in and therefore a computer may offer the ability for rooms to be assigned to particular reservations prior to check-in, especially when specific rooms have been requested by the customer. In addition, the handling of deposits as well as the printing of confirmation slips should be easily accommodated by the system.

In achieving a full house, up-to-the-minute information is needed on the current state of bookings. If the computer system selected has the facility to produce automatic reports on the number of 'no-shows' as well as 'late arrivals' then the hotel can be managed much more effectively. Close monitoring of the overbooking situation will also be a great advantage for the accommodation manager.

Cancellations are a problem where reservations are concerned and it is useful if the computerized system can allow such reservations to be re-activated. There are numerous situations in a hotel of any size where this is necessary and such a facility can save a large amount of staff time.

One other factor to watch out for is that some reservations systems do not allow staff to undertake all the traditional operations that they were used to in the reservations system. This should be guarded against as it can cause problems.

CASE STUDY NUMBER 5

**NOT ALL SYSTEMS ALLOW A HOTELIER
THE NECESSARY FLEXIBILITY**

A south coast resort hotel of top quality boasting 164 bedrooms, that hosts the holidaymaker as well as conference business, possesses an integrated minicomputer system that has only recently replaced a billing machine and a Whitney system. The computer system has three terminals in reception and three in the cashier's office. It deals with guest billing, advance reservations, ledgers, housekeeping and telephone logging. Payroll is dealt with on a separate microcomputer.

Whilst the system has improved speed, given greater accuracy and reduced paperwork it is felt that it is less easy to check room allocations at a glance. "Old clients coming here for 30-odd years need their particular room," says the head receptionist. "When you are blocking off rooms on the computer, you can run into problems with allocations because you cannot see at a glance what is available. You could on the Whitney board," she says.

When the computer has broken down it has 'locked up data' for an entire day in the computer's memory, requiring bills to be mailed on to guests after they have left. This type of problem is not solely restricted to computers as "a power cut or breakdown could have had the same effect on the old system," admits the head receptionist.

The hotel is part of a group and their Systems Controller suggests that mistakes made with a computer system can be more critical than with a manual system. "But they should not happen so often and controls can ensure that mistakes are spotted before it is too late," he says. "Things jump out when in pictorial form, such as on a Whitney board, but manual systems cause mistakes because they are more time consuming and labour-intensive." (Whitehall, 1986)

Watch out for bad design

Some reservations systems show their North American origins by utilizing the American date format as their main method of data entry for the recording of bookings. What this actually means is that the reservations clerks have to enter first the month and then the day, rather than the normal European format of the day followed by the month. For example, 8 January on these systems would be entered as 1/8 and not 8/1, which is totally alien to non-Americans and can lead to great confusion.

This small alteration to the normal way in which the reservations clerk thinks can lead to an enormous number of problems. How many reservations, for example, would be made for 1 August (1/8) by accident? Whilst there may be other design problems, the point should be made that the software should be examined in detail before being implemented.

Reservations reports

The reservations system will be required to undertake the production of some important reports concerning current and future business and these may include:

- reservations summary
- daily summary
- arrival list
- non-arrival list
- departure list
- deposits due
- deposits paid
- group pick-up report
- room blocking detail
- confirmed booking list
- cancelled booking list
- room availability list
- occupancy projection
- audit trail

Security

As part of the overall security of the computer package access to reservations will only be allowed to staff who possess the correct operator passcode. The intention is to stop fraudulent alterations to reservations that may involve collusion between staff and guests. The computer operations will additionally be logged and inspected periodically by management in a number of sensitive fields. These will include the actual placing of reservations, modifications, cancellations and reinstatements.

The reservation sequence

All reservations follow a distinct sequence of:

- initial enquiry
- reservation data collection

In any good computerized reservations system the two parts of the reservation process are closely interwoven, whether they be incorporated on the same screen or follow sequentially.

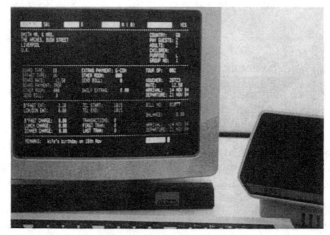

The reservations screen layout must be logical and hold a large amount of information about the guests and stay
Photograph: Megabyte Ltd

Initial enquiry. At this stage the guests will be trying to establish whether they can be accommodated or not and therefore there needs to be a display of the following:

- date availability
- room availability
- alternatives

In many cases the reservation enquiry will go no further as it may not be possible to accommodate the guest in the type of room required on the dates required. Whilst the facility to offer alternative dates or accommodation should be built in, not all guests will be able to accept these. Figure 3.2 shows a sample room availability screen from the Innstar system.

MAY					ROOM AVAILABILITY							28 MAY 09.35		
ROOM TYPE	28	29	30	31	1	2	3	4	5	6	7	8	9	10
	WED	THU	FRI	SAT	SUN	MON	TUE	WED	THU	FRI	SAT	SUN	MON	TUE
SB	21	11	4	10	23	26	19	17	12	11	16	11	5	3
TB	38	30	28	28	23	28	25	26	23	28	33	32	34	34
DB	14	13	14	14	12	11	8	7	12	11	11	11	15	15
DLTB	5	5	5	5	5	5	4	4	4	5	5	5	5	5
STUD	3	4	4	4	4	4	4	4	4	4	4	4	4	4
DUP 1	5	5	5	5	5	6	6	6	5	5	5	5	5	5
DUP 2	2	2	2	2	2	2	2	2	2	2	2	2	1	1
DUP 3	2	2	2	2	2	2	2	2	2	2	2	2	2	2
DUP 4	2	2	2	2	2	2	2	2	2	2	2	2	2	1
PEN 1	1	1	1	1	1	1	1	1	1	1	1	1	1	1
PEN 2	1	1	1	1	1	1	1	1	1	1	1	1	1	1
PEN 3	1	1	1	1	1	1	1	1	1	1	1	1	1	1
BEDDED	95	77	69	75	81	89	75	73	69	73	83	77	76	72
OCCUPANCY	18%	33%	40%	35%	30%	23%	35%	37%	40%	37%	28%	33%	34%	37%
MISC	6	6	6	6	6	6	6	6	6	6	6	6	6	6

Figure 3.2   *Innstar room availability display*

Reservation data collection. Once the dates and types of room have been agreed the system will then need to collect information in a logical sequence about the guest. This will not only form the reservation detail but will also transfer into the guest history. The detail collected may include:

- guest name
- company name
- address and post code
- number of adults
- number of children
- tariff type
- additional charges
- special features
- arrival time
- method of payment
- credit card number
- expiry date
- contact
- phone number
- confirm code
- travel agent IOTA
- remarks
- initials of reservations clerk

Figure 3.3 shows a sample guest information screen from the Innstar system.

```
ARRIVAL DATE      ; 01 MAY 88        ROOM TYPE  ;    SB
                                     # OF ROOMS ;    1
NIGHTS            ; 02               PERSONS    ;    1
RESV ENTERED      ; 29 APR BY I.D.44 RATE          3700
--------------------------------------------------------------------
LAST NAME         ; SMITH            COMPANY    ; GLOBAL COMMUNICATIONS PLC
                                                  CORP #;
TITLE; MR     FIRST; A               GROUP;
                                                  GROUP#;
RESERVATION #     ; AC9D000F         RESV BY    ; MISS JONES
                                                  PHONE 789 8888
                                     SHARE;
*** GUEST ADDRESS ***                TRAVEL AGENT #;  89988
80 HIGH STREET                       *** ADDITIONAL ADDRESS ***
TOWN                                 THE CITY
COUNTRY                              LONDON
PHONE; 0077 777 8888                 EC3
--------------------------------------------------------------------
GUARANTEED? Y        CREDIT CARD #  ; VISA 123456789101112       GUEST TYPE; 1
CONFIRM?    Y        DEPOSIT REQUEST;  10000       DEPOSIT DUE DATE; 30 APR 88
                     DEPOSIT RECEIVED;             VIP? Y  REGULAR? Y  HIST? 0001
COMMENTS; LATE ARRIVAL PREFERS A BACK ROOM                                0000
*** DISPLAY THIS RESERVATION ?
```

Figure 3.3   *Innstar reservations display*
Source: International Guest Systems

Viewdata and reservations

Viewdata has been more widely accepted in the travel trade than in any other industry and services which allow travel agents to book rooms in hotels are becoming more and more popular.

There are three main services enabling the booking of hotel rooms via a viewdata system. Hoteliers are realizing the advantages of being associated with such systems along with the other information providing facilities of viewdata systems.

Prestel's 'Roomservice' is the longest running service and holds information on over 1,800 hotels worldwide which can be located through a geographical index. It is possible for a customer to make a reservation request via Prestel or a telex-link service directly to the hotel concerned. The other two services, which are newer, demonstrate one of the major advances in electronic booking for hotels. They are primarily for use by travel agents and corporate travellers, enabling them to book rooms directly.

Hotels with an automated booking system have, from the spring of 1987, been able to link directly into the system. Hotels without such a facility can use a telex-link to receive bookings on a telex machine or on a viewdata terminal via an electronic mail telex service.

Continuing improvements needed

Unfortunately by no means all hoteliers appreciate the benefits of computerization, perhaps through installing systems that have not lived up to expectations. It is therefore vital that improvements are incorporated into new systems and that the education of hoteliers and their staff continues so that distrust of computers is removed.

CASE STUDY NUMBER 6

DISTRUST OF COMPUTERIZED RESERVATIONS

Some managers still distrust new technology, as does the manager of a luxury city centre hotel of 100 bedrooms. "I've heard horror stories", he says, "of well known hotels with computers showing they have 100 rooms to let when they don't have any or, alternatively, showing they were full up when they have 50 rooms still to let". This he thinks is due to sudden fluctuations in business exposing weaknesses in computerized systems. He believes that vital information can be "invisible" within a computer because, he says, "you can't call up everything all the time, so mistakes which are made – because everyone is fallible – stay there and nobody notices".

"A simple, manual identity chart every time you make a booking shows kinks in the booking pattern for a particular night. That prompts you to find out why – maybe unconfirmed bookings which need checking", he says.

Interestingly whilst reservations are not on the schedule for computerization in this hotel, which is not totally anti-computer, guest history records are, and this will shortly be completed. (Whitehall, 1986)

In-house reservations networks

Holidex – a network of 'dumb' terminals

A computerized reservations network can provide a company with the ability to maintain total control of the business which is an advantage of great consequence. If, after all, every reservation that is taken by the hotels within a company passes through a single location then the executive management have an instant global picture of what is happening. Should the business depend on turnover, as in the case of franchise operations, then a computerized centralized reservations system can provide the basis for accurate monitoring.

One company that has deliberately built up a sophisticated reservations system from early beginnings in 1965 is Holiday Inns. As early as 1969 the Holiday Inns system was the largest in the world with over a thousand Inns being directly linked. The system at that time was claimed to have increased occupancy rates – their occupancy rate was said to be 10 per cent higher than that of their competitors in comparable locations – and to have reduced reservations costs. Holiday Inns also operated at that time *Traveldex* as a computer reservations service for hotels neither belonging to, nor in competition with, the Holiday Inns group.

Holiday Inns has long been regarded as a leader in hotel computerization and their current enhancement of their reservations system first used in 1965, *Holidex III*, boasts no less than 3,000 terminals in 53 countries capturing information on behalf of 1,680 hotels. The centre of the system is Holiday Inns' computer centre in Memphis which takes up to 900,000 messages every day. Thirty-three per cent of Holiday Inns reservations are made through the Holidex system (*Hotel & Catering Technology*, 1986). Holidex III is also a comprehensive management communications system that allows the company executives at Memphis to see exactly how the group is performing on an instantaneous basis.

The Holidex system has all the rooms in the company's hotels in its memory and each hotel issues instructions as to how many can be sold on specific dates through the company-wide network as opposed to by the individual hotel itself. All hotels within the group, with the exception of those behind the Iron Curtain, are linked into the Holidex network whilst there are also terminals with major airlines, travel agencies and corporations. Travel agents are only allowed a Holidex terminal if they can guarantee to book 250 room nights a month with the company. Reservations are totally computerized and are taken for a year in advance. The system can also produce arrival lists, special request lists, confirmations, travel agent commission lists and currency conversions.

If a potential guest is at a location where there is a Holidex terminal, room availability can be checked for him in any Holiday Inns worldwide. In addition the reservations clerk has access to room types and hotel facilities in any of the hotels.

The previous Holidex II system was a stand-alone system utilizing 'dumb' terminals. Holidex III uses the same concept but now the system is designed to interface with existing property management computer systems. Each dumb terminal has a screen, keyboard, printer and modem. A dumb terminal has no 'intelligence' itself; it is purely a device for feeding data into the central computer.

As a large proportion of Holiday Inns properties are franchised the system is particularly useful in producing reports that monitor the flow of business throughout the company. This is particularly important in allowing the parent company to keep a strict control of the overall flow of finance within the group. The system also monitors the productivity of every terminal user in the network.

The impact the system has made on Holiday Inns is demonstrated by the high proportion (33 per cent) of reservations placed via Holidex and shows the benefit of being exposed to new technology from the outset.

Roomfinder – a personal computer network

Another way of handling reservations is to create a company-wide network of intelligent workstations. Each hotel contributing to such an arrangement will have a personal computer to allow reservations information to be passed through the network. This has the advantage of allowing reservations to be handled centrally while also giving each hotel the added benefits of a personal computer when reservations are not being handled.

One such system is the *Roomfinder III* that is employed throughout 600 units in 21 different countries by Ramada Hotels. A total of 96,000 rooms are accessible through the system in hotels that are either owned wholly by the company or franchised (*Hotel & Catering Technology*, 1986).

Ramada initially became involved with hotel computerization in the late 1960s through their subsidiary company Micor and in conjunction with marketing consortia such as Best Western and hotel companies such as Sheraton and Marriott. Ramada International had set up their own separate computing division by 1974 employing 92 professional data processing staff with the intention of providing software for their own properties as well as selling systems to the hospitality industry in general. At that time Ramada's commitment was by far the largest financial investment of any hotel organization in computing. Amongst other commitments they had agreed to purchase

1,000 specially designed minicomputers from Texas Instruments over a three-year period.

When Ramada decided to go their own way they commenced with their Roomfinder I reservations system which was subsequently refined into Roomfinder II in 1982 at a cost of $12 million (1983 value). In common with many systems evolving at this time, Ramada's software staff were largely from an airline background which gave them the expertise to tailor flexible software to cater for the company's needs as evolution of the computer network progressed.

By 1981 Ramada realized that the Roomfinder I system was becoming very 'long in the tooth'. The company had to invest in a large number of spare terminals in order to keep the network operational. These were kept in strategic locations across North America and were rapidly cannibalized to keep the operational terminals in action. Reliability was not the only problem with the terminals, however.

They possessed only a tiny 4K memory which would just about allow a screen of information to be transmitted. The Roomfinder II system had 635 terminals, each possessing 128K of memory and two disk drives.

To make the changeover between systems easier, the first step was to increase the Roomfinder I terminals to 8K to allow for necessary changes to the mainframe computer at Phoenix which held the reservations database. The second step was to convert the main processor at Phoenix and then thirdly the new terminals, which were IBM PCs, were introduced one property at a time over a 90-day period.

Roomfinder II was processing in excess of two million reservations a year by 1984 and had some useful security systems built in. There was, for example, an automatic call-back verification system of the telephone number from which reservations were made to make sure authorized numbers were being used. Also travel agents were given codes that verified all their individual information such as commission rates.

The personal computers used in the Roomfinder III network are actually the same IBM PCs which were installed in each hotel in 1983 and the new system is looked on as a logical step in the progression of this technology. Roomfinder III interfaces with all existing property management computer systems in the hotels thus removing the need to physically transfer information from one system to another, as happened in the past. The time-saving alone is reckoned to be a major benefit of the new network.

Roomfinder III went 'live' on 19 November 1986. Each of the individual units possesses a stand-alone personal computer linked to Ramada's mainframe computer in Phoenix as well as to each of the company's reservations centres. Every reservation placed within the company is passed through the database at Phoenix where it is recorded and confirmed within 15 to 20 seconds. The system also holds details on an inventory of all the rooms that hotels want to sell on particular dates. It is this last feature – the ability of the worldwide network to access the room situation in each individual hotel – that, it is claimed, will allow more rooms to be sold than with other systems.

It is anticipated that the system will allow an increase in annual sales of 500,000 room nights and a revenue increase of $30 million. The comprehensiveness of the system is expected to reduce the number of reservations turned away by 20 per cent because the entire network will be aware of the real situation in each hotel and will have access to the 'last room' in each property throughout the company. Each hotel can produce an arrival list from the computer and registration forms can be printed in advance, along with reports for management on occupancy, booking activity, average daily rates and the market mix.

Through the Roomfinder III system Ramada's reservations clerks have access to comprehensive and up-to-date information on each of the company's 600 locations via a menu comprising the following (*Hotel & Catering Technology*, 1986):

- features list (hotel facilities)
- sales page
- sports and recreation facilities
- tourist attractions
- food and beverage information
- community services (churches and shops, etc.)
- meeting rooms (conferences, etc.)
- meeting support (conference facilities)
- special events
- room types and prices
- package information

The Ramada chain operates the 'Ramada Business Card' system and the holders of these cards should find the level of their personal service increased by the new system. Each time they make a reservation their guest history details will be examined automatically so that their preferences, such as smoking or non-smoking rooms, will be catered for. Lost reservations will also be reduced as mis-spelt names and incorrect dates at check-in will be verified. The guest will be unaware of this level of service but it is facilitated by the network.

Personal computers were chosen for Roomfinder III because the company recognized the benefit of being able to utilize easy-to-use and consequently easy-to-write software. The move to interface existing property management computer systems with the personal computer in each hotel allows many more functions to be handled by the network. These additional functions permit the personal computer to become part of both the front office operation and the reservations system. Not only will reservations be handled but also the production of statistics such as room counts, numbers of walk-ins and no-shows.

In the long term it is anticipated that travel agents and airlines will have direct access to the Roomfinder III system thereby enormously increasing the potential of the system as a selling tool.

Single-site reservations system

Single-site reservations systems almost always utilize a microcomputer and reservations are just one application amongst several that may share the same hardware. Indeed one of the problems of such systems arises at this stage in that if a micro is being used for a number of applications, it may not always be free when required and there may have to be disk changes between different operations.

There is no doubt, however, that a single-site system utilizing a micro or a mini-computer can be of great assistance where reservations are concerned. The typical features on a micro might include (Chart Software Ltd):

- provisional selection and booking of rooms up to 400 days in advance
- booking confirmations with relevant correspondence
- booking cancellations with relevant correspondence
- advance reservations adjustments
- the above functions performed for block or group bookings as well as individuals
- VDU display of advance reservations 'density chart'

- production of advance reservations reports
- guest details stored, including comments and instructions for Expected Arrivals List
- advance deposits recorded and automatically transferred to the guest bill after check-in

COMPUTERS AND THE FRONT DESK

The front desk area of a hotel is probably the place where the guest is going to be most aware of the impact of computerization. Equally, the front desk is where the majority of hotel computer systems have evolved from as it is here that there are a large number of operations that are ideal for computerization.

One should not forget that it is at the front desk that guests form their first impression of the hotel and its staff. The computerized system should therefore be as unobtrusive as possible and should not detract from one-to-one communication with a guest during check-in.

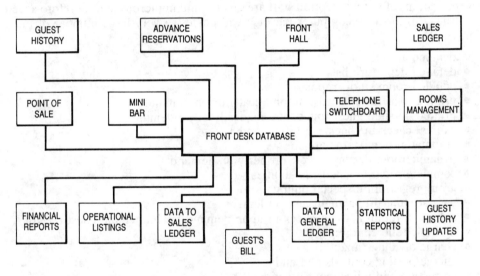

Figure 3.4 *An integrated front desk computer system*
Source: Thorn EMI CHAMPS Systems

A good front desk system will allow the retrieval of the guest's reservation and pre-printed registration card simply by punching in the appropriate guest name or room number, whether the guest is an individual traveller or part of a larger group. Regular guest details will be retained in the system and recalled, thereby removing the need to collect this information again at each check-in.

The system should hold details of the hotel layout and room facilities thereby helping with guest enquiries. This will be of great assistance, particularly to new staff. Bearing in mind the high employee turnover often experienced in reception this could be a very useful feature.

The system will display information concerning the floors, room types and status in order to speed up room allocation and check-in, as well as providing billing details to answer guest enquiries. Even the complications of such situations as groups, room transfers, chance guests and multiple folios should be handled easily by the computer.

The work of the staff in the front office area of a hotel includes the following tasks which may be computerized with ease:

- reservations
- guest check-in
- guest accounting
- guest check-out
- guest history
- sales and marketing
- room management
- management reporting
- sales ledger

Front desk package

The operations of hotel reception staff are diverse and numerous and therefore a well constructed front desk computer package will possess a very large number of functions:

- detailed arrival lists
- detailed departure lists
- detailed room status reports
- printed registration cards, automatically or on demand
- printed detailed guest folios, automatically or on demand
- express check-in/check-out (30 seconds)
- automatic room status update
- dynamic room display – view property on demand
- complete room blocking capabilities
- group registration/special billing
- easy account prepayment and settlement
- auto-post room/VAT at check-in upon demand for immediate guest receipt
- multiple folio charging
- charge-dividing capabilities
- charge-posting controls and audit
- correction and adjustment functions
- end of shift cashier audit
- a total of about 100 charge/settlement keys
- detail folio display
- fully automated night audit and close of day
- guest ledger linked to city ledger
- automatic transfer of guest ledger accounts to city ledger
- fully automated close-month, close-year

SPECIAL FORMS
- Registration Card forms
- Folio forms

Source: Auditel Lodging Management Systems

In effect the front desk package creates a billing account for both rooms and groups, adds charges to and subtracts payments from those accounts, and clears accounts when the guests leave the hotel. For credit customers ledger folios are transferred to the invoicing and sales ledger programs, whilst revenue from the various departments and receipts are kept on the front hall trial balance.

Front desk reports

Whilst a computerized front desk system has 'real time' advantages to the staff there will also be a need to produce a certain number of reports that will be of use in determining business, scheduling staff and anticipating guest requirements.

The basic front desk reports that might be produced with a computer system include:

Arrival list	Departure list	Room status report
Guest list by name	Guest list by room	Credit limit report
Room vacate time scan	Walk-in report	VIP guest list
Roll-away bed report	Cot report	Folio balance report
Changed room report	Vacant rooms list	Room discrepancy list
Cash commission list	Deposits lists	'Off' rooms lists
Tour lists	Currency lists	

Guest messages

With new technology, lost messages for guests may become a memory of the manual past as – in theory – never again should a message for a guest either go astray or arrive illegible. As switchboard operators and receptionists take messages, they simply enter them into the system, cross referenced by name and room number. The message will then be printed at the mail or porter's desk and the message light may be activated in the guest's room. If the message is for a future arrival, it may be printed on the appropriate reservations or registrations file so that the guest receives it at check-in.

Not everything, though, has gone entirely to plan with the installation of computers in front offices. Some problems that have occurred along the technological learning curve are highlighted in the following case study from the early days of computerization.

CASE STUDY NUMBER 7

THE CASE OF THE NEW YORK HILTON

As mentioned at the beginning of the book (see page 20), at an important stage in the emergence of hotel computers the New York Hilton installed a front desk system with disastrous results. The debacle attracted a great deal of publicity and put back the introduction of computers into the industry by some considerable time.

Although this was 25 years ago, it is important to comprehend what actually went wrong as the lessons learned are still of interest and importance to any caterer contemplating computerization.

The hotel itself was the first large establishment (2,100 rooms) to utilize computerization fully in its front office when the system was put into opera-

---

tion in 1963. As with more modern computerized front office systems, the Hilton's 'property management system' (PMS) was intended to allow a speedier arrival and departure for guests as well as handling their bills. The Hilton hoped that it would provide improved control, a reduction in costs, an increase in revenue, the creation of useful management data, and an easier to process system of information within the front office, and enable them to provide the guest with a better service.

In the event this first attempt at front office computerization failed because the computer experts and the caterer did not understand each other. On the one hand the system designers introduced techniques that had worked in an ordinary office environment but that were inappropriate in a hotel, while on the other hand the caterer thought that the computer possessed capabilities that it did not have.

The New York Hilton suffered from being a guinea pig for new techniques. Systems were adopted that with hindsight have been proved inappropriate: for example, the use of a 'batch-mode' system of operation which was then common in other industries. Information was put into the computer on punched cards by key punch operators. The whole system therefore relied upon the key punch operators and when they became overworked in pressure times, such as check-in and check-out, the system itself ground to a halt. The hotel needed instant results, especially during such pressure times, which the system of operating could not deliver. In contrast, systems today operate on 'real-time', providing instant data via terminals and VDU screens for all the users.

As regards output from the computer, the Hilton depended upon a traditional printer and here made a mistake that has subsequently been repeated many times in hotels by installing only a single printer in the front office. As one printer can only handle one cashier and one bill at a time, the result was a long queue of customers in the foyer waiting to check-out, even though the computer was capable of producing information much more quickly. Quite simply, the hotel should have been equipped with more printers in the front office.

Breakdowns proved to be a problem as there was no effective back-up system. One small fault would shut the whole system down and the consequent revenue losses were very high.

The staffing of the computer also contributed to its downfall. The hotel itself was new and therefore the staff had not had the benefit of working as a team in a non-computerized system before the additional unfamiliarity of new technology was thrust upon them. The computer itself generated an extra staffing requirement in the form of 10 full-time data processors so the expected saving on staffing costs was not achieved.

In fact the system was soon costing $10,000 per month (1963 value) and not only because this price was regarded as unreasonable but also because it had been found that the computer had actually reduced guest services it was closed down in late 1964. The computer was replaced by an automated room status system, a manual reservations system and mechanical billing machines. It was to be nearly twenty years before a fully effective computerized PMS was installed at the New York Hilton. (Alvarez et al., 1983)

Guest check-in

The aim of the computer system at check-in is to make the formalities of arrival at the hotel as swift and efficient as possible, ensuring that time is left to greet and welcome guests with a minimum of check-in delay.

A computerized system speeds up check-in by starting the registration process during the night prior to arrival. Registration cards, welcome keycards and envelopes can be waiting for the guests' arrival, while department by department reports on special requests (such as VIPs, cots, hire cars, etc.) and alphabetical arrival lists are ready for the staff in the morning. Chance guests, connecting rooms, room moves, and changes in departure date can be handled more easily because all information relating to guest records or available rooms can be called up on the VDU screens at the front desk. Room records are stored on disk and can be updated from all points in the hotel. The room rack is therefore eliminated and, with it, the tedious task of preparing rack slips and keeping the room rack current.

The computer system must be able to cope with the basic problems of check-in, such as the fact that not all guests have prior reservations and that 'chance' customers must be catered for swiftly. A clear and well organized check-in screen should be available on the VDU so that the relevant guest information may be taken efficiently: the main constraint in these circumstances should be the speed of the receptionist's typing! A fast on-screen room availability display is another essential feature of the check-in package, as is the room status display.

It is important at check-in to discuss with the guest the details of their reservation as it is the last chance to rectify any possible mistakes, such as the wrong room type having been reserved. The computer should therefore hold a detailed display of the reservation information which can appear on the VDU during check-in.

Group check-in

Many hotels deal with a large number of groups and here it may be advisable to use a computer system that allows the automatic production of 'extras' accounts at the time of arrival. Another useful feature may be a rooming list facility that allows an entire group to be checked-in simply by checking-in the group leader.

The entire visit of a group, tour or conference – from reservation to registration through to check-out – may be handled efficiently and rapidly with a computerized package. Each group or block can be easily identified, adjusted and processed. A master folio can be created which automatically controls and posts charges for individual members of a group to either the master account or to individual folios, for improved service and increased accounting accuracy.

Security

Check-in is a sensitive time as far as a computer system is concerned as it is one of the applications where fraud is possible. To overcome this operator passcodes can be issued to staff authorized to use the check-in program and particularly sensitive operations can be individually logged and periodically inspected by management. This can include all check-ins, re-check-ins, room moves, room allocations and re-allocations.

Benefit of an integrated system

An integrated check-in system allows a number of activities to be initiated from a single transaction. These activities would all have to be carried out manually if a traditional type of system were in use. Table 3.1 shows the operations which automatically follow one initial prompt at check-in on a typical hotel integrated computer system.

Table 3.1   *The CHAMPS integrated system*

The check-in of a guest on the *CHAMPS* system automatically:
(a) Prevents the room being allocated by any other member of staff for the duration of the guest's stay.
(b) Changes the reservation from 'expected' to 'arrived'.
(c) Updates the house count.
(d) Changes the status of the room from 'unoccupied' to 'occupied'.
(e) Prints a keycard.
(f) Creates a bill/folio.
(g) Transfers a deposit if appropriate.
(h) Allows any authorized hotel employee to locate the guest.
(i) Updates breakfast figures allowing for accurate forecasting of numbers to be served.
(j) Updates the housekeeping reports so that linen issues are calculated automatically.
(k) Allows for charges to be posted to the room.
(l) Ensures that direct dial telephone calls are charged to the guest.
(m) Increments marketing statistics for business type, nationality, etc.
(n) Adds one night's charges if the arrival is after the hotel's terming routines have been run.

Guest check-out

A computerized cashiering system can enable both swift and courteous service to be offered by the cashiers when guests are checking-out, or even when they simply want to review their charges. Folios may be printed or displayed in an instant and are much more unlikely to be misplaced or lost. Settlements are quickly applied to any number of different payment types. Any accounts not settled in full at check-out may be automatically transferred to the sales ledger for billing and collection. The appropriate information is instantly available throughout the hotel when a guest is checked-out by the cashiers. Security is provided for the cashiers through security codes or sign-in procedures and all charges and settlements are readily identified by the cashier. Displays and reports provide audit trails for swift balancing and verification of charges. The accounts staff are presented with a full range of reports to monitor and control guest credit.

Check-out is the time when a computer is required to undertake the billing routine and to assist in the acceptance of payment from guests. Typical systems may produce bills for guests either 'en bloc' for all guests due to leave or individually by room number as departures actually take place. In some hotels a super-fast check-out facility is available for groups and tours.

Video check-out

There is an increasing move towards video check-out direct from the guest's room and in the United States this is fast becoming a guest preference over check-out units located in the foyer. It has been found that guests feel more comfortable experimenting with new technology in the privacy of their own rooms where they are not pressurized by a queue and where they can operate at their own pace. With the hotel's televisions linked to the existing property management computer the guest may view a display of their bill on the television screen in their room and authorize payment by credit card. This allows the guest to by-pass any queue at reception and provides a swift and problem-free method of check-out. The early systems required the guest to call at reception to pick up a copy of their bill but new systems supply a bill from a printer attached to the television set. Approaching 30 per cent of guests make use of the facility where it is available, whilst even more use the television to view their bill and to settle any discrepancies before leaving.

At the time of departure a bill may be required in a variety of ways and the computer should be able to fit around the guests' requirements. For example, group or shared accounts with a number of folios for each room or split bills for one person may be required and the computer should easily handle these difficulties. The time of check-out may also be unusual and there should be direct contact with the room status part of the system, for housekeeping's benefit, for such situations.

The computer will be expected to produce a clear, comprehensible guest bill that may be quickly and immediately updated or amended during guest check-out.

Totals will be shown at the foot of the bill including such items as:

- total upon which VAT is chargeable
- VAT total
- gross amount
- service charge

Payment may be accepted on the spot or the invoice charged to an account. Problems may occur if the guest has previously indicated that they want their room charges to be transferred to another room, but many computer packages will cope with this situation automatically at check-out.

The master room details will contain a running balance of all charges to be made to the room such as the group or party balance.

Cashiers

The facilities available to cashiers when using a comprehensive computer system will allow the correction, adjustment and transfer of charges once suitable authorization has been received. All the posting categories should be displayed by the computer when charges are placed against a room number so that there is every opportunity for them to be accurately identified.

Guest credit control will be facilitated and guests will be sent reminders when their bill has reached its limit. For this and other purposes it should be possible for a guest's account to be printed for presentation without the guest checking-out. Another useful facility is to be able to reinstate a checked-out guest without major effort.

Currency conversion

In many hotels where a sizeable proportion of the guests are international, a currency conversion module is built into the computer system so that currency exchange rates may be calculated automatically. The facility, if provided, allows for computation of both local-to-foreign and foreign-to-local rates very swiftly. At the time of check-out the folio balance may be displayed in the appropriate currency's exchange rate. In addition a currency conversion system will track payments in each foreign currency for each cashier.

Posting guest charges

The bill received by the guest will perhaps be the single most important indication to them of whether they have stayed in an efficient hotel or not. The ability to produce a bill that includes neither 'undercharges' nor 'overcharges' eludes a large number of catering establishments and hotels, including many that are computerized, where it is often caused by inefficiencies of staff collecting data in peripheral departments. Computerization of the posting of charges goes a long way towards removing many of the problems, including illegible handwritten vouchers and ledgers that lead to many classic mistakes.

Producing a bill for a guest is not as easy as it may appear on the surface as the peculiarities of the hotel trade make billing complicated. Transaction posting, for example, has as an elementary task to allow for charges to be made both to resident guest rooms and for non-resident takings in the form of cash.

Most of the posting transactions within a hotel will be captured automatically by the computer system. Charges incurred by the guest through the use of in-room facilities, such as the telephones and mini-bars, or through point-of-sale terminals in the bars and restaurants will be entered automatically on to the account.

A typical system should allow for VAT and service charges to be calculated automatically, and codes may be used to analyse transactions so that when a code or room number is entered the relative description or guest name is displayed. It will be desirable if values can be entered either gross or net of VAT and service, whilst all transactions should be recorded on an audit trail.

Modules should be available to allow entry of postings via a PLU (price look up) table so that when a quantity and code are entered the computer will look up the price, calculate the total and produce a bill if necessary. This may in addition be linked to a cash drawer.

End-of-day routines

The facility should be available for a daily rate to be charged automatically to the guest account so that a selection of reports relating to the day's business may be produced – in effect, undertaking a night audit.

Room transfers

There must be a facility within the system that allows for the movement of all guest details and current transactional data from an existing room to the newly allocated room.

Credit limits

The system should allow for the alarm to be raised and a report produced for those guests who have exceeded their credit limits. An explanatory letter may even be produced automatically to be sent to the guests concerned.

Overseas guests

It may be desirable, if a large amount of business is undertaken with overseas customers, to build in special parts of the system to cope with their business. For example, a foreign currency calculator can remove many of the problems of currency conversions and calculations. It may also be worth providing a weekly billing facility for international guests.

Security implications

The posting of charges is a sensitive area where fraud can arise and therefore only staff equipped with the appropriate operator passcodes will be allowed to utilize the program. The particular areas of sensitivity will be the postings themselves as well as corrections, transfers and adjustments and these can be logged separately for periodic examination by management.

Automated check-in and check-out

Automated check-in and check-out will never completely replace the hotel receptionist, but it is becoming a more commonly offered facility.

For some years in the United States there have been machines, in some cases direct descendants of automated bank cash dispensers, that have undertaken the automatic check-in of customers, usually on the proviso that they possess a credit card. Although initially guests may have had to book in advance, some machines will now handle chance arrivals, as well as allocating rooms and confirming all booking details such as rate, duration and special requests. Newspapers, morning calls and similar services may be requested at the time of check-in. The machine will, in some cases, issue a computerized key to the guest's room and activate the electricity supply which would have been disconnected whilst the room was vacant.

On check-out, computerized machines can be used to alleviate the problem of queueing and have proved successful in large American hotels where an estimated 10 per cent of guests utilize a credit card payment system submitting their bill details directly to their credit card company. The whole transaction can take as little as two minutes. It has been found necessary to have staff at hand to help guests who have not used the system before or who are unaware that the facility exists.

Some automatic check-in machines allow reference via computer controlled video facilities to the latest international currency exchange rates, restaurant times, menus, the weather forecast and any of the facilities or services provided by the hotel. Thus they become information machines when not employed on check-in, thereby making them more cost-effective.

Automated guest registration system

An automated guest registration system (AGRS) is an electronic device activated by any of the major programmed credit cards (ERS Technologies Inc.).

Customers acquire their accommodation by entering their requirements via a keyboard system similar to those used in bank automated cash dispensers. The system records credit card data, registers the guest or guests according to their needs, dispenses room keys and automatically prepares billing information.

This technology has provided a high-tech solution for several of the most frustrating and persistent problems of operating a 24-hour reception. These problems include:

- *Staff fatigue.* What the Americans call 'operator burnout' applies to all levels of staff, whether they be owner/managers or employees, and is brought on by the constant disruption of a sleep or work pattern. Registering late arrivals is a primary cause. The attitude of even the most courteous member of staff deteriorates with loss of sleep and an automated guest registration system can completely eliminate the problem by removing the need for staff to be on call at all hours. In doing so the system minimizes the inefficiency and high cost that might otherwise result from excessive staff turnover.

The first AGRS in the United States – the 'Night Clerk'
Photograph: ERS Technologies Inc.

- *High operating costs.* A significant percentage of motel managers employ night staff and relief help for times when regular staff are not available. An automated guest registration system removes this need.
- *Lost revenue.* An AGRS should ensure that the 'No vacancies' sign is never displayed when rooms are actually available in the motel or hotel. This situation commonly occurs when fed-up night staff decide to get some much needed sleep, regardless of potential customer demands. In some high crime areas of the United States, many motels refuse to check-in guests after 8.00 pm for security reasons. The AGRS can cater for these situations, thus preventing loss of revenue.
- *Crime.* Crime can be a problem for hotels where a large amount of cash is in the reception tills late at night. An AGRS activated by credit card acts as an anti-robbery device by eliminating the need to hold cash. It also reduces the need for expensive anti-robbery equipment and systems, decreases the threat of violence and may lower insurance premiums.

The function of an AGRS is to register hotel or motel guests without the need for a receptionist or night porter to process the registration. Guests arriving after hours simply insert their credit card, select the desired accommodation, and the machine dispenses the appropriate key. The AGRS verifies each card's credit status and supplies a written record of every transaction via a printer located in the reception office. The constituent parts of the system and their major features are:

- *Self-contained unit* weatherproof
                         vandal resistant
- *Computer*   user friendly
                         software customized to the operator's needs
                         records all vital registration data and prepares billing
- *Card reader*   foolproof and maintenance free
                         accepts all major programmed credit cards
- *Modem*   allows verification of each credit transaction
- *Key dispenser*   allows random access of rooms
                         easily loaded

Automated guest check-out system

An automatic check-out centre combining an AGCS with a guest information facility
Photograph: Bruce Grant-Braham

Automated guest check-out systems (AGCS) have been developed with the intention of making the queue of guests impatiently waiting to check-out a thing of the past. Also busy travellers will no longer have to drop their room keys into an express check-out box then wait for days or perhaps weeks until the bill finally arrives. An AGCS allows guests to process their own check-out from anywhere in the hotel and receive their final bill. Settlement may be undertaken on the spot and in many cases can be transacted in less than thirty seconds, which is a tremendous benefit to the busy traveller.

AGC systems were a development of automatic guest information and registration systems and sometimes incorporate these facilities too. A typical system has an easy-to-use touch-screen and the information storage and retrieval capabilities of laser videodiscs.

An AGCS is completely guest-activated and controlled so that guests process check-out at their own pace. Complete video instructions are displayed to show how to enter room number information, with full security, using the on-screen display. After that the system takes over, communicating directly with the computerized property management system computer and gathering together all guest charges. Within seconds charges from any area of the hotel – front desk, room service, telephones, restaurant and shop – are retrieved and compiled into a final bill.

Whilst an AGCS is obviously used heavily at check-out time, it would be in danger of standing idle during the rest of the operational day unless it were also a system that allowed guest information to be displayed. The better systems incorporate this facility, which may be used to market the hotel's services. It can be used to show guests the restaurants, shops, health and sporting facilities, any special activities or any message that needs to be conveyed. Video sequences are stored on a laser videodisc system and accessed in any order at the touch of the screen. The AGCS, or Guest Services Center as it may be called in America, is therefore working for the hotel throughout the entire day.

An AGCS that also provides guest information may be placed strategically anywhere in the establishment. Typical locations are in the foyer, on VIP executive floors, outside coffee shops and restaurants, or in conference and meeting facilities.

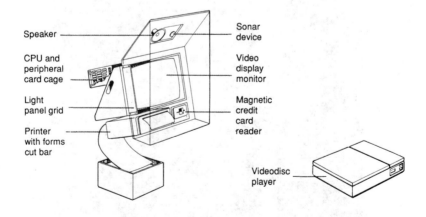

Figure 3.5   *The ECI 'Self-Chek' Guest Services Center*
Source: EECO Computer, Inc.

The ECI 'Self-Chek' shown in Figure 3.5 combines an AGCS and ACRS and makes use of touch-screen and laser videodisc technology. It incorporates a sonar detector into its design which activates the audio portion of a continuous video loop when a guest approaches the unit. When no-one is using the system it reverts to an opening video loop without sound. The touch-screen allows the guest to activate the system by touching the unit screen. All system options are presented in simple screen formats, and any information the guest may need to enter is input using a display generated directly on to the screen. A high-speed bill printer produces a final record of the guest's charges.

Guest information units

AGRS systems owe their evolution in part to Guest Information Units which have been popular for some time in hotel foyers. The idea of such a unit is that guests may obtain a wide range of information on an establishment simply by touching the screen of the unit and watching the video.

By placing their finger over the appropriate location on the screen display the guest causes the unit's computer control to summon up the required information. With a laser videodisc the information appears almost instantly and such systems also offer high resolution pictures and quality sound that may be combined with teletext material. Laser videodiscs do not deteriorate and hold up to 54,000 still frame pages which should be ample for most hotels.

Typical information that may be displayed includes film of bedrooms and restaurants or even of staff. Voice-overs can be provided in different languages for the benefit of guests of all nationalities. Menus, wine lists and tariffs may be displayed in text form and teletext services may also be linked in.

ELECTRONIC FUNDS TRANSFER AT POINT-OF-SALE (EFTPOS)

If there is one part of the traditional operation of hotel and catering establishments that is undergoing change now, it is the area of cash handling. The days of waiting for cheques to clear and demanding payment several days in advance are clearly on the way out with the arrival of 'plastic money' enabling guests to settle their bills instantly. The computer age has removed the necessity for vast mountains of paperwork to be transported around the country from bank to bank or from place of settlement to credit card company, as communications have improved greatly and the whole process may be undertaken by direct links.

The advances in credit and charge card handling have come with the development of EFTPOS terminals which remove much of the risk associated with traditional methods of accepting payment by cards, as well as much of the onerous paperwork. One great advantage of EFTPOS terminals is that they facilitate fast authorization of amounts greater than £50, which is one of the problems that cheque guarantee cards give to retailers in general.

EFTPOS is simply an electronic way for customers to effect over-the-counter payments in retail establishments such as hotels, restaurants and shops.

Operation of EFTPOS terminals

Most EFTPOS terminals require just an electricity supply and a telephone line to function.

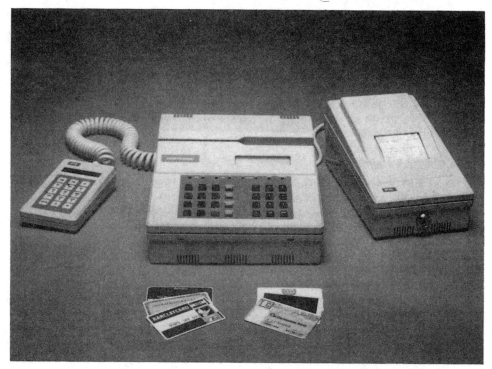

Hotel F75 EFTPOS terminal which may be used in either 'on-line' or 'store and forward' mode
Photograph: Fortronic Ltd

An EFTPOS terminal is quite simple to use. When a guest arrives at the hotel they are asked how they intend to pay. If the answer is by credit or charge card the receptionist 'wipes' it through the terminal's card reader which holds a daily updated list of invalid, lost or stolen cards which is supplied by the host computer or clearing house (the list will be updated automatically on a daily basis by a host computer). If the guest's card is on such a list then the terminal will display the relevant message, such as CARD EXPIRED. Should the card not be on a list, as will be the case with the vast majority of cards, the terminal will prompt the receptionist to enter the appropriate room number. The terminal will then print a verification receipt showing the card details and room number with one copy going to the guest and another copy being retained by the hotel.

At check-out the guest re-presents the card and the cashier wipes it through the card reader again. The total of the bill is calculated and entered by the cashier – some terminals allow separate charges to be coded to show what they were for on the receipt – and checked against the credit limit of the particular card. At this stage the terminal may cancel the transaction or report that the transaction is above the card's floor limit and in both cases it may be necessary to phone the credit card company for authorization in the traditional manner. If the checks and authorizations were successful, however, the EFTPOS terminal will accept the transaction and produce a receipt for the guest to sign which the cashier checks against the signature on the card.

To summarize, EFTPOS terminals:

- validate the credit card
- produce the voucher or VAT receipt
- provide instant totals at the end of the shift and day
- remove the administrative burdens of summaries and banking
- remove the problems of clerical errors such as lost vouchers, overlooked expiry dates, etc.
- give a faster, more efficient service to the customer

Store and forward EFTPOS terminals

With a store and forward EFTPOS system the terminals store each transaction in a protected memory and totals are kept of the daily business undertaken using each separate credit card. The stored transaction charges are then forwarded or transmitted off-line (overnight) via a clearing house to the appropriate credit card company and arrangements are made for the establishment's bank account to be credited with the correct amount.

A store and forward system incurs substantially lower communication costs than on-line systems because communication takes place at off-peak times and is continuous and therefore more time-effective.

On-line EFTPOS terminals

With on-line systems the terminal contacts a host computer at the time of each transaction, and subsequently authorizes and transmits bills for credit and charge cards. If the host computer for communication is the card company or bank concerned, payment will be received very quickly. The main drawback is that line and transmission costs can be high.

EFTPOS operational problems

The use of EFTPOS terminals is by no means totally fail-safe as inevitably the human error element always intervenes somewhere. Amongst the problems experienced is the fact that with some systems staff can make up expiry dates either falsely or through laziness. In addition, the efficiency of an EFTPOS system depends on sufficient terminals being available at the point-of-sale as a queue will build up if there is only one terminal for use by several cashiers.

Smart and super-smart cards

Whilst the majority of cards to date carry information on a magnetic strip, 'smart' cards will soon become more common. These possess a built-in memory (in the case of super-smart cards 64K) and microprocessor and are therefore programmable.

The extra 'intelligence' of a smart card gives it a number of advantages over the standard credit card. The card is secure off-line, carrying out security checks on its user as well as on the terminal that it is 'wiped' through. It can be an 'electronic cheque book', containing a given amount of finance and deducting each transaction from the total as it takes place.

Britain in general has been slow to take up smart card technology, preferring the more traditional magnetic stripe versions. Visa, though, have developed a super-smart card that is completely self-contained with a keyboard similar to a calculator, a display and a battery. The user enters a PIN number followed by the amount of the purchase. The card deducts the amount from the current balance and issues an authorization number to the establishment involved in the transaction. The card may then be 'wiped' to record the necessary information in the EFTPOS system.

GUEST HISTORY

Guest histories and personalized hospitality

When potential customers are faced with a myriad of plasticized and aluminium-filled hotels at which to stay how do they make their choice? There are, after all, several multinational companies chasing the same business in the major destinations and guests must make a conscious decision about where they will spend their often large amounts of money.

In many cases it is the hospitality that they can expect that influences the eventual choice. Whilst some analysts argue that either the location or the price is the most important factor, in reality it is just as likely that the personality of the hotel sways the guest's decision. Frequent hotel users know by experience that at certain hotels they are made welcome whilst at others they are made to feel like meaningless statistics. It is the caterers who run the former type of establishment who will be most interested in the computer applications which can help to personalize their service further. For caterers running the latter, such applications may constitute a new technology lifebelt to help start their staff on the way to creating the cherished air of hospitality that other competing hotels seem to possess.

The computer applications in question are referred to as *guest history* and revolve around the creation of a comprehensive database of guest details that can be accessed with ease. Previously, such information might have been kept in traditional handwritten files, but this meant that reference was often difficult and inconvenient. A computer system can simplify the whole process of keeping track of individual guests and also make that information readily accessible.

A guest history program maintains on-line details of the guest's previous visits to the establishment. The files are created automatically after a guest's check-out and include details of the room number, most recent visit, room rate, special requests, average expenditures per stay, type of payment, outstanding balance and date of birth. With an integrated guest history program future reservations are faster, smoother and automated, because instant access to the history saves input time. It also ensures that repeat customers' special requests can be anticipated. Linked to a printing facility guest history data becomes a ready source of information for advertising and promotional campaigns. For example, the printer can produce labels for a mail shot to all previous guests or specific market segments. It is also possible to target an appropriate audience by post code or nationality.

A computer provides the ability to recognize 'repeat' guests and this is important for the hotel's hospitality image. The hotel can anticipate requests and specific needs, giving a much improved personal service as well as being able to identify those customers who spend most. A good system will produce reports identifying VIPs, nationalities, average spends, number of stays and total revenue. In addition, registration cards may be produced before guests arrive thus greatly reducing check-in time.

The advantages of a guest history program are particularly relevant where regular customers are concerned. To book a return guest into a room they have been complimentary about, or to automatically supply their regular morning newspaper, can make that guest feel personally remembered and welcome. Normally all that has to be done at the time of reservation is to ask whether the guest has stayed before and then the relevant computerized files can be consulted and details confirmed with the customer. Such personalization is not only impressive to the guest but also saves them the time and trouble of having to specify their likes and dislikes and should go a long way towards encouraging repeat business – one of the major aims of most hoteliers.

A typical *guest history* file as it appears on screen or on a print-out is shown in Figure 3.6.

```
           FIRST NAME:   Wheeler
         FORENAME(S):   James, Hubert
            ADDRESS:   12, South Way, Cranfield, Welchester
DATES OF PREVIOUS VISITS:  12/3/85  11/6/85  14/2/86  1/4/87  5/9/87  9/12/87
      MARITAL STATUS:   Married
          OCCUPATION:   Company Director
             COMPANY:   Daler plc, Light Engineering Company, Welchester
              CREDIT:   £1000 ceiling.  All bills settled without problem.
               WHIMS:   Always asks for Moet & Chandon champagne.  Likes
                        breakfast in room.  Tips staff generously.  Non-Smoker.
   EARLY MORNING CALL:   0700 weekdays.
           NEWSPAPER:   Independant and Morning Star
      CREDIT CARD NO:   5966 604 505 027AZ
         NATIONALITY:   British
          PASSPORT NO:   N/A
REASON FOR CURRENT STAY:  Weekend Break
            BIRTHDAY:   10th March 1951
  PREVIOUS COMPLAINTS:   Quality of steak in Hawaiian Restaurant, Had to be
                         moved from room 522 because of noise from lift.
             REMARKS:   None.
```

Figure 3.6   *Sample guest history file*

INDIVIDUAL GUEST HISTORY

The philosophy behind the use of such records is that they should help to cater for all the personal items that a regular customer, for example, would become irritated by if they had to ask for them each time they stayed at an establishment. But what additional sorts of things, other than those above, might qualify for inclusion in an individual guest history?

Guest in-house

Whilst a detailed guest history is useful for a number of reasons there will be a need for staff, such as those at the information desk or the switchboard, to make use of an abbreviated version for quick reference during the guest's stay. In-house guests may therefore only require a display showing:

- guest name
- room number
- company name
- group name

This information should be accessible by either room number or name. In addition, if a general search for a guest is required, then guests with a certain surname or with a

Registration Card:	Name	
	Nationality	
	Address-home/business	
	Previous visits	
Purpose of visit:	Business/Break/Holiday	
Favourite bedroom:	Floor	
	Type	
	Decor	
	Aspect - front/back of hotel	
	- high/low	
	- view	
	- balcony/terrace	
	Position - near lift/stairs for easy access	
	- away from lift/stairs/ballroom	
	for solitude	
	Particular room number _ _ _ _	
	Smoking/Non-Smoking	
Bedroom lay-up:	Non-feather pillows - allergy	
	Bedboard/Hard mattress - backache	
	Extra blanket/pillow	
	Fruit Bowl/chocolates/champagne	
	Welcome back card	
	Flowers	
Complaints:	Leaking radiator	
	Faulty television	
	Unable to book table in restaurant	
Finance:	No problems/problems with payment	
Personal:	No problems/problems with staff/guests	
Grade of guest:	VIP/regular/repeat visit/warn before staying again/	
	do not admit/call police.	

Figure 3.7   *Sample guest history items*

surname beginning with a particular letter of the alphabet can be displayed until the correct person is identified.

Integrated guest history programs

When a guest history module forms part of a larger overall integrated computer system it will prove even more useful than a stand-alone system.

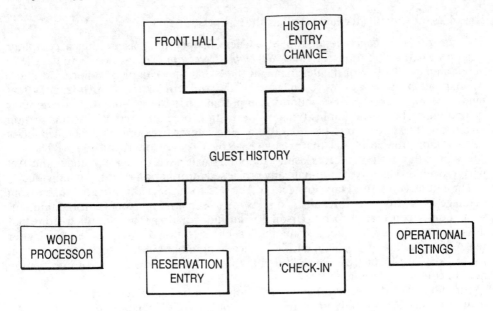

Figure 3.8 *An integrated guest history system*
Source: Thorn EMI CHAMPS systems

Most integrated systems give each individual guest history a reference number which is displayed whenever the particular guest is referred to on a VDU screen or in print-outs. Depending on the arrangement of codings this will indicate to the member of staff concerned that here is a guest who may require different treatment to the others for whatever reason.

It is quite likely that the guest history itself will be divided into two levels: information in the first level will be open to virtually all staff, whilst the second level holds confidential information, possibly of a financial or personal nature, to which access is restricted.

If the guest history module is interfaced with a word processing module this creates the ability to print address labels from specified guest criteria, thus providing a useful marketing facility to target and mail certain types of guests. For example, if the hotel intended to mount a sales drive in France, the sales manager might select the following criteria for guests who could be mailed:

- guests who have stayed in the hotel at least once
- guests who have a departure date during the last four years
- guests who reside in France
- guests who are free, independent travellers (not in a tour, conference or group)
- guests who reserved accommodation either directly with the hotel, via central reservations, or via a travel agent
- guests who booked via a French office
- guests who had an average revenue per stay of more than £200

The combinations of criteria on a good system are almost limitless and offer the ability to mail newsletters or to promote an establishment through special offers, whether of a social or business nature.

How does the Data Protection Act affect the business?

The recording of guest details on to a guest history database within a computer qualifies for the attentions of the *1984 Data Protection Act*, as does any data held about an individual. Whilst caterers might think that they can plead innocence simply by maintaining that they were unaware of the Act, under the British legal system ignorance is no excuse. It is therefore important that the caterer with a computer system understands the implications of the Data Protection Act. Whilst this section gives an outline of the Act, it is advisable for the caterer to examine the detailed terms of the Data Protection Act that was given Royal Assent on 12 July 1984. There is every probability that caterers using computers will have to register under the Act which regulates the use of automatically processed information relating to individuals.

The intention of the Data Protection Act was to protect the private citizen from 'damage or distress' as a result of disclosure of sensitive personal information. Information is considered to be personal if an individual can be identified from that information, through letters and numbers such as National Insurance codes. Under the Act an individual has been entitled, since September 1984, to seek compensation for any damage or distress caused by unauthorized disclosure or loss of information held in computer databases.

Guest history information that caterers hold must be registered under the Act, but many caterers seem totally unaware of their obligations. Since the deadline expired for existing information to be registered on 11 May 1986, a large number of establishments have probably unwittingly broken the law. The maximum fine for not registering relevant information is £2,000.

Any caterer or hotelier registering under the Act has to give the name and address of the hotel and detail outlining the types of individual held on file. The information held on individuals, whether they be guests or staff, must be revealed, as must the way in which it was collected, the way in which it is used, to whom and where it is disclosed, and any intention of revealing information abroad.

The main aim is to protect people from the misuse of information held about them in sensitive areas such as by the police, security services, credit card companies and other organizations of a similar type. The Act allows individuals to find out what information is held about them on computers and how that information is used.

As far as the hotel and computer industry is concerned, problems arise where guest history information is expanded to include *credit worthiness* or where '*black lists*' are held. Such information is sometimes likely to be contentious and so extreme care has to be exercised. Equally, it is important that hoteliers and caterers have registered their files in these situations.

There is no specific information that is regarded as too confidential or personal in nature to be held on computer. The only constraints imposed are that the nine principles of the Act are complied with:

- Personal information must be obtained and processed fairly and lawfully.
- Data shall only be held for specified and lawful purposes.
- The user must specify the purpose or purposes for which the information is kept, giving a description of the data.
- Personal information must not be disclosed in a manner incompatible with the purpose(s).
- The information has to be adequate, relevant and not excessive in relation to the purpose(s).

- Personal information must be accurate and, where necessary, up-to-date.
- Personal data must not be kept for longer than is necessary.
- Individuals are entitled to know from a data-user whether personal data is held on them and, if so, be allowed access to that data.
- There must be appropriate security measures, especially in the case of computer bureaux, taken against unauthorized access to, alteration, disclosure, destruction or loss of personal data. Security measures must also be taken against accidental loss or destruction of data.

During 1987 it became possible to view in public libraries a list of all the computer systems that hold details of individuals and from 11 November 1987 members of the public have had the right under the Act to examine any files kept on them. This places considerable obligations on hoteliers and caterers and whilst only a small number of individuals are likely to want to examine their files the facility has to be made available to them.

To summarize, caterers holding and using data on individuals should be very clear as to how they obtain their information and what they are going to use it for. Bearing in mind the public scrutiny to which guest history records may be subjected, the utmost care should be taken in what is actually recorded so that offence is not caused. The Golden Rule for hoteliers and caterers is – if in doubt, register.

A COMPUTER AS AN AID TO SALES AND MARKETING

> In today's market, it's no longer a question of creating demand – you have to take it away from someone else. (Hogg, 1986)

Many caterers have realized the potential of using computers to assist them in their sales and marketing strategies. What better way to control sales, as well as to undertake market research and analyse present and future business, than to make use of a computer? Whilst the idea may sound intimidating, a suitable database package can probably be added to the facilities of an existing computer to enable a business to identify its existing and future markets.

The great advantage of a marketing database is that it should help put the catering business that has taken the trouble to create it ahead of the opposition by allowing the analysis of the customer base of the business easily, quickly and accurately. The marketing database should allow the maintenance of an accurate profile of customers from which the best potential business prospects can be identified, thereby allowing marketing to be targeted accurately.

Before the use of computers the analysis of customers even into nationalities was a very laborious task. With a computer the rapid analysis that is possible allows a manager to identify trends as they occur, rather than some time after it is too late to take action, and this allows much closer control of the business than would previously have been the case. This is illustrated by the following quotation:

> Because we now have instant accessibility to historic information we have been able to market our hotel more effectively this summer than ever before. (Hogg, 1986)

Many catering companies have found that their sales managers, especially if they have been recruited from other industries, now demand the marketing information that a computer can provide. In the past hotels rarely had the benefit of up-to-date information that a sales or marketing manager could rely on. Sales managers need to identify where their customers come from and, in the case of a hotel, how they made their bookings so that the best sources of prospective customers can be identified.

In starting from scratch, the best initial step is to instigate a series of workshops and meetings of staff to develop the rudimentary design of a program to make the marketing efforts of the business more effective. In a hotel most of the information for the marketing database can be located in the detail already held within the front office records, so it is wise to involve not only the sales staff but also the front office staff in these discussions.

Most hotel marketing databases have a number of basic statistics upon which the complete program rests. These are normally:

- *market segment*
- *source*
- *channel*

The *market segment* refers to the type of business being discussed, for example, a particular customer grouping such as chance, company meeting or tour. *Source* refers to who actually made the booking, which might be a travel agent, the guests themselves or a company. This information is important as a travel agent, for example, can influence greatly the choice of hotel for a customer's stay. The *channel* is the method of communication used to send the reservation to the hotel. This could be a centralized reservations office, Prestel, or the hotel's own reservations department. Gathering the total number of reservations received through the various channels will accurately demonstrate who is handling or controlling particular types of business.

Ideally, a marketing database will allow the facility to project statistics so that a forecast may be built up of what would happen if certain policies were pursued. The sales manager will then have better information on which to decide whether a certain marketing plan should be initiated. A computer with this marketing facility can automatically make the necessary calculations to allow accurate forecasts of the effects of a marketing policy on, for example, average room rates. The staff are therefore released from tedious calculations and can concern themselves more with the actual business mix.

The ideal method of using the statistics produced by the computer is to compare actual figures with those originally forecast. In a hotel actual figures would be produced for each market segment by room nights, average rate, occupancy and room revenue. The production of this information is a vital part of the analysis of the performance of the hotel. Should the hotel be one of several in a company then each hotel may be compared with the others on an area basis or possibly across the whole company. Each hotel can analyse and respond to the trends in its business by comparing figures with those from the previous month, year or whatever period is required.

Usually a print-out called a Marketing Plan Summary is produced for the market segments and period for which detail is required, and at a glance this will show such items as the forecasted average rate figures compared to the actual average rate. Manually this information would have required many hours of calculations but by utilizing the computer the marketing manager has access to the information almost instantaneously.

There will be times when it is necessary to compare detail from more than one market segment. The program should be capable of undertaking this, displaying the results on a print-out or VDU. The overall revenue contribution of each market segment should be produced to include accommodation, food and beverage, and any necessary ancillary services. This information will help set the average room rate for the future when considered in conjunction with other statistics such as the lead time for each reservation, commissions charged and total revenue contribution.

Sales and marketing managers also need detailed information on the geographic origin of all business. The countries, counties and towns that provide the most guests enable the targeting of particular marketing or advertising. The program should also allow for the detailed identification of each source of a booking. Those agents that provide the most business need to be identified as well as the type of customer they are providing. The person booking the reservation must be identified as they have a great influence on the business.

The Hilton International sales management system (Delphi)

Hilton International make use of a computerized sales management system called Delphi which was installed to give the company the competitive edge in the cut-throat convention market. The system helps maximize profitability for each individual hotel and is intended to give the customer the most efficient service possible.

Whilst Delphi has been taken up by Hilton International properties worldwide, it is in fact software that is generally available and illustrates in an excellent way many of the facets of a good sales and marketing computer. It can be operated on either micro or minicomputers.

The Delphi type of system is particularly useful to hotels that derive a high volume of their business from tours and groups, or that have a high percentage of banqueting and catering events. It is common for a sales office to be involved to a large extent with banqueting arrangements and it is therefore good that this is absorbed into the overall sales and marketing package.

In handling a hotel's group sales and function space, a sales and marketing computer system should:

- *Automate the sales and banqueting office*, negating the need for previous manual systems
- *Provide a support system for the sales staff* by presenting a complete picture of room and function space availability
- *Improve customer service* by giving quicker responses
- *Speed up sales decisions* by having information to hand
- *Raise overall hotel profitability* by providing a more efficient service
- *Provide an automatic list of imminent events* giving the banqueting staff the opportunity to be prepared in advance
- *Improve inter-departmental communication* by providing daily, weekly and monthly reports on all booked events
- *Eliminate time consuming work* such as manual preparation of statistics and reports
- *Create banqueting event orders* within the system thus increasing efficiency

Marketing database

The marketing database will include actual and prospective bookings, with a rapid search and sort capability to enable sales activity to be focused on target markets. With a large number of defined codes it will be possible to search the database for characteristics that reflect the hotel's present sales strategy. Examples of attributes on which sales staff may base a search might be frequency, market segment, seasonal pattern, last time in city and next time in city.

The Delphi database runs on either a minicomputer or a microcomputer, and makes use specifically of a booking method report that identifies the channels used for reservations. If the booking method report identifies, for example, that travel agents provide 50 per cent of the business that is booked through airline reservations systems, this would indicate to the sales manager that it might be good for business to include more travel agency-orientated information about the particular hotel within the airline reservations system (Davis, 1986).

By the use of a computer the hotel is able to weigh up rapidly the costs of encouraging any particular type of business, as well as identifying the business that the reservations staff should be concentrating on. It could also help to identify future training needs of staff to cope with the business that is placed with the hotel as it develops.

Even in a large company such as Hilton the marketing database must be sufficiently flexible to allow each individual hotel to maintain its own identity, as well as to hold information on its own specific or peculiar market. For example, the Jerusalem Hilton has a specific market segment called 'Pilgrims' that is peculiar to that hotel and which provides a great deal of business.

Service history

The service history database of a computerized system can eliminate the tedious work related to researching the productivity of groups that have used the hotel. Summary information on past performance can be stored for quick evaluation on future projections.

A good sales and marketing system enables sales staff to keep account histories. These will allow, for example, the sales staff to keep a history of all client bookings, including their average bill settlement, the expected and actual number of guests, the types of functions booked, etc. The system will store these histories thus keeping track of future potential business, and allow sales staff to retrieve specific accounts on the basis of established important criteria, such as:

- marketing salesperson assigned
- convention service manager
- catering salesperson assigned
- postal code
- geographic code
- last use of property
- next trace date
- next time in city
- projected event date
- frequency code
- pattern code
- seasonality code
- peak night rooms
- average check (average spend per head)
- source of record
- booking type
- cover count
- market segment
- account quality rating
   Source: Delphi Management Systems, Inc.

To give a typical example, if there is an obvious gap in business for the establishment during June the sales manager may refer to the computerized records and request details of accounts that:

- meet during the summer months (seasonality code)
- have an average of 50 guests or more (cover count)
- have an average spend of £150 per head or more (average check)

The system should be able to produce a list of such accounts which the sales and marketing manager can contact.

Lost business tracking

In addition to business and accounts that were successfully accommodated, it is important for the system to record details of business that for one reason or another was lost. Business that was passed over or cancelled should be stored along with the hotel's opinion, chosen from at least thirty pre-specified reasons, as to why that business was lost. This database is used to evaluate trends for lost business and to research accounts that may fill need times in the future. Examples of reasons for lost business, together with database codes for recording the relevant criteria, are given in Figure 3.9.

VALID LOST BUSINESS REASONS

1	Other – See Comments	17	Lack – Athletic Facilities
2	Shortage – Guest Rooms	18	Lack – Shuttle Service
3	Shortage – Function Space	19	Lack – Parking Facilities
4	Shortage – Exhibit Space	20	Lack – F&B Outlets
5	Shortage – Suites	21	Lack – Audio/Visual
6	Rates too high	22	Lack – Kosher Kitchen
7	Other Hotel – Rates	23	Turn Down – Poor History
8	Other Hotel – Facilities	24	Turn Down – Space Ratio
9	Other Hotel – Total Package	25	Turn Down – Commission
10	Other City	26	Turn Down – Complimentary F&B
11	Meeting costs too high	27	Cancel – Non-materialization
12	Lack – Specific Function Rooms	28	Cancel – Deposit not paid
13	Lack – Auditorium	29	Cancel – Space given to another
14	Lack – Teleconferencing	30	Cancel – Rescheduled
15	Lack – Ballroom Capacity	31	Cancel – Personnel change
16	Lack – Pre-function Space		

Figure 3.9 *Lost business reasons*
Source: Delphi Management Systems, Inc.

In providing better service to the customer the system should allow guest bedroom and function room availability to be viewed on one screen. This cuts out the problem of liaison between a reception desk and a sales office to find a mutually agreeable date when suitable accommodation and function rooms are simultaneously available. It is also useful to record bookings that are initially turned away because of unavailability. If there are subsequent cancellations such a record provides a ready-made list of customers to contact who might fill the cancelled accommodation.

Being able to view the maximum amount of detail on screen at one time gives a great benefit of flexibility to sales staff. A proportion of business may not be able to be accommodated on the day or days originally intended and a good computer system will provide a clear display of alternative dates which may be acceptable to the customer.

March 1, 19

Mr. Gregg Newmark
Executive Vice President
National Business Machines
115 W. 31st Street
New York, NY   10001

Dear **Gregg,**

Enclosed you will find the complete contract of arrangements for your meeting
scheduled to begin on **Tuesday, April 29th, 1986.**

Attached are two copies of the Program, which contains all of the billing
instructions and general coordination details that we have been discussing.

Events have been scheduled and function rooms set up as follows:

Event Date	Start Time	End Time	Function Type	Function Setup	Agreed Attend.	Room
4/29/	8:00A	5:00P	MEETING	CLASSROOM	60	EXEC-1
4/30/	8:00A	5:00P	MEETING	THEATER	120	CROWN
4/30/	12:30P	2:30P	LUNCH	ROUNDS	120	REGENCY
5/02/	8:00A	12:00P	MEETING	U-SHAPED	60	ROYAL

Also attached is the Banquet Event Order. Please verify the menu items planned and make any necessary changes or comments. Also, promptly sign all
contracts and return them to me to ensure proper handling of your functions.

These attachments represent our complete understanding of your food, beverage
and setup needs. We require that you notify this office by 12:00 noon two
working days before the first meal function date with a guarantee. Charges
will be made according to this final guaranteed number, even if fewer attend.
Please notify **Dan Notman** at 212/563-1001 before the appropriate deadline.

Also, a deposit of $500 is required by **Friday, November 29th** to ensure defi-
nite confirmation of your reservation.

I look forward to a successful Conference for you and **National Business
Machines.** Please feel free to give me a call with any questions.

Sincerely,

Harold Anderson
Sales Manager

Figure 3.10   *Sample standard letter merged with specific customer information*
Source: Delphi Management Systems, Inc.

The computer will really come into its own when handling conference or functions business. Here, provided the correct information has been programmed into the system, it will be able to calculate exact group rates for the meeting planners, including all extras such as additional meals and use of the recreational facilities that take a long time to cost using traditional methods. With the aid of a computer the customer, in this case probably a conference organizer, may be given answers during an initial telephone query. The member of staff handling the sale has before them a clear costed picture that allows an informed negotiation to take place between the hotel and the potential customer. The risks of accepting unprofitable business are as a consequence considerably reduced.

It is sometimes a problem with computer systems that staff who want to view the availability of rooms cannot gain access to a VDU as they actually need it. In such a situation they may resort to daily, weekly and monthly reports printed by the computer. These reports are particularly useful to sales staff working away from the hotel who can carry reasonably up-to-date information in hard-copy form.

It is a distinct advantage if a sales and marketing system has comprehensive word processing facilities. This allows customer proposals, contracts and correspondence to be produced easily by interfacing word processing with the group and functions database. The computer can retrieve data to complete standard letters or contracts with individual information such as contact name, address, scheduled events, function rooms, etc. The system may go one step further to prepare personalized banquet menus, direct mail promotions, invitations, thank-you letters and other correspondence. Figure 3.10 shows a sample standard letter with specific customer information from the marketing database highlighted in bold type.

The MHM system

The Motor Hotel Management (MHM) marketing system (Landry, 1982), is a computerized market analysis program researched in the United States. When it was put into action for the first time in January 1982 it was heralded as the first system to be developed and implemented by a hospitality management company.

The central core of the MHM system was the computerized market analysis report compiled for each of MHM's 45 properties at the end of every month. This required information on all types of reservation such as individual commercial travellers, individual pleasure travellers, group packages, city conventions, etc., as well as additional data taken at the time that the reservation was placed.

The intention of the market analysis report was to present information in an easily digestible form so that the hotel management could see:

- where guests came from
- which of 13 different market segments they belonged to
- how many visits they had made
- how many room nights they had spent
- the percentage of first time visits
- the average reservation lead time
- comparisons for the current year
- comparisons for the previous year

The vast majority of the information needed by the MHM system could be located on the guest registration card; the only additional question that the clerk had to ask was whether this was the guest's first visit or not. Once a month, one clerk at each of MHM's hotels would spend about four hours filling out the computer cards that were sent in for processing.

The MHM system quickly provided the hotel managers with useful feedback. One hotel manager was surprised to discover that 58 per cent of the hotel's total business came from Los Angeles and that the same city provided 70 per cent of the total chance business. The reaction was then to advertise the hotel on hoardings alongside the freeway from Los Angeles which further increased business from that city. Another roadside MHM hotel found that 37 per cent of its chance business came direct from Phoenix airport which was a total surprise for a hotel specifically aimed at the motorist. Again appropriate marketing strategies were created to develop this demand.

Holidex III system

Another comprehensive computer system is Holidex III utilized by Holiday Inns throughout their 1,680 hotels. In addition to handling reservations, it produces masses of reports which help Holiday Inns to identify trends all over the world, from Asia and Mexico, to Canada and South Africa. Holiday Inns identified, for example, the drop in American visitors to the UK early in 1986 which enabled them to formulate their response. Holiday Inns can create marketing programs to go back into the Holidex system and they know, for example, the activities and the productivity of every hotel in the network (Wood, 1986).

Mailing lists

Many businesses are now fully conversant with the benefits of word processors and these can easily be utilized to hold one of the most faithful of marketing tools, namely, the mailing list.

It is quite a simple process with a personal computer to hold guest lists on disk memory and, with the addition of a word processing program and a filing package, to compose and produce all types of marketing-orientated correspondence, including personalized standard letters and accompanying labels.

Standard letters to customers, from whatever market segment, can be targeted to bring a wide variety of promotions to their attention. Whether bargain break weekends, new banqueting facilities or a special menu are being promoted the ability to target specific customers is invaluable and it should be remembered that direct mail shots are widely regarded as an extremely effective marketing tool.

Specific accounts may be selected for a direct mailing based on a number of criteria such as market segment, dates of major meetings or total number of events. A listing can then be produced that enables promotional letters to be sent to those accounts that best fit the profile for a specific mailing. For example, a special banquet theme party mailing may be sent to the 25 largest corporate accounts that have booked bedroom or function space in the last year. Alternatively, correspondence that reminds guests of the hotel's banquet and catering services may be sent to organizations that have not booked function space for more than a year.

Whatever type of hospitality is being marketed a word processor enables a mail shot to be personalized and therefore gives a much better impression. It is also possible to amend the mailing list regularly to take account of contacts who are no longer applicable or to make additions.

Each hotelier will have different ideas as to the categories of customer that might be defined on the hotel's mailing lists. Some suggestions are:

- regular customers
- customers who have stayed at the hotel over the last few seasons
- business customers
- conference organizers
- secretaries of managing directors of local firms
- travel agency contacts
- journalists

Again, the information is collected from guests when they arrive at the hotel by them completing a guest registration card or form specifically designed with the collection of marketing data in mind. In addition to the mandatory '*full name*' and '*nationality*' such data might include:

- *sex*
- *marital status*
- *age*
- *address*
- *reason for stay*
- *mode of transport*
- *length of stay*

Once the initial data has been entered into the database – a major task when starting from scratch – the information then only has to be kept up-to-date. Having a database to hand not only enables marketing statistics and mailing lists to be collated accurately but also allows the guests to be treated on an improved personal basis thereby giving an improved guest history facility.

Whatever its eventual use the database will certainly take the slog out of creating a mail shot. It is estimated that a word processor, that could be left overnight to undertake the chore of printing, works at about three times the speed of a good manual typist when creating personalized letters and labels utilizing the business's headed notepaper. There is little doubt that a word processor enables a caterer to undertake a far more flexible and accurate mailing campaign than would previously have been possible.

Media selection

Another of the uses to which a computer may be put in marketing is in the planning of the relevant media to be utilized for advertising. So complex are the rate structures, circulation data and the media vehicles themselves that a computer can be of great assistance. Certainly advertising agencies make use of media selection models and if a caterer undertakes their own marketing then a similar model may well be useful (Buttle, 1986).

The constituent parts of an integrated marketing system

A computerized sales software package will help maximize profit by automating the paperwork and the functions normally associated with sales, plus making use of some innovations that are only possible thanks to new technology. It is no idle boast to suggest that a computerized sales and marketing system allows the sales manager more hands-on control of present and future room sales than was ever possible before.

In a manual system, past sales performance of a catering establishment was merely tracked, and some projections were made for the future. With a computerized system the future may be anticipated and planned for. To achieve this a complete history is held of every sales contact ever made. Priorities are given to specific individuals and groups with regard to potential, tentative and definite bookings, and each of these may then be matched against the targeted future model.

The sales office is freed and enabled by the computer to concentrate its efforts on the most productive ways of gaining business by targeting the most productive accounts.

Whether the system used is stand-alone or fully integrated there are some common elements to the operation of a marketing and sales package. The main parts of the system are:

- marketing data source
- comprehensive marketing records
- collation package
- identification of new business
- sales action plan
- mailing and word processing

Marketing data source

This enables particular markets to be targeted as well as the existing customer mix to be examined. There will also be a facility to allow information about potential customers to be recorded and accessed quickly. The sales manager, whether operating on behalf of a hotel or another type of catering business, will have the ability with the computer to keep on record a wide range of information on all sales contacts.

There will firstly be a need to record exactly who the potential new customers might be as well as details of their location and company, if applicable, so that their market sector may be ascertained. Whether or not the actual contacts are the people with the power to make a purchasing decision will need to be examined so that time is not wasted and it will be necessary to maintain a record of the quantities, say, of rooms and the frequency with which the customers make use of all hotel and catering facilities. How much they have spent in the past on rooms, covers, meals, and their average room rate, as well as what potential they have for the future and some record of their usage of competing establishments are other important factors.

The aim of the marketing system is to keep a close watch on all sales and marketing activity, whilst helping greatly to cut down on the administrative time needed to record and collate such detailed information that would be needed with a manual system.

Comprehensive marketing records

An integral part of the system will be a comprehensive marketing record which is the central core of information so vital to sales. As the basic elements of this system there will be detailed records on:

- name and title of all business contacts
- company names, address, telephone and telex numbers
- buying motives
- last year's business
- special notes on every contact
- ranking of contacts into market sectors

A comprehensive system will allow the sales staff access to instant on-screen viewing of all the contact details, using names as the search medium. It should be possible for the system to allow quick alterations to customer information held on file and each contact should be given a reference number to make the compilation of mailing lists easier.

There will also be a need for the computer system to store sales details concerning all the business contacts and for these to be instantly available on screen. Many of the sales details will be electronic replacements of the card index systems often used by sales managers in the past. Possibilities include (ADP Hotel Services Ltd, A):

- 'Trace Cards' for sales personnel including customer likes and dislikes, habits, etc.
- 'Sales Visit Records' listing time, place, subject of meeting and outcome
- 'Sales Proposals' highlighting contract prices, elements contained within, discounts, etc.
- Telephone sales calls recording key factors and special requirements discussed
- Next 'action' to progress sale

Collation package

One of the major benefits of a computerized package is that it will allow the sales manager not only to enter details on each business contact but also to classify them for marketing analysis and reporting. The specific classification criteria selected, for example, may be those relating to the geographical location of business and the potential customer spend. Possible segmentation could therefore be (ADP Hotel Services Ltd, A):

- classification of sales opportunity (function, meeting, etc.)
- geographical location of business contact
- annual turnover of contact company
- type of business
- frequency of timing of business
- use of competition property
- booking source
- potential spend

Identification of new business

A marketing system may provide an identification of new business areas, giving impetus and motivation for sales opportunity planning.

With the computer maintaining detailed customer and client profiles it may also schedule the work of the sales team on a diary basis so that business opportunities are not allowed to lapse or be forgotten. For example, it will be possible for the computer to record potential business and prompt the sales team when it is a favourable time to obtain business from specific contacts. The system will also facilitate a record of the special requirements of business contacts so these too are not forgotten.

Sales action plan

A computerized system offers the ability to compile and monitor a complete sales action plan to assist in developing business to its maximum.

To this end the sales manager will be able to track the performance of the account executives and the sales of potential group rooms by using reports which reveal, for example, which accounts should have been contacted that were not and which account executive was responsible for the particular market segment. Equally the sales manager will be able to obtain reports on potential group bookings for a set period and a summary of total advance sales for some time, probably several years, ahead.

It will be possible to jog the memory of sales staff as the computer system can automatically produce details of sales contacts who have not been visited during the last year. This will ensure that contact with customers is maintained. It may even be possible to run such a program weekly so that prompt follow-up action is taken and sales leads are not forgotten.

The computer will enable the sales manager to set up daily sales targets for staff to achieve on products such as group rooms. It may also allow an automatic collation of sales contacts in particular areas or even streets. When a representative is due to visit a specific contact the computer will suggest other contacts in the immediate vicinity who may be called on too.

Mailing and word processing

The records set up within the computerized marketing system provide the necessary information for all forms of communication to customers and potential clients. For mail shots labels can be addressed to all contacts or a selected target market and can be printed directly by the system.

Provided the system is interfaced with a word processing package, the marketing package may be merged with any document or letter set up on the word processor so individual personalized correspondence can be produced. In addition, promotional literature within the word processing database may be addressed to any individual contact who conforms to desired marketing criteria. Alternatively, promotional literature may be linked to personal correspondence and the dual documentation printed, ready to mail out.

Travel agency and tour company business

Major sources of business for many hotel and catering establishments are travel agents or tour companies who expect a commission in exchange for business placed. Whilst travel agencies usually operate on a strict 10 per cent commission, this may vary depending on the individual arrangement. Tour companies, on the other hand, receive a larger discount the more business they place with an establishment.

Travel agency and tour company business will be of particular interest to the sales manager. It is, after all, a major selling advantage to be able to negotiate discounts with potential customers and staff other than the sales manager are not likely to be given this responsibility. To assist the sales manager there should be on-line access through the computer system to all the information concerning particular travel agencies and tour companies. Their performance will be recorded within the system as will their historical record with the establishment, thereby revealing to the sales manager data that is truly up-to-date so that the latest picture is constantly available.

Where the sales manager's decisions on commissions are concerned, which is the meat of the problem, there are a number of alternative strategies that may be employed. The computer may be programmed to cost the implications, say, of a fixed percentage of room revenue by tariff type, percentages of total room revenue or total revenue. Other alternatives include commission rates of fixed amounts per guest, per reservation or per room night. The computer system must be capable of dealing with one or all of these alternatives, as well as issuing commission cheques promptly (with some systems this is automatic) for mailing to the companies involved.

There will in addition need to be a series of statistics provided by the system to enable business to be analysed and assimilated. These statistics will include details of the number of reservations, no shows, cancellations and total room nights, plus the totals of sales revenue, room revenue, commission paid and commission due.

To deal with commission payments there will have to be access to the sales ledger program for the correct handling of VAT. Commission payments to British travel agents will normally include VAT, so the ledger program must incorporate a checking routine that has been approved by the VAT authorities to validate VAT numbers.

CONFERENCE MANAGEMENT

The successful handling of conference and function business is of great importance to a large number of hoteliers and caterers as their reputations depend on this sphere of the hospitality business. The storage capacity of all types of computer, whether mainframe, mini or micro, may be harnessed to smooth the operation of such events.

A conference manager will require the computer to be a comprehensive tool to help with the booking, coordination and execution of conferences, meetings, and events of all kinds from initial enquiry, through quotation, detailed planning and information dissemination, to invoicing and full accounts. A typical conference management computer system might have the following main spheres of operation:

- enquiries
- conference diary
- staff organization
- function list
- quotation and sales forecasting
- bookings
- market research data base
- marketing and mailing
- invoicing
- sales ledger
- reporting

Enquiries

In order to respond effectively to conference enquiries a rolling diary of events will need to be maintained with on-line enquiry facilities covering room availability within certain dates or date availability for certain rooms. Enquiry should also be possible for particular event types and numbers and for specific days of the week (Fretwell-Downing).

Conference diary

The conference diary section of the system is possibly the most important as it permits full control to be exercised over the total number of conferences booked into the establishment. As conferences are booked many years ahead it is wise to have a conference diary that satisfactorily holds information for a long time period: the better computer systems provide a range of at least five years. Historical information may also be required so the conference system should have a memory of at least two years into the past.

The facilities available within the conference diary of a comprehensive system will include the ability to refer quickly to reservations for a particular day or week in the future and to a comprehensive conference listing for any range of dates in the diary. It should also be possible to request from the system details of rooms that are available for specific functions by asking questions such as: which rooms and dates are suitable for a conference of 500 on a Saturday? When making a reservation it will be useful if there is a prompt facility to remind the member of staff concerned if there is a major event or occasion happening at that time. For example, it may be 'Gold Cup week' or the time of another major conference locally so it may be inappropriate to take extra business on. With the notorious situation of bookings not being fulfilled, an overbooking facility will be required as will an analysis of booking status. A detailed cancellations report facility will be useful for checking customer reliability.

Staff organization

In a busy conference centre or hotel an organization system will help with staff rotas, job scheduling, and allocation of staff to individual functions, and details may also be kept of holidays, sickness and special events.

Function list

As part of the operation of the conference diary it would be useful if the computer produced function lists and departmental function sheets to give detailed reporting for each department such as the kitchen, dispense bar, florist, electrician, external contractors, and reception.

Quotations and sales forecasting

A good quotation and forecasting package for conferences should enable the conference manager to have access to client quotations for both conferences and banquets. There should be a fully analysed internal cost and sales quotation report facility as well as the ability to provide gross profit forecasting. The conference manager should have access to details of the sales persons' commission and bonus points forecasting. The reports produced will include monthly, quarterly, and yearly sales forecasts as well as sales analysis by sales person and an analysis of prospective clients and all conference venues in competition.

Comprehensive quotations detailing all the bookings, facilities and services should be reviewable on-screen with the ability to print-out on an *ad hoc* basis (Fretwell-Downing).

Bookings

A single booking entry into a computerized system may cover both meetings and overnight accommodation for a day or a series of days, or even specific times within a day, so the system must be capable of handling this amount and variety of detail. It should be possible to copy events spanning more than one day, thus greatly reducing the necessary input time. Once copied, any changes in requirements for a particular day should be capable of being made and complete events should be able to be moved within the diary or copied in the case of annual bookings.

Facilities should be able to be booked, with or without charge, against individual rooms both before the event in the case of, for example, audio visual equipment, or after the event such as in the situation of electricity being charged on a consumption basis.

Catering requirements should be recordable and chargeable for each room at specified times. A link to a Catering Management Information System will facilitate full kitchen production planning and purchase ordering.

Bar extensions should be recorded and listed separately over specified periods for the purpose of coordinating applications and any special requirements may be detailed on an unrestricted 'note pad' facility against each room (Fretwell-Downing).

Market research database

The market research database should be tailored to a specific establishment with the intention of providing a comprehensive management information and marketing analysis system.

A typical system includes not only a comprehensive market database for, in some cases, up to 90,000 contacts and companies (ADP Hotel Services Ltd, B) but also instant buyer pattern feedback which helps to answer such questions as who buys what, where, how often and with whom. The system will also give statistical analyses of market sectors, types and categories as well as an automatic selection and reporting of any mix of market criteria (for example, banquet organisers with £5,000+ budgets resident in the Greater London area currently using competitor venues).

Marketing and mailing

A good computer system will provide the ability to interface the market research database with a word processing system for brochure mailing or personalized letter production and mailing. A selective sales pitch may also be utilized.

Invoicing

With an interface to an invoicing package the ability will exist for remote or independently controlled conference centres to quickly prepare and print client bills. It should be possible to generate invoices individually or in batches at the user's discretion.

The standard charges maintained for all services and facilities may be overridden to reflect specially negotiated rates or discounts.

Sales ledger

The conference system may include its own sales ledger and credit control system that interfaces with the invoicing and word processing systems to permit automatic personal debt collection correspondence to be created and mailed.

Reporting

The real power of a computerized conference system lies not only with the standard reports that already exist, but more particularly with the flexibility of reporting that allows the user to create and tailor reports to specific local needs. Specialist areas of reporting might include those in Figure 3.11.

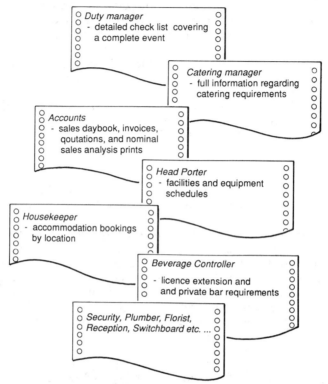

Figure 3.11   *Conference computer system reports*
Source: Fretwell-Downing Computer Group

Teleconferencing

A novel approach to the handling of conferences has been pioneered in the United States where teleconferencing has been in use for some years.

Holiday Inns were pioneers of the teleconferencing philosophy which is to link a number of hotel locations together using a telecommunications network so that they all receive the same information simultaneously. Holiday Inns set up their HI-NET subsidiary using satellite communications for just such a purpose. Some hoteliers could have regarded teleconferencing as a threat to existing business, but when an audience is gathered together they may create business such as the provision of accommodation and food. Apart from corporate use teleconference facilities may also be used for the mass and exclusive viewing of certain prestige sporting events, as is quite common in UK hotels where World Championship boxing matches are a particular favourite.

Some hotels originally used the teleconferencing facility for the much more mundane transmission of in-house movies on what amounts to what is now a normal satellite television network.

Teleconferencing comes in two distinct packages. It may either be *receive only* or *interactive*. The former is generally used by large conferences; for example, it was extensively used by President Reagan to rally party election workers across the country. The ideal development, though, is the interactive teleconferencing facility which allows two-way communication between locations. This is used much more by smaller groups.

BACK OFFICE COMPUTERIZED ACCOUNTS

As number-crunching is one of the applications to which computers are best suited, the organization of accounts forms a major part of their usage in a very large number of hotel and catering establishments. Indeed in these days where cash-flow is so vital to the survival of a business, the capability of handling accounts and to achieve swift results is essential from the very smallest business upwards.

A comprehensive back office financial accounting system specifically designed for the hotel and catering industry is vital to the smooth operation of establishments. Basically, it will be designed to automate and reduce the time consuming back office accounting functions, whilst having the versatility to allow the processing and storage of irregular transactions if required.

The financial accounting program will be interactive and include purchase ledger and general ledger modules. These modules will quickly and efficiently process back office functions and automatically generate the hotel management reports needed for effective decision-making.

The accounting applications that can be handled by computer are numerous but a typical overall package would include the following:

- purchase ledger
- general ledger
- balance sheet
- profit and loss reports
- management information
- financial modelling
- sales ledger
- budgeting and forecasting

Purchase ledger

The intention behind the computerized purchase ledger is to send payments to each supplier for agreed invoices once discounts and any manual payments have been taken into account.

The purchase ledger should share with the sales ledger the advantages of open-time accounting, such as the ability to match the establishment's payment against outstanding supplier invoices ensuring that supplier accounts are always up-to-date and continually balanced. In doing so the general ledger will be automatically updated by the interaction of the overall computerized accounting system.

The purchase ledger contains records of all the catering establishment's creditors, thereby containing details of transactions with them and allowing the printing of remittance advice slips. Purchases will be analysed over a number of categories and reports will be produced of balances on the creditors' accounts. In addition, a good system will allow the automatic production of cheques as well as giving a full 'aged' list of creditors.

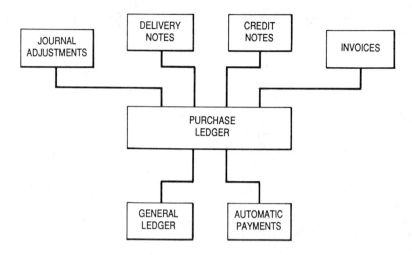

Figure 3.12   *Integrated purchase ledger system*
Source: Thorn EMI CHAMPS Systems

The entire operation of the purchase ledger will depend upon the way in which each supplier's account is constructed. A typical list of data on each supplier would include:

- name and address of supplier
- name and address to whom payments should be sent
- details of goods or services supplied
- payment details (due on invoice or statement)
- discounts (fixed percentages or early payment incentives)

With the better systems, as soon as an account is created for a supplier delivery notes, invoices and credit notes may be handled without delay. With the system users in the control office entering all invoice items against pre-defined identification codes, VAT is automatically separated for the general ledger and cheques may be automatically prepared for payment.

Typical reports produced by a purchase ledger may include:

- aged creditor list
- supplier summary list
- delivery note list
- invoices due for payment list
- supplier type purchase analysis

It may well be useful to interface the purchase ledger with a word processing facility so that suppliers who fall within defined criteria may be automatically mailed with hotel literature or correspondence for marketing or information purposes.

If the sales and purchase ledgers are integrated then there is a useful facility should a supplier also be a customer of the hotel. It is possible to make sure that a cheque is not issued to a supplier who is actually in debt with the establishment. This is one of the many advantages of a fully integrated system.

General ledger

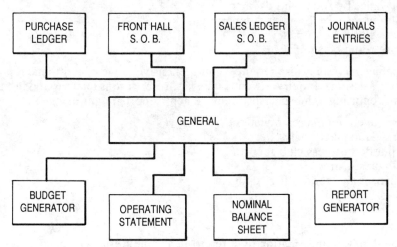

Figure 3.13 *Integrated general ledger system*
Source: Thorn EMI CHAMPS systems

The general ledger will be updated automatically by information from the other main accounting ledgers to give an overview of the accounts and other vital information for managers. An up-to-date balance sheet and profit and loss account may be produced at any time as well as special reports for the restaurants, bars and other hotel or catering departments.

The best general ledger packages make use of the *Uniform Accounting System for Hotels* which may be readily adapted to the requirements of varying types of property.

Facilities that may be advantageous will include the automatic posting of purchase ledger entries and recurring monthly journals. Monthly accruals may easily be made and then reversed the following month, being interfaced with the budgeting system. Indeed the link with a budgeting system is a major managerial advantage of the general ledger system.

The system should make an up-to-date trial balance, daybook and the full nominal account listings available at any time.

The balance sheet and profit and loss account

The balance sheet and profit and loss account on most computer systems will be available with an instantaneous 'last year comparison' and 'year-to-date' display. The computer should provide an automatic comparison of actual results against budget and an analysis by department or group of departments, plus a full departmental summary.

Management information

Front office

As far as the front office is concerned, there are a number of details and reports that may be produced by computer that are essential for the effective management of accommodation. These reports must include:

- daily sales by room and department
- monthly sales by room and department
- future sleeper occupancy
- future room occupancy

The management may also require a comprehensive range of additional reports that provide for sales mix enquiry, revenue analysis, reservations analysis and full transaction audit reporting. The specialist management reports might include:

- travel agent commission analysis
- guest nationality analysis
- corporate business club reporting
- VIP guest listings
- statistical and head office reporting

Accounts

Whilst the details of information required from a computerized management accounting system have been dealt with previously, the point should be made that no two establishments are exactly identical. Therefore although many accounting packages are compiled to an industry standard package (Uniform Systems of Accounting) there are different styles and formats that will need to be accommodated. Some systems, such as ADP's *Innfinance*, therefore merge the nominal ledger with the financial modelling system, so permitting the production and design of customized reports.

Financial modelling

It is a great advantage to the hotel or catering manager to be able to project figures to see the implications of a particular management policy, whether this be required as a comparison against a budget or not. Projection of such figures, which has become an essential management tool, is called *financial modelling*.

The better financial modelling systems provide 'What if?' facilities so that answers to questions that might have taken ages to work out manually can be established swiftly. For example, it is easy to link energy expenditure to occupancy, or the number of 'a là carte' meals to total covers, to establish current trends and to then project them. Accurate answers today will lead to increased revenue tomorrow.

Sales ledger

The control of cash and debtors is vital to any business but nowhere is this more evident than in a hotel or catering business where a substantial proportion of the overall trade is undertaken on a credit basis. The efficient handling of the sales ledger is therefore a prime consideration where computerization is concerned. Figure 3.14 shows an integrated sales ledger system.

In effect, the sales ledger records all the establishment's debtors, whilst maintaining individual accounts for guests and all credit customers. The computerized system will allow details of debtors to be entered, invoices and statements to be produced, sales and cash received to be analysed and sales reports to be produced.

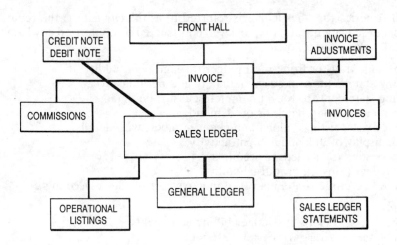

Figure 3.14   *An integrated sales ledger system*
Source: Thorn EMI CHAMPS Systems

The sales ledger may be handled on all types of computer and a typical micro-computer program will contain the following facilities (Chart Software Ltd):

- account name and update (name, address, telephone number and comments may be stored on each account)
- transaction posting
- allocations
- account list
- debtor list
- statements/enquiries
- deletion of allocated transactions
- invoicing

The sales ledger system must be user-friendly and incorporate a credit control system.

A good package should incorporate direct links with the front office system so that automatic guest account posting can take place and advance reservations credit account control may be practised. Before an invoice is prepared all the details of the bill may be checked and compared with the supporting documentation and adjusted if necessary.

Where links are concerned, there should also be a built-in link to a word processing system for personalized debt collection correspondence. The word processor will also be able to selectively mail individuals or companies holding accounts with the hotel. This is particularly important for mailing payment reminder letters or credit authorization letters.

A good system will automatically supply updated statements of account which will be available on demand to the hotel or catering manager for assistance with cash collection. Equally the system should provide a powerful analysis and report of debt collection and aged debtors to ease credit management. Once accounts are cleared there will be the facility for the hotel accountant to delete the balances concerned from the system so that in future the account holder receives a meaningful statement.

City ledger

In North America the sales ledger is referred to as the *city ledger*: the requirements are almost exactly identical. A typical well constructed computerized city ledger package would include the following:

- automatic transfer from guest ledger through night audit
- billing statements printed immediately and periodically
- billing statements to reflect complete guest folio detail
- statements printed batch or on demand
- client master listings, alpha and client number, with detail
- easy display of individual client activity
- easy posting to city ledger accounts
- city ledger transaction journal/audit
- city ledger purge (on demand) of inactive, zero-balance accounts

  SPECIAL FORMS
- Statement forms for city ledger billing statements
  Source: Auditel Lodging Management Systems Ltd

Budgeting and forecasting

The ability to gauge how well an establishment is performing, and to take swift remedial action if necessary, is one of the major advantages of a computerized system for hotel managers.

The challenge facing managers today is to provide better services while returning a reasonable profit on the establishment's investment. The development of new methods for budget preparation and for the modelling of activities has become one of the most valuable computer applications in performance analysis. Effective budgeting, based on sound costs and definitive criteria, assists in the control of costs, whilst variable budgeting algorithms provide accurate financial variances between budgeted and historical costs. The knowledge of what happened yesterday, along with what is anticipated today, may help in planning tomorrow's requirements. Armed with this knowledge, the manager has the information necessary to control costs and, ultimately, gross profit.

The better integrated systems will possess a *budget generating* facility that is linked to the general ledger. This will be capable of storing a number of financial budgets as well as a number of actual results. In printing an operating statement for an establishment it will be possible to impose any of the budgets or actual results to make comparisons between current figures, last year's figures and any of the budgets. It is also possible to link graph plotters to the system to provide a visual picture of the situation.

A computerized budgeting facility will therefore give the accountants the opportunity to effectively monitor and influence the financial stability of their establishments.

Night audit

If a computerized system is going to have an immediate effect anywhere within the organization of a hotel it will be in the night audit where tedious calculations that once, literally, took all night may be settled within minutes. Indeed, in many hotels the job of night auditor has almost disappeared thanks to the efficiency of computers.

A night audit package on computer will balance the day's revenues by processing room, VAT and other charges in a matter of minutes rather than hours. Among other functions a computerized package will provide a full audit trail.

The management will always have fast access to the hotel's financial status through the simplified balancing and reconciliation of guest ledgers and complete summaries of daily activities compiled during a nightly update. Standard charges for groups, ledger transfers, master group billing, employee discounts and other time consuming paperwork will be completely automated for even greater efficiency and accuracy.

The computer will make the work of a night auditor much easier as it will not only calculate and post room charges but it will also produce statistical reports on such items as room occupancy. Guest history details will be updated and all the day's transactions consolidated. During the night audit all the data within the system will be updated on a daily, monthly and yearly basis so that the auditor is then able to produce the morning reports for use during the next day's operation.

Whilst the work of night audit revolves around the balancing of the day's finances and the checking of the work undertaken by the front office, there are also a number of reports that need to be produced and which may be dramatically speeded up by the use of the computer. These reports include:

Room rate report	Posting report	Correction report
Adjustment report	Revenue report	Check-out report
VAT exempt report	No-show report	Deposit report
Cancellation report	Maintenance report	Guest type analysis
Housekeeping lists	Room blocking report	Group lists

A typical integrated computerized night audit package will therefore contain the following features:

- automatically posted room charges and VAT
- detailed transaction journal (audit trail) by transaction sequence
- detailed transaction journal (balance sheet) by revenue department
- automatic transfer of guest ledger accounts to city ledger
- direct billing linked directly to accounts receivable
- batch-run audit reports (occupancy, revenue, hotel statistics)
- automatic audit balance
- automatic close-day
- complete hotel statistics maintained month-to-date and year-to-date for a period of five years
- system date change at end of audit
- batch-run morning reports: room status, detail folios, departures
- advance pay ledger
- travel agency activity reports
- no-show reports
- guest summary reports
- system back-up enacted on night audit

Source: Auditel Lodging Management Systems

Computerizing the payroll

Many computer systems were originally designed to undertake payroll calculations as in the early days this was identified as an ideal application for the new technology. Consequently the methods of operation have been closely defined over the years and payroll handling by computer has now become extremely sophisticated. The point should be made, however, that many computing experts hold the view that small businesses, with less than five employees, are better served by preparing their payroll manually, whilst firms with in the region of 50 employees might use a bureau. It is really above this figure that an in-house computer comes into its own.

It is essential that the computer package one uses for payroll calculations conforms to the relevant government regulations and this should be checked before purchase.

Most systems will be able to undertake the payroll calculations for a catering operation within minutes, with the user simply supplying the details of any changes to the permanent records kept on employees as well as information concerning overtime. If the system is linked to an automated timecard network as outlined later (see page 167) then this simple task may be dispensed with too. The computer should then automatically carry out all the calculations of gross pay, PAYE, National Insurance and Statutory Sick Pay, and produce a payslip for each employee. In addition, a number of reports will be available.

One of the problems with the hotel and catering industry is that the payroll system must be able to deal with a myriad of different ways in which a wage may be calculated, as well as having to deal with all sorts of difficulties associated with specific job tasks. A good system will be able to cope with private, regular, part-time and on-call staff, who may be either salaried or hourly. It will be able to cope with employees who work at an unlimited number of jobs and their wages will be distributed accordingly. The system will also have to support an unlimited number of payments, deductions and benefits, as well as having to cope with unionized situations, where rates may be determined solely by the job, or non-unionized situations where pay may be unique for each employee. Even holiday pay may cause difficulties as it may be calculated on a fixed number of hours per month worked, per year worked, a percentage of gross, or a combination of these. If a regular employee 'moonlights' as an on-call employee, then that vacation information has to be kept separate.

For these reasons the computerized calculation of pay is no easy matter, but there are some very good payroll packages on offer which may be tailored to the individual work patterns of the establishment concerned.

Many computerized payroll systems will be fully integrated with other modules giving a complete picture of the staff utilization in an establishment. Figure 3.15 shows a typical example:

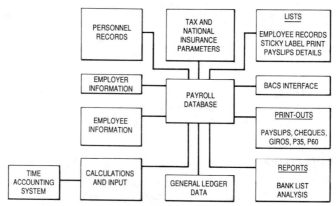

Figure 3.15 *Integrated payroll system*
Source: Thorn EMI CHAMPS Systems

Employer's details

The initial step in setting up a payroll system is to insert the necessary details about the establishment and the employer. This information will include name, address and bank details, and then tax and national insurance parameters will be set.

Staff details

The following details will need to be kept on record within the computer for each employee:

- reference number
- full name
- address
- National Insurance number
- starting date
- leaving date (where applicable)
- National Insurance code
- tax code
- tax class
- previous gross pay (this tax year)
- previous tax (this tax year)
- month/week number
- monthly/weekly pay
- hourly rate
- nett rounding (for weekly pay)
- number of working days in a week
- payment method
- pension deductions
- percentage pension deduction
- fixed deductions (meals, accommodation, etc.)
- bank details for giro payment (bank code, bank name, account number, payee name)

Payroll processing

It will be a distinct advantage if the payroll may be run in a number of different ways. This could entail processing the information for the entire staff in one go, by department, or individually. Once the system is set up with all the employee and employer information alterations will only need to be made to standard information, such as tax code changes or numbers of hours actually worked (for those staff on hourly rates), before the entire process may be set in motion. The system should be set up to produce *exception reports* for those members of staff for whom it was not possible to complete the process through lack of information such as 'no input'.

Payroll reports

The computer will be able to provide the management with a number of reports of great use internally as well as helping to satisfy external regulations. These reports and listings will include:

- *Payroll listing*   gives all employee details
- *Payroll summary*   presents a full analysis of gross pay and deductions made from it
- *Cheque issued list*   gives a tally of cheques against employees
- *SSP report*   lists each employee's statutory sick pay status
- *Monthly deductions report*   gives the total payments and deductions for the month, for those on weekly payroll
- *Employee records*   detailed or brief employee payment histories, as well as records of staff with particular skills who might meet special circumstances
- *Variance report*   lists excessively high or low paid employees
- *Year-to-date employee report*   details the accumulated totals for all employees
- *End-of-year deductions*   this is produced prior to the year-end reset and gives all details required for annual employee deduction cards

Security

There can be no more sensitive information to some individuals than the details of their pay. It is therefore essential that of all parts of an integrated system the payroll is only accessible to selected staff with the correct entry passwords. It will also be essential to ensure that the payroll cannot be printed accidentally anywhere else on the system and that every use of the payroll is separately logged so that management can see who used the system, what they did and when.

Labour analysis (ACOM)

Whilst so far we have accepted that the computer is able to handle the physical side of staff payment, which is presumably one function that an employer intends to undertake, there is also another payroll application for the computer. This is to try to control payroll expenses, whether this be by analysing the labour requirements closely or by undertaking time accounting. Perhaps a mixture of each would be the best solution to controlling what is, after all, the largest single expense in a hotel and catering operation – the payroll.

In analysing payroll expenses a typical package would provide the following features:

- The system will extract information from the front office systems.
- A modelling system will allow calculation of forecasted activity levels.
- Forecasted revenue and labour costs will be provided.
- The system will produce low cost staff schedules for the forecast.
- The user will be able to modify the staff schedules, knowing that additional costs will be incurred.
- Actual activity and man-hours may be automatically polled.
- Actual revenue and labour costs will be available daily, and compared to scheduled costs.
- Optimal payroll costs will be calculated based on actual activity.
- The system will work on either a meal period or a 15 minute interval basis.

These features deal with payroll control and are of vital importance to management. Speedy, accurate information allows immediate action on the establishment's largest expenditure and prevents month-end surprises by carefully monitoring the evolution of the payroll costs.

A typical system will forecast payroll costs and revenues for any time (typically two weeks) in advance and this can be used to produce a monthly payroll forecast of the cost percentage per department and per division.

Revenue statistics will be entered, or automatically calculated, for the month, day by day. These are worked out from covers served in the restaurant, numbers of rooms sold, number of food units prepared and daily financial totals. The forecast revenue will be calculated by exploding these figures by average revenue amounts, such as the average bill revenue for a restaurant or the average room rate for a hotel.

The forecasted labour required is determined by user-designed scheduling charts. For example:

100 arrivals = 1 shift leader + 4 receptionists + etc.
150 covers = 1 Maître D' + 2 station waiters + etc.

This will provide the number of forecasted hours per position per day. The appropriate payroll rates are then applied to give the gross payroll cost. Fixed salaries may also be added, as well as percentages for employee taxes and related expenses.

When both costs and revenues are known the system will then calculate:

- total forecast revenue
- total forecast payroll and what percentage of the revenue it represents.

The system will compare actual daily payroll costs with the forecasted costs, both as a financial amount and as a percentage of revenue.

The revenues will be entered, manually or automatically through point-of-sale devices, daily in pounds. The actual payroll will be entered as a total number of hours worked per category. The appropriate payroll rates will be applied, along with rates for fixed staff, taxes and related expenses, to calculate the daily payroll cost.

Various reports will compare the daily and month-to-date payroll costs. Variances will be highlighted allowing remedial action to be taken. The forecasted payroll percentage will then be compared to the actual.

The system therefore keeps payroll statistics by category for as long as it is necessary and reports can list regular hours and various overtime hours, as well as financial amounts, by week, by month, by quarter or by year. Current information may then be compared to last year or even earlier years.

Data Protection Act

Provided information held on a payroll system is purely for the calculation of wages then Section 32 of the Data Protection Act allows it to be exempt from registration. If additional information is held, however, then registration must be undertaken.

Time accounting by computer

Time accounting is the modern equivalent of 'clocking-in' and 'clocking-out' but the added facility of computer processing gives the caterer the ability to monitor much more closely the times that staff are working.

The basic advantages of a microprocessor-based time accounting system are that it:

- reduces clerical time for payroll processing
- increases payroll calculation accuracy
- improves employee scheduling
- improves labour cost control
- gives tighter control of overtime

The constituent parts of a computerized time accounting system are the timecard terminal, software, data communications and a microcomputer.

Timecard terminal

The timecard terminal is the modern replacement of the old time clock and is in effect a data collection terminal. The terminal stores the staff rotas and collects punch data allowing time and attendance information to be forwarded to the central computer when it is needed. Through its card reader the terminal recognizes a particular employee's card and only accepts authorized punches that agree with employee rotas, including lunch and break policies, and will sound an alarm or refuse a punch if it is unauthorized. As the card is punched the same information is recorded into the system's memory so there are no disputes if cards are lost. Every pay session the system automatically calculates the employee's regular and overtime hours and multiplies them by the proper rate. A good system will allow the terminal to operate off-line, so that the central computer is not tied up unnecessarily, and will hold data on up to 3,000 punches.

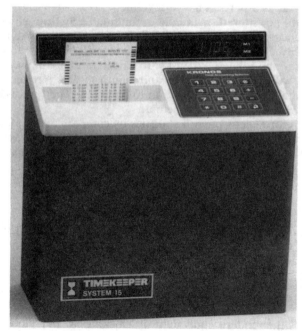

Timecard terminal showing staff timecard inserted on left
Photograph: Kronos Timekeeper Systems

Software

With a microcomputer linked to a number of timecard terminals it is possible to consolidate, store and analyse punch information for up to 5,000 members of staff, which should be sufficient for most catering situations. The information may be used to deploy staff better during peak and off-peak hours and costly extra hours and overtime may be eliminated as a result. It will be possible to produce the following reports:

- *Exception report*   draws attention to missing or unusual punches
- *Approaching overtime*   lists employees who are close to working extra hours
- *Hours report*   includes *approaching overtime*, which enables rota decisions to be reached
- *Coverage report*   shows graphically the hours covered in a particular department (see example in Figure 3.16)
- *Absent report*   lists absences of staff
- *Tardy report*   highlights staff who are persistently late
- *Off-premise report*   shows who is out and for how long
- *On-premise report*   shows who is in

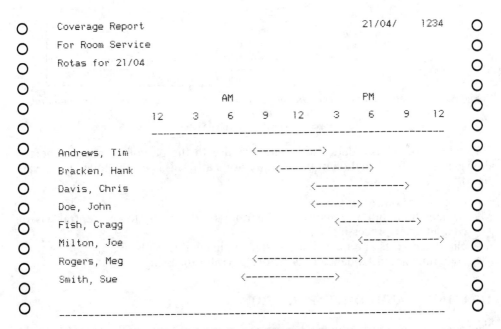

Figure 3.16 *Sample coverage report*
Source: Kronos Timekeeper Systems

Data communications

From one central location it is possible via a network to download the establishment's payroll policies to the timekeeper terminals. Similarly, it is possible to obtain information back from all those terminals to allow data and payroll processing. A typical network is shown in Figure 3.17. Reliance on handwritten attendance records or deciphering information on timecards is eliminated. Of much greater impact, however, is that it has been calculated that it takes on average seven minutes to manually audit and calculate a timecard, but with a computerized system this time is saved completely. It is also possible to generate reports automatically, even in the absence of the microcomputer operator.

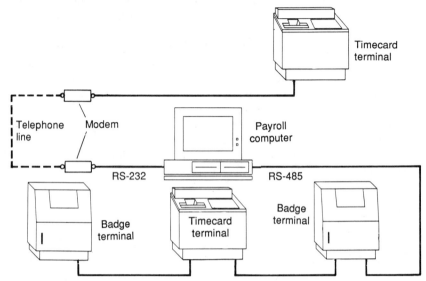

Figure 3.17   *Network of timecard and badge terminals linked to a microcomputer handling payroll*
Source: Kronos Timekeeping Systems

Time and attendance data can be integrated with the payroll computer, thereby allowing the swift calculation of pay cheques for staff. This gives the following advantages:

- centralizes control of payroll
- transfer time and attendance information is fed directly to the central payroll computer for processing
- eliminates costs and delays of transferring manual records
- edits time and attendance data before payroll processing

TELEPHONES AND COMPUTERIZATION

The operation of the telephone has come a long way since 1876 when Alexander Graham Bell invented a piece of apparatus which he called the 'talking wire'. Could he have envisaged that only a century later the telephone system would be used not only for carrying voice messages but also data, and that such concepts as teleconferencing would be reliant on the technology that he had pioneered?

Today the telephone is still the only piece of apparatus to be found linked to the overwhelming majority of hotel and catering telephone lines, and whilst computer and video networks are quite possible, relatively few are actually in existence. There is, however, evidence that hoteliers in particular are using their in-house telephone systems much more effectively by linking them into energy management, fire alarm and video check-out systems to name but a few. Most of these concepts are new to the majority of caterers and hoteliers but it is the existing telephone system that has made them possible and will continue to make modernization possible in the future.

Whilst in-room facilities such as personal computers are regarded as home luxuries their penetration into hotel bedrooms in the foreseeable future is likely to be limited to hotels catering for the business market, but such facilities as television control (volume and channel selection) and room temperature control are becoming commonplace utilizing the telephone handset.

In the foreseeable future it is more than likely that telephones will sprout printers in guest bedrooms so that printed (hard-copy) details of guest bills may be produced for guests, as well as lists of telephone messages. The guest is made aware of waiting messages by a light on the telephone unit, and by acknowledging this the printer produces a list of messages. This facility may or may not be linked into a video presentation on the guest room television.

Many of the current capabilities of telephone systems are due to the sophistication of the computerized PABX (Private Automatic Branch Exchange) switchboards. The complexity of those now available permit the manager to regard the telephone system as a profit-centre as it is quite capable of generating revenue. Equally, switchboards have become much more user-friendly, allowing the receptionist to become the operator rather than having to employ specialist telephonists.

At one time there were very few design differences between switchboards, but now a switchboard and system that provides business benefits to each and every type of user is available from amongst a wide selection on offer. When looking for a new switchboard the caterer will find three distinctly different types of PABX on offer. They are:

- tailor-made hotel systems
- hotel software and multi-purpose hardware
- multi-purpose software, the hotel parts of which are not utilized by office users

General computerized switchboard facilities

With the advantages of computerization, switchboards in general now provide a larger number of facilities in addition to the mere routing of calls. Most switchboards will now offer the following general facilities:

Internal directory display. The facility to examine all internal telephone numbers on a screen saves greatly on the time needed to connect telephone calls.

Extension status display. Tells the operator who is busy on an external number or is out of the office.

Single key dialling. All calls are handled at the push of a single button.

Automatic recall. The switchboard checks all calls are answered so that callers are not left hanging on.

Longest waiting indication. Ensures incoming callers are answered quickly.

Extension to extension calls. The switchboard provides full enquiry, shuttle and transfer facilities.

Conference calls. A number of extensions, usually up to six, may be linked together.

Ring back on busy. If an extension is engaged the switchboard will automatically contact the telephonists or internal caller when the extension is free.

Call diversion. The switchboard will redirect calls to another extension when the member of staff leaves their office.

Call pick-up. Any user may pick up a call for another extension by dialling a pre-determined code.

Call waiting tone. An interrupt tone may be generated when an urgent call is waiting to be connected to a busy extension.

Abbreviated dialling. Dialling time on frequently called numbers may be cut by using, typically, a three digit code.

Last number redial. The last external number dialled by an extension can be automatically redialled via a simple code.

Call barring. There is full control of unauthorized long-distance calls.

The NTX 20 screen-based telephone switchboard console providing the ability, amongst many others, to answer guests by name when they call from their rooms
Photograph: Norton Telecommunications

Specific hotel computerized switchboard facilities

In addition to those switchboard facilities already discussed above a typical hotel switchboard may now offer the following:

Check-in. Used to record the date and time of a guest's arrival at the hotel. Needed to activate the telephone in guest rooms as well as the Illicit Call Alarm.

Illicit call alarm. The system may activate an alarm if someone tries to make a call from an unoccupied room (period between check-out and check-in). This is only needed if the system does not bar calls totally from unoccupied rooms.

Emergency calls. An emergency call made from a guest room will initiate the printing of a record of the call which may be needed for future reference.

Budget alarm. Produced if a guest exceeds a predefined budget during his stay.

Call costing. Exact phone costs are immediately logged therefore removing many of the disputes and confusions that in the past have surrounded phone bills.

Call barring. Outgoing calls may only be made from rooms when the guest is in so unauthorized calls are eliminated.

Wake-up calls. These may be handled automatically at the exact time requested by the guest. The room telephone will ring at the specified time, and when the handset is lifted, the message is delivered in the appropriate language. Should the phone remain unanswered the system will redial a number of times before aborting and alerting the staff or operator of this failure.

Baby listening. Family guests may leave their children in their bedrooms knowing that the phone system will listen for any sound. Alternatively parents may listen themselves from another extension.

Do not disturb. Blocks calls to specific extensions where guests may be tired or ill.

Messages. The telephone system may alert a guest if a message is left in their absence. The guest is either informed by a light on their telephone handset or bedhead, or their phone is rung automatically every 15 minutes until they receive their message (it will be necessary to cut off this facility at night to avoid nuisance to other guests).

Personalized service. On switchboards so equipped, the guest's name is recorded on the monitor along with other details such as car number and nationality. The receptionist using the switchboard may view the status of every guest room (the room number can correspond to the extension number) at the touch of a button and she may tell what services are being used, make changes instantly and even answer guests by name when they call. If guest calls are identified quickly enough on a screen in room service, for example, the room service waiter will be able to talk to the customer by name which will greatly impress.

Abbreviated dialling. Fast calling of hotel services and any local services is assisted by abbreviated dialling helping guests and encouraging them to use the hotel's phones.

Malicious or unwanted calls. Some systems allow for the interception of malicious or irritating calls made within the hotel; a print-out will identify the extension from which they are being made.

These facilities will save the staff time by allowing them to use their time more efficiently, they will keep the hotelier in control of the telephone system by providing the facility to monitor use and abuse, and will also encourage guests to use the phones more. All these reasons may mean that the telephone system can earn money for the hotelier rather than being a necessary facility provided at a loss.

An integrated computer system

A computerized link between a property management computer system and a computerized switchboard will provide instant access for telephone operators to in-house guest information, such as scheduled arrivals and departures. It will improve efficiency, speed of wake-up calls, messages and outgoing calls.

Apart from the switchboard itself and a possible telephone management system the hotel's property management computer system will have certain functions that are of use to the telephone staff as well. The telephonists are, after all, going to be in the business of locating guests and establishing whether they are actually currently resident in the hotel or not. It is therefore essential that they have the facility to look up guests by their name, room number, company name and group name. They must have an overview of all reservations as well as check-outs so that they can quickly establish the location of a particular guest or guests.

To facilitate these requirements a typical well constructed computerized PMS telephone package will possess the following functions:

- easy enquiry: guest name and room number
- guest look-up: past, present, future detail information
- in-house guest lists
- messages may be entered in guest 'comments' field
  Source: Auditel Lodging Management Systems

The major reasons for utilizing a telephone management system (TMS) are to:

- provide a profitable telephone service to guests
- control administration use of the telephone system
- analyse exchange and operator efficiency
- assist with room management
  Source: Tiger Systems

Provide a profitable telephone service to guests. Despite popular belief to the contrary, most hotels (at least those that do not have a telephone management system) make a loss or, at best, break even on the telephone service they provide to guests. This is true even though hotels charge anything up to three times British Telecom's unit rate. Some experiences of hotels that have installed a telephone management system are typified by the following examples (Tiger Systems):

- Following installation of a telephone management system at a large London hotel, it was noticed that the output of the system showed nearly 40 per cent greater revenue from the guest telephones than that of the meters previously used. A thorough investigation showed that the new system was billing accurately and also found the cause of the discrepancy. Despite accurate meter pulses being sent to the hotel from the main exchange, the electro-mechanical meters receiving these pulses were dramatically inconsistent. This was particularly noticeable with long-distance and international calls, where in many cases the pulses were coming in faster than the meters could register. Nor was it uncommon for meters to be totally faulty or to register only intermittently. Another major cause of loss was misinterpretation of meters by hotel staff. Sometimes the wrong meters were read, guests were charged for the wrong accounts and subsequent disputes at check-out caused severe losses on the telephone account. The new telephone management system paid for itself within the first six months of operation, and the hotel was subsequently able to reduce the charge to guests for telephone calls.

- A Leeds Hotel reported that since the use of its new telephone management system the guest revenue from telephones had increased by 50 per cent – with a lower occupancy than in previous months.
- Another hotel in London had budgeted for a £20,000 loss on the telephone system in the year a telephone management system was installed; this was based on previous experience of using meters. The £20,000 estimated loss turned into a £90,000 profit at the end of the first year of the telephone management system's operation.

It can frequently occur that when checking-out of a hotel a person disputes their telephone account, and the hotel capitulates. Then, of course, any other people in the check-out queue at the front desk are likely to follow the same course and the hotel can lose dramatically. The reason for this is that without a telephone management system, there is no concrete proof of the telephone calls the guest has made. With the advent of telephone management systems with a billing facility, hotels have been able to eliminate or reduce:

- meter losses
- human error
- guest disputes

Control of administration use of the telephone system. There is, in all hotels, a certain proportion of administration telephone traffic and, as with industrial systems, staff are often unaware of the cost of telephone calls. With a TMS staff are made aware of this portion of the telephone bill and so it can be reduced.

Exchange and operator efficiency. The telephone management system provides a brief analysis of exchange line usage showing the volume of incoming and outgoing traffic on each line and, perhaps more importantly, the number of unanswered calls on each exchange line. Hotels worldwide spend a great deal of money advertising their service and unanswered calls on the telephone exchange could well mean lost bookings. If calls are going unanswered on specific lines it may indicate a fault which British Telecom can investigate. If problems are occurring across all the incoming lines then a hotelier may need to examine staffing levels. A TMS will produce a 'time to answer' histogram, which will reveal the true picture regarding incoming calls: as these invariably revolve around business transactions they should be regarded as 'income' calls.

Room management. This applies when a telephone management system is connected directly to a front office computer system. It is then possible to use the telephone instrument in the room, via the telephone management system, as a terminal to the front office system. It enables the state of the room to be displayed on the computer as it changes, thus providing an up-to-the-minute service to the hotel management as to whether rooms may be let, and whether they need cleaning or maintenance.

Making a profit from one's telephone system

Until comparatively recently telephones were an accepted charge in the hotel over which there was relatively little control. Telephones were universally regarded as a loss making service in a hotel.

Switchboard operators handled every call and monitored a meter on the switchboard that informed them of how many units of time or duration the call lasted. The hotel fixed a price per unit, involving a small profit margin, and the switchboard operator wrote out a voucher costing the call and sent this to the cashier for addition to the guest's account. All-in-all it was a very time-wasting process and extremely inefficient in any size of hotel.

The system led hoteliers to regard the telephones as a loss maker as many charges were lost, incorrectly calculated or did not arrive on the guest's bill before they checked out. Another problem was over disputed calls, which could have been added on to the guest's account through the cashier misreading the switchboard operator's figures; these were invariably allowed to go unpaid.

So many calls remained unpaid that the profit margin on calls did not cover the telephone system's operating expenses. Also little did hoteliers realize that while they were putting such small profit margins on to telephone calls, many guests were paying their bills by credit card and in effect the commission rate payable on the cards was totally wiping out the telephone profit.

The problem of accounting for telephone charges has eased greatly now that manual switchboards are being replaced by more modern computerized counterparts. A great problem with hotels and catering establishments until comparatively recently, however, was that investment in new switchboards was well down the list of priorities. Now that computerized switchboards are more common the possibility of being able to actually manage the telephone system is becoming reality: many hoteliers are wondering how they ever managed before.

In the United States hotels could only recover the actual telephone company charges before deregulation of the telephone system on 1 January 1983. On that day call accounting systems became almost universal in the United States as they permitted hoteliers to place their guests' long-distance calls at direct-dial costs, whilst still charging operator-assisted rates. Now it is becoming regarded as normal practice for hotels to add a profit on to calls as guests have begun to accept that the hotel has costs other than the charge made by the telephone company.

The expenses involved in providing a telephone service to guests will include:

- leasing of telephone lines
- cost of the switchboard (PBX)
- cost of handsets
- staffing of the switchboard
- cost of collecting charges from guests
- cost of unpaid charges and bad debts written off
- maintenance of the system

The telephone monitoring or 'call accounting' systems, as they are called in the United States, are basically microprocessors linked to a catering establishment's telephone system that remove the necessity for a switchboard operator to identify every call individually. Equally every call may be costed and charged, either in the form of a listing (which is often provided as a back-up anyway) or directly added to the guest's account which may be held on another computer.

In the United States the telephone system boasts a number of telephone companies who charge competitive rates for various distances of call. In this situation, which is becoming more evident in Europe, the telephone microprocessor may also be able to select the most economical company to utilize for a specific call and charge according-ly. This does, though, involve much more regular programming of rates and charges into the charging element of the system and inadvertently expensive calls have been charged at the wrong rates. This has been a problem with some systems in the United States involving complicated software alterations. Such software problems affect pro-fitability and cause guest complaints due to obvious overcharging.

Most telephone monitoring systems will support extra facilities such as:

- compatibility with property management systems
- automatic route selection
- automatic wake-up
- message waiting
- room restriction
- 'do not disturb'
- control of staff phones
- individual accounting for double-occupancy rooms
- stop calls from unoccupied rooms

A problem with some systems is that they can inadvertently bill customers for unconnected calls. It is worth looking, therefore, to see whether a proposed system has a ring-back detection function which will stop a system billing a customer for a call that was unanswered.

As an illustration of the way in which computerized switchboards can save operator time an excellent feature of some of them is that an incoming call to a particular extension is routed to that extension by the telephonist and then allowed to ring automatically. Whilst the telephonist is free to undertake further work the un-answered call is only routed back to the switchboard after several repeated 'automatic' attempts to contact the extension.

Selling

In the United States it has been found quite possible to introduce attractive selling techniques into telephone operation to improve usage, revenue and consequently profits. This sort of imaginative use of a telephone monitoring system is certainly worth contemplating although initially it may seem alien in Europe.

With some research it has been found possible to offer reduced rate calls at off-peak times using the marketing suggestion, for example, that a guest may phone home and receive a specific discount after 8.00 pm. The hope is that the guest will as a conse-quence take advantage of an apparent bargain and make several calls thereby increas-ing revenue. Similarly a policy of allowing a guest a couple of minutes free use of the phone in off-peak times will encourage more telephone usage. It may be worth con-templating, for example, offering a free phone call for any guest placing an order worth more than £10 with room service, or it may be possible to offer three long-distance calls for the price of two. There are many imaginative sales techniques that may be employed utilizing the phone system provided that there is careful program-ming of the microprocessor.

Management of the telephone system

The purpose, as far as the management are concerned, of a telephone management system (TMS) is to increase revenue from guest calls whilst at the same time reducing the cost of calls made by the administration. Increased profits and management control go hand-in-hand with these requirements.

A TMS will either operate independently or in conjunction with a property management system so that calls made by the guest are automatically recorded and charged back to the guest. Guests may be billed on a daily basis, or alternatively, long stay guests may require their call details to be accumulated for the entire duration of their stay and listed only at check-out. The information obtained from the system identifies the time the call was made, the number dialled and the cost.

The Sabre telephone management system
Photograph: Dynamic Logic Ltd.

The information should be in a precise form for presentation with the guest's bill thereby eliminating the majority of disputes over charges and the consequent embarrassment to staff. This should ensure a more pleasant and profitable relationship between the hotel and its guests.

As there are a number of ways in which telephone information will be required it is necessary for an effective telephone management system to produce the information in a number of different ways both on a VDU, which the better systems now possess, and in a printed hard-copy form. The different presentations are for ease of access to information and also to be able to actually demonstrate to guests what their charges were.

Typical reports might be as follows:

- toll ticketing
- full audit

- abbreviated audit
- detailed daily posting
- check-out
- enquiry

Toll ticketing. This is produced on the termination of each guest call and is a print-out detailing the call and costed in accordance with the hotel policies. It is the modern equivalent of the voucher previously written out and costed by the telephonist in the traditional non-computerized systems.

Full audit. The full audit automatically lists every call, by room number, costed at the rate to be charged to the guest and at the rate charged by the telephone company to the hotel. On completion of the run, full audit totals are provided. The full audit may be produced at predetermined times or on demand and shows the revenue from departed guests and that due from those currently in residence. It is of particular use to the hotel management being one of the basic elements of a Telephone Management System.

Abbreviated audit. The abbreviated audit automatically lists by room number the total number of calls made, costed at both the rate to be charged to the guest and the actual cost from the telephone company.

```
                              AUDIT
  ROTHESAY HOTEL                                    24:01:86
  FOR 24:01:86                                       11:28

  EXCEPTIONAL CALLS

  DEPARTMENT ADMIN
    EXTN   DATE       END  DURATION DIALLED NUMBER    COST   UNITS
                     TIME    m:s
      152 24:01:86    9:04   0:13   9019284567        0.00     0
                     10:15   0:47   9018394092        0.10     2

      153 24:01:86    8:37   0:10   90223356935       0.00     0
                      8:40   0:11   90223356935       0.00     0

                              AUDIT
  ROTHESAY HOTEL
  24:01:86                                          24:01:86
                                                     11:31
  ROOM TOTALS

   ROOM    EXTN   CALLS  DURATION      COST    UNITS   CHARGE    REVENUE
   330     121      3      3:39        0.30      6      0.48       0.48
   331     122      1      6:10        0.60     12      0.96       0.00
   332     123     17    114:01       10.90    218     15.42      10.25
   334     124      0      0:00        0.00      0      0.00       0.00
   335     125      4      3:56

                              AUDIT
  ROTHESAY HOTEL                                    24:01:86
  FOR 24:01:86                                       11:31

  ROOM CALLS

   ROOM    EXTN   DATE       END  DURATION DIALLED NUMBER   COST  UNITS  CHARGE
                            TIME    m:s
   330     121  23:01:86   17:58   1:49   921122          0:05    1      0:08
   330           24:01:86   9:30   0:54   921122          0:05    1      0:08
   330                     10:05   0:56   9010612811624   0:20    4      0:32

   331     122  24:01:86   11:19   6:10   9058238581      0:60   12      0:96

   332     123  23:01:86   20:44   9:23   930481          0:10    2      0:16
   332                     20:53   2:22   90201458334     0:45    9      0:72
```

Figure 3.18 *Typical audit sheets from Tel-Tag 'Teller' system*
Source: Systems Reliability plc

Detailed daily posting. Automatically lists details of every call by room number, costed at the rate to be charged to the guest, and provides a total. This enables posting to the guest account. This information is the same as would be produced by the check-out facility.

Check-out. Provides a list of calls made by a guest from a particular room since the last posting and is provided on demand. These are detailed on a call-by-call basis and costed at the rate to be charged to the guest, either as in the detailed daily posting above or as a total only. Once a guest has checked-out the system will prohibit use of the telephone in the room until another guest has checked-in, thereby helping to eliminate some of the private calls made by staff from unoccupied rooms.

Enquiry. Lists all calls made by a guest from a room, both for the current and the previous guest. All the information may be displayed on a VDU, allowing reception staff to offer a fast enquiry service to guests. Printing can take place concurrently with the VDU display to provide the guest with a list of the calls made. At any time guests may be shown the current state of their accounts, thereby helping to eliminate any contention over what they will be charged for their telephone calls.

Guest telephone handsets

Whilst we have paid a lot of attention to the overall telephone system provided in a hotel and catering establishment we must not forget the handsets themselves. The effects of cellular telephone networks are being felt in the business world and there are already implications for the hotelier. Business users have specific requirements of the telephone handsets in their rooms if the experiences of the United States are to be felt here too.

Telephone handsets with built-in dataports

In the United States telephone handsets have been developed to provide the busy business traveller with an access point to connect a portable computer to the telephone line. Many travellers are now carrying portable computers with them on business trips and these devices must be connected to the telephone network to access a database or transmit information.

Until now, travellers have been obliged to carry a set of tools with them in order to connect a portable computer to the phone line in their hotel rooms. Most often this was accomplished by taking the telephone apart and attaching a separate modular jack to the network in the handset. The traveller then re-assembled the telephone and connected the computer to the jack. In other cases, the traveller would undertake a similar exercise with the telephone line connection at the wall jack. In either case, the exercise was time consuming and often resulted in the guest causing damage to the telephone or its wiring. Often the guest would simply disconnect the computer on check-out and leave the wiring in disarray to be repaired by the hotel maintenance staff.

The new telephone handsets allow connection to the telephone line by way of a standard modular jack plug right on the handset. When there is a two-line installation the computer user is able to talk to one location whilst the computer communicates with another. It is easy for the user, and the hotel benefits from additional telephone usage and lower installation and maintenance costs. Equally the traveller will have been attracted to the hotel offering this facility rather than to another establishment without it.

Radio telephones for guests

One of the more recent additions to the telephone services on offer to guests in hotels has been the hire of a portable radio telephone so that they do not lose touch with their base or important callers.

The intention is that any customers, whether staying for business purposes or on holiday, may visit a hotel and then inform their office or customers that that is where they may be contacted. There is nothing unusual in this procedure but the ability to hire a portable radio telephone adds a further dimension. Should telephone calls come into the hotel for a guest who is not contactable via the switchboard system, because they are out of their room or out of the hotel itself, the telephonist can give the caller the number of the guest's portable telephone. The guest may then be contacted via this facility whether in or out of the hotel, thereby keeping them constantly in touch.

The hotel can offer portable telephones for hire by the day, week or month. The guest would be required to leave a substantial deposit to cover loss or damage which may be reclaimed when the telephone is returned safely. Metered units are charged at a standard rate, that could include a profit element for the hotel, and an accumulation meter clearly shows guests the total number of metered units that they will subsequently be charged for. The system will not register unanswered or engaged calls.

Some hotel groups have now extended this service to their preferred regular customers who do not necessarily have to be residents to qualify.

Management of the staff telephones

Many hoteliers find effective control over the use of administration telephones just as important as guest billing. A range of reports is therefore required from the telephone management system to identify any areas of misuse or abuse, as well as to apportion costs to those areas responsible for generating them.

The problem of staff misuse of telephones, through either uneconomical business use or private calls, is not peculiar to hotels but is a problem that faces any employer. The use of a computerized telephone management system gives a distinct benefit to the astute manager in cutting down on the wastage experienced through such misuses of the telephone system.

With a comprehensive system the manager will have access to information that will help telephone management in the following ways:

- cost accountancy
- cost control
- communications efficiency

Cost accountancy

By breaking down the charges for telephone calls to individual departments or extensions reports may be produced that show the actual usage against an allocation. By examining these reports realistic budgets for telephone usage may be set for departments and for the hotel or catering operation as a whole, and overspending may be spotted and corrected.

Cost control

Individual extension reports mean that individual members of staff may be made aware of their telephone costs and encouraged to use their telephone more efficiently and economically.

Communications efficiency

The statistics and graphs produced by computerized telephone management systems provide data on the use of all the circuits in the complete telephone system and will help in spotting problem areas where a redesign may be necessary or desirable. Such problems as over or under utilization of certain extensions, insufficient incoming lines, or an inadequately manned switchboard may be shown up in the reports. The manager will therefore be able to take action on sound statistical information.

It is claimed by manufacturers, and backed up by government research, that a telephone management system may achieve the following:

- 10 to 15 per cent drop in call duration
- 10 to 15 per cent shift in traffic from peak to standard rate
- 20 to 30 per cent drop in telephone charges
- 20 to 30 per cent decrease in the number of calls made

Telephone usage and operation analysis

The statistics and reports that may be presented to a manager by a computerized telephone management system might include the following:

USAGE
- By extension – total report or selected extensions only
- By department – total report or selected departments only

COST, DURATION AND NUMBER OF CALLS
- For all exchange lines
- By extension
- By department

ANALYTICAL STATISTICS
- Ten most expensive calls
- Analysis of calls to a selected dialled number
- Analysis of calls within a selected time band
- All lines simultaneously

GRAPHICAL ANALYSIS OF SWITCHBOARD WORKLOAD AND RESPONSE
- Histogram of incoming call traffic against time
- Histogram of outgoing call traffic against time
- Histogram of operator response to incoming calls
- Histogram of lost (unanswered) calls against time

Voice messaging

Whilst the use of telephone answering machines has become commonplace, the availability of such a system for hotel guests has almost seemed an impossibility until comparatively recently.

A voice messaging system allows anyone in a hotel, whether guest or staff member, to pick up their telephone, punch in a simple code, leave a message for anyone who might call whilst they are out, and subsequently retrieve any messages left on their return. Guests may be advised that messages are awaiting them either by means of a message light on their telephone handset or by means of a portable bleeper issued by the hotel.

A major advantage is where guests are of various nationalities. Using traditional message collating schemes confusion could arise due to the person recording the message being a different nationality to the person making the incoming call. With a voice messaging system the telephone response may be recorded by the guest in the required language. This also removes the possibility of a message being mis-translated for a guest as they will listen to any messages personally.

Confidentiality is maintained with guests setting their own access codes so that even hotel staff cannot gain access to messages left on such a system.

Whilst we have so far examined the philosophy behind an in-house system, it is also worth mentioning that British Telecom offer a much wider service called *Voicebank* by which a subscriber rents a 'mailbox' facility for messages on a central computer system. The system provides an alternative telephone number and allows messages to be left if there is no reply from the original number.

SECURITY

Security in its widest sense is of major importance to caterers and hoteliers, especially as it has become accepted that guests have a right to feel as secure in their hotel bedroom as they would at home. Total security is difficult to achieve in catering establishments and hotels which are of necessity public places, with large numbers of people moving in and out, and which are therefore much more open to abuse than the normal residential property.

The major security areas where computers may be of assistance are:

- fire
- robbery and assault

It is perhaps worth looking initially at some of the extreme problems that might occur in these very difficult security situations.

Fire security

As established in chapter one (see pages 20–24), the twin Las Vegas hotel fires of 1980 and 1981 focused attention in the United States on the apparent weaknesses at that time of existing fire precautions. These were after all two ultramodern high-rise hotels that caught fire, resulting in heavy loss of life.

The fear and worry that these fires were to instill in the domestic American traveller in the ensuing months prompted American hoteliers to turn to computer companies to help with fire precautions. It is therefore worth looking in detail at the occurrences and consequences of these two disasters.

MGM Grand Hotel, Las Vegas – 21 November 1980

The 26-storey MGM Grand Hotel in Las Vegas boasted 2,000 rooms and on the morning of the fire the hotel had at least 3,500 guests (some reports put this figure as high as 8,000). The fire started at 7.00 am and, as Las Vegas is a resort where people tend to go to bed late and consequently get up late, most guests were still asleep when the fire started.

The seat of the fire was apparently in a construction area over the restaurant in the casino and its cause was faulty electrical wiring. The ensuing fireball fiercely erupted with devastating effect and within a very few minutes the entire casino, nearly 140 metres long, was completely gutted. So fierce was the heat that slot machines were reported to have melted into pools of metal. However, the lethal problem was the dense, choking, black smoke which the fire sent spiralling through the floors above. The smoke spread quickly through the hotel's air conditioning vents and lift shafts and entered guest rooms under doors, and through ventilation system outlets, bathroom vents, room joints, electrical outlets and windows.

It took the fire department until midday to get the fire under control. Six helicopters were employed to rescue the many guests who had made their way to the roof of the hotel or on to balconies to try to escape the dense fumes. Indeed loud hailers on the helicopters had to be used to warn many guests not to jump from balconies. Furniture was thrown through the hotel's large glass windows by guests trying to escape the smoke. Five hundred people were injured in the fire.

It was alleged by witnesses that the hotel's manual fire alarm had failed to go off and that only three floors of the hotel possessed a sprinkler system. It was also alleged that the hotel's switchboard was quickly destroyed by the fire and that as a consequence worried guests could get no information as to what the state of the fire actually was; as a result many guests panicked or wandered around not knowing how to escape.

Most of the 84 deaths occurred on the upper floors due to smoke inhalation, particularly of fumes from burning synthetic materials contained in furniture in the casino. Sixty of the victims were on the nineteenth floor or above, illustrating that smoke was the major problem as the fire itself only affected the first two floors. It was further alleged that the hotel's air conditioning system continued to run and this was blamed for pouring fumes into bedrooms on the upper floors whilst guests slept.

As far as fire precautions were concerned, the hotel only had ceiling water sprinklers on three floors but as the MGM Grand had been built in 1973 this conformed with the building regulations at that time. In addition, the hotel did not have an automatic fire alarm system and it was alleged that the manual system was disabled early in the fire so that sirens did not sound and fire doors did not close.

Las Vegas Hilton – 11 February 1981

Less than three months after the MGM Grand fire a similar disaster hit the neighbouring Las Vegas Hilton; mercifully on this occasion there were only eight deaths and 242 injuries. Of the fatalities, seven were caused by smoke inhalation and one through jumping from a high window.

The main difference from the MGM Grand was that this second disastrous high-rise hotel fire was a case of arson. Four separate fires were started on the eighth floor, which was just about as high as the fire department's ladders could reach and this posed the same problem for the guests on higher floors of how to escape. Helicopters were again used for evacuation of guests from the roof.

One of the reasons that there were fewer casualties at the Las Vegas Hilton was that the hotel possessed sprinklers on all floors. Also, the fire alarms were definitely operational.

The effect on hotel guests of Las Vegas's two 'Towering Infernos'

These two fires were quickly seized upon by hotel fire precaution critics as being distinctly similar to events in the film *The Towering Inferno*. Just as public outrage at the MGM Grand fire was dying down, the whole debate was rekindled by the events at the Hilton.

There is little doubt that for a considerable time after these two fires the attention of potential hotel guests in the United States was focused on fire safety. Indeed, even a year later hoteliers were experiencing a strong customer preference for hotels better equipped with fire precautions and better able to withstand a fire. Many hoteliers found that they were having to reassure customers on arrival about the safety of their establishments, whilst some customers would only stay if they could be accommodated in rooms near fire exits. Other customers were deliberately choosing modern low-rise hotels which were seen as safer because 'modern' meant 'equipped with the latest fire precautions' in their minds and 'low-rise' indicated that fire department ladders would be functional in the event of a fire.

To be able to demonstrate adequate safety precautions was a definite marketing asset at this time for hoteliers and the fire precaution theme was exploited greatly in advertising.

In response to the 'fire safety lobby' hoteliers were forced to look at fire precautions in the widest sense and high on the priority list was the introduction of new automatic computerized fire systems. The attitudes of hotel users and the responses of hotel management were reflected in surveys carried out in October 1981 (Romeo, 1981). Some of these are reproduced in Table 3.2.

Table 3.2   Hotel & motel management consumer survey (October 1981)

How important a consideration is a room on a low floor when checking into a hotel?			
Extremely important	25%	Not very important	16%
Very important	22%	Not at all important	17%
Moderately important	15%		
Somewhat important	5%		
Total % of 'important' responses	67%	Total % of 'unimportant' responses	33%

How important a consideration is the presence of fire prevention and detection devices when checking into a hotel?			
Extremely important	58%	Not very important	3%
Very important	34%	Not at all important	0%
Moderately important	3%		
Somewhat important	2%		
Total % of 'important' responses	97%	Total % of 'unimportant' responses	3%

How important a consideration is a room near an exit or escape route when checking into a hotel?			
Extremely important	57%	Not very important	1%
Very important	38%	Not at all important	0%
Moderately important	3%		
Somewhat important	1%		
Total % of 'important' responses	99%	Total % of 'unimportant' responses	1%

What kind of hotel do you look for when you travel?

Modern low-rise structure	68.2%
Modern high-rise structure	18.2%
Older low-rise property	18.2%
Older high-rise property	3.4%

(Total exceeds 100% because of multiple responses)

Hotel & motel management hotel managers survey (October 1981)

What are you currently doing to combat the threat of fire at your property?

Training staff	92.1%
Installing new safety devices	57.3%
Waging promotion or advertising campaigns	31.5%
Retrofitting older areas of building with modern equipment	30.3%

(Total exceeds 100% because of multiple responses)

With statistics showing 97 per cent of customers thinking that the presence of fire prevention and detection devices was important, it was hardly surprising that the computer industry soon capitalized on the perceived market. With 57.3 per cent of hoteliers installing new safety devices the market was both large and lucrative, and was the catalyst for the creation of a large number of microprocessor controlled fire systems.

Robbery and assault

Many of the systems in use in Europe have been developed as a result of experiences in America where hotels in some locations have had a history of violent robberies and assaults to combat.

It has been known for hotels to be fined substantial amounts if found negligent in cases of robbery and assault, and in a country where damages are considerably higher than in Europe this is a great incentive for hoteliers to make use of the most up-to-date security devices.

In some cases rapes and robberies have taken place and the hotel management has been found negligent in allowing such events to happen on their property. Some hotels in this situation have been found to have no key control system whatsoever. As many as 100 emergency master keys have been issued to various members of staff with many being lost and the only follow-up being that when a master key was lost a new key was cut. These keys, of course, gave access to all rooms, even overriding the double locking undertaken by guests who thought themselves safe. It has also been found that some hotels had not changed their locks since the establishment had originally been built, which again was hardly security conscious.

One hotel in America was losing 500 guest bedroom keys a week which works out at 26,000 in a single year. With the attached tags proudly identifying the room to which the key belonged, it is almost certain that many of these keys were used for robberies.

Against this sort of background it has been necessary to find ways of minimizing the effects of lost emergency master keys and guest bedroom keys. The use of electronic keycard systems has gone a long way towards helping the situation.

Computers and fire security

Computerized fire-protection is now looked upon as essential in all modern hotels, so dangerous are the consequences of a conflagration. It is essential, though, that the system installed not only affords guests and staff the maximum possible protection, but also that it is versatile, in the sense of being installed with the minimum of physical alterations as well as being capable of expansion at a later date.

Systems must satisfy the elementary requirements of fire precautions. A system must:

- provide detection and notification of a fire
- alert guests to the best means of escape
- provide the guests with the maximum time to escape
- help where possible with the extinguishment of the fire

A computerized fire system will in many cases also be part of a wider security system handling both fire and intruder alarms, as well as energy management applications. It is unlikely that a fire system will be exclusively used for fire precautions. A typical configuration is shown in Figure 3.19.

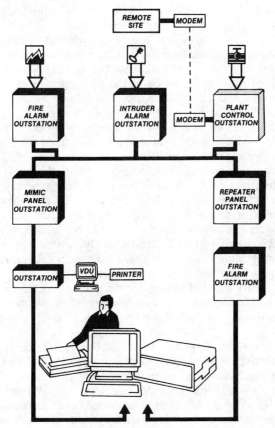

Figure 3.19　*Typical schematic computerized fire alarm system*
Source: Zettler Fire Detection Systems, Zettler UK

Central control panel

The comprehensive systems that are being installed of late boast a vast number of essential features and the central 'core' of the system will undoubtedly be the *central control panel*. This panel will be linked directly to fire detection and control devices such as:

- heat detectors
- smoke detectors
- telephone emergency warning system
- fire alarm 'break the glass' points
- sprinkler controls
- sprinkler water flow meters
- air conditioning fans
- heating system controls
- lift isolation controls
- direct link to fire station

The central control panel of a fire security system will utilize microprocessor-based components linked to all the other parts of the system, and be capable of sending messages to them as well as responding to data received from them. In addition, the circuits within the central control panel will constantly monitor the operation of the entire system, so that it is always maintained at constant readiness and faults are immediately located and rectified. In many cases the panel will possess its own printer so that details of alarms, as well as the status of the various devices within the system (whether they work or not), is produced in the form of a print-out in addition to a display so that there is a recognized back-up. The printer is also there to constantly record the activity of the system.

A feature of the better systems is that they may be programmed in the language of the caterer concerned. This is so that there is a minimum of confusion in the seconds after an alarm has been raised. The location of each device linked to the central control panel is programmed into the computer using the exact terminology that would be used in the premises concerned. For example, there might be a number of foyers and landings and each can be defined exactly so that, in the event of an alarm, the visual display and printer will produce a precise report such as 'Alarm-smoke detector, Mountbatten banqueting suite foyer, 13.05'. Staff and management then know instantly where the problem is, thereby vastly improving the reaction time.

Typical displays that might appear simultaneously on VDU and in hard-copy form on the printer might be as in the illustration opposite.

A fault spotting facility linked to precise definitions of locations programmed into the microprocessor will facilitate much easier and speedier maintenance of the system, and obviate the necessity to examine a large number of devices before finding the faulty one.

Externally there is usually very little to see of the central control panel: a typical system will only outwardly display a small number of lights and buttons. Whilst inside the panel are all the functions of a computer, including a central processing unit and the necessary interfaces with external devices such as the hotel sprinkler system, externally the panel is deliberately kept as uncomplicated as possible.

One of the major problems with fire alarm systems that rely on heat or smoke detectors is that there are certain locations within a catering establishment or hotel where they are prone to go off at the slightest excuse. There will, for example, be bars

Emergency alarm display
Photograph: Zettler Fire Detection Systems, Zettler UK

where smoking is common or restaurants where flambé work is undertaken, and these will be common locations for sensitive detectors to be activated. In some fire systems it is therefore possible to alter the sensitivity of detection devices from the central control panel itself. If a device is found to be too sensitive for an area then its sensitivity can be reduced or vice versa. It is important, though, that access to this facility is strictly limited by means of security codes given only to very senior members of staff.

In the event of an alarm sounding

If a fire is detected the automatic system will take over but there has to be a manual intervention at some point to take care of false alarms, of which there will undoubtedly be many.

The sequence of events with a typical system might be:

(1) Alarm sounds. Fire station automatically receives alert from system and dispatches appliances.

Alarm messages played automatically over loudspeakers (at least 85 decibels) on floors or each telephone rung automatically and tape message of emergency instructions communicated by this method.

Smoke doors throughout hotel allowed to close by switching off electro-magnetic restraints.

Lifts isolated.

Stairwells pressurized by stairwell fans.

Air conditioning and heating fans are automatically shut off.

Separate exhaust duct system activated to suck smoke from building.

Progressive subsequent activation of heat/smoke detectors or sprinklers monitored.

Water flow in sprinkler system monitored.

(2) Receptionist identifies location of problem from central control panel printer and display.
(3) Receptionist alerts security staff (made much easier if personal radios carried) who check whether it is a false alarm or not. Staff who have been contacted confirm to reception that they are investigating.
(4) Duty manager takes decision whether to evacuate or not depending on findings of security staff. If it is obvious that there is no threat or that it is a false alarm fire brigade recalled. Decision helped by arrival of fire brigade who are also presented with a print-out by the central control panel's printer of the operation of all fire security related devices.
(With some alarms the hotel will not go into full evacuation procedure for a short period to give the staff and fire brigade time to shut off the full alarm if there is no problem. After the short period, which in some hotels is as long as eight minutes, the general evacuation alarms are sounded automatically.)

What did the MGM Grand and Las Vegas Hilton do?

The MGM Grand reopened in July 1981 following a major eight month refurbishment which included a $5 million (1981 value) computerized fire safety system, which amongst other features boasted a smoke detector, alarm and sprinkler in each guest bedroom. The system was designed to monitor the entire building using 1,300 sensors; the primary aim was, of course, to sound the alarm effectively in the event of a fire.

The nucleus of the MGM Grand's new system was a control centre manned constantly and equipped with its own emergency power supply. This centre was built of fire resistant materials and could be entered directly by firemen from outside the building.

Situated within the control centre were two computers and, as is normal practice, one of these was maintained for back-up. These two computers were linked to nearly 90 information collating panels throughout the hotel. In the event of a fire information was immediately displayed on the terminal in the control centre, on a display board, and as a print-out. The information was also displayed at the switchboard, at another location, as an extra back-up device.

When an alarm was sounded this operated sirens on the affected floor itself, as well as on the floors immediately above and below, and information and instructions could be given utilizing any of the 6,000 loudspeakers positioned around the hotel. As an extra confidence inspiring device, the Hollywood star Gene Kelly was hired to make a video about the hotel's fire safety and this was played regularly on the hotel's television sets.

With the computers linked into a water sprinkler system covering the entire hotel, as well as to energy management and security controls, this was a great improvement on the older system.

In the case of the Las Vegas Hilton, the management there were to spend $15 million (1981 value) on upgrading their computerized fire system which was to boast three sprinkler outlets in each guest bedroom and up to eight in suites. The system was housed in a block house in a separate building from the hotel itself, and sensors were so prolific that even minor cupboards were equipped with smoke detectors.

Lifts at the Las Vegas Hilton were equipped so that if an alarm sounded they would not open their doors on an unsafe floor but, relying on sensors, they would select a safe floor to stop at.

Robbery and assault

In tackling the problems of robbery and assault the hotelier will firstly try to deny access to persons who may have this intent. It is often the case, though, that the only firm barrier is to improve door locking systems, such are the problems. After all it is not just guests and outsiders who may be a security risk; the staff themselves may succumb to temptation if an opportunity presents itself.

Preventing access

One of the best means of preventing robbery or assault on hotel premises is to try and keep undesirables out of the building to start with.

In most establishments this means keeping strict observation over the foyer area by means of not only the security staff but also the porters and receptionists. There are, however, less obvious means of access to a building. These may include not only staff and delivery entrances, that must be watched, but also fire escapes which may be utilized by the determined thief. In all these cases one may rely on the vigilance of staff, but it may also be beneficial to utilize computerization to control an alarm system connected to the fire escapes, as well as closed-circuit TV cameras that may monitor access routes.

Lifts

Lifts are a main means of access to a building and provide a major route for undesirables to penetrate a hotel.

One of the best ideas here is to employ a lift attendant purely as a means of security. Whilst this may appear superfluous, as most lifts are quite easily operated by the guests themselves, the security angle is obvious whilst also giving guests a feeling of luxury into the bargain.

Another simple rule here, in the circumstances where a lift might run from a basement car park past the ground floor to floors above, is to program the system so that the ascending lift is made to stop automatically every time at the ground floor even if nobody wants to get out or in. This at least allows the security staff an opportunity to examine all those passengers who are travelling to the guest floors.

If lifts run from the ground floor to a rooftop bar, it would be foolish to allow those lifts to stop at all the bedroom floors thus allowing undesirables ready access. At the design stage a single express lift could be allowed for thereby removing the problem.

In-room safes

The hotelier is under a legal obligation to provide means of safe custody for guest valuables and the traditional way of satisfying this requirement has been to allow guests to make use of the hotel safe.

In recent years it has started to become more commonplace to replace this somewhat clumsy and unpopular system by providing guests with their own safes within individual bedrooms. The safes on offer range from those with traditional locks to those making use of electronic systems. The electronic safes usually allow the guest to program in their own self-selected six-digit code which can in an emergency be overridden by the hotel management. Some are linked to alarm systems which sound if the safe is tampered with, and most are large enough to at least hold valuables such as documents and a camera.

Guest room key control

Some hotels admit defeat in the sense that they feel unable to stop potential undesirables from getting to the floors due to the difficulty in spotting a thief, say, amongst a large number of anonymous and quite legitimate customers. They quite often resort purely to protecting guests once they are installed in their bedrooms.

Some hotels lose as many as 12 keys for each room every year, necessitating the locks to be changed on a complete floor every month. Hotels responded to this costly security problem by installing locks with removable cores so only the cylinders needed to be changed each time a key was lost. Other hotels chose to utilize bigger and bigger fobs, whilst some charged deposits refunded on the return of the key.

The main problems that hoteliers face are that many hotel bedroom doors rely on old mechanical locks that can be easily picked, forced or even slipped, and that keys are frequently lost, including master keys. Some keys may well have landed up in the hands of staff who are less than trustworthy, whilst it is not unknown for guests to 'rob' themselves with the intention of trying to claim insurance.

To try to cure the majority of these problems it was realized at an early stage that the possibility of being able to keep a tighter control on keys, perhaps issuing each guest with a personal key, and of recording who entered each room during the course of a guest's stay would improve security greatly and save a lot of money on replacing both keys and locks. The obvious solution was to tailor the computerized systems already in use in industrial locations to the hotel industry.

Computers have been increasingly employed in controlling access to rooms and there are a large number of similar packages on offer to hoteliers and caterers.

Essential features of a computerized door locking system

In selecting the appropriate computerized key control system for a property it is important to have several considerations in mind:

• *Reliability*	so every key works every time
• *Speed*	for fast guest check-in
• *Simplicity*	so that a computer expert is not needed to issue a key
• *Control*	to limit room access and track who issues keys and who uses them
• *Easy installation*	for cost-effectiveness
• *Software integration*	to communicate with other computers and hotel systems
• *Expansion and upgrading capability*	so the system is never obsolete
• *Comprehensive training program*	so that staff turnover does not pose a problem
• *Responsive service and support*	to back up the investment

Computerized systems have many features in common. As far as outward appearances are concerned, they all utilize reprogrammable locks that are activated by either:

- keycards   magnetic strip
              punched hole
- replica keys   reprogrammable metal
              plastic disposables

The locks themselves will be either:

- stand-alone
- wired directly to the central processor

Magnetic strip key cards

Uniqey magnetic strip keycard and room lock
Photograph: Uniqey

Magnetic strip keycards are the latest development of computerized electronic door locking systems and demonstrate many of the features of the various types of computerized key systems.

Most systems share the philosophy that each individual key that is issued is programmed with a specific code that supersedes that previously accepted by the lock. The combinations of codes are literally endless with the possibility of billions of lock combinations. Indeed it is the boast of at least one supplier that:

> the most powerful supercomputer in the world would have to work for years to crack a single keycard combination – and might not even succeed. (Schlage)

As each lock will be capable of accepting an infinite number of different combinations, a replacement key may quickly be issued should the guest lose their initial key. The room will then be protected against the thief who might find the lost keycard and try to gain access to the room as that initial keycard has in effect been totally invalidated. Equally the old problem with traditional metal keys of replacing locks when easily identified room keys were lost is removed, thus saving a large amount of finance. A great benefit of keycard systems for the reception staff is that, it is claimed, it is possible to create and issue keycards in a mere four seconds which greatly speeds up the check-in process.

Locks are obviously the most important part of these systems as they were what had to be changed in the past when a traditional metal key was lost. It is essential to look for heavy quality locks that are a deterrent in themselves to potential thieves. Locks should be stand-alone – some early systems required complicated and expensive wiring running to individual locks from the central processor. The microprocessor and card reader within the lock are powered by batteries with a life of several years. If batteries are running low then often an indicator light will flash, and if this is ignored then a typical solution is for a battery pack to be plugged in and the door lock activated in this manner.

The neat folder in which a keycard may be presented to the guest
Photograph: Schlage Lock Company

The locks will be activated by keycards that are programmed to operate on a number of access levels. The normal access levels are:

- Grand Master or House Master
- Area Master
- Floor Master
- Maid
- Guest
- Emergency
- Maintenance or One-shot
- Power Down or Back-up
- Guest Lock-out

Grand Master or House Master. This keycard will operate locks independently and separately from all the other levels. It will usually give access to all guest rooms in the hotel, provided the guest has not activated their 'deadbolt' or privacy facility.

Area Master. This keycard will open locks in a specific area only. The area will be defined by management but might, for example, be a particular wing of the hotel. Staff who have a card of this type might include valets, room service waiters or mini-bar service personnel. The important feature is that these cards bear their own encoded identification so that use may be recorded within the microprocessor locks.

Floor Master. Typically issued to floor housekeepers these cards allow access to rooms on a specific floor for room-checking purposes. They will not give access to rooms on other floors.

Maid. This keycard permits access to a specified number of rooms allocated by the management. Within this facility duplicate keys might be issued if two or more maids are required to work a larger section but they will still only open the assigned rooms.

Guest. Each guest is issued with their own unique keycard at check-in that will only allow them access to their own bedroom. Each new keycard automatically cancels the previous keycard for that room at that level. Duplicate keycards may be issued for family or group use.

Emergency. The purpose of this management keycard is to provide the ability to override the deadbolt or privacy function on guest bedroom locks so that rooms may be evacuated in the case of fire or a similar problem.

Maintenance or One-shot. This keycard gives limited access to a specific room only as the lock will only allow it to be used once. The typical situation would be where an outside contractor, such as a television engineer, needed one-time access to a room.

Power down or Back-up. In the event of a power failure or during computer maintenance pre-prepared power down or back-up keycards are issued to guests checking-in. These keycards are normally kept in a secure place by the duty manager.

Guest Lock-out. This keycard may be issued to block a guest's return to a room after check-out. A new guest keycard for the room will return the lock to its normal mode.

The basic equipment needed in a typical system starts with an *encoder* that is required to transfer the new lock combination for the guest's bedroom on to the keycard. The encoder may be attached to a microcomputer or be stand-alone, and there is the additional option of having a hard disk and printer to further enhance the system. A typical configuration would consist of a VDU with a built-in authorization card reader and magnetic writer, a standard keyboard and a central processing unit.

The blank credit card-sized *keys* will possess the industry standard magnetic strip. All the issuing member of staff has to do is to enter the appropriate room number to create a new keycard. A verifier may be used to check that the operation has been undertaken correctly.

The possibilities are there to make normal keycards, duplicate keycards (handy where several guests are occupying one room or suite), deadbolt override keycards (for parents to be able to enter their children's rooms), or emergency access keycards. Additionally a high security keycard may be made to allow a business person to control access to a hospitality suite or lock out hotel staff. It is even possible to program a keycard so that the lock makes an audible bleep so that customers with impaired sight can hear that the lock has activated.

The encoder may have the facility to issue warnings, for example, when a new keycard has already been made for a specific room that day. This will remove the possibility of double-rooming guests.

Security is important where encoding is concerned. Without control staff collusion would be possible; for example, a receptionist could issue master keycards to maids who would then have an opportunity to steal guest valuables. It is wise, therefore, to make use of a system that requires authorization cards to be inserted before various levels of keycard may be produced. For example, a Grand Master Authorization Card will be in the possession of the duty manager for emergency use only and will be the only card to permit the encoding of further Grand Master keycards should that prove necessary. The receptionist, on the other hand, will hold a Guest Authorization Card allowing her to produce guest keycards as a normal check-in activity.

In a typical system the guest takes their key to their room door where the substantial lock, which contains its own microprocessor and card reader, firstly accepts the 'old' code that the encoder placed onto the new card. The lock then tells itself to accept the 'new' code until another card comes along possessing the correct instructions in the possession of the next guest who will subsequently use that particular room. The computer provides the security in possessing and encoding the two 'old' and 'new' codes that give the lock its instructions.

The guest slides their card into the slot in the lock. In some systems this is greeted by a number of coloured lights on the lock which have specific meanings:

- green light   Lock is released and the guest may enter the room
- yellow light   A guest is already in the room with the deadbolt thrown and maids, for example, know they cannot enter
- red light   The card is not valid for that room or the lock's batteries are running low

In some systems the lock simply will not activate if an invalid card is used, whilst this could also be the indication that an 'inhibit' facility is in operation. The 'inhibit' facility means that the guest is denied entry to their room and obliges them to return to reception in situations where, for example, they have exceeded their credit limit or some similar problem.

The point should be made that there may well be a period of time, whether hours or days, between the old guest checking-out and a new guest checking-in. The old guest's keycard will, with many systems, still operate the room lock in that time, making it feasible that the last guest that checked-out could return to the room and gain access. It is advisable, therefore, to have a facility to cancel a guest's keycard after check-out.

The computer should be able to provide some analysis of keycard usage that will be of use in security monitoring and management control. The print-outs or screen displays will provide information as to which cards were issued by a specific receptionist over a period, or the number of keys that were issued for a specific room. It is possible with some systems to add in a clock calendar to each door lock so that the times and days that keycards are used may be controlled. With the addition of an audit trail capability to each door lock it will be possible to find out who the last, say, 10 people were who entered the room. The information for such reports will often be retrieved from each lock by means of a handheld portable computer.

Absolutely every operation of the encoder, even mistakes, will be recorded on a print-out located in a secure place. This facility is utilized to keep a complete record of every keycard issued, who issued it and to whom, the rooms concerned and even the time of issue to the nearest minute, so investigations of problems may be made with ease.

Where staff are concerned it will be possible to monitor areas other than just guest bedrooms. For example, the manager will be able to find out who goes into the liquor stores and when. A maid's access to certain floors and wings may be restricted as well as access to the linen room. The maid's keycard could additionally be programmed to work only on certain days, during certain hours, for a certain number of weeks and months. There is even the ability to make a one-time-entry keycard which expires in a time limit, say 15 minutes, thereby controlling such users as delivery drivers.

In the event of a complete power failure it is important that guests are not locked in or out of their rooms. As the locks themselves possess their own battery power supply they will not be affected but the encoder may go out of action. In this situation it is commonplace to have temporary power down keycards that override the existing codes and may be used by new guests checking-in. These keys are kept in stock and issued using a manual record until the system is back to normal and power is restored, when the usual method is used to give new keys to new check-ins. The guests may make use of these keys until the completion of their stay when they are replaced in the usual manner by new keys in the hands of new guests.

Time controlled keycards

There are hotel door-locking systems that provide many of the facilities of the previously described magnetic strip keycards but operate through a clock located within the lock itself. The keycard for the room is issued at the time of check-in for the duration of the guest's stay so that the card ceases to be valid at a pre-determined time on the day of departure. This type of system removes the need for sequential coding of keycards.

Punched hole keycards

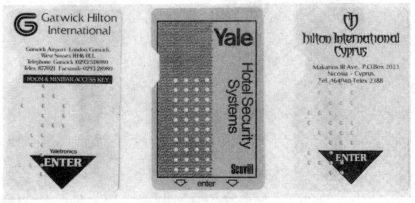

A selection of punched hole keycards
Photograph: Yale Security Systems

Door-locking systems that use keycards with magnetic strips are not the only systems available. There are equally good systems utilizing keycards that make use of punched holes. These systems have been around for some time; Uniqey, for example, were instrumental in using such keycards in the UK before more recently updating their system to make use of magnetic strip keycards.

Outwardly the keycards look very similar to the magnetic strip variety, but the randomly selected combination code might or might not be visible in a series of punched holes on or in the keycard. The only difference is that the card-reader within the door lock recognizes a series of punched holes rather than the magnetic 'signals' on a magnetic strip.

The encoder is more correctly described as a 'keymaker' with these systems: it actually punches holes into the keycard rather than transferring magnetic signals onto a strip.

The facilities of this type of electronic door-locking system are otherwise identical to the magnetic strip system.

Door-locking systems that utilize replica keys

Whilst so far we have examined systems that use various types of keycard, there are systems that rely on different means of access to door locks. They almost all utilize plastic or metal keys which physically resemble a traditional key, but which provide most if not all of the advantages of a computer operated system with re-programmable door locks.

In one such system the re-usable keys are made of nickel silver. Each key is inserted into a command console at check-in and, in the same way as for the magnetic strip, a new combination is placed on the key. The advantage is that when the key is handed back the code can be erased and the key re-programmed for subsequent use. It is even possible to go back to using key tags to identify rooms as a 'lost' key may be replaced with another and the original combination erased, thereby invalidating entry to anyone who had stolen or picked up the missing key.

Plastic replica keys illustrating the notches that make up to 250 million combinations possible
Photograph: Guestkey

Another system utilizes plastic replica keys with an additional option that all the locks may be directly linked to a central processor by two-core cable. As far as the guest is concerned, they receive a plastic key that has a number of notches cut on the sides and these notches make up the combination code for their lock. The keys are supplied ready made to the hotel with the notches already cut out and are introduced into the system at random. By using notches 250 million combinations are possible; the key itself is disposable and may be taken away as a souvenir at the end of the stay as a matter of course (Guestkey).

An added advantage of this type of system is that it was one of the first (although magnetic strip keycard system manufacturers are not far behind) to allow functions other than room access to be undertaken. If the system is linked to the property management system computer for billing purposes, then small terminals can be fitted at points-of-sale. If guests make purchases at the bar or in the restaurant, for example, their key is placed into the terminal as a means of identity and their charge is transferred straight to their bill. This in effect allows immediate guest identification, which has long been a problem in hotels, and greatly enhances the control of all cash or credit transactions.

Room status may also be undertaken with this system as housekeeping staff may use special keys to identify the status of rooms – such as ready to let, vacant, not ready, clean or inspected – by means of cabling linked directly to the reservations system and front desk. Indeed energy control, mini-bar monitoring, morning call and message waiting facilities may all be added, thanks largely to the fact that each door lock is connected by cables to the central processor.

Another feature which the cabling allows for is an alarm on each bedroom door. If there is an attempt to force the door, tamper with the lock or use an invalid key, the system can raise the alarm and even page security staff to intervene swiftly.

Advantages and disadvantages

Whilst there is little doubt that electronic door-locking systems have greatly improved the control over keys in hotels, they do not provide total security as there is still the human element that may intervene. These systems do not, for example, stop the maid from leaving a series of doors open on her section whilst she changes the linen, and they do not stop staff from innocently letting a person into a room whom they believe to be a customer who has forgotten their key.

Likewise, we should not forget the human element of the guests themselves. The guest will put their keycard into their back pocket, sit on it, bend it, and expose the magnetic strip to magnetism and static. Also, how will the guest who is slightly the worse for wear, having perhaps been celebrating, cope with a card that has to be inserted gently into a narrow slot without causing it damage? The human element is always there.

Some of the systems have proved unreliable, which is hardly surprising when one thinks about the large number of microprocessors involved in a complete system. By the law of averages, with individual microprocessors in every guest door there are always going to be some that are out of order or faulty.

The expense of systems should not be underestimated either. New locks will prove expensive to install, and systems requiring wiring will prove even more expensive, but against this should be balanced the lower insurance premiums that are attainable, the lower cost of replacement keys, and the fact that there will no longer be a need to employ a locksmith on a regular basis.

The future

Whilst the trend today is towards locking systems that make use of keycards with magnetic strips, it is quite apparent that in the near future keycards will be replaced by the guest's own credit card. Before long the guest's Access card, Barclaycard or American Express card will double as their room key, in addition to being a guest identity card and allowing the guest to pay their bill.

COMPUTERS AND THE HOUSEKEEPING DEPARTMENT

The major implication of a computer for the housekeeping department will be in the area of communication to establish room status. A typical computerized housekeeping package will allow room status discrepancies to be quickly identified, as well as providing information on those rooms that are occupied, vacant or out of order. An additional feature will be the opportunity to keep track of Z-beds (roll-away beds) and cots which might otherwise not be fully recorded.

The computerized system allows the housekeeping department to directly update room status into the central memory so that reception is made aware of room availability. This enables the reception staff to see at a glance exactly which rooms are prepared for the arriving guests.

Whilst reception have the task of letting rooms, the housekeeping department has to maintain a constant flow of information outlining current room status and availability. In the opposite direction will come details from reception outlining requests for bedboards, for example, or late departures. The computer will therefore have to act as a two-way communication medium.

From the memory of the system the housekeeping department will access lists of room types and status, as well as lists of arrival and departure rooms for the particular day. In addition there may well be maintenance check-lists to be referred to. From the information contained in these lists the housekeeper is able to schedule the staff along the most effective lines, whilst coping with sudden changes and requests.

Once a room has been cleaned and checked the room status is updated, perhaps by use of a housekeeping terminal or via the telephone in the guest room which is linked to the computer. In addition the computer may be required to keep track of items loaned out by housekeeping including cots, ironing boards, irons and hairdryers, to ensure that they are returned even though a new shift may be on duty. A typical housekeeping package will therefore include:

- complete room status report
- automatic update of guest room status
- 'portables' assigned, system-charged to guest account
- maintenance codes to generate work repair lists
- 'out of order' and 'out of inventory' capabilities
     Source: Auditel Lodging Management Systems

The computer may also be used by housekeeping for linen reports and stock control. It can additionally be used to eliminate tedious maid scheduling and generally allow for more efficient scheduling of housekeeping services.

Maintenance

As the housekeeping staff are quite often the first people to locate maintenance problems in guest bedrooms and public areas, there is a need for close liaison with the maintenance departments. This may be helped considerably by computerized records.

Most housekeeping systems will allow a maintenance problem to be entered by way of a description so that work orders may be created. The system also allows maintenance staff to check on room status (i.e. whether a room is vacant or not) through their own terminal before undertaking work. They are subsequently able to set the room status back in order when they have finished.

The problem with maintenance undertaken in a busy hotel where rooms are required for occupation is one of wasted time. If maintenance requests are collated by computer then a number of similar jobs may be identified and carried out in a specific area at the same time, thereby cutting down the organizational and logistical problems that might otherwise have occurred. Urgent jobs may be brought to the attention of the maintenance staff thus assisting them to identify priorities.

Monitoring room status by computer

The utilization of a computer to monitor room status in a hotel requires good integration in design and farsighted management who are able to perceive the advantages of a computer system during the design stage.

The purpose of a room status system is to connect the front office departments of reservations, reception and cashiers with the housekeeping department so that all concerned know whether rooms are occupied or not, or whether they are free to let or not. Other departments, such as the porters and maintenance, may also need access to this information.

It is possible to establish room status by making use of the telephone lines to each guest bedroom; the floor housekeeper phones a specific number to indicate that a room has been checked and is ready to let. The message will be picked up by the telephone logging hardware of the system and either transmitted directly to a VDU in reception, or be available if the receptionist interrogates the system at the time of check-in. On some systems it may be left to the computer to select appropriate rooms for guests and in this case the information upon which the computer bases its decision will include the room status messages from the floor housekeepers.

The computer system may in addition be programmed to spot illogical changes in room status, as well as providing housekeeper's check lists, an instant head count and expected occupancy reports.

It is becoming common for room status software to incorporate housekeeping functions such as linen stock control, mini-bar stock issues and even maid location.

MINI-BARS OR IN-ROOM REFRESHMENT CENTRES

Mini-bars have been provided in hotels for many years. The reason for their existence has always been either to stimulate extra liquor or snack sales to guests, or to replace traditional room service.

Computerized mini-bars provide an instant beverage and light snack room service for guests whilst allowing room service staff, where they still exist, to be deployed solely for the provision of larger and more profitable orders.

They are resilient guests indeed who can resist the temptation of an impulse purchase of cool drinks from the refrigerated bars in the privacy of their rooms, and which may be obtained without the embarrassment or delay that might occur when ordering from room service. All they have to do is to press a button and their selection is instantly delivered. Not only will they remember the facility but hopefully it will help create satisfied guests who will return again. Mini-bar systems can provide the guest with an extra service, while generating extra revenue for the hotel which might not otherwise have been spent.

Market research has revealed that mini-bars are particularly popular amongst female business travellers in the United States – the fastest growing segment of the hotel market. Sometimes these travellers are reluctant to go to the hotel's lounge unaccompanied. Mini-bars, with their large selection of drinks and sometimes snacks, provide the perfect solution to their refreshment needs. Business and holiday travellers spend much of their time in their rooms, working or just unwinding, and whether one is referring to resort, airport, city-centre, suburban or convention hotels, the time spent by guests in their rooms can leave a lasting impression.

In-room entertainment is being used deliberately to encourage guests to spend longer in their rooms and the mini-bar is one of the sources of revenue targeted with an in-room entertainment package. It is the extra sales from mini-bars that are the incentive in many cases to hoteliers to make use of in-house movie systems, and satellite and cable television systems.

Whilst there have been many varieties of mini-bars in guest rooms for some time, they have often been operated without the benefit of computer technology and have therefore been subject to a large number of problems. Sometimes the honesty of the customer was relied upon to reveal on departure which drinks they had consumed; with other systems the housekeeping staff were required to undertake a stocktake and report the consumption to reception before the guest had left. Both these types of operation frequently led to losses and were extremely unreliable.

With computers, though, it became possible not only to monitor mini-bars remotely, but also to calculate consumption and to automatically charge guests for their drinks by adding details on to their bills even as the drinks were being consumed.

Mini-bar systems

The most recent mini-bar systems, or as the Americans would say 'in-room refreshment centers', involve full computerization which utilizes the existing MATV (television distribution) system to instantaneously transmit purchase details to the guest's account. The software programs in the system interface with the existing property management system so that not only may guests be billed instantly but also a variety of print-outs, such as sales reports, re-stocking reports and diagnostic information, may be provided.

A computerized system removes the problem of 'honesty' mini-bars and the requirement for staff to stocktake them. In addition, a typical computerized system can be programmed to comply with local liquor laws and regulations, a common problem in the United States, and to prevent access to liquor by minors.

Many hoteliers have been unimpressed by the unsightly nature of some mini-bars, but nowadays recognized companies commonly supply a variety of finishes to choose from, so that the heat, stain and abrasion-resistant external high pressure laminates can blend discreetly into any decor or colour scheme. Custom finishes and real wood cabinets may be obtained from some companies.

Mini-bar systems can be purchased outright by the hotelier, or alternatively some suppliers offer what is called a 'revenue sharing plan'. By this method both the hotel and the company receive a percentage of the income generated from guests. The mini-bar supplier charges sufficient to cover the cost of installation and make a profit, and the hotelier receives an extra profit centre without any outlay. Whilst generating extra income the hotelier also benefits from a major extra in-room facility which will increase guest satisfaction, eliminate single drink room service calls and, at the same time, increase the perceived value of guest rooms.

If a hotel is over 300 rooms, some suppliers will install the whole mini-bar system, including the computer network or a link into an existing computer, completely free of charge. They will then manage the system at no extra cost and every week, or more often if trade demands, they will re-stock each bar. At the end of each month they send the hotel a bill for the drink consumed. Subsequently, the firm will refund to the hotel as much as 30 per cent of the revenue earned by the system.

Operation

The typical computerized mini-bar system is controlled from a terminal at the front desk which activates mini-bars in rooms when guests check-in. In practice, the receptionist is able to control access to the alcoholic beverage dispensing part of the mini-bar from the front desk and can therefore deny minors access to that part of the service. Minors occupying rooms can still obtain soft drinks and snacks, thereby maximizing the revenue earning potential of the mini-bar.

The guest is issued with a key which they insert into the mini-bar when they want to take a drink or light snack. The guest then makes their selection, usually from a choice of about 24 items, by pressing a button. Some systems have a rotating carousel display to help guests view the range on offer. Pressing the button opens the appropriate vending door which activates a message to the computer telling it what has just been purchased. The purchases are instantly recorded on to the guest bill, where an interface with a property management computer is in existence.

The computer's software, with most systems, has the ability to store and allow retrieval of charges whilst providing a complete print-out of purchases tracked through a variety of means, for example, by room type or product.

In many systems remote management reports are easy to create as the necessary modems are part of the computer. This allows a central accounting office of a hotel chain to have immediate access to sales and accounting reports from the vending systems installed throughout its properties.

Three sample costings

- A 100 room operation at 70 per cent occupancy with a mini-bar average gross revenue of £1.50 per day per room can generate an annual net profit of £15,330.
- A 200 room operation at the same revenue rate and 70 per cent occupancy would show a jump in annual net profit of £30,660.
- For a 400 room hotel at the same £1.50 per day per room and 70 per cent occupancy the yearly profit would increase by £61,320.

Reports

Typical reports that may be produced by a mini-bar system include:

- *Refill report.* This calculates the complete refill requirements for any given room, for a section, a corridor or a floor.
- *Turnover report.* This calculates the revenue per room per day, on a product basis.

- *End-of-day report.* For audit purposes this gives information of revenue, opening balance, closing balance and printing of all departure bills.

Ghost bar sales

One of the problems with mini-bars is that they are sometimes vulnerable to fraud. Whilst it is often the customer who is blamed in such cases, it is more often likely to be the staff who are at fault either accidentally or deliberately.

The intention, as already explained, is that every time a shelf or door on the mini-bar is opened a message is sent to the CPU of the computer system and the correct charge is automatically added to the guest's account. One problem, however, is that mini-bar systems have been known to send pulses to the CPU even if the bar has not been used at all and none of the contents have been consumed.

Guests in hotels have been known to complain at the front desk about overcharges and refuse to pay until the extra amounts have been subtracted from their bills. Unfortunately, sometimes the staff concerned in the front office are more prepared to believe the computer than the guest and then a nasty situation develops, probably resulting in the management having to settle the complaint which has mushroomed into a major confrontation. The end result, even if the overcharge is subtracted from the guest's bill, is to leave the guest with the impression of a hotel with an ineffective computer system and unhelpful, mistrustful staff.

It is quite clear that either the management of the hotel is totally unaware of the problem, or that no reconciliation of stock takes place to check whether more money is being taken by the computer system than actual usage should demand. The other possibility is that the staff filling the mini-bars understand the problem and are keeping stock for their own personal consumption.

The extra revenue that can be earned by these 'ghost' sales can be considerable. One frequent visitor to a hotel in Geneva stayed there 14 times in a year and was overcharged on 12 occasions. The average overcharge was about 40 Swiss Francs. If we assume the hotel had 200 rooms and operated on an occupancy rate of 80 per cent and that half the guests use their bar, the total in the course of a year could be as high as a million Swiss Francs (£250,000), which is not an inconsiderable sum to just fall out of the sky. (*Computer Fraud & Security Bulletin*, 1982)

ENERGY MANAGEMENT SYSTEMS

When one examines the energy problem that faces caterers it is clear that opportunities exist for the application of new technology to energy wastage, leading in turn to catering businesses being more profitable. These are largely in the area of Energy Management Systems (EMS) which rely on computerized, automatic control to efficiently oversee the use of energy within a catering business.

Prudent caterers will find the opportunity to reduce energy consumption very attractive as it gives them the ability to cut one of the prime overheads of their business. The only problem is that this perceived aim has to be balanced against the wishes of customers, who certainly want to stay in a luxurious and convenient environment.

There is, therefore, an opportunity to reduce overheads, but this must not be at the expense of the customer and the service that they expect. It is, however, a common complaint from hotel customers that their rooms are too hot: frequently the blame is laid at the feet of the hotelier for accommodating a large quantity of Americans who, we are led to believe, have a higher cold threshold than us hardy Europeans! The unhappy truth of the matter is more often that existing heating systems are out-of-date, set at the wrong temperatures, and hopelessly inefficiently operated.

A problem that an EMS will help to overcome is the supply of heat to different areas of the hotel at different times. It is a constant fact in hotels that an expensive boiler is producing heat for the whole building when in fact the public rooms are in use but the bedrooms are unoccupied and vice versa. A basic arrangement provided by an EMS will be a switch to distribute heat to zones of the hotel as guests use them, channelling heat that might otherwise be wasted away from unoccupied areas.

A typical EMS would consist of a master controller and processor linked to a number of input devices monitoring information and output devices controlling functions strategically located around the catering establishment. The system would monitor minute-by-minute the energy situation throughout the premises. The moment the temperature departs from the desired level, the system would switch on fans, valves or radiators as appropriate and then cut them out when the temperature has been restored.

A typical establishment would be divided into a number of zones where individual temperature levels may be maintained. For example, the temperature requirements of a wine cellar will be vastly different to those of leisure facilities, and therefore zoning is essential. The EMS will store and print out historical information so that a picture can be built up of energy use and the effect of this energy on the environment of the establishment. The system can also point out defects, such as certain areas not receiving sufficient heat, and remedies may be speedily applied.

There are a number of ways in which EMS computers can be applied to solving the problems of energy management.

An integrated energy management system

The installation of an energy management system is not cheap and therefore one would expect a significant reduction in energy costs. Normally one can, as a rule of thumb, hope for an installation to have completely paid for itself within two years; in many cases this has been achieved much more quickly.

Many systems have been initially contemplated to help solve a relatively local problem, and then expanded when it has become apparent that a fully integrated system will give even wider benefits if installed right from the beginning. It is quite common, for example, to find that an EMS has been thought of purely for the improved control of a boiler by monitoring and switching plant at optimum times. Only during the initial research stages has it become apparent that the EMS could play a much bigger part in the efficient operation of a building by being expanded into other areas such as heating services control.

The sort of benefits that an integrated EMS can give will quickly outweigh the scepticism with which a new system will be treated by the existing staff. The system will soon give rapid access to a large amount of operational data that has a varying number of uses. It will be possible for the manager to see on VDU the temperatures in various rooms, which will indicate whether certain items of plant are working correctly or not. This can, of course, be done without leaving the office. Also the manager may obtain a comprehensive overview of the working of the energy systems within the establishment: with the benefit of this overview solutions to problems can be forthcoming and better control strategies can be employed.

It is quite normal for a number of large steam raising boilers to be the centre-piece of a catering establishment's energy system. These will often be gas-fired with perhaps only 1 per cent of their annual fuel consumption being oil. Steam from the system can be used not only for the establishment's ducted warm air or radiator heating systems, but also for baths and wash basin use. The EMS can save energy by accurately controlling the various fans and pumps. At quiet times, when the public areas are not heavily used, the EMS will switch the fans in some areas down to low speed whilst turning some off completely. At the same time the water circulation pumps are turned off, cutting the supply of hot water to the central heating in these zones.

The EMS will, in addition, monitor a number of radiator heated zones by controlling the pumps and mixing valves thereby achieving a constant temperature of hot water.

At the start of each day the EMS will automatically restart the pumps and fans, or switch the latter from low to high speed, and bring the rooms up to the correct ambient temperature, having monitored the internal and external temperatures and compared them with the programmed internal level of warmth.

Remote energy management

It is quite possible for energy to be monitored in a number of catering establishments or hotels some distance away from the central control point. Indeed some catering organizations, notably breweries, have appointed energy conservation managers whose job it is to keep energy consumption as low as possible throughout a large number of geographically dispersed establishments, and therefore remote monitoring of these properties is essential.

The systems used involve the installation of an EMS in every property, and let's for sake of argument assume in this case that we are concerned with public houses. Coupled to the EMS will be a master controller, which in turn possesses a modem through which the energy conservation manager at the regional head office can interrogate the system over the public telephone system.

Once connected to the master controller, which in effect is a microcomputer, the energy conservation manager can print out an analysis of the temperatures in the bars, public areas, dining rooms, and the cellar and refrigerators. In addition, there will be detail of equipment such as radiators, coolers and ventilation fans showing the times that they have been running as well as information concerning any faults.

The advantage of remote monitoring is that not only does the unit manager have access to energy monitoring information in-house, but that an expert in energy management can also be watching over the property always ready to step in with advice and assistance. With the best will in the world the pub landlord, for example, is unlikely to be fully trained in energy management analysis, but with remote monitoring an advisor is always close by.

Individual room temperature control

When one stands outside a hotel and looks at the total structure, it is quite apparent that the majority of the building is comprised of guest bedrooms. Relatively small areas in total volume are devoted to the public areas and these are generally on the ground floor. In the energy expert's worst nightmare, all those floors of bedrooms have all their radiators switched on using valuable energy when, in effect, it is only during the night that bedrooms will be occupied and even then a proportion of them will not be sold. The potential cost of all that wasted energy is enormous and therefore the astute and energy conscious manager will devote a substantial amount of time and effort to trying to control the energy use in the guest bedrooms by an effective EMS.

The ideal situation is to have a system by which the temperature of every individual guest bedroom may be controlled centrally. Indeed it used to be the case that the only control, where the hotelier actually bothered, was to ask room maids as part of their work to adjust the temperature controls on each bedroom radiator when completing the servicing of each room. This proved to be a lengthy and highly inefficient means of controlling energy, particularly as changes in radiator settings could only be made at best once a day. In addition, sometimes room maids forgot, not to mention that complaints were often received from guests who found rooms too cold or too hot, especially when there was a sudden change in weather conditions.

Equally, bedrooms are often empty or unoccupied and to be able to shut off heating or ventilation at these times offers a tremendous saving in energy costs. Some systems are interfaced directly with the computer handling the hotel's reservations and room status and will shut down the heating in vacant rooms and turn it on when a guest actually arrives.

The systems have a central processor that constantly monitors the temperature in every bedroom by means of sensors. In some cases these wall-mounted sensors are linked, using the existing telephone, to the computer operated from the reception desk. The computer registers the ambient temperature in each bedroom and should this fall below the preset level it automatically opens the valve on the room's radiator.

Temperature levels can be set from the VDU in reception to suit the requests of guests and the receptionist can see exactly what the temperatures actually are at any time in any room.

One installation of an energy management system of this type linked to every bedroom in a large London hotel was budgeted to make a saving of £23,000 in energy costs during its first year of operation.

Room sensors

The temperature sensors that are actually utilized in each guest bedroom are of varying types depending on the EMS installed. Whilst a simple thermostat is common there are more sophisticated devices that may be used. An infra-red sensor may be used which monitors the room's infra-red energy level. It will automatically distinguish between human occupancy and non-human movements, and eliminates the need for room temperature control to come direct from the reception desk. The infra-red sensor is triggered when the bedroom door is opened and shut and this sequence of events instructs the device to look for human movement. If the device determines that the room is in fact unoccupied the heating or cooling unit is turned off.

An alternative to the infra-red sensor is the movement detector. Triggered in the same way by the opening and closing of the bedroom door, this device scans the room for motion. Should motion be detected the room heating and ventilation devices are set at a locked 'occupied' state which allows the guest control of the temperature. One such device has to register motion once every 16 to 32 minutes to remain in the 'occupied' state and it is sophisticated enough not to cut off should a guest be asleep. In the 'unoccupied' state the movement detector will set the heating or ventilation back to the temperature required when guests are not in residence.

The fourth alternative for monitoring temperature in a guest room is an ultrasonic device that is again switched on by the opening and closing of the door and which has to detect motion to give the guest control of the heating and ventilation. In passing it should be mentioned that some systems not only work on the opening and closing of the bedroom door to record the occupation of a room but also make use of pressure sensors under the room's carpeting.

Whilst many automatic detector Energy Management Systems give the guest some control over their own room atmosphere, it is important that there are controls preset into the EMS to ensure that rooms are not allowed to get too hot or too cold. A limiter that will cut off heating or ventilation will have to be built into the system in each room so that guests do not get carried away using too much energy.

The normal temperatures that will be maintained when a guest is not in residence in a room, as it would be unwise to let a room overheat or freeze when unoccupied, would be 16 °C (60 °F) for heating and 30 °C (86 °F) for air conditioning.

Other ways in which individual room temperatures can be controlled include linking the hotel's key rack in reception into the heating system. The key rack controls the heating in each bedroom through special fobs attached to each key. The philosophy is quite simple in that when the key fob is taken off the rack, in order to allow a guest to go to their room, a sensor is activated and the heating switched on in that room. When the key is handed back in at reception and placed back into the rack the sensor is again activated and the heating switched off as the room is now unoccupied.

The guests themselves should be allowed to influence the heating in their room and indeed there are now systems that allow the temperature to be controlled just by pressing a button on the telephone receiver.

Corridors and public areas

The sort of system needed here is a small set of microprocessor controls that thermostatically manage the heating in the corridors and public areas once the correct temperatures have been programmed into the control panel. Indeed the same system would be able to monitor exactly the frequency and length of time for heating to be switched on. The optimum time for switching on heating is the last possible moment that still allows sufficient opportunity for those rooms to be at the right temperature before guests occupy them.

Some energy management systems are installed purely to monitor public areas; these are common in restaurants and public houses. A typical EMS of this sort might be installed at the same time as the telephone system to economize on wiring and would cover the foyer, meeting rooms, corridors and up to four food and beverage areas. The system would assist the conservation of energy by scheduling as much power usage as possible for off-peak hours when lower rates are charged and by cutting back usage during peak hours. The system would also shed power loads at peak times to reduce the possibility of a Maximum Demand Tariff (see page 209).

A typical system would be linked into nearly 60 sensors. A terminal in the management office would be able to monitor, program and produce print-outs of energy consumption and remedial action. The EMS would heat the building up during off-peak hours during the night and run down consumption during peak times. A realistic saving in energy consumption could be as much as 30 per cent.

A side use of the energy management system is as a foul air or pollution detector. In this situation, common in bar areas for example, when a build-up of cigarette smoke has occurred, the fans will be automatically switched on to freshen the atmosphere.

Scheduling of electricity purchase

One of the major possible savings, apart from reducing the consumption of electricity, is to actually purchase electricity at the cheapest time whenever possible. The sort of saving that an EMS can provide might involve making sure that non-essential plant is switched off during the night, such as air-conditioning, ventilation, boilers and immersion heaters. The EMS might also allow non-essential equipment to be scheduled for operation during off-peak tariffs where this is possible within the operational requirements of the catering establishment.

Whilst electricity tariffs vary from one regional electricity board to another, a common factor amongst all of them is the *Maximum Demand Tariff*. This tariff is operated to try to limit the amount of electricity purchased during peak periods which are very expensive to the CEGB (Central Electricity Generating Board) as it has to keep stand-by generating capacity on hand to cope solely with these peaks. This stand-by capacity is financed by commercial users, such as caterers and hoteliers, and is charged as the Maximum Demand Tariff on the basis of units consumed as well as on the average rate at which electricity power is used.

Maximum demand is measured on an electricity board meter that records the highest reading over successive half-hour periods and the tariff charged is based on this maximum demand reading. If the hotelier or caterer were unlucky enough to record a very high reading in one particular half-hour period this could affect the electricity charges for the whole month. It is therefore essential for the EMS to make sure that two or more major items of plant cannot run together, which if it were allowed to happen would enormously increase the amount of electricity purchased at the maximum demand rate.

TELEVISION PROVISION

Many hoteliers have recognized that in providing guest in-room entertainment it is no longer adequate simply to supply a television.

In the same way as retailers and manufacturers who constantly seek out new ways of attracting their customers and retaining a brand or shop loyalty, hoteliers too have examined their customers to find out what features of the 'hotel experience' they appreciate. Where guest entertainment is concerned, the hotelier's motivation is to provide a service that attracts the more lucrative business guest and to develop his or her loyalty.

The second motivation that the hotelier has is to develop further revenue earning opportunities that attract the guest to spend over and above the room charge. Therefore anything that will make guests more aware of, or prompt the use of, other hotel facilities and services is valuable.

A unique market

Hotels are a unique market for in-room entertainment systems for a number of reasons. Hotels, especially in London, have a high percentage of North American and European guests with some hotels drawing heavily on other foreign markets such as the Japanese and Arabs. Viewing times range all over the day and into the early hours of the morning, with the average stay in many hotels being very short – in the region of two to three days.

Traditional broadcasting services in Britain are not orientated towards these markets. There is a high British programme content and transmission focuses on the prime time between 6.00 and 11.00 p.m. when guests classically are not in their rooms.

The whole attitude towards provision of guest in-room entertainment and television in hotels has changed enormously over recent years as traditional television broadcasting has been usurped by new technology. Whilst domestic television viewers throughout the country have been accustomed to the television aerial on their roof receiving BBC and ITV channels from their local transmitter, hotels have welcomed the concept of supplementing the traditional TV channels by the use of three methods, namely:

- in-house movies
- cable
- satellite

Hoteliers have indeed been at the forefront of installing such new systems, perhaps partly through having the purchasing power and economies of scale that the average domestic user does not.

Hoteliers have also moved towards new television ideas because of the demands of their customers many of whom, especially Americans, are thoroughly familiar with satellite and cable as established and widely used alternative television technologies. There has also been the influence in this country of the video recorder which has become an accepted piece of equipment in many homes, allowing a much more relaxed attitude towards television viewing because viewers no longer have to stick to the rigid schedules of the national TV companies. If sophisticated equipment may be found in the domestic lounge, guests are increasingly going to expect more of their hotel bedrooms.

The influence of the video recorder cannot be overestimated. The penetration of this piece of technology in the UK has been greater than anywhere else in the world and the proliferation of shops renting video tapes has demonstrated that UK viewers want, and are prepared to pay for, alternative programming of their choice.

Clearly television viewing habits in the UK are changing, and following the pattern of the USA and Europe, as the public actively asks for what they want to see rather than what the broadcasters have provided. A market for more television undoubtedly exists.

There are two other reasons for the interest shown by hoteliers in alternative methods of providing television entertainment. The first is a direct reflection of customer demand, and will become obvious when it is realized that to date the majority of satellite and cable installations have been in business hotels. Business guests are usually alone and require much more in the way of entertainment than, say, a family group. Business people stay in one hotel after another night after night and therefore exposure to new entertainment through their bedroom television will be greatly appreciated to enable them to kill tedium.

This reaction in itself has the desired effect for the hotelier as the primary aim has been achieved of keeping guests in the hotel making use of the room service and restaurants, rather than going out and frequenting other establishments. Quite bluntly, the hotelier is maximizing revenue thanks to the attraction of the entertainment provided by these systems.

Both cable and satellite television systems allow a much wider range of programmes to be available in a guest bedroom. Not only is there a wider range of entertainment but the hours of transmission are longer than traditional television channels and undoubtedly this is very attractive to many guests.

Such is the popularity of these systems, as already witnessed in the United States, that before too long they will almost certainly become the norm in hotels catering for the business guest, who appreciates this type of system for business purposes as well as entertainment. A business customer will expect, for example, to be able to obtain instant access to financial information from banking centres throughout the world via the guest room television, which may also be connected to a microcomputer in the foreseeable future.

An essential of all of these television enhancements is that hoteliers make use of televisions which have handheld remote controllers that enable access to a large number of channels and services without the necessity for complicated re-tuning. It is also an added luxury for guests that they do not have to get up whenever they want to alter the television service.

An interesting by-product of the increased usage of television in rooms has been experienced by at least one major hotel in London which has noticed an increased use of room service. Snack meals have been increasingly ordered by guests in their rooms since satellite TV was installed, perhaps indicating a return to the 'TV-meal' that was so popular in the early days of television.

The appeal, therefore, of alternative types of television technology to a hotelier may be summed up as follows: They:

- provide the guest with greater service and satisfaction.
- improve the hotel's image by showing that it is technologically advanced.
- lead to higher occupancy.
- promote an increased usage of hotel services, particularly room service and mini-bars.

Installation considerations

What is common to all three alternative methods of providing television services is that they ultimately feed into an existing hotel network of television sets fed from a master aerial and receiver. These networks, referred to as MATV systems (MAster TV), have until recently depended upon the traditional TV aerial but with the new systems this has been supplemented by a video recorder (in-house movie channels), a network of external cables (cable TV systems) and a satellite dish aerial (satellite TV channels).

Apart from the extra receiving equipment needed particularly by the cable and satellite systems, the existing MATV will have to be examined closely as if the hotel possesses equipment or television sets that need to be changed this could lead to a very high expenditure. Most of the more modern hotel TV distribution systems have equipment capable of handling 20 extra channels and these are more than sufficient for the extra cable and satellite requirements. Some systems have a total capacity of only eight channels and when these are already accommodating existing television programming there are insufficient channels to cope with either cable or satellite. In this situation the television sets themselves will have to be replaced, increasing the cost of the system enormously.

In-house movie channels

Satellite and cable television have been turned to after many hotels have made wide use of in-house movie channels on their televisions. These have been found to be very popular, although sometimes technically rather problematical.

The great advantage of in-house movie channels is that they require the minimum of technology to allow them to be 'plugged' into the hotel's existing television system. All they require is a video recorder, a modulator and a timer, to be able to provide taped films to all the televisions in the hotel at specific times during the day and night.

A typical system will have three main components:

- film selector
- system controller
- front office terminal

Film selector

The film selector, positioned in the guest bedroom, converts one channel of the TV set into three channels. It normally sits on the TV set, bearing simple instructions for the guest on how to obtain the film programmes. Featured on the film selector is a 'confirmed purchase' button. This is used by guests after a two minute preview when they definitely decide to watch the channel selected. If they fail to press the confirmed purchase button the picture will scramble. On pressing the button, the picture returns to normal and a bill is created for the guest's account. A 'parental control' feature may disable the film selector should parents not wish their children to see the films.

System controller

The typical system will allow the controlling and monitoring of up to 2,040 rooms and a billing structure that allows on-site changes from pay-per-day to pay-per-view. The software can produce:

- individual room bills printed at time of purchase
- end-of-day billing summaries
- daily billing analysis of all three channels
- automatic monthly invoices
- diagnostics to advise the status of film selectors in every room

The controller will be of modular design, for easy replacement of circuit boards, and will contain 2,000 hours of battery back-up in the event of power failure.

Front office terminal

The front office terminal, together with its associated printer, provides the ability to communicate with the system via the computer. The printer produces the room bills and other reports generated by the computer, such as up-to-date statements on programme viewing levels.

The terminal is the input mechanism for control of the entire system, including the video players. It is through this terminal that rooms can be disabled for parental control on an individual basis and through which questions can be asked of the status of the system.

Some hoteliers maintain that the choice of films on in-house movie channels is limited, whilst others regard video recorders as unreliable and temperamental and judge the picture quality to be inferior. In addition, it is difficult to suit all tastes as children may require one type of film, the business person may require another, thus forcing some difficult programming decisions. Where contractors have been running systems on behalf of the hotelier they have found that the need to increase the guest buy-rate has led to them depending heavily on soft-porn or risqué movies, but even with these included the buy-rates have averaged only about 10 per cent.

Some in-house movie systems depend on staff in the front office to switch them on and off and insert specific film videos at particular times. This in itself can be a problem as it provides a weak human link in the chain. Some hoteliers, however, like to provide an in-house film channel in addition to cable and satellite transmissions, so there is still a place for this type of system. One cannot overestimate, though, the effect that these systems have had, in advance of satellite and cable, in encouraging a wider interest in the utilization of televisions in guest bedrooms.

Free or pay TV?

Another aspect of these systems to consider is the method by which the hotel is going to be reimbursed for use of the movie channel. In some hotels the service is provided entirely free of charge to the guest; the hotel stands the installation, maintenance and hire of film costs. Some hotels try to raise revenue by advertising placed either between films or on the programming notes provided in the bedroom, but if this source is relied upon totally to fund the film hire then the programme will almost certainly be extremely limited, as many hotels have found. The overall cost of the 'free' movie channel may in reality be reflected in the overall room tariffs, forcing them up, but to all intents and purposes as far as the guest is concerned the service is free and consequently a bigger attraction.

Pay TV has also proved very popular around the world in large numbers of hotels as a method of enhancing the entertainment on offer to guests, and encouraging them to stay in the hotel. The point, though, should be made that the hotelier receives very little of the revenue from these systems, and only really benefits from the largely intangible spin-off spending from the customers who are encouraged to remain in the hotel. The hotelier, in effect, receives either nothing at all from the contractor or a small percentage of the viewing charge as revenue; the bulk of the income from guests goes to the pay TV operators to recover their hardware investment and to pay a licence fee to the movie distributor. On the other hand, the hotelier does not incur any costs either as the service is provided entirely by outside contractors – unless, of course, there have had to be alterations to the MATV distribution system at the time of installation.

The contractor installing the pay TV system will be taking a large gamble as these systems are expensive. The hotelier may be assured that the best possible programme of films will be provided, if only in the interests of the contractor's business: for the system to be successful as far as the contractor is concerned, it must encourage the hotel guests to make great use of it.

Payment may be made by the guest in a number of different ways. Firstly, there may be a direct link to the hotel's property management computer so the charge is automatically added to the guest's account each time a film is watched. Secondly, some systems permit the insertion of a card with a magnetic strip into the room TV mechanism that records viewing details. The cards may be read at reception to enable a bill to be produced on departure. Thirdly, payment may be made by means of an overall daily charge which allows the guest a complete day's viewing. This daily charge may be paid at the reception desk and the system activated from there, usually on a midday to midday basis. Fourthly, the pay television system may print a ticket outlining the charges which may then be placed with the room folio and added on to the guest's bill by traditional methods on departure. Amongst these various methods there is a suitable system to allow a pay television service in almost any type of hotel.

The only problem with a pay movie channel is the question of whether the guests will be put off by the charge and therefore will the potential for them to stay in their rooms and use the mini-bars or room service be lost?

Cable television

Cable television is another alternative in those geographical areas where this transmission system operates. The limiting factor currently is that only those hotels situated in certain towns and cities that possess a cable network have the opportunity of connecting to such a system.

Basically cable television provides television pictures from cables run along the street which any subscriber such as a hotel can link into. The cables usually run in 'tree and branch' style from a central studio known as the 'head-end' which originates the programmes. These programmes have been collected from various sources including satellite, studio, video tape player, land line, and off-air pick-ups, and are assembled at the head-end for injection into the system. In the 'tree and branch' type of system, which is the most cost-effective type, the trunk cables run outwards from the head-end in strategic directions and the branch cables then run into the side streets to allow individual subscribers to insert 'drop cables' to connect them to the system.

All the programmes on offer to subscribers are transmitted along the tree and

The control room or head-end of Westminster Cable Television where input and output of satellite and video channels are monitored
Photograph: Westminster Cable Television

branch system's cables simultaneously, and are available to all the subscribers who select their choice of viewing by means of the tuner on their television.

Another variety of cable television network – the one which the Government prefers – is called the 'switched star' system. This involves much more expensive cabling. Each subscriber is linked to an intelligent video switch in their locality which in turn is connected by cable to the head-end. The implication of the intelligent video switch is that it receives details of subscriber choice, checks that the subscriber is authorized to receive that choice, and then sends it into the subscriber's premises.

The cabling in the switched star network permits the system to be interactive, thereby creating a complete two-way communications facility which can carry services such as electronic mail and teleconferencing in addition to entertainment. This type of communications system is also useful to hotel management for transmission of data, whether this be reservations or financial returns, from hotel to hotel, or between a hotel and the head offices if they are linked into a switched star network.

It is claimed that cable permits the best possible picture quality, especially as the latest cabling technology is used such as fibre optics and built in self-diagnostic features.

Westminster Cable Television

In October 1985 Westminster Cable Television started operating as the cable service franchise-holder in Central London: the company is regarded by many as the market leader in this country. The Westminster Cable network represents the first significant application of the technology in a major metropolitan area and provides an opportunity to take an early, if not pre-emptive lead in establishing the credibility of British cable technology.

By 1987 the service was available to 19,500 homes and hotel rooms in the City of Westminster and over 4,500 customers were contracted to receive transmissions. This represented a 23 per cent penetration in the cabled area.

Signals from satellite television channels are received by dishes such as this and then fed through the Westminster Cable system to subscribers' premises
Photograph: Westminster Cable Television

Area served

Westminster Cable's franchise area is the City of Westminster in its entirety, where the resident population according to the 1981 Census is 163,892 and private households total 96,000. There are 22,753 commercial and government rated premises in the area and a further 1,273 recreational, educational and entertainment premises.

Westminster itself is the centre of national government, is host to tourists from all over the world, contains the headquarters of many businesses with national and international interests, and embraces a large number of the nation's cultural, educational, professional and research establishments.

In this national and regional role, Westminster provides around 60,000 bed spaces for business visitors and tourists in 500 hotels, accommodates half of Central London's workforce amounting to 500,000 people, and contains 60 per cent of Central London's shopping floorspace.

Strategic considerations

Westminster is a place of regional, national and international importance. Westminster Cable is therefore using an advanced cable network with fibre optic switched star technology, which permits a highly sophisticated range of services and is designed to evolve into a fully integrated communications network. The network has benefited from the fact that British Telecom is a joint licence holder and has therefore made its facilities and ducts available for the miles of necessary cables.

To illustrate the variety of entertainment and information available through a cable network it is worth looking at the variety offered by Westminster Cable on both their programme, broadcast and text channels.

Programme channels

Premiere – the movie channel. Presents a selection of recently released films featuring world renowned stars and internationally acclaimed films, blended with films for the whole family. The programming includes special features, reviews and interviews with the stars.

Westminster home video channel. An all movie channel showing popular films.

Bravo. This provides a monthly selection of the best movies from the golden age of Hollywood, including film 'festival' featuring specific actors and directors.

The Children's Channel. Offers programme material suitable for both pre-school children and older children at different times and includes fun-to-learn programmes, magic shows, cartoon films, quizzes, guest appearances and competitions.

Matinee Channel. A popular American daytime drama every afternoon, with a weekend omnibus for those who missed an episode during the week.

TV5 – the French Channel. The best of French language television entertainment and news production from France, Switzerland, Belgium and Canada.

The Arabic Channel. Provides a broad range of films, dramas, documentaries and current affairs for the Arab community including live news, via satellite, from Dubai.

Worldnet. Breakfast television and a daily report on viewpoints from the USA covering topical events, current affairs and the American way of life.

Reuters. A 24-hour rolling text service covering the latest national and international news, financial information, sports and weather reports.

European Television Network. Covers major financial news stories live from Europe and New York.

Cable News Network. The world's only live 24-hours-a-day, seven-days-a-week television channel of news and information, available at present only to commercial premises and hotels.

Westcan. A complete at-a-glance thirteen screen display which conveniently presents what is happening on each channel at any one time.

Sky Channel. A family entertainment channel with broad programme appeal offering a mixture of sports fixtures, action and adventure series, children's programmes, dramas, comedies, documentaries and nature programmes as well as the *Sky Trax* pop music programme.

Screensport. Screensport carries over 40 hours per week of sports and leisure events from Britain and around the world. The format includes action coverage, documentaries, interviews, sport news, competitions and a full results service.

Super Channel. A 24-hour service combining a wide variety of BBC and ITV programming with popular music from the Music Box team and Super Channel's own productions. The channel provides comedy, drama, sport, news, documentaries, music, wildlife and children's programmes.

The Arts Channel. Covers the visual and performing arts and includes classical and jazz concerts, ballet and opera, drama, exhibitions and festivals and a weekly arts round-up with interviews and profiles of leading personalities in the arts.

Lifestyle. A TV 'magazine' programme with broad family appeal. Lifestyle is particularly aimed at the daytime audience. The channel includes health and fitness, holidays, cooking and wines, gardening, photography and many other leisure interests.

Broadcast channels

Television. The service provides BBC1, BBC2, ITV and Channel 4 with assured high-quality reception.

FM Radio. A host of radio channels are provided, both local and national, to the cable subscriber's FM receiver, with assured high-quality reception.

Text services

Westminster Today. Local headline stories from the London Newspaper Group. Lunchtime and evening stories during the week and additional weekend features.

Weather Window in Westminster. Daily forecast for Central London area.

About Cable. News and notes, competitions and helpful hints, all keeping the subscriber in touch with the network.

Programme Guide. The Cable Programme Guide and cable news tell the subscriber what's on cable television and introduce enhancements in services.

Westminster Community Information. Bulletin board of news, events and information from local groups; where the subscriber's help may be put to good use in Westminster; City Council information for residents and visitors.

Cable Nosh. By using the interactive screen the subscriber may order a take away meal from the comfort of their home.

Fitness. Subscribers can get fit using 'Ready Steady Go' – a fitness programme designed with convenience in mind that even provides a signed certificate when the fitness programme is completed.

London Zoo. Zoo gossip, events and book reviews; how to adopt an animal and other ways of helping the Zoo.

Football. A way of keeping in touch with London's First Division soccer teams.

Chinese Horoscopes. Chinese predictions for the year ahead.

Shopping. A display of goods and services for sale, including special offers.

London fire line. The local fire brigade gives weekly news and safety hints.

VCR Settings. A guide giving multiple settings for the subscriber's video cassette recorder.

The future

Whilst Westminster Cable provides the comprehensive services outlined so far, the proposed future developments of their cable network indicate that they have just scratched the surface of the full potential of the system.

The fibre optic switched star cable network can provide the high-speed, high-quality communications which will be required by business in the future. This capability will provide a wide range of innovative interactive services for both the private customer and commerce.

The interactive facilities that can be provided include both those with a primarily entertainment based function as well as those with social, educational, information and commercial functions. The scope for interactive services includes:

- local electronic newspaper
- access to national databases
- telebanking
- teleshopping
- telebooking
- alarm services
- educational services
- interactive games
- opinion polling
- meter telemetry
- electronic mail
- telesoftware

Local Electronic Newspaper. A 100-page magazine consisting of the following material:

- latest local news
- local sports results

- features on the Westminster area
- what's on and where in Central London
- community contacts and advice
- classified advertisements

Access to national databases. As well as locally generated data subscribers will have access to national databases as a great deal of information is only meaningful in a national or international context.

Telebanking. This is the facility by which subscribers can make use of 24-hour home banking.

Teleshopping. The first step here is to initiate a user response facility, so that users can indicate when an item interests them and they wish to receive more information or have a salesperson visit them.

Cable systems of the switched star variety can go much further than this by the use of *photovideotex*. This consists of a computer system with stored data and pictures, and display terminals which can call up the data and visual images. Usually pages have a picture, in full colour and of TV quality resolution, as well as text. This is especially appropriate for teleshopping applications, as the picture can show the item while the text describes its features, price and availability. Unlike some technologies, alteration of both text and pictures is cheap and easy.

The first application of such a service is likely to be a house buying channel. Most people have experienced the difficulties and frustrations of searching for a new house. Unlike most items that are purchased, houses are of almost infinite variety, and equally varied locations, and usually can only be seen in detail at most inconvenient times. Estate agents' detail sheets and newspaper advertisements sometimes give an adequate textual description, but rarely have an adequate photograph of even the outside of the house. How much more convenient, then, to be able to sit at home and see a series of full colour pictures of houses for sale, showing front and back views and the interiors of all rooms, backed up by detailed text. This service will be infinitely more satisfactory than a visit to the estate agent. Serious viewers could follow up their interest by filling in a response frame to ask the estate agent to send full details or to contact them to arrange a live viewing of the property.

Once this service is mastered it is envisaged that the technology will move on to create similar services for car sales, boats, antiques and groceries. Even pet sales or advertisements for local entertainments could use this facility if demand warrants.

It does not take much imagination to see this facility being extended to hotel reservations so that hotels, their facilities and even individual rooms may be viewed and booked from the comfort of the potential guest's lounge. This may, of course, be an additional enhancement of the telebooking facility below.

As both telebanking and teleshopping operate through viewdata systems, it is intended that the booking service for hotels be extended using this technology.

Telebooking. Telebooking is a service which allows subscribers to remotely book and pay for holidays, hotel rooms, air flights, theatre tickets and various other services.

Telebooking has as much potential as teleshopping. Currently one can telephone in a booking, but for some services there is no central clearing agency, so one has to ring a series of separate numbers to find what is available and what it costs. Payment over the telephone is difficult: some organizations will accept credit card bookings, although they seem to dislike doing so as they have no means of checking whether the numbers they are given are valid. Even this limited facility of remote booking is unavailable to people who do not possess credit cards.

With telebooking all these disadvantages are removed, thereby simplifying the booking process for the subscriber.

Alarm services. Alarm services are one of the major potentials of any advanced cable system. Public anxiety about burglary is considerable, as is concern over household fire potential. Old people and others living alone in Westminster – and elsewhere – could benefit from an emergency medical alert system, sending out an alarm signal over the cable system when an emergency button is pressed at home.

An alarm system attached to the cable network would offer the following major benefits:

- connection to the emergency services would be immediate and direct
- interfering with the alarm system would in itself alert the remote centre
- any fault in the alarm system would be rapidly detected by the remote centre

Educational services. Cable systems should be capable of adding to the quality of the educational environment of school age children, college students and adults. With education being a two-way process, the interactive capabilities of the switched star system can add a new dimension to the formal and informal educational process.

The first step will be to invite simple viewer response through button presses. For example, many viewers watching a programme on a complex subject, such as most Open University broadcasts, often have the feeling that they would like to say 'Wait a moment! Can you repeat the last bit?' With a response capability, the audience could communicate with a lecturer who could stop and go over the difficult bit again. Even if the programme were broadcast on videotape, the channel programmer could ask the audience at the end of the programme if they required a repeat of any part and they could reply through the keypad.

Another way of using the keypad would be to have instant tests at the end of a lecture. The lecturer could thus get almost immediate feedback of the parts of the lecture that had not been understood and could amend the presentation accordingly.

Interactive games. Well designed interactive entertainment services can play a very useful role in introducing people who suffer from 'techno-fear' to the use of advanced information technology. The image of the home computer as the modern equivalent of the train set – something that parents and children can both enjoy – is useful in this regard as the initial stage of learning to operate a computer should not discourage people.

Westminster Cable believe that interactive games and similar amusements on the cable system could play a similar role. The provision of interactive games and amusements on the cable system will not only be a valuable service in its own right, but will also be an effective method of ensuring that users become involved with the facilities from the earliest possible moment.

In addition, a large number of microcomputer games, generated from a bank of micros at the cable head-end, will be provided as well as interactive videodisc games.

Opinion polling. The response facility may be used to increase audience involvement or for serious market research. In the latter case it is very important that a demographically representative group is selected and viewers will often be paid or given other incentives to ensure a high response rate.

Westminster will be using the talk-back facility as an amusement to increase audience enjoyment of, and participation in, local or regional programmes. In other contexts, such as the Eurovision Song Contest, the facility will be of great value in giving viewers something that they have always missed – the ability to talk back to their television.

Meter Telemetry. Telemetry is a system by which remote devices may be monitored and in some cases activated or controlled from a distant location.

There is a wide range of possible uses for telemetry systems that Westminster Cable would like to see applied. Examples are:

- remote reading of electricity, gas and water meters

- electricity load shedding, by which a central point can switch off water heaters and other electrical devices in homes, thus reducing peak load and electricity costs

- remote control of domestic appliances, so that cookers or lights can be switched on or off remotely

Savings for the utilities companies could be considerable, and both businesses and householders could benefit as well.

In addition to those services mentioned, Westminster are committed to providing a 'Mailbox' and a 'Telesoftware' service. The latter is a facility by which computer programs are stored in a central computer and transmitted to a subscriber's home or small business computer.

Satellite TV

Satellite technology, when applied to the distribution of television programmes, allows transmissions from a source satellite to be beamed down to receiving dishes on approximately one third of the earth's surface. The technology removes many of the problems of existing television transmissions, from the top of tall masts, which frequently cannot reach locations shielded by hills or the curvature of the earth.

Signals are sent at high power from a large earth station to the satellite which is located in a stationary orbit some 35,000 kilometres (22,000 miles) above the equator. To remain stationary the satellite is spinning at the same speed and trajectory as the earth. On reaching the satellite the signals are converted to a frequency in the 11 GHz (gigaHertz) band before being beamed back to earth at approximately 30 kW. The pictures will have travelled over 72,000 kilometres (45,000 miles) since being originated to the time they are actually viewed on a television.

At the time of writing there are actually two satellites used by services in the UK: these are Intelstat V and Eutelstat-1 F1. These two satellites are direct descendants of Early Bird and Telstar that were the pioneers in broadcasting technology but that were in low orbit, thereby only being usable for a maximum of eight minutes at a time. Both Intelstat and Eutelstat are primarily utilized for telecommunications, and television transmission is really only carried because of some spare capacity. It is planned to launch a number of totally dedicated broadcasting satellites in the near future. Had there not been the accident to the NASA Space Shuttle *Challenger*, there would have been more dedicated broadcasting satellites in orbit by now, but the consequent delay in the Shuttle programme has put new satellite plans well behind.

*IVS satellite reception dishes on roof of May Fair Hotel, Stratton Street, London W1.
This was the first satellite TV system to be installed in a UK hotel, in May 1985.*
Photograph: IVS Enterprises

TVRO

The Television Receive Only (TVRO) earth station consists of three parts:

- the antenna
- a low noise converter (LNC or LNB)
- the receiver

The antenna is dish-shaped to collect and concentrate the signal from the satellite. The low noise converter amplifies and converts the frequency to the usual 1 GHz band, and the receiver tunes into the required frequency and provides a video and audio output.

Most TVROs, in collecting and focusing the signals from the satellite, currently use a 1.8-metre (6-foot) or 2.3-metre (7½-foot) diameter antenna, and the more easily erected versions are petallized so that they can be carried more easily to the installation site. The size of these 'dishes' will reduce considerably – to less than one metre – when the planned new dedicated television satellites are launched. The structure for the antenna can be either self-supporting, using the weight of the base to prevent excessive movement in high wind conditions, or it can be bolted directly to the roof. The only constraint is that the dish must be capable of being trained at the correct part of the sky, so unless mounted high up it is possible that it could be in the shadow of trees or a tall building. The further north the installation in the UK the lower the satellites will appear to be against the horizon.

The signals from the antenna are carried along coaxial cable to the receiver rack where they are split to serve a number of individual receivers. The receiver contains, sometimes, a low gain amplifier to make up for the loss in splitting the signal. Each receiver is tuned to a single channel, and frequency selection is controlled by a microprocessor that picks out pre-programmed channels. Video and audio output is provided separately at the rear of the receiver.

The signals, known as baseband, are modulated and transmitted to the televisions by the coaxial cables which are already installed as part of the regular hotel television distribution system.

One cannot pretend that there have not been some problems with satellite systems during their initial stages. One is that a separate receiving dish is needed to receive signals from each of the main satellites, so at present that could mean two antennae on the hotel roof if reception is to be uninterrupted, or a motorized swivel can be used to train a single dish on to more than one satellite. In the future, unless a universal antenna is produced, each new satellite will require an additional antenna. These antennae themselves may be a problem as they require planning permission from the local authority. Generally, as long as they are not the highest point of the building and are not visible from the street below a planning authority will look favourably upon them. Bad weather conditions, such as heavy rain or snow, can sometimes cause fading of the signal.

Information channel

Some satellite television systems have developed a special feature for hotel use which is an in-house information channel. The channel is a computer generated colour text and graphics system, fed through the television distribution system just like any other channel.

The information is attractively presented in full colour, high definition graphics, and usually contains up to one hundred pages of information that may be watched on a continuous turning display. Each page may be displayed for as long or as short a time as the viewer wishes.

Hotel applications for this extra service include:

- promoting special events
- publicizing restaurants and other facilities (in-house sales)
- keeping viewers informed of the programme viewing schedules
- informing viewers of emergency procedures

The hotels that utilize this type of extra facility usually display the information on a 10 minute continuous loop, but the viewer may intervene at any time and examine a particular page for a longer period.

The satellite television companies that provide this service will help the hotel management in the initial stages to design the displays and then train the appointed hotel staff how to update the information as necessary.

This type of channel has proved very popular, not only in hotels but also in apartment blocks and similar locations.

News service

Some satellite television systems also provide the facility, for use in hotels and hospitals, of a continuous news service in text and graphics. This is provided through an international news gathering agency, such as Reuters, and with the aid of a page cycle controller linked to the agency's database provides a continuous flow of the following information, which is being constantly updated by their reporters:

- news
- weather
- sport
- financial information

Programmes

Of the general programming on offer the best mix may be obtained by taking transmissions from both the Intelstat and Eutelstat satellites. Whilst the former specializes in most of the English-language broadcasting stations, the latter handles a number of the European broadcasts.

The two satellites can offer the hotelier the following services:

Intelstat

Premiere – 12 hr film channel (3 am–3 pm)
Screen Sport – All sports channel (5 pm–midnight)
Arts Channel – opera, ballet, etc. (6 am–9 am)
Children's Channel – cartoons, etc. (7 am–3 pm)
Lifestyle – general interest (9 am–1 pm)
Cable News Network (CNN) – 24 hr USA news

Eutelstat

The Music Box – 24 hr pop and rock (6 hr programme repeated 4 times)
Superchannel – 24 hr general entertainment
Europa – subtitled entertainment
World Net – USA news service
Filmnet – films
Teleclub – German film channel
New World – religious channel

Finances

With the hotel guest apparently receiving a free service, the pricing of this extra service is left largely to the discretion of the hotelier involved. Whilst the hotel is obviously paying for the provision of the satellite service it is up to the hotel management what charge is going to be passed on to customers. Quite often the cost is reflected in the price of the room as the tariff is adjusted to allow for the new service.

Whilst the cost of a satellite TV licence from the Department of Trade and Industry is minimal (currently £10), there are various additional charges apart from installation that hoteliers will find themselves involved in. Depending upon which programmes are accessed, as some satellite TV companies are funded directly by advertising at source, there may well be a programme charge per room per night (which is subject to VAT) which is billed irrespective of how many guests actually make use of the service.

The best of all worlds

We have looked at the television transmission systems separately, but the opportunity exists to merge various systems to find a package that is ideally suited to a particular hotelier. Such systems are quite popular and have the advantage of perhaps offering the best of a number of worlds to the hotel guest, and possibly tempting them to make the most use of the in-room entertainment facilities.

The typical mix of technologies would be to provide the guest with the following:

- a NEWS channel by satellite
- a SPORTS channel by satellite
- a MOVIE channel by in-house movie system
- a PROMO channel initiated by in-house computer and video recorder

A typical selection of hotel programmes utilizing this system is illustrated in Figure 3.20.

AMSTERDAM
Marriott.
HOTEL

Television Channels

1	Information Channel	Details about the Amsterdam Marriott
2	Nederland 1	Local Dutch Channel
3	Nederland 2	Local Dutch Channel
4	Germany 1	German National Channel
5	Germany 2	German National Channel
6	Germany 3	German National Channel
7	CNN – News Channel	24 hour international news
8	Music Box	Pop Videos
9	Screen Sport	International Sport from 16.00 'til late
10	Sky Channel	General Entertainment (English)
11	Belgium 1	Belgian National Channel
12	Belgium 2	Belgian National Channel
13	Movie Channel	See Opposite for this month's selections
14	Unused	
15	TV5	General Entertainment (French)
16	BBC 1	British National Channel
17	BBC 2	British National Channel

Movie Channel Selections   CHANNEL/KANAAL 13

OUT OF AFRICA   a SYDNEY POLLACK film
WINNER OF SEVEN OSCARS
Meryl Streep, Robert Redford
Based on a True Story and filmed entirely on location in Kenya
Meryl Streep stars as Karen Blixen and this is an account of her extraordinary love affair with Africa and with the maverick adventurer Denys Finch Hatton (**Robert Redford**)
Showing - January 20th, 24th, 28th, February 1st, 5th, 9th, 13th, 17th, 21st, 25th
Start Times - 10.00, 13.00, 16.00, 19.00, 22.00, 01.00   Run Time - 154 mins approx

BACK◄═════ TO THE FUTURE   STEVEN SPIELBERG Presents
a ROBERT ZEMECKIS Film
Michael J Fox, Christopher Lloyd
One of the top grossing box office comedies of all time !
Steven Spielberg presents this comic fantasy which sends a typical American teenager of the Eighties back to 1955 in a plutonium powered Delorean time machine.
Showing - January 21st, 25th, 29th, February 2nd, 6th, 10th, 14th, 18th, 22nd, 26th
Start Times - 10.00, 14.00, 16.00, 18.00, 20.00, 22.00   Run Time - 112 mins approx

BEVERLY HILLS *cop*   Starring EDDIE MURPHY
Ranks in the TOP TEN box office hits in history !
Eddie Murphy's hilarious portrayal of Detective Axel Foley a brash, street smart, Detroit detective who follows the trail of a friend's murderer to the posh area of Beverly Hills.
Showing - January 22nd, 26th, 30th, February 3rd, 7th, 11th, 15th, 19th, 23rd, 27th
Start Times - 10.00, 14.00, 16.00, 18.00, 20.00, 22.00   Run Time - 104 mins approx

Terms of Endearment XX   WINNER OF FIVE OSCARS
SHIRLEY MACLAINE
DEBRA WINGER   JACK NICHOLSON
Dazzled critics and audiences alike !
The story, spanning 30 years, of two captivating people, mother and daughter, played by Shirley MacLaine and Debra Winger. Ranges from grand and slapstick to deep sentiment.
Showing - January 23rd, 27th, 31st, February 4th, 8th, 12th, 16th, 20th, 24th, 28th
Start Times - 10.00, 13.00, 16.00, 19.00, 22.00, 01.00   Run Time - 126 mins approx

Marriott Craftsmanship	**Marriott Vakmanschap**
A blend of local influences and a proven understanding of our guests' needs	's Lands aard gecombineerd met de reputatie in te kunnen spelen op de wensen van de gasten.
We've created a group of very special, but very individual hotels CHANNEL 1	Dit is de basis van zeer speciale, maar, ook zeer individuele hotel. KANAAL 1

Figure 3.20   *Amsterdam Marriott Hotel – television channels*
Source: Vista Satellite Ltd.

This configuration has the advantages that it allows guests several choices. They can 'dip in' and be brought up-to-date with current international news, or watch some sport during short periods in the room, or they can settle down to watch a current hit movie and make use of the mini-bar or room service. Additionally, with a Promo Channel the guest may be kept abreast of the hotel services and facilities, be prompted to use the hotel restaurant or bar, or to make onward reservations within the hotel group.

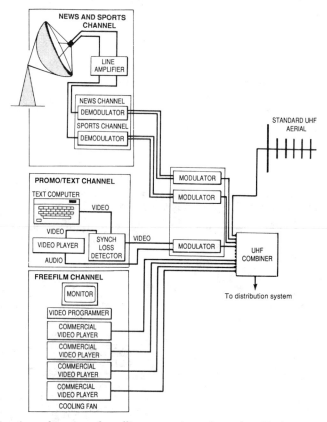

Figure 3.21　*A combination of satellite, promo/text channel and in-house movie channel as offered as a total system to hotels*
Source: Vista Satellite Ltd

Whilst we have already referred to the facilities of News, Sports and Movie channels, it is important now to examine the Promo service to guests.

The Promo channel

The Promo or promotional channel may be either purely text or a text and video film channel. The text terminal will be a microcomputer handling software that will scroll, typically, up to 60 pages of text from programmable memory and a further 20 from a fixed cartridge. The content may be anything relevant that needs drawing to the guest's attention, such as details of facilities, restaurants, bars and emergency instructions.

A feature that may make the scrolling more attractive is if the pages can be drawn on to the screen rather than simply appearing whole. This is much more eye-catching and therefore holds the interest better.

The 60 pages are simply created through a keyboard and the size of the text is expanded to fill the screen. The operator can define which of the 60 prepared pages should be displayed and in which order so that just a small series can be selected from amongst the standard pages held within the memory.

With the promotional text and video playing continuously whenever there are no other signals being fed to the television, there must be a facility built into the system to automatically rewind the promo videotape. A month is regarded as the maximum time that a videotape will last in continuous use before the picture breaks up.

Viewdata (Videotex)

Viewdata, or Videotex as it is known internationally, is a computer-based technology that allows information to be displayed in words and pictures on a television or computer screen. It is seen as a cheap way of making information available to a wide audience.

One might have expected viewdata technology to have originated abroad but the British *Prestel* service, conceived in 1971 and introduced in 1979, has long been regarded as the most extensively researched and used viewdata system in existence. It was Prestel that was copied and later introduced into Canada, where the videotex system is called *Telidon*, the United States (NAPLPS) and Europe (CEPT).

Prestel evolved because the telephone communications side of the Post Office (now British Telecom) wanted to find a way to encourage a wide audience to make use of their telephone lines during quiet or off-peak hours. Since the early days of Prestel many copies have emerged; the main difference as far as the user is concerned is that a different telephone number is dialled and even then it may well be carried out automatically by a modem so there is no perceptible difference. Originally designed as an information display, viewdata is now interactive so information may be passed back by the user, whether this be a request for a brochure or a reservation of a hotel room. The quality of picture will improve once the current modernization of the telephone line network is completed, making a photographic display possible. The introduction of 'gateways' has allowed the system to access remote independent computer databases, which has greatly widened the choice of information available.

The travel and hotel industry was one of the prime early users of Prestel and remains so today, with a large number of hotel chains as well as private establishments displaying information for customers via the system. There are several ways in which hoteliers make information available to specific markets. Some only make information available to subscribers so the general public are not privy to the contents of the pages. These hotels tend to restrict themselves to travel agents and tour companies who are, in effect, the subscribers. Other hotel and tour companies provide information in what is really an electronic brochure form and give an address for further information. Lastly, reservations may be placed via the system by using it as an electronic mail facility. The potential customers, who may be from either the general public or the travel industry, send a reservation request via their Prestel terminal which is then transferred to the hotel's reservations system and confirmed the following day. There is not a direct computer link as the Prestel information has to be input manually to the hotel's reservations system, which may or may not be computerized, on receipt of the viewdata request.

Guest information

Viewdata is a colourful and easy-to-read method of providing guests with information. Common uses in hotels include:

- Pages of information on such items as menus and films can be created and then carouselled on monitors placed in key positions such as the foyer and bar.
- The viewdata terminal may be connected to the hotel's UHF TV signal amplifier so that the same carousel of pages may be viewed on the television in every bedroom.
- A full interactive private viewdata system can be run on a PC in the hotel which, with a viewdata adaptor in each bedroom, allows guests to retrieve the information they want. The initial cost of such a system may be offset by selling advertising on the system to local businesses.

Having access to a viewdata service such as Prestel opens the door to a host of information which will not only be of use to the hotel management, but also may be used to provide the basis for a guest information service.

The range of information that may be accessed includes:

- Travel   – airline, rail and coach information including timetables and fares
- Leisure   – news, weather, entertainment, restaurants and much more
- Business – business news, financial information, company information, credit management services and electronic banking

Electronic reservations

This is a very popular viewdata service being provided by such systems as Prestel. For further details see the section on reservations in Chapter 2 (page 116).

Electronic mail/telex

Viewdata terminals and modems are capable of taking advantage of the many electronic mail and telex services that are available.

- *Electronic Mail.* This enables hard-copy memos, letters and reports to be sent instantly to colleagues and clients. A special written link can be established between major clients, thereby providing them with a more personal and professional service (Tandata).
- *Telex.* One of the main features offered by electronic mail services such as Prestel, Telecom Gold, One-to-One and Easylink is the telex-link facility. This allows telexes to be sent and received without the need for a dedicated telex terminal and telephone line. For users who send telexes infrequently, the telex-link is usually more economical than investing in telex equipment, whilst charges on the telex-link system are standard. It is therefore a convenient way to provide guests with a telex service.

Liaison and management control

Networked viewdata systems have made a large impression in major breweries where at least one uses the system to receive regular, accurate and up-to-date information from its nationwide network of 1,800 public houses, restaurants and specialized food retailers. The information collating process used to take three days but with viewdata it is completed in a matter of seconds.

Using frequently changed passwords, house managers input their details of sales, labour and profit every Sunday. The data, which is in the form of a weekly cash sheet, is formatted automatically at head office and is immediately made available to management. The information may also be summarized at district, regional or operating company level. Up to 128 reports may be produced. Of specific interest is that stock-taking is entirely on-line, so a shortage or surplus is shown up within four seconds compared with the previous norm of three days.

Not everything went smoothly at first as cash registers were the only new technology that most of the pub managers had been exposed to up to the time of viewdata's introduction. Viewdata, though, was found to be easy to assimilate and was not beyond the inexperienced user. Once contextual editing and validation against master files had been built into the system, the information produced became reliable. It also became possible for all the managers to input their bar, restaurant and hotel trading data on a Sunday afternoon and for regional managers to interrogate the system from their own homes to gain an overview of company trading.

Photovideotex

This enhancement of existing viewdata systems permits the illustration of subjects by the use of colour TV quality pictures, which are a distinct improvement over the rather 'lumpy' displays that characterize the present viewdata displays. Users will have the advantage of being able to display video presentations of a hotel or restaurant in a potential customer's home or at a travel agent's desk. It will provide, in effect, a 'video brochure' of establishments amongst other uses.

To work effectively, however, the system cannot use telephone lines. It requires leased lines of the Kilostream variety or the forthcoming System X and when this network is fully operational photovideotex will undoubtedly prove more popular than now.

References

ACOM Computer Systems Ltd. Detail of Labour Analyst system.

ADP Hotel Services Ltd, A. Detail of Innmarketing system.

ADP Hotel Services Ltd, B. Detail of Innconference system.

Alvarez, R., Ferguson, D. H. F. and Dunn, J. November 1983. How not to automate your front office. *Cornell Hotel and Restaurant Administration Quarterly*.

Buttle, Francis, 1986. *Hotel and Food Service Marketing*, p. 350. London: Holt Saunders.

Chart Software Ltd. Overview of Check-In system.

Computer Fraud & Security Bulletin, August 1982. Mini bars – maxi bills. Elsevier International Bulletins, Oxford, UK.

Davis, Emily, June 1986. Marketing database – a secret weapon. *Hiliner*.

ERS Technologies Inc. Information on Night Clerk system.

Fretwell-Downing Computer Group. Detail of Space Manager system.

Guestkey. Overview of system.

Hogg, Alan (General Manager, The Londoner Hotel, Welbeck Street, London), October 1986. *Caterer & Hotelkeeper*.

Hotel & Catering Technology, December 1986. Reservations systems.

Hotel & Motel Management, January 1985. Computer says 'No Vacancy' at empty prop.

Landry, Don (Senior Vice President of Marketing and Administration), July 1982. Motor Hotel Management – Eastern Regional Meeting.

Romeo, Peter, October 1981. Public still pressing for 'safer' hotels. *Hotel & Motel Management*.

Schlage Lock Company. Overview of Intellis system.

Tandata Ltd. Detail of Viewdata.

Whitehall, Bruce, 23 October 1986. Hotel systems: pros and cons/all systems go! *Caterer & Hotelkeeper*.

Wood, Richard (Regional Vice President Holiday Inns Reservations and Holidex Europe), Quoted in Reservations systems. *Hotel & Catering Technology*, December 1986.

4 Selecting a Computer System

INTRODUCTION

It seems that every day more computer systems come on to the market to tempt the caterer. Where purchasing is concerned one would expect that the decision making process would be getting easier with all the experience that has been built up. Everywhere new technology is evident, whether it be in the opposition's hotel, or in the fast food hamburger bar in the high street. 'Shouldn't my business be computerized,' the caterer might think, 'after all everyone else is using new technology profitably, aren't they?'

The truth of the matter is that there is an increasing amount of computerization on offer which in itself is quite a problem to a caterer wishing to investigate computerization for the first time. There is a baffling array of hardware and software being sold by various experienced and inexperienced manufacturers and their respective dealers. The wise caterer will have to sift carefully through a multitude of systems before making a particular choice. Careful research will have to be undertaken to make sure that what is likely to be a substantial capital investment is not wasted: there have been many before who have been put out of business because their new technology 'strangled' their operations, for one reason or another.

There is also the problem that whilst there might appear to be a great amount of experience with new technology, out there in the computerized world it is notoriously difficult to locate. There are many individuals who have specific experience of their own particular system but who have little idea of what similar systems might offer. Neither can one rely totally on computer salesmen, as whilst there are very reliable household names involved in the computer industry, there are also those who are attracted by the opportunity to make a quick profit and who have no experience whatsoever of the catering industry. Many caterers have fallen foul of the promises made by 'sharks' who have taken their money and left, leaving the caterer's business more confused than it ever was initially.

It is also a sad fact that the computer industry is not alone in having bad ambassadors. Catering contains a large number of unimpressive and unreliable managers who possess management techniques that are not compatible with new technology.

> The effectiveness of an automated property-management system is directly related to the quality of the management using it: it cannot compensate for management shortcomings and will only accentuate them. In a well-managed hotel, a system is perceived simply as a tool for better performance, while in poorly managed properties, a system often serves as a convenient excuse for all operational problems. (Marko and Moore, 1980)

The caterer's attitude itself can help or hinder the success of computerization. The eventual outcome may be anticipated largely by examining the caterer's existing attitude to work. If the caterer is totally disorganized now then it is unlikely that a computer will greatly assist, but if there are already well established organizational methods then computerization will be that much easier.

> It's better to computerize a good existing manual system. It's no good doing something in a totally different way or the staff will end up on their backs. (Ferrar, 1986)

The problems, therefore, of selecting an appropriate computer system for a particular catering application are considerable but not insurmountable. Caterers are well advised not to rush decisions and to involve themselves with manufacturers and dealers who have a proven track record with catering establishments and who are likely to remain in business long enough to give the very necessary back-up services.

There is no one source of infallible information open to the caterer that can offer impartial advice concerning every possible configuration of computer system on offer. The range and variety of systems does not permit this. Professional advice may be obtained from organizations such as the HCIMA, the HCITB and a whole host of consultants, but it is best for caterers to sit down themselves and draw up specifications and then investigate the field. This is, in the long term, the most reliable method.

Even the smallest of family-run guest houses which currently has an index system, a filing cabinet or a telephone, could benefit from a computer. Quite simply every business can afford a computer. Basic systems are now extremely cheap and becoming commonplace in the home, bringing an elementary word processor well within reach. An elementary business-orientated system can be obtained very reasonably.

We shall discuss the steps the caterer should take in detail in this section of the book.

WHY CONTEMPLATE USING A COMPUTER?

Before we look at buying computers in detail, we should establish some of the benefits that will undoubtedly be the goals of catering managers who are intending to deploy new technology.

In order even to contemplate computerization the caterer will want to know how the proposed system is going to justify its costs and what tangible benefits it will bring to the business and customers. If cost-effectiveness is not proven then there is little purpose in entering a blind alley just for the sake of making use of new technology.

Computers are marvellous machines for undertaking repetitive number-crunching jobs as long as these jobs are logical and well structured. With the benefit of good programming they will provide information that can be processed both quickly and accurately.

Whilst to a new technology cynic there may be some negative aspects to utilizing a computer, these are far outweighed by the benefits that computerization can bring. These potential benefits should be taken into account when the caterer is contemplating the selection of a computer system. The computer, therefore, may bring about a number of essential benefits to the catering business, otherwise new technology should be avoided.

Computer benefits

(a) *No tea-breaks*. Being an inanimate object the computer does not take a tea-break or go on holiday so it undertakes its function as long as it is switched on.

(b) *Donkey work*. The computer can undertake the monotonous paperwork and data collection that has constituted a lot of mundane work for staff in the past. This should free staff for more interesting work and will probably create a more satisfying work existence. Repetitive tasks are made easier.

(c) *Reduced human error*. A computer will cut out many of the opportunities in manual systems for human errors to occur. No longer will there be the need to manually copy certain documents, all of which will be carried out by the computer from the original input. This is especially helpful where accounting applications are concerned.

The very nature of communication by computer takes decisions out of the human mind which has the ability to mis-read figures and transpose them, as well as make other mistakes already mentioned. The more information that is handled by staff the more opportunity there is for error. The computerized system, by relying almost entirely on electronic communication, minimizes these problems.

(d) *Forecasting*. From the build-up of historic data on the business it is possible to produce forecasts of future business which will be more accurate than was previously possible.

(e) *Modelling*. The caterer may well be able to test theories on a computer model before actually placing his actual business at risk. This might show the financial risks or benefits that might be achieved through taking specific policy decisions. A spreadsheet is a common way of undertaking this type of application.

(f) *Access to information*. By providing a central database accessible to a number of staff the computer gives better access to information than might have been possible previously.

(g) *Management efficiency and control*. The management may receive much more relevant information more speedily, enabling them to take managerial decisions that much quicker. A computer will produce a large amount of management information much more rapidly than is possible with manual systems. This should give the manager a clearer picture of the business and facilitate strategic decisions much earlier, thereby improving the overall control of the operation.

(h) *Quality of information*. Information that was difficult to obtain may be accessed more readily provided the computer is programmed correctly.

(i) *Enhanced image*. The work of any member of staff who is involved with paper, such as a secretary or clerk, will be enhanced as the computer can utilize a word processing package to undertake the repetitive work involved in dealing with multiple letters or forms. The presentation of both internal and external documents will be much improved creating a better image.

(j) *Better guest service*. Certainly where important applications such as reservations are concerned, the information held by a computer system should be an improvement over that held by manual systems. Check-in and check-out should be speeded up, as should the complete guest billing system. The accuracy with which computers work will allow the provision of a much better service to one's guests and customers. Bills presented to customers at the completion of their stay are more likely to be accurate, and it should also be possible for reservations to be handled more efficiently thereby reducing the possibility of guests being forgotten or being allocated incorrect accommodation. A much improved personal service can be given to guests by fully utilizing a database for guest history information.

(k) *Cost-effectiveness*. Most caterers will be looking to a computer system to save them money as their primary objective. Savings may be expressed in staff terms or in improvements in cash-flow, such as more efficient operation of the sales ledger.

(l) *Increased revenue*. Whilst this may be similar to cost-effectiveness, the computer should increase the revenue accruing to the hotel as a direct result of many of the advantages outlined in this list.

(m) *Paperless environment*. The old manual paper orientated systems may be largely replaced by the use of a computer which will improve communication throughout a catering business. No longer will pieces of paper be physically transferred around various departments, but electronic messages will be transmitted instead between printers and VDUs.

(n) *Reduced costs*. By the arguments already expressed increased efficiency within the business should undoubtedly reduce costs overall and increase productivity.

(o) *Scope for expansion*. By using a computer system many possibilities will be opened up that would not or could not have arisen otherwise, perhaps revealing opportunities for expansion that previously would not have been evident.

The suppliers themselves will be keen to draw the attention of the caterer to the benefits of their system and a typical justification might be as listed in Figure 4.1.

Some of the benefits to be gained through the HOTEL system include:

- Ease of operation and staff training,

- Fast, efficient guest handling procedures,

- Legible and accurate folios and invoices,

- Accurate information at all times,

- Data need only be entered once,

- Totally integrated hotel operation,

- Extensive analysis and management reports,

- Guest and staff satisfaction,

- Efficient use of staff and improved guest service,

- Lower costs and improved revenue,

- Accurate profit and loss statement,

- Flexible budget and forecasting programs,

- Lower cost to install and operate,

- Greater revenue control,

- Comprehensive sales and marketing reports,

- Faster payment to and from clients,

- Reliable system security and operation,

- Accurate availability and letting at all times,

- Less Manual clerical procedures,

- Efficient support and maintenance from supplier,

○   ○
○ *The full extent to which the HOTEL system may benefit each hotel varies* ○
   depending on the style of management, size of operation, business
○ *pattern and the degree of computerization undertaken, but it is true to* ○
   say that most of the HOTEL system customers have achieved considerable
○ *savings from day one of the system operation and have recovered the*   ○
   initial outlay in a very short period of time.
○   ○

Figure 4.1 *The benefits of the HOTEL systems (CHAMPS, 1986)*

What the caterer has to decide is which particular system gives the most benefits for them and which is therefore the one to buy. As the greatest computerization risk for caterers is often taken when initially selecting the most suitable computer system, they should be aware of some of the potential problems that computerization can bring once installed.

THE SELECTION PROCESS

Caterers should be aware of the inherent problems with computers

Whilst computers in the catering industry have thrown up all sorts of problems over the short period of time in which they have been used, many of these originated from the complete ignorance that caterers had of the technology. This ignorance was unwittingly, or in some cases deliberately, capitalized on by over-zealous salesmen with the result that unreliable hardware and inappropriate software was frequently installed.

Through their ignorance caterers perceived computers as being little more than money savers and hardly realized the implications of applying new technology to a catering situation. In many cases they went for the cheapest products, many of which were totally inadequate. Some installations were undertaken in a rush to get abreast of computerization, without stopping to consider the implications or even what was required of a system.

Whilst many caterers in the early days failed even to identify what their new system would be expected to do, there were and still are some easily overlooked problems in utilizing a computer that are common to all types of catering business. It is quite possible in an initial gush of enthusiasm to be swept along without realizing that there are simple pitfalls to watch out for.

Some computer pitfalls

(a) *Over dependency.* Whatever caterers do they should not destroy all their existing systems that presumably have served the business adequately in the past. It is mistaken to believe that a computer will instantly create an electronic office totally devoid of paper. The caterer will need back-up systems in the event of the computer going down, which will happen despite everything one is told about reliability.

(b) *Resistance to change.* A psychological problem in the implementation of a new or replacement computer system is that the existing staff have been used to carrying out work by their traditional methods. Resistance to change, a common element of human nature, will therefore have to be overcome in installing a new computer system.

(c) *Loss of motivation*. It is quite possible that staff who have happily undertaken a job in the past that they have regarded as challenging will lose their motivation when faced with supplying a faceless machine with data.

(d) *The computer can become a god*. The computer could take over the catering business, becoming more important in the minds of staff than the applications that it was installed to undertake. Computer systems themselves can prove addictive once staff are exposed to them.

Make an initial investigation

It is a common problem with many computer installations that caterers did not really know what they wanted from the computer before they went ahead and bought their system. Numerous computer consultants have been involved in baling companies out of the inevitable results of not defining what they wanted before purchasing their system. Another problem linked with the lack of a clear specification of what was wanted initially is the common failure to realize the true cost of an effective system: many caterers, perhaps as many as half of those who have invested in systems, have found that they are severely undercapitalized. In other words, their system eventually cost about twice what they had originally bargained for.

It is essential from the inception of the computerization project that the caterer select or appoint a single member of staff to act as project leader and coordinate all aspects of system research, specification preparation and eventual installation. This individual will become the focal point for all communication throughout the investigation and eventual running-up of the system so that there is a smooth operational transition. Hopefully the chosen computer supplier will make a similar appointment to ease communication.

Before jumping straight in at the deep end and tailoring the work of the hotel around a computer system, the caterer's project leader should identify the areas of the business that may benefit from computerization. It may well be that a feasibility study will be initiated that should show not only the cost advantages but also the consequent benefits of installing a computer. It is most unwise to rely on intuition.

It would be as well to select those areas of the catering business that lend themselves to computerization and to concentrate on those. The jobs undertaken in a manual system that might be suitable for computerization can be identified as follows:

Repetitive work. Those time consuming jobs that attract large quantities of paper which need to be filed sequentially and referred to regularly for information. Reservations is a typical hotel application of this nature that involves correspondence, confirmations and the production of lists of guests. This is an ideal area for computerization.

Calculations. There will be many financially orientated jobs in the catering business which may involve billing or invoicing of customers. Both income and expenditure may be strictly controlled. There will be the possibility of introducing computerization both to keep track of costs and to maintain the cash-flow of the catering business.

High staff costs. It may well be the case that the business is incurring extra staff costs or that too much overtime is being worked by existing staff because of the cumbersome nature of the present system. In this case a computer may satisfactorily modify the system to the benefit of the overall wage costs.

Draw up a specification

In considering installing a computer it should be remembered that it is potentially a very potent force in helping to manage the establishment and, used properly, will allow a much more economical and efficient method of work. No one should contemplate installing a computer purely because the opposition possesses one or because it is fashionable to own one.

Before one even reaches the time for installation one must go through an intense period of work covering the selection of the right system after the needs of the business have been identified and an analysis made of whether computerization is the right answer to the perceived problems.

Before even contemplating the purchase of a computer, whatever the size, hoteliers or caterers should analyse in detail exactly what it is that they would like the machine to do. This will take the form of a specification against which the range of potential equipment may be compared.

For those caterers familiar with job specifications, as used in the personnel department, exactly the same criteria are applied. For a new member of staff a job specification would list the *essential* qualities and qualifications that would be looked for at interview, as well as details that are *preferred* but not mandatory. In the case of a computer exactly the same process may be undertaken: there will be several requirements considered *essential* as far as the new system is concerned and some facets of the operation that may be *preferred*. The specification will form a vital checklist against which the offerings of the various suppliers may be gauged.

The very first idea that should be firmly fixed in the minds of caterers is to introduce the business to computerization gently and not to invest in too much 'kit' initially. This is not to say that one should not allow for expansion, but one should be modest. Having identified the applications that need to be computerized stick initially to those and purchase extra add-ons when it can be established that they will be useful. Caterers should not try to run before they can walk.

In suggesting to caterers that they should computerize gradually this is not to say that they should not allow for future expansion. In this context, just because a supplier demonstrates a system running on, say, two screens simultaneously, their word should not necessarily be taken that when the company expands the system will run with ten screens.

How shall I start?

One of the worries for busy caterers is how to construct such a specification and fit together a strategic plan for the installation of a computer system which they may be committed to but which may not be so readily acceptable to their colleagues and staff.

The following schedule may help:

- Identify and educate influential decision making people within the business and include them in the plan.
- Analyse in detail the requirements of the computer system in the particular workplace asking such questions as:
  - What is needed?
  - What must the computer system do?
  - Should I examine one system that can undertake many tasks or should I go for a modular system that can be built up, application by application, over a period of time?

- Make use of information from experts in the industry such as consultants.
- Look closely and methodically at all the products on offer that seem suitable to the needs of the business.
- Make direct comparisons between the alternatives and draw up a short list.
- Draw up a cost justification analysis of the short-listed products as the cost implications are always paramount.
- Once a product is selected draw up a carefully worded contract so that sales promises are translated into actual product performance.
- Be sure that the installation schedule is practical within the operational requirements of the business.
- Make one person wholly responsible for the management of the installation.

THE SUPPLIERS

The number of hotel and catering computer system suppliers seems to be constantly on the increase and therefore the array of hardware and software is often baffling. An estimate was made in 1986 that there were 29 UK companies actively involved in the sale of large front office systems to hotels, whilst there were 38 companies offering microcomputer-based systems. This makes the British front office system marketplace one of the most hotly contested in the world (Gamble, 1986).

With this statistic in mind, it can be seen how important it is for caterers to know clearly in advance what they want in their system so that they can best benefit from the purchasing situation rather than being at the mercy of the supplier. The caterer should also be aware of the potential problems of buying from a selection of suppliers rather than solely from one (*Which Computer*, 1984).

It is often beneficial to use one single supplier for the complete computer system. One will therefore be obtaining the software, hardware, installation, training and support from the same company, which can only cut down on the communication problems that might be involved if separate companies were involved. If different parts of the system are obtained from different suppliers who can be blamed if something goes wrong? It is a distinct benefit with a single supplier that all the parts of the system will be compatible and there will be no opportunity for the supplier to blame somebody else if one part of the system fails.

On the other hand, some caterers will argue that they have good systems because they have bought separately and one must respect their views. If one shops around, though, despite the attraction of the lower prices that may be achieved it may mean that at least one supplier is remotely situated, which will possibly reduce their ability to give a swift and reliable maintenance service. Whether one buys centrally or from a selection of sources the supplier or suppliers must fulfil certain criteria before being selected.

- long-term stability
- performance to date

Where suppliers are concerned their *long-term stability* should be examined as it is not uncommon for new technology companies to go into liquidation or to cease trading. This is not going to be much use to caterers if they are left with a system for which there is no maintenance cover or which cannot be repaired or enhanced.

The first major question, which will allow a list of potential suppliers to be drawn up, will be to ask them for their *performance to date*. It is wise to establish that the company has successfully installed its products in a range of similar establishments and therefore knows what it is doing. The potential supplier should be asked outright how many systems they have installed.

Specific installations should then be investigated to see whether in reality they match up to the supplier's claims. A reputable supplier will willingly furnish a list of previous customers and these will be excellent contacts to check what a system actually does in practice, whether it is the type of system required, and whether the salesman has been making rash claims or not. Something to watch out for in investigating previous installations is whether the system has been upgraded, evidence of which will indicate that there is long-term satisfaction with the equipment.

Most computer users will be more than willing to talk about their system – the benefits as well as the problems – knowing full well that they may be in a similar situation themselves one day. The sort of questions to ask the existing user include:

- Would you consider purchasing the same system again?
- How long did it take to get the system operational?
- What sort of assistance did you receive from the supplier?
- How much did you know about computers before installing the present system?

By formally contacting these people, without involving the salesman, caterers can make sure that the details of maintenance agreements, the cost of stationery and the amount of training required by staff actually match up to what has been indicated. They will obtain a very clear picture of which systems are worthy of more detailed investigation for their particular range of applications.

It would generally be very unwise to be a guinea pig for a new system, as even though it may be cheap it will be tested at the potential expense of your business. You do not, after all, want your business to suffer whilst the supplier irons out the bugs in the hardware and software.

One useful way to compare computer systems on offer from suppliers is to construct a spreadsheet with comparative statistics and costs so that easy reference may be made to the disadvantages and advantages of each individual system. This arrangement of information will reveal areas for future discussion with the supplier where, for example, gaps in the comparative detail might exist.

Compare computer systems at a trade exhibition

One of the best ways to compare equipment on offer is to attend a computer exhibition where it will be possible to examine similar systems under the same roof. By establishing in advance the areas of the business that require computerization time will not be lost in visiting irrelevant stands and a true short list will be created. Whilst a large amount of information will be gathered, remember that any demonstrations given will be designed to highlight the best features of the system under examination. There will also be too little time to gain a complete insight such is the pressure of time at an exhibition.

Whilst talking directly to a manufacturer rather than a supplier there are a number of questions that it is important to ask so that a clear picture may be obtained:

- How many users do you have in the UK?
- How much does a working system cost, including all extras such as interface cables?
- What is the delivery time?

- How long is the guarantee period?
- Who provides engineering and training support?
- Is installation on the caterer's premises included in the price?

Purchasing considerations

In what sort of package can I buy a computer system from a supplier?

There are several ways in which a system may be purchased and it is not necessary for all the components to come from a single supplier. Indeed it is not even always necessary to actually purchase and to be able to make use of a system might be sufficient. The most common ways to arrange the use of a computer are as follows:

(a) Buy time at a computer service bureau.
It is quite possible to find a service bureau with spare computer space for hire. One must be careful, though, to ensure that there is total unrestricted access to the computer at all times. It may be the case that it is cheaper to use a service bureau for specific functions that are not available on the in-house system, such as a ledger payment facility. This type of arrangement was very popular in the early days of computing when the costs were much higher. Nowadays, it is probably more cost-effective to utilize a minicomputer or a series of microcomputers.

(b) Buy hardware and commission own bespoke software.
Buying hardware and tailor-made software is a popular option amongst those caterers who want to fashion programs around their own business. The drawback is that relatively few caterers have either the time or expertise to program their own systems, and the cost of hiring a programmer or a software house often proves too high when comparing bespoke software with package software.

(c) Buy hardware and software, the latter being capable of modification by the caterer.
The idea of being able to modify an existing package software program appeals to those caterers who have the expertise to modify programs themselves. The advantage is that most of the major decisions will already have been taken in producing the package software and the caterer will only have to undertake the fine tuning. If the caterer does not have the expertise himself, however, the costs of hiring qualified staff can prove a drawback, although probably not so serious as in option (b).

(d) Buy hardware and pre-prepared package software from different suppliers.
Being provided with hardware and software from different sources may not be a bad thing, but it does bring the problem of having separate support agreements. Arguments can occur when the hardware manufacturer blames the software manufacturer for a problem and vice versa.

(e) Buy a complete system from one supplier.
Buying a complete system from one supplier is probably the ideal way administratively to make use of a computer system. Provided the supplier is reliable then there is only one person to deal with when support is required. If caterers require as simple a life as possible with computerization then this is the method for them.

Are there any hidden costs that I should watch out for?

Whilst the hardware and software costs of a system are usually straightforward, there are some extra financial aspects that must be examined. These include any building alterations that might be required to facilitate installation, training of existing staff, special stationery, maintenance agreements and insurance.

COMPUTER INSTALLATION

It must be appreciated by the caterer that, whatever the size of the system, it will be impossible to install it instantly. Sometimes quite impossible deadlines are promised to senior management by inexperienced staff charged with the installation of new technology. These are often younger staff who, because of their age, are supposed to know about computers as far as wary senior executives are concerned. Potential users often make this mistake and expect the impossible. Whilst senior management may want computerization to be instantaneous, this is never a practical possibility as the whole system, whether mainframe or micro, will have to be run-in gradually, even though the eventual changeover may take place at a specific time.

Experienced suppliers who have installed a large number of computers can help immensely with scheduling the introduction of a new computer system. This will undoubtedly be one of the benefits of using a well known company specializing in the catering field.

The supplier can advise on how to phase the installation of a system that may involve a series of departments and therefore separate computer modules. If the department initially selected for computerization shows swift benefits, this can be of psychological importance in putting other departments in the establishment in the right frame of mind for their eventual computerization.

The most important consideration when choosing the time to install the computer system is when it will create the least possible disruption. Never, for example, plan installation for the same week as the year-end accounts are required or when there are similar peaks of business. The caterer will presumably want to arrange installation for a slack or quiet period. In a resort hotel this is not too much of a problem, but in a popular busy catering outlet there may be some difficulty in finding an appropriate time. In coming to a decision it is important to keep the supplier informed so that delivery of the system is worked into the supplier's schedule around the date required. Failure to do this will lead not only to operational problems but also to a probable spiralling of costs.

Other options are to install the system whilst the business is running normally, whilst alterations are taking place anyway, or ideally when the catering business itself is in its construction phase.

Installation whilst the business is fully operational

It is more than likely that the installation of the system will have to take place whilst the business is operational and the majority of systems are, unfortunately, installed in this way. It will still be necessary to pick as quiet a period as possible to 'go live': some caterers prefer to make the actual changeover itself at night.

Installation during alterations

If the computer is installed while alterations are being made, this will presumably be during a quiet period in the business. Apart from anything else, it will be better to have the two sets of engineers working at the same time and consequently out of the way quicker, rather than having to endure interference to the business for two separate periods of time. It is also an excellent idea to run-in a system at this time while there is a limited amount of business going on. There will be fewer possibilities of mistakes being made as there will be a lower number of transactions to be recorded in total.

Installation during construction

To be able to install a system when the building for a new catering operation is being constructed would be ideal, but is by no means always possible especially when an existing system is being replaced. Any caterer lucky enough to be in this situation should make the most of it. A major point is that all capital costs can be included in the building and a clear budget for the costings established. Should any departments need to be designed around the system then this will be possible at the outset rather than having to adapt existing facilities. Also the costs will be more easily absorbed at this stage.

Where installation is concerned, the actual staff involvement should be considered carefully. Whilst it will be beneficial for a single member of staff to be the initial project coordinator or leader, once the system has arrived it would be dangerous to leave that person in sole control. What would happen, for example, if the project leader were to go sick or take a holiday? The staff left behind would inevitably flounder. If the same member of staff holds the security codes in their head, this could lead to the whole system grinding to a halt in their absence.

It is beneficial to have manuals containing all codes and operational details available to management. One should not rely purely on the manufacturer's manuals – which are frequently inadequate – but should draw up one's own manual tailored to the individual business that is easily understandable by all the staff. At least three senior members of staff should have a complete working knowledge of the system to cover the possibility of one or more being incapacitated. If any should leave the caterer's employ then another member of staff should be trained to take their place.

PHYSICAL ALTERATIONS THAT A COMPUTER MIGHT NECESSITATE

High profile or low profile?

One of the major decisions in the installation of a computer system is whether the customer should be made aware of its existence or not. Some hoteliers feel that the presence of computers tends to remove the personal nature of their business, whilst others see computer systems as partly a public relations exercise illustrating that their business is modern and businesslike.

Whilst there is no specific answer to this question, the policy decision has to be made. If the system is to be hidden from view this has to be catered for at installation time, remembering that the staff must be able to work in as efficient a way as possible.

Is a separate computer suite needed?

The term 'computer systems' often conjures up the picture of a huge computer centre with a strictly controlled environment. Whilst it is true that the initial systems were very sensitive to heat and humidity this is no longer always the case. Mainframes need to be allocated their own suite, not necessarily for environmental reasons but for security. Specialized air conditioning may therefore not be necessary, although some suppliers do stipulate that their systems should operate within specified heat and humidity tolerances.

It is certainly the case, though, that every computer system should be exposed to as little dust, grease or grime as possible as a build-up of these can lead to major problems. Some hotel computer systems have gone out of action purely because of a build-up of dust. Quite often the heat extractor fan on the computer itself not only performs the function for which it was designed but also draws dust into the machine. The best policy is to isolate the processor in as dust-free a room as possible.

In creating a computer suite one of the considerations should be prevention of fire, especially as so much electrical equipment is involved. The normal ways of extinguishing a fire are of no use; for example, sprinklers utilizing water would completely destroy both the hardware and software. Major computer systems should be capable of being isolated so that a fire extinguishing gas such as Halon can be flooded into the confined atmosphere.

The importance of the carpet

Whilst most computer users are well aware of the importance of maintaining a suitable atmosphere for their computer systems few would actually contemplate details such as the carpet that the machine will be placed on, but this can be most important (Van de Pijpekamp, 1986/7).

It is not widely realized that a floor-covering that is unsuitable could result in the following problems that might affect the data processing capability of the computer:

- static electricity
- static discharge

More than 60 per cent of computer downtime is caused by static electricity, and nearly 25 per cent of systems are 'retired early' due to static damage. (D.P. Media Services)

The first question that caterers might ask themselves is what is static electricity? The simple answer is that it is a form of electric charge created when two dissimilar materials are rubbed together and then pulled apart. This can happen when people walk on carpets and their shoes are lifted. The charge is released when the person touches a conductor such as a metal stair rail giving a tingling sensation. Temperature and humidity affect the amount of the charge given off but it can be as high as 35 kV. Table 4.1 gives some typical static voltages created in a working environment.

Table 4.1 *Typical static voltages (at 10 to 20 per cent relative humidity)*

Static source	Voltage
Walking across carpet	35,000
Walking over vinyl floor	12,000
Worker at desk	6,000
Picking up a polythene bag	20,000
Work chair with a polyurethane padding	18,000

Source: D.P. Media Services

As can be seen from Table 4.1, static electricity is part of everyday life in a catering establishment, and in most situations it is completely harmless. However, the latest microchip computers operate on currents of less than 10 volts. Whilst all humans generate static to some degree, and this must be discharged somewhere, the computer could be the unwitting recipient of over 20,000 volts. A charge of less than 250 volts can in some circumstances cause memory loss, resets and permanent damage to microchips.

Realizing this problem some carpet and mat manufacturers now produce 'permanent' antistatic carpets made of polyamide yarn, the pile material of which has carbon modified components. Unfortunately these carpets will allow a discharge of 2 kV which is still enough to affect some computers.

If a carpet is not suitable for a situation then there are antistatic mats which come equipped with a 3-metre earthing lead and a 1-megohm resistor to conduct high voltage charges safely out of harm's way. Some mats are made from a black conductive carbon-based vinyl, whilst others are made from transparent vinyl with an inlaid carbon grid to drain static instantly.

There are now carpets that ensure permanent elimination of the adverse effects of static charges by containing antistatic additives. Combined with a conductive backing system these carpets are claimed by the manufacturer to be very effective and should be seriously considered for any room containing sensitive computer equipment.

CLEAN ELECTRICITY

One of the most common causes of data loss from a computer is fluctuation in the electricity supply which, despite being very reliable from the CEGB, is subject to a number of problems (D.P. Media Services, 1987):

- electricity consumers receive on average 1,000 peaks of over 2,000 volts per annum
- there are over 40 supply interruptions per minute
- over 46 million consumer hours are lost in one year

When one also considers the problems of Radio Frequency Interference (RFI or 'noise') which can corrupt data within a computer system then there is a potential problem for all caterers reliant upon new technology.

If one operates a hotel or catering establishment in an area such as the Caribbean then electrical surges and 'brownouts' are so commonplace they become a way of life. Unless the establishment is blessed with a universal power supply, downtime as a direct consequence of bad electrical supply may be considerable. Even closer to home the problems that PCs experience due to electrical surges are illustrated by the following quotation:

'With many PCs and add-ons, it is estimated that about 50 per cent of all faults are caused by power supply irregularities. Most larger machines have provision for this but smaller units are often neglected or forgotten as far as the importance of power supplies goes.' (Turner, 1987)

Devices to protect a computer system and particularly microcomputers are readily available and range from a basic plug that fits into a normal socket which the computer is then plugged into, to major battery packs which maintain a system in the total absence of power. Some devices promise a clean uninterruptable supply of power to a computer for 13 minutes from a sealed maintenance-free battery. The battery back-up is intended to give the caterer time to shut down the system 'softly' without data loss. The back-up waits off-line and should a power loss occur it cuts in after 2 milliseconds and before the computer is affected.

67 DAYS TO INSTALL A RESTAURANT COMPUTER SYSTEM

The particular restaurant operation in this case study was a busy lunchtime business offering a silver service restaurant and a coffee shop. These services possessed separate kitchens but shared a bar.

The total operation already possessed a property management system (PMS) minicomputer which handled the accommodation function. It was decided at an early stage that the new computer system for the restaurants should interface with the PMS as a matter of priority so that residents' food bills could be posted directly to their main accounts.

Past problems

The restaurant operation had previously installed a Local Area Network utilizing PCs, but this had proved unreliable. The staff had therefore turned their backs on the system, preferring their manual method of work. The restaurant had actually been a 'guinea pig' for the system, but the time and finance that could be justified to make the system reliable finally ran out.

In effect the restaurant management had made most of the classic mistakes in installing the Local Area Network. They had failed to:

- use hardware and software from a recognized market leader in the restaurant business
- recognize the specific skills needed to run-up a system using staff in-house
- appoint one single person to oversee installation and implementation who had a knowledge of both computers and food and beverage management
- look into the future to anticipate the need to link the network with other computers in the establishment
- appreciate the operational problems of using a 'guinea pig' system
- create an adequate budget for full implementation of the system and accurately estimate the finances that would be required

System selection

The management of the restaurant and coffee shop were aware that if computerization were one day to be successfully applied to their operation then they had to keep abreast of the latest systems. They visited exhibitions and avidly read the trade press in the UK and USA to see which systems would eventually be applicable.

Day 1 – The decision to replace the existing system is made

As luck would have it, the decision to replace the unreliable network came unexpectedly at the end of a financial year when the necessary budget became available. The only problem was that purchase and implementation had to take place rapidly in order to take advantage of the finance available.

At least the management had not been caught off guard and were well aware of the systems on the market. Indeed they had examined several systems operating in similar establishments and knew the advantages and pitfalls. They also had a good idea as to which was the best system on the market for their purposes.

Because of the importance of the interface with the PMS the range of possible systems was necessarily limited. One system stood out but to make sure management sought advice from the PMS minicomputer supplier as to what systems would best interface with their equipment. A short list of four firms was eventually drawn up. Three of these firms had existing interfaces available, whilst a fourth firm's system did not interface but so good was their computer that it was hoped that they might agree to construct an interface if they were chosen.

After detailed analysis of the four companies two were disregarded. Their total packages were considered mediocre and in both cases there was little opportunity to expand the systems in the future to take on further applications. The two remaining systems included the one lacking an available PMS interface; the other was the market leader in restaurants whose equipment was familiar to many of the staff as well as the management.

The final selection of supplier was largely taken out of the hands of the restaurant management. The remaining field of two was whittled down to one when the company that at the time did not have an interface for the PMS minicomputer promised to make an appointment to discuss their system. This company took too long to come back to confirm an appointment with the result that they deselected themselves as they had run out of time if implementation were to be completed by the necessary deadline.

Contact was made with existing users

It had been decided at the outset that any potentially useful systems would be checked out before any sales people visited the restaurants. Even though the field had been reduced to one runner it was still felt necessary to contact existing users of the system. The names of users were listed in the supplier's sales material and therefore the management of one establishment was contacted for their remarks.

The response was positive. The establishment contacted had found the system to be an excellent one that interfaced easily with other computers and was far simpler to use than any other computer system designed for restaurants. The training offered by the supplier was very good and the response to maintenance calls was very swift. The system required the full attention of a computer supervisor each day to set it up and there were opportunities for it to be mis-used if the hotelier was not vigilant. The only parts that needed replacing regularly, which were expensive, were the ribbons; stationery was expensive too. It was always important to keep the paper rolls in the remote printers topped up otherwise the whole system would shut down after a period of 45 minutes. To be fair, though, the computer did give adequate warning of the shut down well in time to alert staff. It was possible to add-on the facility to cost menus and undertake food and beverage control but the establishment did not make use of this. Overall the system was excellent and had been running successfully at the establishment for six years.

A personal visit was made to view a system in another establishment with similar requirements. There too the response was encouraging where practical usage as well as overall operation of the computer was concerned.

It was therefore decided to investigate this system further, even though it was felt ironic that the opposition had in effect disqualified themselves. The restaurant management still needed to be convinced that the system could be installed effectively and at the right price by the deadline. The option after all was still there to ignore computerization and continue with the manual method of work. The supplier was invited to visit the restaurants as soon as possible to make a presentation and discuss implementation.

Day 8 – Supplier's visit

The selected supplier arranged a date for their head office consultant to visit the operation within eight days of the initial enquiry. It was regarded as significant that the supplier was motivated sufficiently to arrange a personal visit so quickly, as this indicated a favourable attitude towards the urgent installation that would be required. This impression was indicative of the way the supplier worked and no customer could accuse them of being either tardy or lacking in enthusiasm. The schedule agreed with the consultant for the day was as follows:

- 11.00 am–12.30 pm   Examine existing restaurant operation and discuss possible configurations and options.
- 12.30 pm– 2.00 pm   Meeting with middle management over lunch to form policy and select options.
- 2.00 pm– 3.00 pm   Meeting with senior management and directors to hopefully reach final decision and discuss implementation.

11.00 am–12.30 pm

On arrival the consultant was met by middle management and briefed on additional criteria that needed to be fulfilled by the new system. The criteria included:

- rapid implementation
- an interface with the PMS minicomputer
- full training for a sufficient number of staff
- an adequate maintenance contract
- a limited budget

The consultant was shown around the operation by the member of staff entrusted with the implementation of the system. Detailed examination was made of the layout and the number of customers served on each station in the à la carte restaurant then the coffee shop. The number of staff involved was taken into account in planning the quantity and positioning of peripheral hardware such as terminals. In each restaurant the way in which cash was handled was examined to see whether there would need to be any change in operational policy or whether the computer could be tailored to the existing work methods.

Next each kitchen was visited and finally the bar which was to be equipped with a link to the computer system. The bar rarely served cash drinks, although there had to be a facility to cope with this infrequent eventuality which only really occurred when functions were held on the premises. The bar was normally concerned with serving drinks to restaurant customers to accompany their meals and was therefore mainly a dispense bar. A location for the main processor was identified in a small office alongside the restaurant where the management terminal and screen could also be sited. This was regarded as ideal because of its close proximity to the potential sites for the terminals which would cut down considerably on the amount of cabling required.

In each area the possible location for terminals and printers was discussed, as was the availability of an electrical supply. This is when one of the extra costs of installing the system became apparent. The computer supplier undertook neither the work of altering the mains electrical supply to reach each terminal nor that of running the cabling between the processor and the many peripheral devices. The restaurant was expected to organize both of these elements of the system and indeed a separate electrical ring main to provide 'clean' electricity was recommended. The computer supplier would fit the system devices once all the wiring had been completed.

The housing of the various terminals and printers was also of importance as the existing hot cupboards in the restaurant and servery areas in the kitchens were felt unsuitable. They tended to be too close to working areas where hot food and liquids were handled which could in extreme circumstances prove harmful to the terminals. If sited incorrectly the terminals could also severely reduce staff working space which was at a premium. A carpenter was therefore required to customize the housings for the various devices.

Detailed questions were put to the consultant concerning the operation of the system, including:

- Was the system compatible with the existing electricity supply?
- Would the eventual price cover:
    - insurance?
    - warranty?
    - installation?
- What would the cost of stationery be and did it have to come from the computer supplier?
- What would be the cost of maintenance and would there be a 24 hour service?
- What back-up was there if the system went down?
- How 'idiot-proof' was the system?
- Were menu items selected by pre-select keys or by the use of numbers on the keyboard?
- How flexible was the system to cope with menus that changed daily?
- What information would the system give on:
    - sales mix?
    - theoretical gross profit?
    - gross profit for each menu item?
    - analysis of sales?
    - analysis of productivity?
    - sales per member of waiting staff?
- Would the system eventually link to a facility for volume forecasting, purchase orders and stores?
- How does the system raise a bill and how effective is this?
- How many covers can the system handle?
- How secure is the system from theft?
- Would the system one day allow the use of handheld terminals?

12.30 pm–2.00 pm

Over a social lunch with the middle management the consultant roughly costed out the various configurations of system that could be considered. The options discussed included:

- Installing a total system as soon as possible.
- Installing a system in the coffee shop only and in other areas in future financial years.
- Reducing the number of terminals to a bare minimum to keep costs down.
- Installing a system omitting the bar.
- Installing a system without the facility to handle cash in the bar.

All of the above alternatives were costed but it was decided to approach the directors with a request for a complete system. The main element of all the options was the central processor which was the single most expensive piece of hardware, and it was therefore decided that the small cost savings offered by the other scenarios were too insignificant to contemplate.

2.00 pm–3.00 pm

The meeting in the boardroom commenced with an internal discussion while the consultant waited outside. The conclusions of the morning's discussions were analysed and broad agreement reached. Whilst it was accepted in principle that the particular company was offering a system that was well worth installing, there were elements of the costings that needed further examination. For example, the individual costs of some peripherals seemed very high compared with the prices paid for similar equipment in other non-catering applications with which the directors were familiar.

On being invited to join the meeting the consultant was asked to justify the costs of certain items of equipment such as the terminals. The higher cost was because they were specifically designed for a catering situation, being liquid- and heat-resistant and also protected against deliberate damage in most cases. This led on to a discussion of the maintenance agreement which specifically excluded vandalism or negligence by restaurant staff. Insurance should cover this problem, as had happened at one existing installation where a member of the waiting staff had felt threatened by the new computer and attacked a terminal with a knife. A very positive point regarding maintenance was that the agreement allowed a spare terminal and printer to be kept on the premises so they could be installed quickly in the event of a hardware failure, thereby obviating the lengthy wait for the engineer to arrive and restore the system.

The details of staff training were discussed, as well as the practicality and costs of interfacing with the PMS minicomputer. Eventually overall agreement was reached and the consultant requested to submit a written quotation as soon as possible confirming all the details.

Day 10 – The full quotation is received

On examination this matched exactly with the discussions during the consultant's visit and there were no surprises. The quotation was rapidly signed and accepted to allow installation to go ahead.

Day 21 – The installation site visit

With the paperwork signed and tied up the next step was for a site visit to be undertaken so that all the necessary parties to installation could get together. Unfortunately, it was impossible for the electrical contractors to be present at the agreed time and the meeting had to go ahead without them. The site visit therefore included the systems consultant and installation manager from the computer suppliers, the system supervisor and heads of section from the restaurant, and the computer wiring contractor.

A tour was made of the restaurants, kitchen and coffee shop identifying the locations of all the hardware for the installation manager who was new to the site. Points were raised as follows:

Management centre

This was to be in an office between the restaurant and the kitchen. As it stood this location was too warm as there was a large number of hot pipes in one wall. Ventilation was therefore required to keep the temperature below 30 °C (86 °F) which was the maximum operating temperature of the management centre. The system also needed a dedicated external phone line so that remote fault diagnosis could take place as part of the maintenance and support package.

There was a need for a 'clean' electrical supply at this source, from which a dedicated ring main would run to each peripheral device. It was emphasized that if a dedicated ring main were not provided, as per the supplier's instructions, this would affect the maintenance agreement. All the wiring linking devices would run from the management centre base on a 'star' arrangement rather than on a ring.

Restaurants

Discussion here centred on the precise location of each terminal, printer and cash drawer and the experience of the heads of section was solicited. It became apparent that specialized furniture would have to be made and therefore a carpenter would have to be consulted, which could be a hold up to installation.

Kitchens

Whilst the kitchens only required the siting of printers these had to be located away from busy work areas but close at hand for the chefs producing the orders received. It was deliberately decided to avoid cutting into stainless steel work tops on the grounds of cost and to locate the printers in their own furniture.

Day 24 – Installation details arrive from supplier

Very detailed instructions, including a sample of the necessary wiring, were received from the supplier enabling detailed electrical and carpentery contracts to be negotiated. So good was the information that very little had to be added to the technical drawings in order to put potential contractors in the picture. The swift and detailed paperwork back-up speeded up the whole process tremendously and demonstrated the wisdom of utilizing an experienced system supplier.

Day 27 – Meeting with electrical contractor

With the aid of the supplier's excellent wiring diagrams the electrical contractor was briefed on the dedicated 'clean' circuit that was required and an acceptable quotation was received. As luck would have it, electricians were already on-site working on another electrical installation and therefore the computer installation could just be added to the work schedule already in hand.

Day 29 – Meeting with carpenter

The restaurant's carpenter was called in to inspect the sites for the various pieces of furniture that were required. The main problem here was communicating the need for such furniture to someone who was not familiar with computers. Very detailed drawings, based on those provided by the computer supplier, and instructions had to be given as to the locations and usage of all the required pieces of furniture. A sample drawing can be seen in Figure 4.2, followed by a photo of the finished installation. Those items that were to be in public view had to be made of materials that would fit into the decor, whilst those in kitchen areas had to be constructed with hygiene in mind.

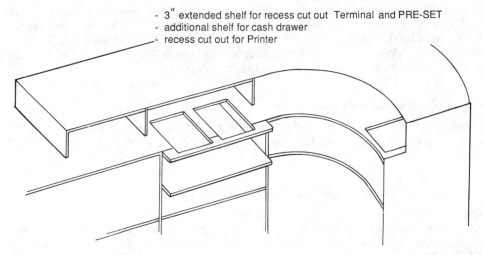

- 3″ extended shelf for recess cut out Terminal and PRE-SET
- additional shelf for cash drawer
- recess cut out for Printer

Figure 4.2 *Detailed drawing for the carpenter from the computer system manufacturer of the bar installation. The required server terminal, preset keyboard, cash drawer and order printer required holes to be cut in the existing shelves*

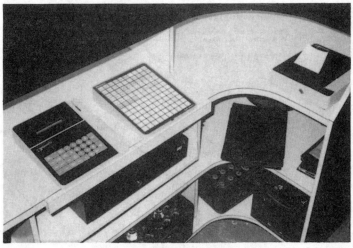

The finished bar installation
Photograph: Bruce Grant-Braham

Days 35 to 37 – Electrical installation

The dedicated 'clean' electrical system was completed using top quality fittings, especially trunking, bearing in mind the health and safety requirements in working and public areas.

Day 44 – Meeting with software supervisor

The supplier's software supervisor met with the restaurant's system supervisor on-site to discuss the codings to be used by the system to identify such details as the various drinks and dishes that the computer would be recording. A sheet was left for completion and subsequent return to the supplier containing all details of menu items. This was completed by the restaurant's system supervisor.

Day 53 – Data cables installed

The data cabling between the site of the management centre and the various peripherals was installed in one day. The engineer labelled each cable so that the supplier's field engineer could save time connecting the system up the following week.

Days 56 and 57 – Furniture and hardware installation

With the supplier's field engineer in attendance, the necessary furniture was assembled and fitted. It was a great advantage to have both the carpenter and field engineer there at the same time so that detail could be discussed and catered for, rather than the carpenter going ahead and then alterations needing to be made at a later date. The field engineer's experience in installing many similar systems was invaluable. It was also appreciated at this stage how detailed and useful the drawings were that had been sent by the supplier.

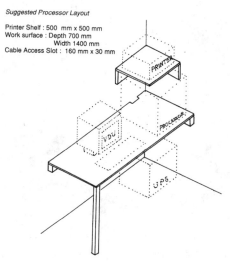

Suggested Processor Layout

Printer Shelf : 500 mm x 500 mm
Work surface : Depth 700 mm
Width 1400 mm
Cable Access Slot : 160 mm x 30 mm

Figure 4.3 *Whilst following the installation diagrams to the letter . . .*

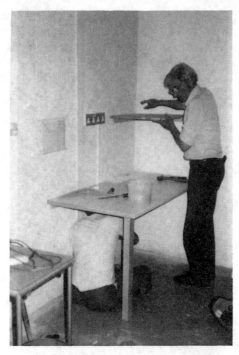

. . . the carpenter works on the management centre shelving as the field engineer makes the electrical connections
Photograph: Bruce Grant-Braham

The only problem encountered at this time was the need to stop work during meal service when the noise of drills and electric jig-saws would not have been compatible with the restaurant operation.

Once the management centre was connected to all the peripherals the field engineer left a test program running for several days to fully test the cables, terminals and printers. This was to run non-stop until day 64.

Days 64 to 66 – Staff Training

For three days the supervisors of the system from the restaurant and coffee shop were given detailed on-site training by the staff of the computer manufacturer. The training involved detailed simulations of every aspect of the system so that they would be able to operate fully from the start-up date.

Day 67 – The system goes 'live'

With the computer company's training staff in attendance the system went 'live' during service. The staff in general had been given an induction course of about an hour's duration before service and they found this quite adequate. Whilst there were one or two teething problems these were minor and were staff-orientated rather than stemming from the hardware or software.

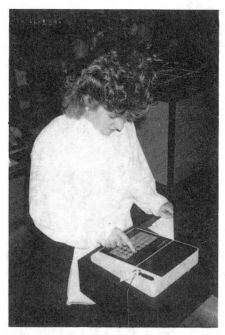

Server terminals are used for the first time . . .

. . . and the management centre runs its first service analysis
Photographs: Bruce Grant-Braham

Summary

Whilst the system went live within 67 days from the first embryo idea there were still a couple of additional features to be added which came a few days later. These included a modem to allow direct connection of the management centre to the computer company headquarters for direct diagnostic help in the case of problems. This was not installed until the final maintenance agreement had been signed and agreed. Also the interface to the PMS computer was to come some time later once problems of distance between processors had been overcome.

As regards the eventual cost of the system this worked out proportionally as follows:

- computer hardware and software   76%
- furniture   5%
- dedicated 'clean' electrical installation   5%
- cables   2%
- stationery   1%
- annual maintenance charge   11%

SUPPORT

Not only should the capacity of the potential new system be examined but also such criteria as the supplier's reliability record.

- Is there an adequate maintenance agreement that will provide a fast and yet efficient service in the event of something going wrong?
- Does the manufacturer offer sufficient support to cover the computer for its entire working life even when newer technology overtakes it?
- Can the supplier provide adequate training facilities for staff?

If the supplier can offer adequate support for his system this should mean that his staff are distributed at strategic geographical locations and there should be sufficient of them to cover the total number of installations. An adequate response time for hotels in particular is necessary as, like many catering businesses, they operate throughout the day and night. If the computer were to go down and the maintenance response was too slow untold harm could be done to the business. A maximum response time of as short a period as possible should be insisted upon. Most reputable companies will react to a call out extremely quickly, but the caterer should watch out for the costs involved. Full maintenance agreements are not cheap.

Once the computer is installed the supplier must be able to demonstrate that there is a commitment to the future and that the caterer is not going to be left on his own. Both the hardware and software will require continuous support and this should be costed in at the commencement of the negotiations so that there are no sudden shocks where labour or parts charges are concerned. These costs should be included right from the start.

Where overall costs are concerned one has to be realistic in the estimates reached at the time of purchase. The caterer should examine whether a large microcomputer is a more cost-effective solution than a minicomputer as it may well cost much less. It should also be born in mind that package software will be much cheaper than having special software created for the establishment.

What will the computer be required to do?

It is a very common error when analysing the demands that will be put on to the computer to overlook potential growth within the business. Whilst the catering company may have plans for expansion, often this is not allowed for at the time that the computer is purchased. It is therefore always necessary to look ahead so that the system purchased will cope with what is being contemplated. It would be unwise to install a system that needed to be replaced rapidly because the business had outgrown the computer's capacity. It is too easy to base plans for a computer system on history rather than the future.

Another of the problems commonly identified with all types of computer system are the unexpected demands actually created. Once staff become used to a computer system it is not uncommon for them to demand new and unanticipated applications so that the original capacity is quickly exceeded. Equally, management will suddenly be presented with such comprehensive information that they themselves may create an insatiable demand for information that clogs up printers with immense print runs of management reports.

The possible links that the computer may be required to fulfil in the future are of importance in selecting the correct machine. Is the computer compatible, for example, with existing personal computers already in use in the business, or will it link happily with the head office computer or the marketing consortium's central reservations computer that the hotel utilizes? Is the computer flexible enough to cope with the demands that may be placed upon it in the next five or six years?

One of the best policies for an establishment that is unsure of the future may be to invest in a modular computer system. This means that one area may be computerized initially and then added on to in other areas as the need arises and as, perhaps, the initial applications are mastered. It may even be possible, provided the correct choice was made at the outset, to add on new applications without having to replace the central processor.

The caterer would be wise firstly to examine the software that is on offer and if this suits the establishment then move on to examine the hardware on which it may be run.

THE IMPORTANCE OF COMPUTER MAINTENANCE

One of the first questions that the potential user of a computer system should ask is how reliable is the system?

If the purveyor of the system tries to maintain that it is totally reliable and will never go 'down' then there is something wrong: no computer on its own is totally reliable.

The catering industry, anyway, will impose major strains on any computer system. If, as in the case of early catering computers, a system developed in outside industry where a cosy 9.00 to 5.00 existence is the norm is suddenly exposed to constant hotel use throughout the day and night, then the time taken to come across the first faults will be dramatically reduced. Simply, the system will be put under much more pressure and quantity of work in a much shorter time than would have been the case in other industries. It must be remembered that whether we are referring to the largest mainframe or the smallest micro, in the hospitality industry the computer will take a tremendous battering in a comparatively short period of time. There is therefore considerable need for a maintenance contract to be drawn up.

It could be argued that parts of the system, such as the processor itself, will be needlessly covered by a maintenance contract as they will hardly ever go wrong. The high risk parts are the printers and disk drives and it is likely that these will show up faults, if there are going to be any, during the guarantee period.

Luckily, common sense usually prevails over such arguments. Maintenance need not just allow for emergencies or random calls to the engineer but also for scheduled maintenance visits throughout the year to undertake preventative work. By definition some of the common problems will be averted by preventative maintenance which may take place four or twelve times during the year.

If one accepts that the computer is going to go out of action at some time or another it is essential that a proper maintenance arrangement is entered into so that problems with both the hardware and the software are either solved rapidly or hopefully prevented.

Many computers are very reliable indeed, but that being said there are others that were almost certainly built on the proverbial Friday afternoon shift in the factory. It is almost certain that in true loyalty to Murphy's Law those computers that have been covered by an excellent maintenance agreement will turn out to be the most reliable, whilst those not so generously covered will go down in the middle of the hotel's busiest check-out thereby aggravating the maximum number of guests possible and losing the most revenue.

The caterers who will need the most comprehensive maintenance agreements will be those operating systems constantly and those for whom the loss of the computer for any time would bring their business to a complete halt.

Accepting that something will go wrong sometime, the caterer has to contemplate how to rectify the situation. It is very unlikely that anyone on the catering establishment's staff will have the ability to undertake even the most minor of adjustments to the system so an expert must be called in.

Analysts are sometimes very complimentary about the total support service, including maintenance, offered by some suppliers:

> In addition to their 24-hour-a-day support unit and the secondary telephone line for other problems, we like their 'two-day audit' service, carried out once a year. The user is visited and the installed system is monitored to ensure (a) it is being properly exploited and (b) it is fulfilling the needs of that particular hotel or restaurant. (*Hotel & Catering Technology*, 1986)

What sort of maintenance contract should be used?

It is essential to have an *on-site maintenance contract* so that an expert engineer can be called in when required.

In many cases the engineer will firstly try to sort out the problem over the telephone and will talk through the symptoms being experienced and try to establish a possible diagnosis. In some cases there may be a direct telephone and modem link between the computer supplier and the processor in the catering establishment so direct diagnosis and assistance may be given. It is a great advantage to deal with an engineer who is an expert in the caterer's system, as undoubtedly he will be aware of problems that are occurring in similar computers and will know quickly what the actual problem is. If the problem cannot be solved rapidly over the phone or by direct link then a visit by the engineer will be essential. If we are dealing with a microcomputer then some maintenance contracts will allow for a similar machine to be substituted while the problem computer is taken away for repair. Obviously this is not possible with mini and mainframe computers where maintenance must be undertaken on-site.

O   • Are the hardware and software used seperately or together?   O

O   • Is preventative maintenance covered and who is responsible for   O
              implementing it?

O   • Is the maintenance engineer based locally?   O

O   • Who will carry out maintenance if the usual engineer is   O
              unavailable?

O   • Does the agreement show the name and adress of the organization   O
              carrying out the maintenance?

O   • Is the complete system maintained by a single company?   O

O   • What is the guaranteed response time?   O

O   • What is the length of the contract?   O

O   • Does the agreement allow for a replacement computer if this is   O
              possible?

O   • Does the agreement cover spare parts as well as their shipping   O
              costs and repair?

O   • Does the Agreement provide higher levels of maintenance for   O
              priority parts of the system?

O   • Is accidental or deliberate damage by the operator covered?   O

O   • Would a labour and parts agreement be sufficient?   O

Figure 4.4   *Maintenance agreement checklist*

Looking at the *Maintenance Agreement Checklist* in Figure 4.4, there are several important points that should be emphasized.

The agreement that is eventually entered into by the caterer will rely on an engineer being close at hand. A caterer cannot wait an indefinite time to get the computer back in action as every moment means revenue lost. The caterer should therefore examine the location of the engineer as well as how many systems that engineer will have to cover. Almost certainly when the caterer's computer goes out of action the engineer will have other work on which may lead to a delay in having it repaired. The point should also be made that with a labour and parts agreement the caterer may be charged on an hourly basis for the engineer's travelling time in addition to time actually spent repairing the computer. An engineer from nearby is obviously an advantage in this situation.

It is often best if a complete system is maintained by a single company so that there can be no squabbling between firms, each blaming the other for the poor standard of work. This is easy to say in a textbook but, of course, with larger systems a number of peripherals may well be added on to a computer system from specialist manufacturers who may be the only ones able to provide specialist maintenance. The moral, though, is to try to ensure that maintenance is standardized wherever possible, if only to make life less complicated for all concerned.

In addition to emergency cover it may be beneficial to allow for preventative maintenance to be undertaken at various times throughout the year. The engineer may then tackle such tasks as cleaning paper particles out of the printers before they reach sufficient quantities to clog the works. Such items as the spring mechanism on the disk drives may be examined for wear and the print heads might be re-aligned. All the circuits may be tested so that any problems can be identified before they become the subject of an emergency call.

Often a maintenance agreement will quote a number of hours within which an emergency call will be answered. It should be examined closely to see whether hours quoted are 'working hours' or not, as a misunderstanding here could well mean that a computer is left idle all night or over a weekend despite a relatively short guaranteed response time. It should also be remembered that the time quoted is that within which an engineer guarantees to be able to come and look at the problem – it is *not* the time within which the computer will be back in action.

It is ideal, if possible, to word the contract so that it states that within a certain number of hours the maintenance engineer will either rectify the problem or substitute another similar piece of equipment whilst the faulty item is taken away and repaired.

It may well be a feature of a computer system that certain parts are more unreliable than others. For example, the mechanical parts within printers are notoriously more unreliable than other parts of a computer system. If this is the case it may be necessary to concentrate maintenance on the weak links and have a higher level of maintenance agreement for those than for the other parts of the computer hardware.

How much does maintenance cover cost?

Quite often the standard maintenance charge will provide the caterer with all the system updates as they become available on general release and provide guidance and support when required during normal office hours. It will possibly require an extended maintenance option to acquire the extra security of the supplier's staff being available on a 24-hour-per-day, 365-day-per-year basis.

It is possible to negotiate when finalizing a maintenance agreement and the caterer should examine the costings carefully. If, for example, the computer concerned is renowned for its reliability then rather than investing in the most expensive 'Rolls Royce' maintenance cover, which in practice may never be recouped if the engineer is hardly ever called out, it may be preferable to negotiate a parts and labour agreement. This type of agreement only involves payment when a problem actually occurs rather than spending money in anticipation of problems happening. It is really a matter of choosing the best agreement to suit the individual situation and the financial package available, but correct judgement often only comes with experience.

The cost of maintenance is always regarded as extraordinarily high by those not used to new technology, but it must be appreciated that the skill and knowledge of a competent computer maintenance engineer does not come cheaply.

Maintenance costings are basically worked out as an annual percentage of the original purchase price of the equipment and they will add a large amount of money on to the total cost of operating a computer. For example, the more expensive maintenance agreements will work out at 25 per cent of the cost of the hardware per annum which is no small amount. This type of percentage will apply particularly if a short response time of say, two hours, is required. The type of costing more normally reached is for an eight-hour response time which will usually be provided annually for between 10 and 15 per cent of the cost of the computer. The age of the computer will also be taken into account, as will its configuration. The more peripherals, for example, the higher the maintenance charge as there is more equipment to look after.

Computer systems purchased from well known suppliers are usually well proven and all new enhancements strictly quality controlled. Unfortunately, failures may still occasionally occur. For software failures some systems incorporate a built-in modem link so that the external engineer can rectify the problem without actually visiting the catering establishment. This can be a great advantage and is well worth taking up if offered. The only additional facility required will be a dedicated telephone line for the processor.

Third Party Maintenance (TPM)

Up till now we have assumed quite correctly that the majority of maintenance cover is provided by the manufacturer of the hardware and software. Many manufacturers in fact have kept their firms financially viable through the follow-up maintenance of existing installations. In practice there is a growing market for third party maintenance (TPM) which is provided by specialist, and yet unconnected, maintenance firms.

The advantages of third party maintenance are:

- reduction in cost of between 20 to 30 per cent
- one firm will maintain a selection of different manufacturer's equipment

Potential users of TPM should mainly satisfy themselves that the firm they are contemplating utilizing carries sufficient spares for all their types of equipment. It is also worth noting that satisfactory TPM companies will be approved by the Computer Services Association (CSA) Third Party Maintenance Group and may also satisfy the British Standards Institute quality assessment schedule (QAS 3302/187) (Turner, 1987).

It is quite possible these days to obtain insurance for a computer that will cover repair bills provided the system has actually stopped working. Wear and tear is not insurable and the premiums for repair are likely to be in the region of 6 per cent of the cost of the hardware.

One of the best solutions to problems of reliability is to set up a mutual-aid arrangement with another catering establishment similarly equipped with the same hardware and software nearby.

WHERE CAN THE CATERER GO FOR IMPARTIAL ADVICE?

If the prospect of wading through a mountain of brochures and sifting a vast array of statistics is too much to contemplate then there are people and organizations in existence that are equipped to help the harassed caterer.

It should never be embarrassing to ask for advice. Nothing is worse than an ineffective system being installed by a caterer who thought he was an expert merely from reading a few journals. It is far easier to call in a consultant than to spend time programming a system that is not going to be good enough for the job.

There are a whole host of experts, including the major hotel consultancy companies who have built up invaluable experience over the years. Unfortunately there are also some who have jumped on the bandwagon and who do not possess the necessary industry knowledge, without which it is impossible to advise on a correct solution.

Making use of a consultant is worth contemplating if caterers have not the time or expertise to devote to the selection process themselves. It should be remembered, though, that a consultant does not come cheap and therefore there is going to be extra expense involved. Another important consideration is that the hotel and catering world is very specialized and a consultant, despite a proven ability with computers, should have the necessary expertise in the catering industry too.

One of the problems with consultants is that they are often offered 'introductory fees' or similar amounts of money by manufacturers in exchange for recommending their particular system. The danger is that unscrupulous consultants may recommend the systems that offer them the biggest personal rewards rather than the systems that are actually best for the caterer concerned. The answer to this problem is either to only employ consultants who are known to be impartial, or to get consultants to draw up a shortlist of systems rather than asking them to make the final decision.

It is wise therefore to make use of consultants who possess both computing and catering qualifications and who can demonstrate an up-to-date knowledge of the latest computer technology. Perhaps the safest way is to only make use of consultants who have been recommended by similar organizations who have made use of their services. The consultant should be checked out if necessary. Figure 4.5 gives a checklist of points to follow in choosing a consultant.

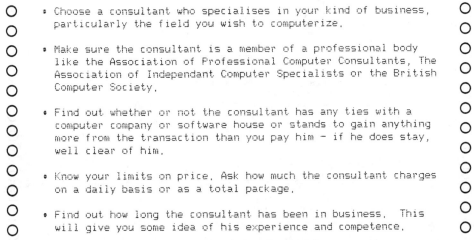

* Choose a consultant who specialises in your kind of business, particularly the field you wish to computerize.

* Make sure the consultant is a member of a professional body like the Association of Professional Computer Consultants, The Association of Independant Computer Specialists or the British Computer Society.

* Find out whether or not the consultant has any ties with a computer company or software house or stands to gain anything more from the transaction than you pay him - if he does stay, well clear of him.

* Know your limits on price. Ask how much the consultant charges on a daily basis or as a total package.

* Find out how long the consultant has been in business. This will give you some idea of his experience and competence.

Figure 4.5 *Five recommendations for choosing a consultant*
Source: *Which Computer*, 1984

It is best if the consultant selected has sufficient knowledge to be able to compare both computer and manual systems. Not only a historical knowledge of systems should be possessed but also an up-to-the-minute comprehension of the latest systems on offer.

One of the best sources of information is the Hotel and Catering Training Board (HCTB) who organize a very useful consultancy service from their Wembley headquarters. They provide the caterer with a useful selection of in-house courses at their headquarters, or as an alternative the caterer could become involved in their Open Learning scheme, details of which are shown in Figure 4.6.

The HCTB's Open Learning Scheme is for those caterers who want to improve their knowledge without having to formally attend a course. The units that are offered allow the caterer a realistic way to manage work alongside study at their own speed and when time allows.

In the case of new technology the open learning program that is most applicable is number six entitled *"Using technology to aid managment decision making"*, and especially module three *"Choosing a computer system"*

USING TECHNOLOGY TO AID MANAGEMENT DECISION MAKING

This unit gives the caterer experience of using a micro computer and how it can be applied to hotel and catering operations.

Module 1: Getting started.

This introduces the caterer to computers and specifically the BBC B microcomputer. The caterer also begins to use some general managment system packages produced by Gemini Marketing Ltd.

Key points covered in detail are

- working through a program designed to help the caterer with a particular management function - STOCK CONTROL
- setting up a computer filing system by using a DATABASE management program
- SPREADSHEETS - another common type of management program
- using a GRAPHICS program, enabling the presentation of spreadsheet data visually

Module 2: What do we want from a computer system?

- gives some idea of what a computer can do
- distinguishes between data and information
- shows how to compile data flow diagrams
- analyses a business in terms of the two principle ways a computer can help
- identifies management information needs
- applies the techniques learned to a case study

Module 3: Choosing a computer system

This module shows how to choose the appropriate computer hardware and software for a business.

Key points covered in detail are:

- learning what sort of computer capacity the caterer is going to need
- re-evaluating one of the software packages already worked through
- technical specifications of computer hardware and comparing one with another
- computer storage capacity
- applying what has been learned in modules 2 and 3 to a business situation

Module 4: A case study in how not to introduce a stock control program

This module asks the caterer to follow the misadventures of a mythical character, Tom Sweeter, in introducing a stock control package. Although light hearted it contains some serious lessons to enable the caterer to consolidate what he has learned in the other three modules.

The first section sets the scene of the catering service of Midshire University and its need for a stock control program.

The caterer then discovers the dangers of buying software and hardware before he has adequately specified his requirements. The final section puts the caterer (and Tom!) right about planning, training and implementation.

What do you get?

• Self-instructional loose-leaf text
• A software pack (either on cassette or dual 40/80 track disc)
  prepared by Gemini Marketing Ltd., containing their database,
  spreadsheet, graph plot, and stock control programs.

What do you need?

A BBC B microcomputer, monitor and either a single or double disc
drive with interface or cassette recorder.

Full details of this and other courses are available from The Open
Learning Unit, Ramsey House, Central Square, Wembley, Middlesex, HA9
7AP.

Figure 4.6 *HCTB Open Learning scheme*

Through their Micro Systems Centre at their head office in Wembley the
Hotel and Catering Training Board offer a range of courses for
caterers which provide an excellent introduction to and appreciation
of new technology.
  Undoubtedly the HTCB offer a good series of courses that are most
relevant to the situation that we have been examining, the various
types of courses are outlined below.

TRAINING IN SELECTING MICRO COMPUTER SYSTEMS FOR SMALL BUSINESS
SYSTEMS FOR THE HOTEL AND CATERING INDUSTRY

Aim of the Courses

To provide an understanding of the micro computer systems that are
available and suitable for business use in the hotel and catering
industry.
  To give an understanding of, and practice in applying, methods
needed to evaluate the benefits and advantages of introducing micro
computers into a business, including assessing the time, training and
financial commitments entailed, and their justification.
  To provide an understanding of the management planning and control
required to install and develop useful and efficient micro computer
based systems in stages, with measurable and comparable performance
objectives and standards.
  To give basic training in the uses of general purpose software for
fundamental business functions.

PART 1 - Consultancy and Advisory Service
PART 2 - Appreciating Micro Computers
PART 3 - Applying Micro Computers in Small Business
PART 4 - General Purpose Software - Business Uses
PART 5 - Hotel and Restaurant Software Systems
PART 6 - Promoting and Marketing

Full details of these courses are available from HCTB, Ramsey House,
PO Box 18, Central Square, Wembley, Middlesex, HA9 7AP.

Figure 4.7 *HCTB microcomputer training courses*

Perhaps the best piece of advice is to make use of those equipment manufacturers
who have a long understanding of the industry. Their sales forces should be able to
answer all the detailed questions that the caterer may put their way. Also, always
investigate existing installations and seek out the unbiased view of staff already using a
similar system to the one required.

References

CHAMPS Hotel System Product Description, December 1986.

D.P. Media Services, 1987 catalogue.

Ferrar, Dave (Executive Director, CHAMPS), October 1986. *Hotel & Catering Technology*, p. 1.

Gamble, Paul, October 1986. Technology: host to the future. *Computer Solutions for Hotel & Catering.*

Hotel & Catering Technology, October 1986. Profile of Kalamazoo Hospitality Systems.

Marko, Joseph A. and Moore, Richard G., May 1980. How to select a computing system. *Cornell Hotel and Restaurant Administration Quarterly.*

Turner, Annie, April 1987. Searching for the benefits of TPM. *Computer Systems.*

Van de Pijpekamp, J. M. (representative of Enka carpets). Carpets for software. *HCIMA Yearbook 1986/87.*

Which Computer, October 1984. Educating yourself.

5 Computer Hardware and Software

HARDWARE SELECTION

In using the term 'hardware' we are referring to the inert equipment that comprises the total computer system. This invariably consists of:

- processor
- keyboard
- visual display unit (VDU)
- store/memory
- interface
- printer
- modem

Hardware is the term given to the collection of metal and plastic items which require the necessary software to convert them into a functional computer. We shall deal with software selection later.

During the evolution of the computer the electronic circuitry that makes up the hardware has undergone a tremendous amount of development both where components and manufacturing technology are concerned. The introduction of the silicon chip, in particular, facilitated a great reduction in the overall costs of computers. It has therefore become possible to utilize computers in situations that would previously have been regarded as uneconomical and it is common to see microcomputers fulfilling functions that would at one time have required a mainframe.

Second-hand hardware

Until comparatively recently the second-hand computer market was almost irrelevant to computer users and only new hardware would be considered. However, now that computers are commonplace and being upgraded regularly many purchasers are looking at second-hand equipment as a viable alternative to the most modern offerings from the manufacturers. Whilst the catering industry has no single major manufacturer at the time of writing, one can envisage in the not too distant future that the experiences of other industries will be felt by the catering industry and second-hand equipment will become commonplace. As an example, in 1987 the European second-user IBM market alone was estimated to be worth £150 billion annually (Turner, 1987).

Many manufacturers initially openly discouraged the second-hand market but if purchasers of replacement equipment can be assured of obtaining, say, 50 per cent of the initial purchase price back by trading it in then they are much more likely to purchase initially. The quality of second-hand equipment has also improved as three to four years is now the period for which most new systems are expected to operate. They are much more reliable than their predecessors which means that they have a longer useful life in them for the second user. In the 1970s computer systems were expected to run for six to seven years and with the small quantity of systems the number actually coming on to the second-hand market was much smaller than is the case today.

The main pitfalls to watch out for where second-hand equipment is concerned are the arrangements for:

- transferral of software licences
- maintenance contracts
- copyright of manuals/architecture
- availability of spare parts

Minicomputer or microcomputer?

Whilst the decision to computerize the functions within a catering business will have been taken after a comprehensive feasibility study, the further decision will ultimately have to be faced of whether to make use of mainframe, minicomputer or microcomputer hardware. The situations in which a mainframe would be contemplated are obvious, but confusion may still exist as to whether a minicomputer or a microcomputer may be applicable in certain situations. Minis and micros do in fact possess similar capacities and therefore can legitimately be regarded as competitors.

It will almost certainly be cheaper if microcomputers can be utilized. Also micros are generally not susceptible to temperature changes whilst minis often only function properly within a narrowly defined atmospheric band.

A number of micros on a network provides in effect multiple processors so that if one goes out of action the whole network is not necessarily affected. With a mini-computer, if the central processing unit goes down then the whole system follows suit.

Micros, because of their volume sales, often have the advantage of being available off-the-shelf whereas this is not always the case with minis. Whilst we are not strictly dealing with software here it should be said that software packages are sometimes more readily available for micros than for minis. Minis can be difficult to integrate into an office environment whereas micros often fit in with ease with a multitude of accounting and word processing packages being readily available in addition to the specific catering packages.

Questions that must be asked about hardware

Whether buying new or second-hand hardware, potential computer users are faced with a wide selection of equipment and, bearing in mind the importance of making the correct choice in an industrial situation, there are a number of questions they should ask about the proposed hardware so that they may be sure of making the right choice.

How quick is the computer?

Invariably in a catering situation the computer user is under pressure. When dealing, for example, with a reservation over the telephone, or the settlement of a bill in a busy restaurant, the speed with which the computer operates is most important as often the customer cannot wait. After all, one of the major perceived benefits of computer systems, as far as the user is concerned, is the speeding-up of various processes so that the customer receives better service than was possible before.

The speed with which the computer operates is largely down to the power and performance of the hardware and is reflected in the time that is taken to process a particular application.

This will depend on the volume of information to be inserted into and retrieved from the store. The processor therefore must first of all be capable of handling the required volume of data. The speed of the store is very important in this regard; for example, a micro with a hard disk is much faster than one with a diskette. The size of the microprocessor is also important as a 16-bit processor can, in some circumstances, perform twice as quickly as an 8-bit processor. This last statement must, though, be qualified as there are constraints other than the processor that could reduce this speed advantage. The size of the wires carrying information between the processor, the store and the memory are another contributory factor. These wires are known as the 'busses'.

It is often the case that a particular computer may be faster than a similar machine when working on one job and yet slower when undertaking a different process. One computer might be quicker than a contemporary at handling a stocktaking run and yet be slower at compiling a guest bill than the other machine.

The reason for this difference in speed can usually be found when the particular application is examined. For example, one computer may have greater capacity for handling a large number of mathematical calculations, whilst the other may process the input and output of information more readily. It is wise, therefore, when contemplating purchase to examine the computer under all circumstances and not to rely purely on the application demonstrated by the manufacturer or dealer. The only recommendation that can be made is that the system be tested at length, actually in a live situation, before purchase is finally agreed. Most reputable manufacturers who have confidence in their products will be pleased to oblige.

Does the computer possess sufficient capacity?

Where mainframe computers are concerned there is usually very little problem with the quantity of information that they can hold in their main memory. It is extremely unlikely that the average catering applications could overload the memory of a mainframe. The problems really occur at microcomputer level where it becomes apparent that a particular computer cannot cope because the memory capacity is inadequate.

A computer has two types of memory which are called RAM and ROM.

Random Access Memory or RAM refers to the quantity of memory that allows the operator to use it 'at random'. In the RAM program a certain quantity of memory capacity will be required to facilitate an operation, leaving an amount of 'user memory' free for use. It is this free amount of space that can be utilized by the user program that is all important. In other words, RAM can be expanded. A typical quantity of RAM on a dedicated word processor might be 256 Kb, which in fact means 256,000 characters of information capacity within the memory.

Read Only Memory or ROM is the type of memory that is totally committed and contains functions that are programmed in advance. These functions cannot even be changed when the computer is disconnected. ROM cannot be expanded.

Is the computer compatible with other machines?

It is obviously useful if your computer can run programs that are available for similar but not necessarily identical machines. Many micros possess a compatibility option that increases the potential number of programs that might be utilized. There can, though, be a decrease in operational speed when running a computer in compatibility mode.

It is also of great use if the computer can 'speak' to other computers and exchange information. For example, it may be thought necessary to link a telephone logging computer to an existing guest billing system in a hotel. Even if this is not thought necessary at the time of purchase it may become apparent as the catering business expands, so future compatibility should be considered.

What configuration of computer would be best?

There are a number of different ways in which the hardware may be arranged (configured) to cope with catering applications. The caterer should be aware of these various configurations which may be summarized as follows:

(a) *Basic configuration.* This is a very common configuration now that cheap computers have been developed for catering applications and consists of one processor and one disk drive. The problem is that there is no back-up system. Whilst disks can be copied at a later stage, if the system crashes during an operation there is a great danger of losing the information being processed at the time. This will not be a risk worth taking in a large business.

(b) *Integrated back-up.* As a modification of the basic configuration this is an improvement as there is always a back-up system in operation. In this configuration there are *two processors and three disk drives.* The intention is that only one processor operates at a time, with the second ready to take over as an instant back-up in the case of failure. With the disk drives the primary disk is utilized for processing whilst a second disk is utilized at the same time running in parallel. This second disk is described as having the information 'ghosted' on to it. If the primary disk fails then the 'ghosted' disk can be used as a back-up very rapidly.

(c) *Distributed processing.* In this configuration a number of PCs, for example, may be networked together with each PC possessing its own specialist function. The intention is to distribute functions so that access time is improved and the system will also continue operating if one element is out of action.

(d) *Remote links.* If the computer system envisaged is going to need to be linked to remote terminals, or to other catering units or even head office, then there is going to be a need for some hardware to allow physical links to be established. This will include such items as *modems* which will help the transmission of information. It is important to establish that the equipment selected is suitable for the application and will interface with other equipment.

(e) *Catering hardware.* There will be specialist hardware on offer that is peculiar to the catering industry. This may, for example, include items of hardware such as point-of-sale terminals designed for beverage areas boasting keyboards that are impervious to liquids and that can be wiped down easily. There are great advantages in utilizing dedicated catering hardware rather than hardware developed for other industries.

Some manufacturers offer a variety of configurations to suit certain sizes of establishment and types of business. Where a reputable supplier is concerned these recommendations can be relied upon and can be very useful to the caterer who is inexperienced in computer systems.

Figure 5.1 shows system configurations relevant to four sizes of hotel as recommended by a highly reputable North American supplier.

ITEM	PROPERTY SIZE (ROOMS)			
	50	100	200	300
COMPUTER	IBM PC	IBM XT	IBM AT	IBM AT
MEMORY	256 Kb	256 Kb	512 Kb	512 Kb
Ports	2	4	8	8
DISK DRIVE -				
Useable Capacity	20 Mb	42 Mb	60 Mb	160Mb
Avg. Access Time	40 Ms	30 Ms	30 Ms	20Ms
TAPE DRIVE -				
Capacity	N/A	60 Mb	60 Mb	60 Mb
Modem Auto Dial/				
Answer	1200 Baud	1200 Baud	1200 Baud	1200 Baud
120 CPS Printers	1	1	2	3
160 CPS Printers	1	1		
290 CPS Printers			1	1
Amdek Terminals	1	1	1	1
Wyse Terminals	1	2	3	5
SOFTWARE				
Hotel Software including:				
-Reservations	Yes	Yes	Yes	Yes
-Check-in	Yes	Yes	Yes	Yes
-Check-out	Yes	Yes	Yes	Yes
-Travel Agent Acct.	Yes	Yes	Yes	Yes
-Night Audit	Yes	Yes	Yes	Yes
-City Ledger	Yes	Yes	Yes	Yes
-Accounts Payable	Yes	Yes	Yes	Yes
-General Ledger	Yes	Yes	Yes	Yes
-Financial Acct.	Yes	Yes	Yes	Yes
-Management Stat.	Yes	Yes	Yes	Yes
-Marketing Stat.	Yes	Yes	Yes	Yes
-Envoy Electronic Mail	Yes	Yes	Yes	Yes
	-------	-------	-------	-------
	£10,000	£14,000	£23,500	£33,000
	-------	-------	-------	-------

```
OPTIONS AVAILABLE

Guest History            N/A        £1,500     £2,000     £2,000

Automatic Call

Accounting Interface     N/A        £1,500     £2,000     £2,000

Automatic P.O.S.

Interface                N/A        £2,700     £3,500     £3,500

Word Processing          £500       £500       £600       £600

Spread Sheets            £300       £300       £400       £400

------------------------------------------------------------------------

The above systems, in whichever configuration is a multi-user, multi-

tasking system.  The system provides performance more normally associated

with a mini-computer.  However, the cost is in line with microcomputer

prices  The system is currently implemented in 130 installations all over

North America.  Each system is installed complete with a modem so that

support can be handled via the telephone communication lines.  In addition

for those organizations that are decentralized it allows them to

communicate with their individual properties to transfer either reservation

data or transfer operational data.

------------------------------------------------------------------------
```

Figure 5.1 *Sample configurations*

It will be the detailed data that is collected when comparing computer systems that will eventually determine the exact configuration of the computer selected. One of the most important aspects, certainly as far as the user is concerned, is the configuration of peripherals such as printers and VDUs.

A typical configuration for a 600-bedroom hotel might be as in Figure 5.2 shown opposite.

The number of peripheral devices will depend greatly on such factors as the average length of stay, the market sector of the hotel, and the physical layout. The following departments, though, will have to be considered:

Advance reservations. At least one VDU should be set aside in a hotel to allow for information input on group bookings as well as management control of reservations. As most reservations will be taken over the telephone sufficient terminals should be provided to cope with demand, as well as a character printer for lists, reports, confirmations and letters.

Front desk/cashiers. Staff here may share terminals as long as the layout allows this. A rough guide is three terminals and printers for 300 rooms and another terminal and printer for every extra 150 rooms.

Location	Terminals	Medium Speed Printers	High Speed Printers
Reservations office	4		1
Registration desk and			
cashiers desk	6	2	1
Telephone switch board	2		
Housekeeping	1	1	
Accounting office	3		
Points of sale:			
Gift Shop	1		
Coffee Shop	1		
Restaurant	1		
Bar 1	1		
Bar 2	1		
Golf pro shop	1		
Manager's office	1		
Sales office	1		
TOTAL	24	3	3

Figure 5.2 *Typical system configuration for 600-room hotel*
Source: Marko and Moore, 1980

Accounts receivable. One terminal should be sufficient for most hotels but due to the bulk of paperwork a line printer may be preferable here.

Accounts. One terminal for accounts payable and one for general ledger with a shared printer should be sufficient.

Switchboard. A VDU for every two operators so they may refer to the enquiries module.

Housekeeping. One terminal to handle room status information, if a telephone call logging system is not in use to undertake this task direct from guest rooms.

Enquiries desk. One terminal for enquiries if felt necessary.

Management console. This terminal is required for control and security purposes.

Can I use a fully integrated computer system?

Where complete integration of systems is concerned, it has been a source of consternation to many catering system users that it has taken so long to be able to link different aspects together to provide a total picture of a business. In hotels, for example, until recently it has been quite normal to see a large number of separate computers working side by side handling different applications but in many cases physically unable to communicate with each other.

One could find point-of-sale terminals and telephone call loggers both compiling valuable information, but having to rely on this being punched in to the front office computer manually before the relevant bill could be produced for the customer. Far from increasing efficiency, in these situations the relevant computers and their manual communication physically slowed down the hotel's operation.

It can be argued that for some time the major obstacle was that computer manufacturers could not or would not agree to a common method by which their particular machines could communicate. We shall look at interfaces later, but the problem was that all the computers seemed to have different interfaces. Recently a common standard of communication has started to be agreed with standard interfaces being introduced.

Once standard interfaces were agreed it became possible to create software that would allow two separate devices to swap information, but in the catering industry there was still a limited number of manufacturers, many of whom saw each other as direct competitors and distrusted their perceived opposition. Of late attitudes have changed and improvements have come about in relationships. The hardware and software involved has become much more reliable and therefore integration is becoming much more widespread.

What do managers think of integrated systems?

Honeywell Inc., which manufactures integrated electronic systems, decided in 1986 to conduct a survey of 300 managers of hotels in the United States with at least 300 rooms. The definition of an integrated hospitality system as far as the research was concerned was '*one that integrates a hotel's computers, communications and controls*' and included '*property management, energy management, automatic temperature control, telecommunications, and fire-safety systems*'.

Three out of five hotels did not possess an integrated system, but most managers thought that installation would be inevitable in the future. The managers' responses to the survey are shown in Table 5.1 (Breen, 1987).

It's the way of the future	84%
It pays for itself	68%
It's absolutely necessary for large hotels	65%
It's a necessary evil	24%
The technology is not there yet	22%
I can't afford it	17%
I don't understand it	8%
It's too complicated	7%
It scares me	2%

Note: Figures total more than 100% because of multiple mentions.

Table 5.1 *Reaction to the term 'Integrated Hospitality System'*
Source: Honeywell, Inc.

From the research it was apparent that managers who already claimed to have an integrated system thought that it was the way of the future and absolutely necessary for large hotels. Managers of the smaller hotels were more likely to agree that an integrated system is a necessary evil.

The survey went on to ask managers what they thought were the most important reasons to integrate hotel operations and the responses are shown in Table 5.2 (Breen, 1987).

Table 5.2 *Most important reasons to electronically integrate hotel operations*

Improved service	32%
Productivity improvements	26%
Guest comfort	19%
Cost savings	16%
Hotel image	1%
Improved turnover	*%
Other	6%
Total	100%
* Less than 0.5%	

Source: Honeywell, Inc

Amongst many other items the survey established that hotels operating an integrated system paid less for hiring and training a single employee ($850) than those without integrated systems ($1,260). Also, managers had found no resistance from suppliers where integrating their systems was concerned.

The managers stated that the *most* attractive guest facilities that could be tied into an integrated system were the following:

- in-room safe 36%
- in-room bar 33%
- electronic voice messages 30%
- in-room check-out by TV 28%

The *least* interesting amenities included:

- in-room personal computers 11%
- shopping by television 9%

Amongst the facilities looked upon as being very important and that should therefore be tied into an integrated system were:

- fire safety
- housekeeping room-status
- energy management
- electronic door-locking system
  (Breen, 1987)

What is the situation regarding integrated systems in the UK?

Research in the UK in 1986 revealed that there was still a lot of room for improvement where integrated systems were concerned. Less than 20 per cent of hotels in the survey admitted to having fully integrated systems, whilst most possessed partially integrated systems. (See Figure 5.3 overleaf.) With the moves in technology forecast for the future the number of establishments with integrated computer systems is likely to increase dramatically.

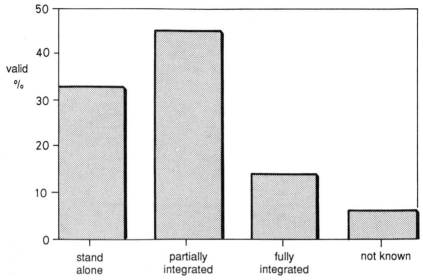

Figure 5.3   *Degree of integration*
Source: Whitaker, 1986

The processor

The heart of every computer is the central processing unit (CPU). In a microcomputer the CPU is often a 'chip' which is a piece of silicon containing integrated transistor circuits and measuring about a quarter of an inch square. The chip usually has two purposes: to control the operation of the flow of data and the machine program and to perform the actions defined within the pattern of its circuitry.

The central processing unit therefore contains the instructions (in machine code) which allow the computer to add and subtract in a variety of sequences to facilitate the tasks that it is required to undertake.

It is the software that the processor is able to handle that will often determine the hardware that is purchased. The speed of the processor, especially in a micro, will be a limiting factor with regard to the usefulness of the complete computer system. Whilst blaming the processor for speed limitation, in truth it is often the input of data by human hands using a keyboard and the output by mechanical printer that slows the entire system down, but this is not helped by the additional problem of a slow processor.

What is important about the keyboard?

The keyboard is of great importance to the computer user as it is usually the main method by which the computer can actually be operated. It enables control to be exercised over the various functions, applications and programs by way of commands.

The keyboard is deliberately designed to ease operation. The basic alphanumeric (both letters and numbers) layout is based on the QWERTY keyboard. This is identical to a typewriter and actually refers to the arrangement of the first six letters on the top line. The QWERTY layout was never intended to be the most efficient of layouts but came about in the 1870s when mechanical connections for a reliable typewriter dictated this particular arrangement of the keys. The basic QWERTY layout is shown in Figure 5.4. Additional keys, whether to print other characters and signs or function keys, are then arranged round this layout in logical fashion for ease of use.

Figure 5.4 *QWERTY keyboard*

Whatever the layout of the keyboard non-glare keys will help the comfort of the operator and the keys themselves may have concave surfaces to help the operator's fingers to fall naturally on to the correct keys. Also it is of importance that the keys are easily readable for swift identification.

The keyboard will usually employ *full travel keys* which means that they can be pressed right down to operate the *auto-repeat* facility; this repeats the letter when the key is held down for a period of time. If there is no auto-repeat facility then there may be a separate *repeat key* that has to be held down in conjunction with the key that is going to be repeated.

Computer keyboards of the QWERTY variety only really differ in the number of additional or control keys that are provided to allow functions over and above the normal requirements of letters, numbers and basic punctuation. These extra keys will differ greatly from one computer to another, but one can always expect there to be cursor keys to allow the cursor to be moved around the screen.

User comfort is important

It is important that the operator is comfortable with the operation of the keyboard and it is therefore helpful if the keyboard is on a flexible attachment so that it may be moved about. It is useful to have a separate numeric keypad if large amounts of figures are going to be entered.

It should be realized that when a keyboard is being used constantly it may be subjected to between 10,000 and 12,000 keystrokes per hour, which is not only putting the hardware under pressure but also the wrists, hands and fingers of the user. It is possible for this level of usage to lead to muscular problems (Hammond, 1986).

The features a catering computer keyboard should possess

In a catering situation it may be useful to employ a *touch-sensitive* keyboard. Keyboards are normally sensitive to dust, dirt and grease and therefore to attempt to locate a terminal with a keyboard in a kitchen or bar might be unwise unless a touch-sensitive option is available. The surface of this type of keyboard is completely flat and responds to the light finger touch of the operator whilst being capable of being wiped clean without ill effect.

It is also important to employ keyboards that are really durable as they will take a lot of punishment in a busy restaurant or kitchen. Punishment may not always be accidental: at least one restaurant system sales manager relates that it was once known that a member of staff in a restaurant, who felt threatened by computers, tried to vandalize the terminals by stabbing them with a knife. Whilst such abuse of the hardware can hardly be foreseen it is always a possibility and therefore is another reason why durable keyboards must be employed.

What should I look for in a Visual Display Unit?

The Visual Display Unit (VDU), of which there were approximately two million in the UK in 1986 (Hammond, 1986), is the only means of access that the user has to the operation of the computer where many systems are concerned. It is therefore the work-horse of the computer, allowing the input and output of information. It allows the user to interact with the program and therefore control the operation of the computer. By the display of instructions the user may be guided through a sequence of operations in an application which can considerably simplify the use of the computer. A system that utilizes an easy to follow, sympathetically written series of instructions is described as user-friendly.

It is of interest to note that originally VDUs, or terminals as they were known in the early 1970s, were described as 'dumb' as they could only be utilized to communicate directly with a mainframe or minicomputer. They were purely receivers and transmitters. It was only with the advent of the microchip that terminals became 'intelligent' so that with the aid of their own microprocessors they could undertake their own limited processing. Information and data could be held at the VDU locally before being transmitted to the central processor, thereby freeing the latter to control the network of VDUs.

In selecting the correct VDUs to complement a computer, as it is no longer necessary to buy the same make as the computer itself, design will no doubt feature greatly in the decision. The ergonomic requirements of the user are of primary importance, as are the considerations of compatibility and cost. It is certainly worth examining all the potential VDUs on the market that are 'plug-compatible' as big savings might be possible for the caterer buying sufficient quantities.

Is the size of the screen important?

It is important right at the start to understand that the larger the screen the more data that may be displayed for the user. It will be of great assistance to the user to be able to see as much as possible of the complete information that is being worked on.

The size of the screen is determined by the number of columns and lines of characters that can be displayed simultaneously. Screen format is most important, being defined as the number of characters that will fit on to the screen. The most common business computers use a format of 80 columns with 25/25 lines, which gives 1,920 possible locations on the screen at any one time. Eighty-column width (also known as character or screen width) is essential for word processing and should be borne in mind if this is a requirement of the computer system, although 132-character width is necessary when dealing with spreadsheets. Home computers frequently only allow 40 characters per line. Screen height is the number of characters that will fit vertically on to the screen.

One of the more recent improvements has been to design a VDU screen on which a whole document may be displayed. In the past it was sometimes not possible to view an entire document at one time but this need no longer be a worry. What is provided is a 15-inch screen vertically mounted with a 64-line screen height and an 80-character screen width.

Of late graphics and colour have become very important as far as VDU users are concerned:

> In 1983, of the 800,000 VDUs sold in Western Europe, 80 per cent were graphics terminals. (*Which Computer*, June 1984)

The majority of these terminals were bought to utilize business graphics making use of the much higher resolution screens, the colour of which allows attractive displays of histograms, pie charts and graphs to illustrate financial and marketing information.

The resolution or density of a screen depends on the number of *pixels* that can be illuminated. A pixel is each individual dot that may be illuminated on the screen to create a piece of graphics. The larger the number of pixels on a screen the higher the resolution.

Amongst other VDU features of importance is the ability to scroll. This is the way the computer fits in text at the bottom of a page by removing the top line. Similarly, the ability to wrap or start a new line of text when the original line proves too long to display on the screen will be another feature if word processing is seriously considered.

Will my health be affected by my using a VDU?

Over the years there have been some health scares centring on VDUs, especially the assertion that the radiation given off could be harmful to health. Equally, some operators have complained of ill effects such as headaches, neck discomforts and sore eyes. Apart from radiation there were scares concerning the possibility of epilepsy, as well as fears concerning miscarriage amongst pregnant VDU users.

It is true that the cathode-ray tube within a VDU gives off X-ray emissions and there are also radio frequency, ultraviolet and microwave emissions. In addition, a positive electrostatic field is given off by the screen. The National Radiological Protection Board has investigated all complaints and surveyed apparatus with the eventual conclusion that radiation emissions are far less than international and national safety limits. These safety limits are, though, being constantly reviewed as VDUs become more common.

> The emissions from a VDU are of a similar order to those of a luminous wristwatch. . . . There are not any measurable emissions from a cathode-ray tube. . . . One thing X-rays do is destroy static. . . . The front of a cathode-ray tube has lots of static. . . . if there were any significant X-ray emission the static would not be present. (Bushman)

Where epilepsy is concerned the flickering of the screen can affect those suffering from the very rare condition of photosensitive epilepsy, but ordinary televisions affect sufferers in exactly the same way and it is very unlikely that someone will suffer their first attack from exposure to a VDU.

Many regular VDU operators may feel that their eyesight is seriously at risk, but there is no evidence to corroborate this assertion. It is certainly the case, though, that prolonged work with a VDU will induce fatigue of the ciliary eye muscle and that consequent eye-strain will result. The brightness or luminosity of the screen and the fact that information is presented in most cases in green, amber or white on a black background may well be confusing as it is the direct opposite of the normal black on white printing to which we are accustomed.

The foreground and background colours on a VDU are relevant to the ease with which the data may be read by the operator. The foreground and background are sometimes also known as the ink and paper and these colourings are deliberately chosen to help operator's eyes. The colour combinations vary from one system to another.

One of the major solutions to glare is to fit a protective anti-glare screen which eliminates up to 95 per cent of the problem. The best anti-glare screens have a metal frame which is earthed to the back of the computer. The positive electrostatic field that the VDU produces (often 5,000 to 20,000 volts at half a metre) will then pass through the mesh of the screen harmlessly to earth. It is argued that the electrical force of anything up to 30,000 volts per square metre generated by a VDU will drive any debris in the air straight at the operator's face. When one realizes that some people suffer headaches during electric storms, then it becomes obvious that the removal of the positive electrostatic field will help similar people who happen to be computer users. In addition, the VDU will give a softer image to the eye without affecting the contrast.

The effect of a VDU without a non-glare screen and highly reflective surfaces is to increase the likelihood of eye discomfort. When one mixes in the possibility of dot matrix characters that are not only difficult to read but shimmering too then problems will almost inevitably occur. Whilst eyestrain may well be a phenomenon suffered by VDU users, this is just the same as might be experienced on any intensive piece of work that requires close concentration. Anti-glare screens will help considerably.

The characters displayed are a major factor in the clarity of the information to be read. The letters themselves should be adequately spaced for easy reading and clearly defined. The letters should be of an adequate size to be legible and there should also be a clear space between lines. If colour is displayed there should be adequate brightness control. The rate at which characters are refreshed when an image has been changed is important so that the image does not fade from the screen and flickering is reduced. The VDU should therefore not operate at a refresh rate of less than 50 Hz.

As the eyes are the main problem with the operation of VDUs, it is a good protective measure to give regular eye tests to staff to ensure that damage is not occurring and that existing conditions, which the member of staff may not be aware of, are not being aggravated. Staff should also be allowed regular breaks from their screens, for perhaps five minutes every hour, so that the intense concentration needed to operate a VDU does not irritate the eyes.

> The single most important thing is posture, the height of the keyboard and VDU in relation to the user with no glare on the screen from other light sources. (Bushman)

As regards the operator's back, arms and neck being strained, this may be avoided by utilizing the correct posture. Operators should have adequate legroom and it should be remembered that muscle fatigue will set in when only the arms and wrists are being used to operate the workstation.

The VDU should be capable of being adjusted so that the user is comfortable in its operation. A tilt and swivel facility should be built in and the keyboard should be flexible enough to be attached at variable distances and heights from the screen, so that the operator can be comfortable. Some VDUs incorporate a tilt and swivel facility powered electronically to be of assistance to disabled users. It is evident, though, that many apparently minor ailments are caused by poorly designed or maintained equipment.

The environment in which the computer is situated will either help or aggravate any apparent health problems. Of greatest importance is the overall lighting which must not cause glare or reflections or reduce the contrast on the screen. A golden rule is never to work at a screen with one's back to a major light source. All the surfaces in the room where the VDU is situated should have matt finishes.

From available evidence it would appear wise to permit pregnant employees to undertake duties other than using a VDU, if they wish to, until their pregnancy is complete.

A checklist of VDU features

Colour of screen	affects clarity. Dark green with light green characters or white with black characters is best.
Large dot matrix	the larger the dot matrix of each character the better the clarity.
Full screen editing	eases operation with cursor free to move everywhere.
Lower and upper case letters	essential for word processing.
Audio signals	help indicate mistakes.
Multiple colours	useful for graphs and charts.

The importance of the memory to a computer operation?

Where computers are concerned there are two types of memory that are commonly found. They are:

- main memory
- external or backing store

Main memory is normally made up of silicon chips that are directly linked to the central processor (CPU). They hold the programs and data required for immediate processing.

Main memory can be described as Random Access Memory (RAM) where information can be written on to the chips and read from them. Often when information is read off a disk it is written into RAM. It is the size of the RAM that limits the size of the programs that can be run by the computer. One Kilobyte can hold 1,024 characters in memory. Typical microcomputer Random Access Memory sizes are:

64 Kbytes	65,536 characters
128 Kbytes	131,072 characters
256 Kbytes	262,144 characters
512 Kbytes	524,288 characters

Information can be written to and read from RAM when the computer is in operation but it is lost when the machine is turned off. The only alternative where information in RAM cannot be lost, usually where portables are concerned, is to have sufficient battery power and therefore current to keep the RAM activated. An option in development which may be available in the future is 'bubble' memory which will retain information in RAM even when the machine is switched off.

The other form of main memory is Read Only Memory (ROM) which can only be read from and cannot be changed.

External or *backing store* in business computers is usually held on disks. Where microcomputers in particular are concerned, both programs and data are held on disks which are subsequently deciphered through disk drives connected to the computer itself.

The speed and reliability of the disk drives themselves is crucial to the overall functioning of the system. Hard disks, as opposed to floppy disks, are often the fastest option.

The most common memory storage media for microcomputers are:

- floppy disks
- hard disks
- tape cassettes (inappropriate and very rarely seen on business machines)

Floppy disks

Floppy disks or diskettes are made out of magnetically treated circular sheets of flexible plastic resembling a 45-rpm record, usually sheathed in a vinyl jacket for protection. They hold data magnetically on a concentric series of 'tracks' in a series of sectors and each of these sectors can be accessed directly. The normal diameter of a floppy disk is either 5¼ inch which are found on most PCs, 8 inch which are common to mainframe and minicomputers, or 3½ inch which are found on newer PCs. The latter have become popular as they are not only more robust, being encased in a plastic case, but they are also particularly useful with portable systems. The density of the recording depends on whether the floppy is single or double. One-sided and two-sided disks are available. It is unusual for a floppy disk formatted for one computer system to be compatible with a rival system.

In practice a disk with less than 200 Kbytes of storage capacity is not worth considering for a business system: the usual standard is 1.2 Mbytes on a standard hard disk and 600 Kbytes on small floppy disks.

The major drawback, if there is one, with floppy disks is that they are prone to wear as the head that reads information from and writes information on to them actually rests on the plastic during these processes. It is quite often a problem with floppy disks that they just do not hold sufficient information and soon outgrow their usefulness, as illustrated by the following case study.

CASE STUDY NUMBER 8

HOTEL COMPUTER SAVES TIME BUT THE MEMORY IS TOO SMALL

An independent business hotel with 21 bedrooms in the Midlands has utilized an integrated front office and back office microcomputer system for two years. The system is linked to the telex network and undertakes all billing as well as profit and loss accounts. It retains a file of 600 standard menu items and can produce a new menu in 20 seconds. Extra programs include spreadsheet planning and general word processing.

The system has allowed major savings on the sales ledger, making it possible for the hotel owner to issue statements and balance ledger cards three days earlier than was previously possible.

As the reservations program requires the disk to be changed it is described as 'very cumbersome' and is therefore not used. 'Unless you have a hard disk machine and can run different programs at the same time, facilities like reservations can be very cumbersome if somebody phones up to make a booking and you have another set of disks in the machine', points out the manager. He finds the system in total a 'tremendous asset' and is considering upgrading to a hard disk system with two VDUs.

(Whitehall, 1986)

Hard disks

Hard disk drives or 'Winchesters' are commonly offered by manufacturers when existing storage proves inadequate as they can store anything from 5 Mbytes to over 100 Mbytes. Hard disks are similar to floppies except that they have several layers or inflexible platters linked together by a spindle. In microcomputer systems these hard disk drives are generally of the Winchester type, meaning that the disk cartridge cannot be taken away from the drive itself so that programs or data must first be copied on to a floppy disk before being stored off-line. Because Winchester disks cannot be removed from their drive, their manufacturing tolerances can be much finer and the disk can therefore hold higher quantities of data than their floppy equivalents.

Winchester drives can be ten times as fast as floppy disk drives, depending on their rotational speed, thanks to the rigidity of their aluminium construction. As a consequence, getting information from a disk can take one tenth of the time or less compared with getting information from a floppy disk. The speed of the hard disk is made possible by the fact that the read/write head does not actually touch the surface of the disk, thereby removing the comparatively lengthy up-and-down movement. Hard disks can also store as much as ten times more information than a floppy disk and indeed a 5¼-inch Winchester disk can be expected to hold 10 Mbytes of data.

Although hard disk drives are often compatible with other machines, if the right interface is used, it is recommended that the same disk drive is used as produced by the actual manufacturer of the computer allowing fewer possible problem areas to occur. Hard disks are generally more reliable than floppy disks and are therefore highly recommended for business use.

Questions a caterer should ask about storage

How many characters will a storage medium hold and how many will I actually have access to?

Where floppy disks are concerned they will vary in total size from 100 Kb (102,400 characters) to 1200 Kb (1,228,800 characters). Disk drives with a double-density option are well worthwhile even though costlier as the increased capacity will assist greatly in the usability of the computer. In theory, about 90 per cent of a floppy disk's capacity should be available for an application, with the remaining 10 per cent being for system overhead.

The system overhead refers to the quantity of memory allocated to the operating instructions, or in other words the operation of rather than the content of the program. Whilst the disk will be sold as containing so many thousand or million characters, in effect the user is only going to have access to a percentage once the operating instructions have been subtracted.

With the operating system taking up room in the memory it is quite possible for a manufacturer to use as much as 12K (12,000 characters) of a 36K memory to make the computer function. It is therefore important to ask the supplier how many Kbytes are actually going to be available for storage.

The sort of practical problem with which a potential purchaser of a new system may be faced is shown in Figure 5.5, taken directly from a manufacturer's brochure. In this case the manufacturer has given some indication of the relevance to certain sizes of hotel of his particular software which helps a potential purchaser greatly.

```
The software will run on most MS DOS business computers which have at least
256Kb of RAM memory.  The program information is stored on magnetic disk
and the size of the establishment will determine the disk storage
requirement.

The following is an approximate guide, for detailed specifications please
contact your dealer.

HOTEL SYSTEM

No. of Bedrooms       Minimum disk storage required
up to 20              1x720Kb or 2x360Kb
20 to 40              2x720Kb or 1x720Kb plus 320Kb RAM disk
40 to 100             At least 5Mb (hard disk)
100 plus              Contact your dealer

Typical Installation
These are typical transaction numbers for a 40 bedroom establishment.
Front office - Full transaction details retained for one month.
Occupancy rate                                     100%
Number of chargeable items per day per room          3
Duration of stay - average days                      2

Sales Ledger
Account Customers                                  100
Invoices (per month)                               100

Purchase Accounts - Details retained for three months.
Supplier accounts                                   60
Supplier Invoices per quarter                      600
     average of three lines per invoice

Menu Processor - 500 menu items.

General Ledger - 3000 automatic transactions + 50 manual entries.

Total space required 720Kb data disk.
------------------------------------------------------------------------
```

Figure 5.5   *Hotel system requirements*

How many floppy disk drives can be used at the same time?

In business situations it is often necessary to have two drives being used simultaneously, helping to avoid frequent insertion of disks. Sometimes the on-line capacity is expressed in characters rather than drives.

What types of hard disk are there?

The number and capacity of hard disk drives is important in some applications such as general ledger or stock control. A number of hard disk drives will help reliability and there are combinations of between one and four, or even more. This could give a capacity of between 5 Mb and 20 Mb, less system overhead.

Should I use magnetic tape?

Magnetic tape cassettes as a means of storage are very slow. They have a limited storage capacity and can only assimilate information sequentially, which makes them almost useless in business situations.

What can go wrong with floppy disks?

The floppy disks, being electro-mechanical, provide the weakest link in any micro-computer system. It is estimated by the manufacturers that a disk should survive 160 hours of individual access to a track. It is because disks can fail that it is essential to always make back-up copies.

How can I safeguard data held on a disk?

Information held on floppy disk is almost certain to be of great value to the caterer's business and therefore every care must be taken to avoid accidental or deliberate destruction. It is essential to regularly copy disks. This only takes a short period of time (perhaps only a few minutes) and should be built into normal working practices. One day this might represent the most valuable few minutes that the computer operator spends on behalf of the catering company.

How can I take care of the floppy disks?

In order to ensure that the disks are well looked after the following guidelines should be followed:

(1) Always make sure the disk is kept in its cover.
(2) When inserting disks into the drive do so carefully and do not force them.
(3) Do not bend the disks in any way.
(4) Do not touch the surface of the disk that is visible through the read/write slot.
(5) Keep disks out of temperature extremes.
(6) Keep disks away from any source of magnetism.
(7) When writing on the disks to label them press gently.
(8) Do not let disks get damp.
(9) Do not try to remove disks whilst they are being read or written upon by the computer.

What is an interface?

Once involved with computers, before long the caterer will want to connect the machine to some other equipment. The computer may need to be linked to a printer so that hard copy can be produced, or maybe the computer is to be linked into a network; a point-of-sale till may need to be linked to the computer, or maybe a modem to enable the computer to communicate along telephone lines needs to be connected. If any of these happen to be the case then an *interface* is required.

An interface is the circuitry that allows any external devices (peripherals) to be attached to and to communicate with the processor. Physically, interfaces are the actual places where peripherals are attached at the side or back of the computer.

The interface works as an interpreter allowing the signals from the processor to be understood by the peripheral. Another function of the interface is to regulate the speed at which data flows between the computer and the peripheral equipment. The same functions are performed by the interface in the reverse direction. Peripheral devices connected via interfaces might include such items as printers or disk drives.

There are two types of interface:

- serial
- parallel

The type of interface fitted to the computer depends on whether the peripheral piece of equipment itself is run in parallel with the processor or in serial.

A *serial* interface is where the data from the computer flows down the communication line in bits – one after another. By contrast a *parallel* interface allows the data to flow simultaneously down parallel lines.

There can sometimes be problems in synchronizing a peripheral with the processor because of a number of variables. A typical example is where a printer is attached to the processor. In this case the interface will simply be a plug and a matching socket. It is important if contemplating utilizing a peripheral from a different manufacturer to the computer itself that the interfaces are identical otherwise the two will be incompatible. Whilst most printers, for example, are equipped with at least two interfaces the computer itself may only have one. The connecting circuitry must therefore be synchronized to ensure proper communication and the correct print messages to be interpreted. Specific designs of interface are therefore required to link certain devices to computers.

It is becoming common practice for the major computer systems manufacturers to provide their systems with interfaces that permit compatibility with most of the other well recognized systems. Figure 5.6 shows the possible computers that could be linked to a sample hotel property management system and a sample restaurant system.

The printer

The printer is the part of the business computer system that produces the 'hard-copy' output or print-out that is necessary in many applications. After all, it is not possible to carry a large amount of information on the VDU screen and it may be far more convenient to produce a print-out of information that can be referred to at leisure. Whether this information be the daily trading results or the production of a bill for a guest, a printer of one sort or another will be required.

Whilst there is a large selection of printers on offer, their usefulness in a catering application may only be judged by their speed, print quality and reliability. The caterer has to strike a fine balance between these requirements when selecting an appropriate printer. Unfortunately selecting a printer is almost as difficult as selecting the computer itself, such is the variety of technology available.

Printers themselves vary immensely in *print quality*. The caterer is unlikely to need a high-quality printer for the production of internal information for the sole consumption of staff, but for word processed external correspondence the best possible 'corres-

TWO EXAMPLES OF THE INTERFACE POSSIBILITIES OF COMPUTER SYSTEMS

HOTEL INFORMATION SYSTEMS (HIS) Property management System

The following 83 systems will readily interface with HIS systems:

CALL ACCOUNTING SYSTEMS: Alston's Tel Charge, Bitex, C-Com,CAI, CIT Alcatel, Com Dev's Dynacall, Computerware's TFMS, CP National, Digital, Ericcson ASB900, FM 5000, Focus, Hassler, HOBIC/HOBIS, HOMISCO, HOTAC, MICROCALL, MOSCOM, 5000/4000E, NCR 3250, NEC's Neax 12 (CDR), NEC's Neax 22 (CDR), NEC's Astro, Northern Telecom 503 (CDR), Omnifax, Plessey, Ronco, Siemens 601, SL-1 (CDR), Sodeco, Softel, Stromberg Carlson (CDR), Summa Four, Sure, Sykes, TC-3, Telesphere Microtel, TFM, XETA.

ENERGY MANAGEMENT SYSTEMS: Robertshaw, Scientific Atlanta.

VIDEO CHECKOUT: EECO, Spectradyne.

TELEPHONE MANAGEMENT SYSTEMS: C Squared Systems PBX, Dimension 600 and 2000 PBX, FCS-6201, GTE OMNI Series II/III, Hitachi EX-10, Hitachi DX-30/40 EPABX, Hoteltag, LEXAR UTX-1001, NEC's Neax 22, NEC's Neax 2400 via IBM PC, OKI PABX, PARC 24 via I Bw P/C, ROLM CBX 8000 and CBX 9000, S.C. Telecom, SL-1 via IBM PC, STC Starswitch, Telectron, TN 6030 PABX, Unimat 4080 PBX.

POINT-OF-SALE SYSTEMS: CTC's System 1000, DTS 571, HRC, Micros 470, NCR 2160, Remanco 1500/1700 Series.

IN-ROOM MOVIES: Bitex, CATV C-8000 (MAT Sushita), DBC, Domestidyn, Spectradine, Toshiba.

BEVERAGE CONTROL SYSTEMS: Barvendor, Bell Captain, CIT Alcatel, Roboserve.

MAID SERVICE: Guest Key, Plantronic, Teleport 3000.

GENERAL PURPOSE COMPUTER LINKS: Spectradyne, Telectron.

REMANCO Restaurant System

The following 30 systems will readily interface with REMANCO systems:

ADP Infront, Aptech, Applico, Arms/Ritz, Bank, Berkus CLS, Burroughs, Champs, Connect, EECO, EECO Enhanced, Encore Lodging, Galler/Micor, HIS, Hogatex, Honeywell, Hoskyns H2, Hotman, Information, JBA, Lodgistix/IHS, Micro Z, Most by Walvis, Optim Hotel Manager, SARA, Servitech, TAJ, Team Data, Telegraphix, Televerket.

Figure 5.6   *Interface possibilities of catering computer systems*

pondence quality' standard of print will be necessary. The caterer or hotelier may have a requirement for a near letter quality (NLQ) printer for output that does not need to be of very high quality and there are printers especially aimed at this application. Many of the standard computer printers are dot matrix and here the readability will depend upon the size of dot matrix used. Different standards of print quality are therefore a prime consideration in different applications.

Some printers actually use pressure on the paper to print in the same way as a typewriter and these are referred to as *impact printers*. Both dot matrix and daisy wheel printers are of this type and they are of particular use if, for example, the caterer is using multi-ply forms with several copies as they possess the required 'force' to print all the way through. There are also printers that are *non-impact* where thermal transfer and ink-jet processes are used. In addition there are laser printers.

Whilst there will be some information that may be produced during the night, such as back-up print-outs, there will also be the requirement for customer bills to be produced instantly as the guest is waiting to pay and leave. The *speed of a printer* is described as 'cps' or characters-per-second. Manufacturers normally quote the maximum possible cps which, depending on the quality of printing being undertaken, could actually reduce by as much as a third in the practical situation. It should also be noted that in most cases the faster a printer operates the noisier it becomes. This noise can be quite irritating in a public area such as a busy reception and potential purchasers should be aware of this possible source of annoyance to guests and staff. Printer hoods or housings can minimize this problem.

There are almost certain to be differences in speeds between printers even if the speeds are advertised as being identical. The only true test of the cps is to set each printer a task of producing, say, two sides of identical A4 printing and then compare the times taken. The quality of test given is important as a daisy wheel printer, for example, needs time to position the carriage and to spin the character required to the correct position for printing. The speed achieved will therefore depend on the distance that the carriage has to travel in order to position the characters to be printed. Laser and matrix printers, by contrast, will have a uniform print speed.

There are some standard tests that may be quoted on the data sheet supplied with each printer. The two standard tests are:

(1) The 'Triple A' Test – a line of A A A A A A A A A.
(2) The Shannon Test – seven lines of text.

Some comparison of printers can therefore be made if references to these tests are outlined on the respective data sheets.

It should also be noted that the take-up speed of paper will affect the speed of a printer; this is known as the *paper slew feed*. A printer capable of 90 cps and with a slew feed of 8 inches-per-second will obviously be faster than one with a paper slew feed of 1 inch-per-second.

The *noise* level of the printer will be an important consideration for many potential users as this may not be complementary to the luxury surroundings of many catering and hotel locations. The standard test applied by manufacturers here is to locate a microphone and a noise meter one metre in front and one metre above the printer. Needless to say, the impact printers tend to be much noisier than the non-impact varieties.

The *width of the carriage* on the printer is just as important as it would be if an ordinary typewriter were being purchased. The more columns available the better, with 132 horizontal print positions being useful whether compressed on to 8½-inch paper or on 15-inch width. Some offer eighty columns on 8½-inch paper which is in fact more than adequate for most catering applications.

Consumable items related to printers, such as the ribbons, should be chosen carefully as a multi-strike cloth ribbon will last far longer than the single-strike carbon variety that the supplier will be keen to sell. The improvement in print quality of as little as 10 per cent will not compensate for the tedium of changing ribbons every day, but for high-quality correspondence the expensive carbon ribbon will prove necessary.

The caterer will also have to decide whether to use printers that handle single sheets of paper or continuous fanfold paper. The printer, ideally, should be capable of handling both but it is important when examining the tractor mechanism to check that paper cannot fold back on itself and overprint, which can be most aggravating. It is worth remembering that mechanisms that pull the paper through are much more reliable than those that push.

One minor tip: watch out for the £ character on printers manufactured in the USA. It is possible that # will replace £ on some US printers and the caterer will then only be able to use one or the other of these. If the caterer produces print that requires both then there may well be problems, so US printers should be examined carefully.

It is quite common for a printer produced by a different manufacturer that fits the necessary specification to be attached to the computer. Indeed few computer manufacturers actually make their own printers, most being made by specialist printer manufacturers. It is quite likely that the printer is of older technology than the latest equipment available and therefore it is worth examining the different types on the market that may demonstrate the new refinements or improvements.

Where maintenance is concerned, printers are undoubtedly more unreliable than the computer itself as they have moving parts. It is estimated that an average printer would have a 40 per cent duty cycle with a minimum life of three years continuous use at this cycle. What this actually means is that in an eight hour working day the printer would be in use for 40 per cent of the time which is about three hours. Printers should be covered by a maintenance agreement and be prepared to pay as much as 18 per cent of the original cost per annum for this service. (Maintenance of the computer itself will cost between 10 and 12 per cent.)

The selection of the correct printer will require a calculation of the quantity of printing that the business requires. This will involve examining the priorities for printing in different locations, some of which will require fast, high-quality printing such as in the cashiers, whereas in other locations slow and draft quality output will be adequate. Caterers should ask themselves whether it is worth paying twice as much for a printer (not forgetting the recurring cost of maintenance) so that, for example, they can obtain weekly reports five minutes or monthly reports 20 minutes earlier.

Manufacturers' terminology can confuse the issue. There are both 'rated speed' and 'true speed', as well as speed being indicated by characters-per-second or lines-per-minute (lpm).

Where speed is concerned, whatever the rating claimed the printer will undoubtedly operate at a slower one. A character-per-second printer is calibrated on the number of characters it prints on each line. By contrast a line-per-minute printer supposedly prints at a constant speed regardless of the number of characters per line.

The last point is to consider a 'buffer' if considerable use is to be made of the printer. It is certain that the printer will work at a slower rate than the computer itself and a buffer will store data to be printed until the printer becomes free, whilst allowing continued use of the computer itself.

Dot matrix printers

Until comparatively recently it was argued that correspondence quality printing could only be produced by daisy wheel printers but with the constant improvement of dot matrix printers this philosophy is fast disappearing.

With a dot matrix printer the printing actually takes place when the needles or wires on the print-head are physically impacted against a ribbon, thus making an image on the paper, just in the same way as a typewriter.

The quality of a dot matrix printer depends on the density of dots or the size of the print-head matrix. The way the printer operates is to set a certain number of

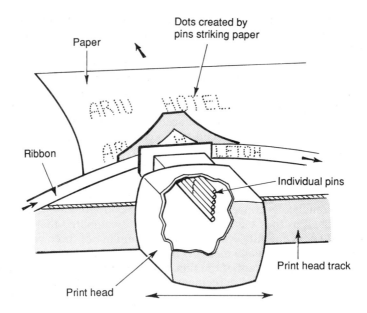

Figure 5.7   *Dot matrix printer*

dots to a given area or matrix, usually on a 7 × 9 design. The size of the matrix determines the ratio of the height of the character to the width of the character. The more dots in the matrix, the sharper and crisper the character image. If you cannot see the dots on the paper, except on magnification, then you are looking at a very good quality printer.

The great advantage of a dot matrix printer is that usually the printer can change from one typeface to another instantly, giving great flexibility.

It should be remembered that the dot matrix printer, being of the impact variety, does make a noise as the wires hit the ribbon and then the paper. They are at least as noisy as daisy wheel printers and some people find their high-pitched buzz more annoying, but at least the print duration is not as long as with a daisy wheel.

Daisy wheel printers

These used to be the only type of printer capable of producing good looking paper-work and correspondence quality letters and until recently were invariably the first choice for word processing systems. They are now, though, being rivalled by the improvement in print quality of the dot matrix printer and by the perfection of laser printers.

A daisy wheel has a full set of characters on the individual petals or spokes of an interchangeable wheel. These characters are embossed on to the paper when rotated electro-mechanically into the correct position to be struck by a hammer through a carbon ribbon at a speed of 50 to 80 characters-per-second. Daisy wheel printers are rather slow because of the mechanics rather than the electronics used, but they do produce good print as well as a large selection of typefaces. Some daisy wheel printers use a concave 'thimble' configuration for the spokes rather than a flat wheel.

Figure 5.8   *A typical daisy wheel*

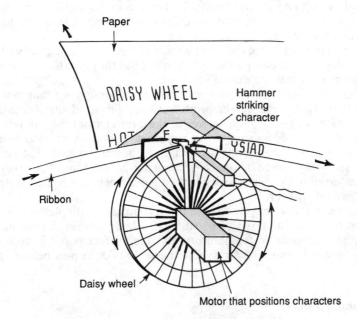

Figure 5.9   *Daisy wheel printer*

The daisy wheels themselves are often interchangeable and therefore a large selection of different typefaces is usually available. This is a distinct advantage but it can be irritating to have to change wheels every time a new typeface is required. This inflexibility rules out the use of graphics which are becoming increasingly important in business applications.

Laser printers

> 'Although laser technology is still relatively young, laser printers are expected to be one of the biggest single growth areas in computing . . . A great deal of excitement is now being generated by the new intelligent laser printers which some are predicting will have a similar impact on industry and business as the rise of the personal computer.' (Hanks, 1986)

Only comparatively recently the only choice where printers was concerned was whether to buy a dot matrix or a daisy wheel. The choice was then between flexibility or high-quality reproduction. The emergence of laser printers has removed this basic decision.

There are two types of laser printer:

(1) Laser printers that replace the old impact printers.
(2) Intelligent laser printers.

Whilst intelligent lasers are expected to revolutionize the printing industry and any application involving publishing, it is the former category that is of primary interest to caterers.

Laser printers can reproduce a wide variety of copy ranging from all types of text to graphs and drawings. As an added bonus, they are extremely fast and much quieter than impact printers. They are often so quiet that the only noise to be heard is from the fan cooling the printer.

Laser printers not only have the great benefit of being fast and quiet with their print production being regarded as publication quality, but they also have automatic paper-handling capabilities that are difficult to beat.

Most of us are familiar with photocopiers, even though we may not appreciate exactly how they work, and a laser printer utilizes almost identical technology. The way they operate is that the data arrives at the printer from the computer as digital information. The printer interprets this information and its beam is aimed on to a spinning drum where it traces out the images to be reproduced. The surface of the spinning drum is magnetized by the laser beam and allows toner to be picked up. The toner is transferred to the paper which is then passed between heated rollers that fuse the image on to the paper.

As regards reliability laser printers are often compared with photocopiers that have a reputation for breaking down. In reality, if a laser printer is kept in a dust-free atmosphere at a reasonable temperature and the correct paper is used there is no reason why it should not last for five years or 100,000 copies before requiring an overhaul.

Thermal transfer printers

Thermal transfer printers are peaceful and quiet compared with other printing technology. The way they work is to transfer ink to paper using the dot matrix principle with a heating element inside the print-head moving across a heat-sensitive ribbon which transfers the image on to the paper.

Invariably these printers utilize special heat-sensitive paper rather than ribbons, but this tends to make the process much more expensive and heat-sensitive paper is not recommended for business applications. Some models have started to appear that do not need heat-sensitive paper and these are making the whole process more viable.

Thermal transfer printers are particularly useful in offering reasonable quality printing and inexpensive colour facilities. They are, however, notably slower than dot matrix printers and they cannot be used for applications such as addressing envelopes, labels or printing requiring special stationery. Sometimes the printing will fade in certain storage conditions.

Ink-jet printers

The ink-jet printer is non-impact and operates by pumping electrically charged particles of ink in a matrix through the print-head on to the paper. Absorbent paper is required. These printers give good draft quality print inexpensively, but if the wrong paper is used the print may go blotchy on coarse paper or the ink may take a long time to dry on shiny varieties. Ink-jet printers are quiet and fast, managing 210 characters-per-second. As they are non-impact, multiple ply forms cannot be handled.

Disposable cartridges of ink are used that should last for up to six million characters. A development being worked upon is the use of solid ink which will mean that the ink is only in a liquid state as it passes from the print-head to the paper. This will make the ink-jet printer less messy and allow more readily the use of colours.

Line printers

Frequently found on mainframe computers, *line printers* can print a whole line of characters simultaneously thereby giving very high speed printing. Many line printers can produce up to 1,200 lines a minute. The most common line printers are of the 'barrel' or 'chain' variety.

Word processing

Word processing is perhaps the one major application that has brought computers to the notice of a large number of users. The ability to merge and alter text, to personalize correspondence and to save enormous amounts of time where standard letters and forms are concerned, has been accepted as a major advantage of computerization.

Of necessity, most word processing in the hotel and catering industry takes place in the front office as this is the location where there tends to be staff with typing and secretarial skills. It is therefore highly relevant for us to examine word processing, whilst also referring to other areas where word processing may be put to good use.

The following are some of the major application areas of word processing in a hotel and catering environment:

FRONT OFFICE
- Personal replies to all enquiries and reservation requests from guests
- Text may be transferred for telex transmission

MARKETING AND SALES
- Personalized letters for mailing lists as well as correspondence
- Text merged for telex transmission to selected customers

ACCOUNTS
- Preparation of debt collection correspondence
- Mailings produced for sales ledger customers

FOOD AND BEVERAGE
- Menu printing

CONFERENCE AND BANQUETING
- Printing of delegates' luggage and lapel badges
- Mail shots to target groups, previous clients or regulars

Text printing

Where word processing is concerned there are a number of factors that the caterer should consider which may improve immensely the quality of the final product produced by the hardware.

The first facility that a caterer should watch out for is the physical size of the printer as the catering trade has some specialist needs, such as the printing of à la carte menus and wine lists. Too small a printer will not permit a non-standard size of paper to be handled. The type of printer linked to the word processor will also determine the speed with which the system will operate and it will be of great benefit to have not only a choice of print style but also the ability to choose high-quality print where necessary. Where print character sets are concerned it will be of use in some operations to have access not only to script, but also italic, classical and modern text presentation.

Spelling checkers

It is all too easy to insert text on to a document on a screen and then print it before realizing that there were a number of spelling mistakes. A spelling checker facility helps greatly with this problem by automatically checking the spelling and pointing out obvious errors. Each word that has been used is compared with a dictionary held in the computer's memory and attention is drawn to any words that are thought by the computer to be incorrect.

One of the problems is that the hotel and catering industry uses a large amount of jargon that will not appear in a standard dictionary. It is therefore advisable to use a word processing system which allows new words to be added to the dictionary thereby covering an individual establishment's vocabularies. A supplementary dictionary may be useful which may be set up by the user so that culinary terms, for example, may be added to the main dictionary.

Text manipulation

It is useful to consider how text may be manipulated once presented on a word processing system. A merge facility, for example, will open up a number of ways that may make the system far more useful as a management tool.

It is common for word processing facilities to be used either independently for the production of letters and memos or in conjunction with the accounts program, in an integrated system, for the production of advertising mail shots, letters to debtors, etc. The names, addresses and account details are extracted automatically. Reports may also be sent directly to the word processor for editing and mailing list labels can be printed.

Menu production

One task that is made much easier with a good word processor is the production of menus. Quick and easy printing of menus, tariff cards, or any price lists may be undertaken by word processor as these are all items that require frequent changing. A list of items will be kept, which may be grouped into categories with a description, cost and selling price. It is simple to select the items for the day and they will then be printed out in the format of a menu under the appropriate headings, with a description and selling price which can be tailored for an appropriate menu if necessary.

Useful word processing system features

- It should be possible to load the program into the machine quickly.
- Text should be easily edited.
- The instructions should not require the user to need prior knowledge about computers.
- It may be advisable to purchase a word processor that allows other additional computing functions.
- The screen should be easy to read.
- What is seen on the screen should be what is printed.
- Document length should be flexible, as required by the user.

Security

One of the maddening problems with some word processors, especially those that are based on personal computers, is that text may be accidentally erased if the computer is switched off or if a disk fault is encountered. Some word processing systems will allow each page of a document to be saved as it is completed; this can slow the process down but slight loss of speed is a penalty worth paying.

What is a modem?

A modem is a device that allows two computers to communicate with each other through a data communications telephone link. In addition to allowing two computers to communicate, modems also facilitate the communication of peripherals with the computer should they be physically separated. Literally, the word 'modem' stands for 'modulator–demodulator'.

All data equipment uses digital language, otherwise known as binary because it consists of just two entities, 1 and 0. These are easy to represent electrically as 'on' or 'off' conditions. Information is therefore transmitted and received in streams of 1s and 0s, called binary digits or bits. The telephone network currently is analogue and carries information as continuous rapidly changing tones (rather than individual bits), which is ideal for carrying the human voice. Digital data, though, has to be converted into analogue form for transmission across the telephone network and then back to digital form at the receiving end. These two processes are respectively called modulation and demodulation, and both are performed by single devices known as modems which connect a computer to the telephone. Some modems come as small separate boxes which attach to the computer, but increasingly they are being built into terminals.

In practice computers can either be linked via analogue telephone lines, which is the most common method, or via digital core networks such as 'Kilostream' or 'Megastream'. Long term, and probably not for a period of at least ten years, British Telecom will introduce their integrated services digital network (ISDN) which will provide national coverage and then the public switched telephone network (PSTN) will no longer be needed for digital communication.

The modem facilitates communication by translating the computer's digital signals into tones (analogue signals) that can be transmitted over the PSTN using normal telephone lines or leased dedicated analogue lines. A similar modem is required at the other end to translate the tones back into digital signals that can be understood by the second computer.

There are two basic types of modem:

- acoustic
- direct connect

With *acoustic modems* users dial the telephone number of the modem with which they wish to communicate and then place their receiver's handset into the relevant cups on top of the modem. The problem is that the handset can sometimes confuse data during transmission because it is prone to picking up background noises. Modems that are *direct connect* are preferable as they hook directly on to the telephone line and in some cases even have the facility to dial automatically.

The transmission speed of data is important when contemplating a modem and this is measured in bauds. Where microcomputers are concerned the usual transmission speed is 300 baud, which means that about 30 characters per second of information can be transmitted or received. Some modems are designed to operate at a variety of speeds so that different computers may be accessed. Amongst the slower systems using modems, for example, is Prestel. The very advanced modems will detect automatically the speed of the modem it is communicating with and adjust speed accordingly.

When contemplating the purchase of a modem it is important to check whether it can both send and receive information at *full* or *half duplex*. It is a feature of many modems that they can do both, but half duplex modems cannot do both simultaneously. A full duplex modem can, and will therefore enable much speedier operation.

The difference between multi-user computers and computer networks

There is often confusion amongst caterers as to what the real difference is between multi-user computers and computer networks.

A *multi-user computer* is one where each user has a terminal and these are connected to a single microprocessor or computer. The computer itself arranges its work so that it shares its time between the various users, but this happens so swiftly that each user actually feels that they have the computer to themselves. With a multi-user computer, unlike a computer network, all users share the same computer.

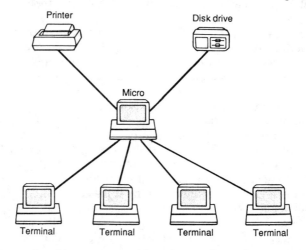

Figure 5.10   *A multi-user system with a micro as the single processor*

A multi-user system is best suited to catering applications where there will be several users making use of the same files, such as in the situation of reservations or accounts. It should be remembered, though, that a multi-user microcomputer will normally only cope with between 10 and 12 peripherals, whether these be terminals or printers, and the more that are connected the slower the system will be due to the time sharing method.

A *computer network* is subtly different in that under this arrangement a chain of microcomputers can be linked together along with peripherals such as printers. Each user has in effect an 'intelligent workstation', or what others might call a 'local computer', which is connected to the network whilst sharing the peripherals. One sort of network, a Local Area Network (LAN), permits users to share data and to pass information from one computer to another.

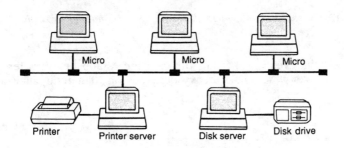

Figure 5.11 *A 'bus' network that connects together all the micros on a single cable*

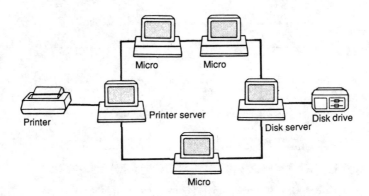

Figure 5.12 *A 'ring' network where all the micros are connected in a circle*

Of the various types of network configurations the *star* version is the slowest as well as requiring the most wiring; the *bus* improves on this, provided there are not too many collisions between instructions flowing in different directions; the *ring* is a further improvement. Coaxial cabling is much faster than *twisted pair* cabling, although the latter is easier for adding extra connections.

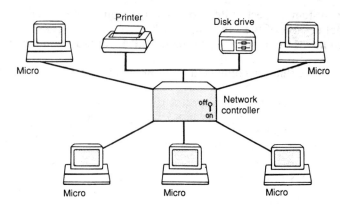

Figure 5.13   *A 'star' network where all the micros are connected to a central controller*

Networks, of whatever variety, suit the catering establishment where users have mainly separate tasks which make heavy demands on their individual microcomputers.

A multi-user micro is good for:

• people based in a single office or department

• no more than 10 people

• a staff with limited need to use the computer,except at scheduled peak times

• a staff that needs to work from the same data resources, like accounts and customer records

• departments that are unlikely to expand beyond the capability of the computer to support them

----

A network can:

• link micros to other micros, minis to mainframes, or any computer to any other, as well as to data storage devices like disk and tape drives, and shared peripherals like printers

• link together with any number of computer users simply by joining network to network

• link together adjacent offices and buildings using physical cable connections and distant office sites using remote telecommunication lines

• link equipment from a wide variety of suppliers, running a wide variety of software

• allocate work from one processor to another elsewhere on the network in order to smooth out peaks and troughs

• help cut down the cost of printers, which can be shared by different suppliers

• unify the computing power of equipment from different suppliers

• keep in contact with colleagues who are often out of the office

• smooth the operations of a company that is expanding rapidly

----

Figure 5.14   *Multi-use and networking at a glance*
Source: *Which Computer*, October 1984.

The main advantage of a network over a multi-user system is that each computer connected to it may also operate independently, so that a failure in one machine does not affect the operation of the other parts of the network.

Local area networks (LAN)

A local area network is a communications system usually consisting of a number of microcomputers which are linked together within the same building allowing the distribution of voice, video or data. It is the inability of a LAN to use telephone lines for communication that usually restricts it to one building. This configuration of computers is certainly worth contemplating if there is sufficient use to which a local area network can be placed.

Typical LANs already in use in hotels may include point-of-sale billing systems and central television reception systems.

Some of the LANs available necessitate the dedication of one of the micros to solely controlling the functions of the network; it is therefore lost to general use and this often makes the arrangement less financially attractive. Perhaps a local area network should only be contemplated where there are more than five users. As an alternative to making use of a complete micro, a dedicated 'file-server' may be used. This is often a hard disk of the Winchester variety, along with a processor that effectively acts as a central controller making use of software that controls the activity of the network.

The simplest LANs make use of either a T-switch or an X-switch to allow a number of peripherals to be shared by various micros.

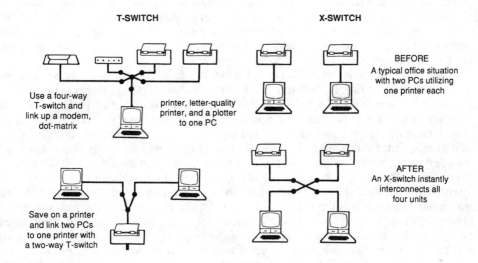

Figure 5.15   *Simple LANs make use of T-switches and X-switches*

Most LANs now make use of networks of the *Ethernet* variety which consist of coaxial cabling linked to boosters and modems that keep data circulating.

One of the features of networks, and particularly those of the LAN variety, is that the response time of the system slows when a large number of users are actively involved with the system. The reason behind this slowing down is that the software controlling the network is of necessity complex in order to permit the system to:

- allow micros to check if they are receiving messages
- control the switching of messages to a variety of users
- stop two users changing the same data simultaneously on a disk

The advantage of a local area network to a caterer is that it provides a flexible system to which it may be possible to add extra peripherals as and when it is evident that they are needed.

Wide area network (WAN)

Wide area networks mean a harnessing of computer power between establishments around a town, country, continent or worldwide, and in the latter case involve the solution of some complex communication problems.

Invariably to date these systems have made use almost exclusively of telephone links, but with new data systems coming into operation there will soon be many more dedicated data transmission lines throughout the UK at least.

In contemplating a wide area network it may be perceived by hoteliers, for example, that instead of being restricted by the relatively limited computing power of a microcomputer-based system, there are considerable benefits offered by a multi-site system. It is therefore becoming more common to find a number of hotels in different locations making use of such wide area network systems.

Such an idea is extremely useful to, say, a small hotel group as not only does each individual hotel profit from the larger number of facilities that are available, but the group management may monitor the total performance of the group or of individual establishments. The better systems allow this without compromising the control security of each individual manager or hotel.

A WAN would allow centralization of many of the administrative functions of the hotel group and the first area of interest would surround advance reservations. It will be possible to set up a centralized advance reservations office to make individual reservations in each of the hotels as it would keep an individual file for each of them. Close liaison would have to be maintained between the central reservations office and each hotel so that availability changes, such as chance arrivals, early departures and extended stays, were updated on the computer system immediately. If the central reservations office access the same file within the computer as the hotel staff then the potential for accidental overbooking due to the time lags involved in conventional communications will be eliminated. Additionally, the central reservations facility will allow accommodation availability within the entire group to be viewed, thereby giving the opportunity to offer alternative hotels if the original choice is already booked, or to take conference bookings using several hotels to accommodate delegates.

A WAN within a small hotel group would also allow centralization of the sales ledger function so that invoices and statements are issued centrally rather than from individual hotels. Staff expertise is increased and credit control and debt collection uniformly applied by utilizing a centralized sales ledger office and staff. The general ledger and purchase ledger may be similarly operated.

A WAN in this situation may considerably benefit the operation of a small group and need not necessarily be the domain of multinational operations.

Hilton's in-house communications network (Bennett, 1985)

Hilton International's *Hiltonet* network illustrates the complexities of establishing a worldwide means of communication, and the complications of linking a number of locations together using various speeds and sophistication of device to link computers effectively.

Firstly, it should be explained that Hilton International had a problem and that was how to set up a communications system between the 90 hotels in the company, 40 of which were situated outside North America. An added complication was that Hilton International was a separate company to Hilton Hotels which itself ran more than 250 hotels in the USA alone. The difference between the two companies was not evident to the customer, and indeed it was regarded as important for both companies that the operational difference should not be emphasized. The communications network would therefore have to operate a reservations service that was common to both, as well as a central database containing room availability for both companies so that customers would not become confused.

Since the early 1970s Hilton had made use of a reservations system in the United States and Canada called Hiltron. This was the first hotel system to possess two-way terminals in each hotel allowing both the making and placing of reservations to be undertaken. Outside America, an airline network called SITA and commercial telex systems were used to maintain contact. SITA was a system, in common with many of the time, which had its origins in the airline industry and was operated by Transworld Airlines.

The SITA system proved relatively cheap for the hotels where it could be utilized, but in many locations telex had to be used instead. There was therefore confusion within Hilton as different hotels could only be reached by either Hiltron, SITA or telex.

Having three avenues of communication created problems, especially in locations where SITA terminals were not actually on the hotel premises. In some of these situations communications had to be carried by messenger between the nearest TWA office and the hotel, which was hardly conducive to efficiency and totally unsuited to reservations. It was also a problem that whilst memoranda and administrative messages could be readily communicated, SITA terminals and telex terminals were only equipped to receive messages. In the absence of a confirmation being transmitted when messages were received, people placing reservations were often uncertain as to whether their booking had been accepted or not.

It was because of problems such as these that a private in-house network was investigated, costed and found to be both desirable and within the budget available.

The intended new network was required to improve reservations specifically and the following requirements were decided upon:

- *Reliability*. Every message or reservation had to reach its intended destination. There had to be report methods and reports to verify arrival.
- *Quality*. All transmissions had to arrive accurately. There was to be no manual intervention, and there had to be methods to check for transmission quality.
- *Speed*. All messages had to arrive within a specified period of time. Urgent messages should be delivered within minutes anywhere in the world.
- *More reservations functions*. The international locations had to be fully integrated into the existing North American Hiltron network. Any location in the world had to be able to book a reservation and get immediate confirmation from the central database in Dallas of dates, room types and rates.

- *Cost-effectiveness*. The cost of the network had to be competitive with other commercial alternatives. Furthermore, as the company grew, the network had to be easily expandable with minimum cost. (Bennett, 1985).

The new Hiltonet system was to operate from two IBM 3083 mainframe computers (the second computer providing back-up) situated in Dallas, Texas, and after much investigation of the existing flow of messages London was identified as the correct location for a computerized message switching device. London was not only geographically central for the many European locations in need of networking, but it also boasted excellent data circuits and low cost telex facilities and all Hilton International locations would communicate through this device.

The initial Hiltonet system still required three levels of communication in order to reach all locations.

- On-line terminals and printers were to be used for the 25 hotels geographically nearest to London. Separate leased lines ran to Belgium, France, The Netherlands, West Germany and Switzerland and then spurs (multidrops) ran to each individual hotel. This system ran at 2400 baud.

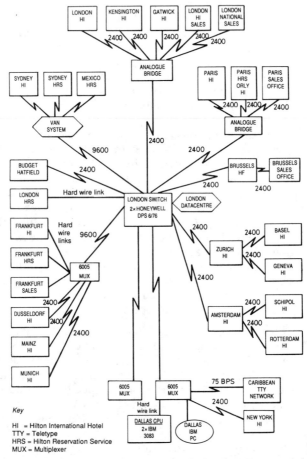

Figure 5.16   *Hiltonet Network (May 1985)*

- Teletypewriter circuits using leased lines were connected to 32 other locations in countries such as Israel, Barbados and Australia, running at a relatively slow speed of 50 to 75 bits per second.
- Commercial telex facilities were used to communicate with the switching device in London from the remaining 40 locations, which were either very remote or did not have sufficient volume of messages to warrant even the low cost teletypewriter service.

The London switch was in fact a pair of minicomputers each with 512K of memory and two 256 Mbyte disk drives. The second minicomputer acted as a back-up. The switch could either be used in 'message' or 'reservation' mode and was able to translate data coming in from any of the three types of input device used by the system. An electronic mailbox facility was provided for all users and confirmation was sent out when a message was received not only by the switch but also by the destination.

For reservations the switch would automatically, on receipt of a keyword, connect a Hiltonet user to the Dallas mainframe utilizing a 19.2 kbit/s data circuit. Interactive on-line reservations communication was therefore possible, with the switch adjusting the varying speeds of devices and amounts of data as well as carrying out error checks so that the London/Dallas link worked effectively.

As if that was not enough Hiltonet provided the company with monthly costs and traffic reports so that managerial control over the system could be applied.

In the future it was envisaged that more locations would operate with higher speed devices and the facilities would be provided to carry not only accounting data for Hilton but also marketing information.

The SITA system (Hotel & Catering Technology, 1987)

Whilst Hilton pulled out of the SITA system, preferring instead to utilize their own private in-house network, SITA remained very much in existence.

As already mentioned, the SITA system, known as SAHARA (SITA Airline Hotel Advanced Reservations Automation) had its roots with airlines. Of late the largest user of the system has been British Airways who made the decision to link in their own international computer network called Babs. This merging of two computer networks allowed travel agents and offices worldwide to make flight and hotel reservations at the same time.

The merging of the two networks was looked upon as a great benefit not only to customers but also to contributing hoteliers who immediately benefited from access to the extra 38,000 computer terminals on the Babs system.

Hotels making use of the SITA system have several ways in which they can be incorporated. These are by:

- direct link between the hotel's reservations system and SITA

- indirect link between the hotel's reservations system and SITA via either: (a) booking agency; (b) representational agency

- a link via the British Airways database

Funding of the system is undertaken by a registration fee, an annual database maintenance charge and a booking fee for each guest name record.

```
STATUS AS AT APRIL 1987

Total hotels using SAHARA in UK            150
Total hotels using SAHARA in Europe      1,000
Total hotels using SAHARA world-wide     2,200
Total hotels contracted to SAHARA        7,853
```

Figure 5.17   *SITA's SAHARA hotel booking system*

Communications

There are a number of new technology communications services that make consider-able use of networks of one kind or another and a variety of some of these are outlined here.

Telex

Telex was the original electronic mail system, having evolved out of the old telegraph network of the nineteenth century.

The more modern telex machines are in effect word processors with a message transmission facility tagged on. Messages may be edited, transmission may be de-layed, automatic retry is available and incoming messages may be stored if the machine is already in use and printed out later.

Dedicated telex machines are available or personal computers may be utilized instead with the addition of extra hardware and software.

Fax

A fax or facsimile machine combines the image reproduction capability of a photo-copier with the communication benefits of a telex. It allows exact copies of documents to be transmitted to other fax machines via the telephone network.

Fax machines may possess a memory which will store up to thirty pages of docu-ments, to be transmitted at approximately 11 seconds per page.

The most modern fax machines possess 'sequential broadcasting', which is the ability to send a number of documents simultaneously to a number of different loca-tions. This may have a number of business applications within a catering business. For example, from the sales manager's point of view a promotional 'mailing' may be sent direct to a number of customers, or from the regional manager's viewpoint an impor-tant memo may be distributed to a number of units within the region without having to wait for the traditional postal service.

A facility called 'relay broadcasting', which permits a document to be sent to multi-ple locations, is both fast and money-saving for a large business. Instead of paying long-distance charges from a central head office, the catering business may broadcast the memo to regional sites and then have them re-transmit to branch offices at lower local rates. With some of the better fax machines this means that in theory an impor-tant document may be relayed to an additional 100 locations from each of the 100 originally broadcast locations, giving the ability to send a document to thousands of units with one easy operation.

It is possible for a fax machine to 'store' incoming messages in a personal mailbox, the contents of which may only be viewed once a security code has been entered so confidentiality is maintained should the machine be in a public office.

As with telex machines, there may be an autodial facility for the most commonly used numbers.

Some of the most common reasons for using fax machines include:

- to reduce telex, phone and courier costs
- to reduce labour-intensive preparation of telexes
- to reduce inaccuracy due to transcription errors
- to overcome postal delays
- to transmit stock/sales/account information on company's own pre-printed forms

Intelpost

One of the aggravating situations that caterers may find themselves in is that they possess the necessary technology but the person with whom they are trying to communicate does not. This need not necessarily mean that communication must fall back on traditional methods as there are services such as *Intelpost* that cover this very situation.

Intelpost is a UK Post Office service that has immediate access to a network which offers same day delivery of telex and facsimile messages to many parts of the UK, as well as to Europe and North and South America.

The service is quite simple. Companies with facsimile, telex or computers equipped for communications can transmit copies via the Intelpost network to reach their contacts who have no such machine. All caterers have to do when they want to get information – on paper – to a contact is to prepare the contents of the message, adding the destination and delivery requirements, and then transmit it from the terminal to Intelpost. From there the global network is accessed and the message is transmitted to the nearest receiving centre, from where it may be collected or delivered by messenger.

Datel

Datel is British Telecom International's worldwide data transmission facility which allows computers in the UK to communicate with compatible equipment around the world through a telephone call connection.

Data can be sent throughout the world between almost any kind of terminal equipment so that, for example, a personal computer in Milton Keynes can exchange files with a similar machine in Munich, receive a document from a word processor in Montreal, access a database in Melbourne, and interact with a large mainframe computer in Minneapolis.

Provided the transmitting modem and receiving modems are compatible then data transmission may take place between them using the Datel facility wherever they happen to be situated.

Telecom Gold

Telecom Gold is a sophisticated messaging and electronic mail service that can link various networks together, thereby passing messages internationally. It is more sophisticated than viewdata and possesses the telex advantage of being able to prepare a message first and then transmit it at speed. The system may be accessed by personal computers or even electronic typewriters to send messages to the receiver's mailbox. It is also possible to program your PC to automatically download messages from a mailbox at certain times so messages are not overlooked.

The electronic mail system is quite simple. Each user has their own electronic pigeon-hole or mailbox on the central computer. The mailbox is identified by a particular code. Other users can send messages to this mailbox, once they know the code, and the owner of the mailbox retrieves messages at frequent intervals. The mailbox will either be interrogated daily by the owner or the owner's attention may be drawn to the fact that a message is waiting by means of a radio-pager.

As an electronic mail system Telecom Gold has a number of advantages and disadvantages when compared with the traditional telex service.

Advantages
- cheaper (10% of telex cost)
- wider print range
- large number of destinations may be reached in one go (500 UK)
- easier to use
- more facilities
- terminals are smaller

Disadvantages
- have to retrieve messages as they are not automatically delivered
- electronic mail users not as common as telex

Viewdata (Videotex)

Networked viewdata systems such as Prestel have made their impression most in hotel companies, for reservations, and in the major breweries where the technology is used to receive regular, accurate and up-to-date information from their networks of up to 1,800 public houses, restaurants and specialized food retailers nationwide. This information collating process used to take three days but with viewdata is now completed in a matter of seconds. The facility utilized by the breweries includes data collection, stocktaking information, payroll and electronic mail.

The necessity for back-up

One of the major problems with computers is that they are fallible: they are not 100 per cent reliable all the time. Accepting, therefore, that a computer in a hotel and catering situation is often required throughout the day and night, then there has to be some procedure to counteract the inevitable problems that will occur when the computer goes down.

The industry is well aware of hotels where, for example, the entire reservations record has been lost thanks to a disk being corrupted. The ensuing chaos has taken weeks to sort out and even then a percentage of bookings have never been found, causing problems of guests arriving who are not expected.

With the improvements in software and hardware that have been made throughout the 1980s many computer suppliers have recently turned their attentions to procedures that can be carried out that will prevent a hotel or catering operation from becoming paralysed when a computer goes out of action.

The point should be made that not all computer failures are accidental or caused by malfunctions as there will be scheduled times when the computer is taken out of action to allow necessary maintenance to be undertaken. The actual timing of maintenance will be difficult to programme as the computer will undoubtedly be required through-out the working week, both during the day and during the night. It may well be that the system will deliberately be shut down during the day and then the question is posed as to how the hotel or catering establishment is going to cope.

An added dimension to the problem is that many staff these days have not had experience of manual systems and therefore it is essential that there is a planned procedure for dealing with the consequences of a computer failure. Some suppliers suggest that to counteract this problem caterers should schedule downtime during each operational shift and actually carry out normal work without the computer during these planned practice sessions. The intention is that the staff will then be able to cope manually if the computer should go out of action due to a malfunction. An added benefit is that it is then also possible to timetable scheduled maintenance periods without the fear that the staff will not be able to undertake their duties.

Other suppliers are already insisting that prior to a new computer system being installed the establishment's existing manual operating procedures are recorded and incorporated into a permanent record which is kept on file in case of a computer failure. In some cases caterers have never formally recorded their methods of operat-ing before and the record may well have to be created from scratch. This information is kept both at the catering establishment and at the office of the computer supplier so both locations know what is happening in the event of a failure.

The night audit in a hotel will provide most of the reports that are needed to run the establishment manually, although it may well be an advantage to refer to other reports too that can be distributed to the various departments to form a hard-copy back-up. The reports that will be needed will be those that show the following:

- expected arrivals
- expected departures
- room availability

The departments that will need this information will include:

- reservations
- reception check-in
- housekeeping
- switchboard
- cashiers
  (Mable, 1987)

The last department named, the cashiers, will undoubtedly be affected most by the loss of the computer system as guests may well have to check-out without being given a bill. This is where the greatest difficulty occurs, but there are various ways of overcoming the problem.

How can the configuration of a computer help?

In the event of equipment or power failures it will be the intention of the better hardware suppliers that their system should allow recovery and halt the potential disastrous loss of data.

There are basically two configurations of computer system which assist this inten-tion greatly:

- single processor system
- dual processor system

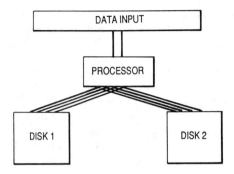

Figure 5.18 *Single processor system*

Single Processor System. Where this type of system is installed this will provide a dual disk updating facility. This will ensure that all the data being processed is recorded simultaneously on to two disks. In the event of the corruption of one disk the total system can be recovered with ease and the caterer can continue on the second disk without loss of data.

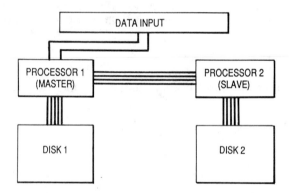

Figure 5.19 *Dual processor system*

Dual Processor System. This system provides full dual processing capabilities and ensures that all transactions are processed by each computer concurrently. In the event of equipment failure the entire system may be operated from the second processor without loss of data or significant time lapse.

In addition to the configuration it is a wise precaution to make at least a daily copy of all the data and programs for storage outside the system. In the event of a complete system failure, prompted by fire or some similar disaster, all information up until the time of the copy can then be retrieved.

At regular intervals throughout the daily operation of the hotel a program might be run which prints the minimum information necessary for the functioning of the hotel without the computer.

Disasters

Whilst the word disaster may seem rather emotive the caterer or hotelier must be aware of the possibility of the total loss of the computer system due to unforeseen circumstances. Many users just turn a blind eye to the fact that computers in general have been put out of action by fires, explosions, lightning, power failure, water, as well as by building defects.

There are firms that will provide standby facilities. They usually depend on a wide number of users of similar computers investing in a stand-by machine, on the assumption that they will not all go out of action at the same time.

Insurance is another answer to disasters covering damage, the cost of operations immediately after a failure, and the overall cost of recovering the lost data.

SOFTWARE SELECTION

> The best computer without the right software is as dangerous as a drunk in charge of a Rolls-Royce. (*Banking World*, 1986)

The term *software* is used to describe the many programs that computers can utilize. Programs themselves are the instructions that the computer follows that allow it to carry out its various tasks. These tasks can be relatively simple, such as receiving information from a terminal keyboard, or as complex as running a complete night audit function for a major hotel.

Whilst hardware has fallen dramatically in price over the years thanks to improvements in the components, notably the introduction of the silicon chip, and cheaper manufacturing methods, software is still an expensive part of any computer system. The production of software (computer programs) for specific catering applications, or indeed applications in general, is still a labour-intensive operation and necessarily exposed to increases in inflation. After all, programmer salaries will continue always to rise at least with the inflation rate.

There are basically three types of software that a caterer will need to know about. These three types of software are:

- operating systems software
- applications software
- integrated software

Operating systems software

The first type of software that should be examined when a system is being considered is the operating system which controls the computer's internal housekeeping. This software coordinates and integrates the work undertaken by the silicon chips within the computer that in turn operate the central processor, as well as the input/output processors for the printers, screens and storage disks.

Specific operating system software is designed to run particular computers. The software contains instructions that tell the computer how to handle standard commands, such as reading from and writing on to disks.

The operating system is similar to the nervous system in the human body in controlling what the computer does with the information placed in its memory. What the operating system does is to ensure that the computer follows instructions. The most common operating systems are:

- UNIX   Initially used for scientific research with mainframe computers UNIX and its derivatives are now available as operating systems on smaller computers.
- XENIX   Microsoft's version of UNIX.
- CP/M   (Control Program for Microcomputers) The creation of Gary Kildall of Digital Research, this operating system is versatile and used both on home computers and particularly for word processing on business machines. This was the most popular operating system for microcomputers until the uptake of MS/DOS.
- CP/M-86   A speedy, friendly and improved modification of CP/M.
- CONCURRENT CP/M-86 A version of CP/M-86 that is multi-tasking.
- MS/DOS   (Microsoft Disk Operating System) This is the operating system that runs on most large micro-computers and is regarded as both competent and easy to learn. It is an improved and more powerful version of CP/M and has become very popular. Unfortunately MS/DOS only allows a computer to do one thing at a time (single-tasking) and can only be used by one person at a time (single-user). It is therefore problematical for users who have heavy computer usage requirements.
- PC-DOS   An IBM modification of MS/DOS with variants numbered 2.1, 3.0 and 3.1. It should be noted that a computer operating with PC-DOS 2.1 will not operate, for example, with PC-DOS 3.1.
- BOS   (Business Operating System) Not used to any great extent in UK.
- UCSDp   Not used to any great extent in UK.

Applications software

Applications software is the term given to programs relating to specific tasks such as word processing, spreadsheets or databases, and it is the real reason that a caterer will purchase a computer. After all, the user is not really interested in how the computer works – in other words what operating systems software it uses – but wants to know what the computer can do for the business. The applications software is therefore vital to the caterer.

Whilst word processing, spreadsheets and databases are examples of common general purpose applications software, there are also specialized applications software packages specific to the hotel and catering industry. Typical examples of applications software of this type would include:

- reservations
- guest history
- menu compilation
- liquor stocktaking

Whatever the applications software, the point should be made that they will only operate with specific operating systems software. If, for example, a reservations applications software package has been written to work with the MS/DOS operating system it will not work with the other operating systems.

Integrated software

Integrated software contains a number of applications that share identical data. A typical integrated software package might contain word processing, spreadsheets, graphics, database and communications. The integrated software in this case might allow the caterer to print information from the database utilizing the word processor.

What should be watched out for when choosing software?

The software should demonstrate that it has been written by people familiar with the operation of a catering business so that it is therefore of practical use. The procedures that are required should be feasible in the pressure of the work situation, and above all the software should be easy for the operator to use or, in other words, user-friendly.

The best way of testing the validity of the claims of the software salesman is to actually contact and interrogate existing users.

When investigating a potential supplier of software it should be established that there is a wide selection available which will indicate a competence with the catering industry. If the same software can be used in a range of establishments it will benefit the purchasing decision within a group as staff will be capable of being relocated without additional training.

One should also establish that the software being offered is modern and therefore up-to-date and that the supplier has the commitment to keep on modifying it as systems and technology progress. If the supplier shows a positive attitude in this way it will be evident that one is dealing with a firm that has the right attitude.

In what forms can the caterer purchase software?

There are basically four options that caterers have to consider when contemplating the purchase of appropriate software. These options are:

(1) To buy package software
(2) To commission tailored software
(3) To commission bespoke software
(4) To write software for themselves

To buy package software

Package software will have been produced for a large number of similar establishments by a well established supplier and it will therefore be exceedingly reliable, having had all the bugs removed. As there will be a large number of copies in existence it will be relatively cheap. In many cases package software will cover many of the problems that may crop up in an establishment and in most cases it is quite satisfactory. Package software is very useful for general accounting and payroll applications, but it might be inflexible in other situations which may not suit all catering operations.

The main criticism of package software is that no two establishments are identical in their method of operation and therefore inevitably the establishment will have to tailor its operation to suit the computer. In some cases this may be no bad thing as the experience of the software designer elsewhere may give caterers the obvious solution to problems that have previously eluded them.

To commission tailored software

Some caterers make the best of both worlds by installing package software that may be modified or enhanced. This solution, which is often necessitated by the inflexibility of package software, is called commissioning tailored software. This is software that is pre-prepared (in other words a large amount of the programming has already been completed) but contains sufficient space within its framework to allow the addition of the specific catering establishment's detail. For example, in a restaurant package there will be the opportunity to use the detailed menu items for that restaurant and bills will be printed with specific detail individual to the establishment.

Similarly, reservations software will possess a framework of the dates into the future for which bookings will be handled but there will be the opportunity to add in the specific bedroom and tariff arrangements for the hotel concerned.

In some of these cases the catering establishment's computer manager or other staff may possess the ability to modify or tailor programs to the establishment's requirements, but as may be imagined this usually only occurs in the largest of organizations that can afford such luxuries.

To commission bespoke software

Where it is impossible to utilize package or tailored software, possibly through the difficulty of fitting the catering establishment's work processes around the constraints that are imposed, bespoke software is the answer.

Bespoke software entails writing programs specifically for an individual catering establishment. This may be the ideal solution in theory, but it is actually very expensive and labour-intensive in practice. It is also necessary to make sure that the programmers are expert in the field of catering and therefore understand the task they are undertaking, otherwise great problems may be created.

To write software for themselves

Whilst caterers always have this option the number who are practically equipped to undertake such a task is relatively low, and of those the few who actually have the time are even more thin on the ground. Except in a very few circumstances, therefore, this is an option that one would imagine would be out of the question for the majority of caterers.

In the United States, however, research by the respected magazine *Restaurants & Institutions* has revealed that a surprising number of North American restaurant caterers have in fact written their own software. The results can be seen in Table 5.3.

Table 5.3 *'Have you written your own software?'*

	Segment			Type of establishment		
Program	Full service	Fast food	Hotel	Independent restaurant	Chain restaurant	Institutional
Accounting	–	50%	11.1%	14.3%	11.1%	23.1%
Menu analysis	20%	–	–	14.3%	–	15.4%
Inventory control	40%	50%	33.3%	57.1%	22.2%	38.5%
F&B cost control	–	–	22.2%	–	22.2%	15.4%
Word processing	–	–	–	–	–	23.1%
All of above	20%	–	–	–	11.1%	7.7%

Source: Tougas, 1986

Modular software

Just as it is important to consider the purchase of hardware that is capable of being expanded, software too must be able to accommodate enhancements as the business grows and more reliance is put on to the computer system. Software can be extremely expensive and to have to renew it every time the hardware is enhanced can be a very costly business so proof should be requested at the time of purchase that the system is in effect modular. A modular arrangement will also permit caterers to select the applications particular to their business needs and ignore those that might not be applicable.

A typical example of grades of enhancement may be seen in Figure 5.20.

```
CHECK IN 1                CHECK IN 2                CHECK IN 3

Front office              Front office              Front office

Advance Reservations      Advance Reservations      Advance Reservations

Room Enquiries            Guest & Room Details      Guest & Room Details

Checking-in               Checking-in               Checking-in

Checking-out/Billing      Checking-out/Billing      Checking-out/Billing

Transaction Posting       Transaction Posting       Transaction Posting

Daily End Routines        Daily Routines            Daily Routines

Management Information

Room Transfers            Room Transfers            Room Transfers

                          Back Office               Back Office

                          Sales Ledger              Sales Ledger

                          Management Information     Management Information

                          Room Maintenance          Room Maintenance

                                                    Guest History

----------------------------------------------------------------------------

Single user micro         Multi-user networked      multi-user minicomputer
System for 120            micro system for 100      system for any size of
bedroom hotel             to 200 bedroom hotel      hotel

----------------------------------------------------------------------------
```

Figure 5.20 *Check-In hotel systems overview*
Source: Chart Software Ltd

A modular approach allows hoteliers a number of alternatives where software and hardware are concerned. Figure 5.20 demonstrates how software may be used on more than one type of hardware so that it may remain familiar to the users as the establishment purchases more powerful computers. The second alternative is to build up modules gradually, as business requirements permit, or to tailor modules to the operations of a particular establishment.

One of the integrated systems that has been developed along modular lines is CHAMPS from Thorn EMI. This system has been structured in a modular way to allow it to be configured to suit the exact requirements of each hotel in which it may be used.

Each module and sub-module is fully integrated with all the other modules at all stages so that data need only be entered into the system once; thereafter the information is instantly available to the relevant departments and in the appropriate form.

The various modules and their software descriptions are as follows:

Reservations. Availability and reservations satisfy the requirements of a hotel to aim at selling 100 per cent of available beds every night at maximum revenue. Future forecasts and past analysis programs are also provided.

Front hall. The front hall module creates a billing account for rooms and groups, adds charges to accounts, and clears the account as the guest(s) leaves the hotel whilst maintaining complete, accurate audit control.

Sales ledger (accounts receivable). Automatic verification and printing of invoices updates the accounts receivable, which operates in open item mode. Facilities exist to match payments against invoices and detailed, on-line aged analysis is available.

Guest history. Details of any guest's stay(s) in the hotel may be recorded and updated automatically to provide increased service and marketing information. A word processing facility is also available.

Bought ledger (payable). This module produces automatic payments to each supplier for any validated invoices, taking account of pre-defined discounts and manual payments. There is an on-line enquiry for individual suppliers and transactions.

Nominal ledger (general). The code structure and reports conform to the American Uniform System of Hotel Accounting. The hotel may superimpose its own code structure to retain comparability: automatic updating is provided.

Interfaces. The system incorporates facilities to receive information from a wide variety of telephone exchanges and telephone monitoring equipment. Full records are maintained and analyses provided. Full control of room status is ensured via the telephone message system, which enables housekeeping staff to transmit vacant, let and ready status as soon as the status changes. Discrepancy and information lists are available. There is a direct link with some existing makes of room bars for billing and information purposes. In addition, a facility has been implemented to enable bar staff to directly input charges via the telephone system. Several manufacturers of POS terminals have developed suitable links.

Payroll and personnel. A payroll and personnel suite that meets all UK statutory requirements and allows for all payment periods. Includes SSP and direct links to BACS if required.

Office administration. Includes personal diaries, 'to do' lists, electronic messages, calculator, word processing, sales records, business cards and many more programs to automate and streamline the functions of office administration.

Stock register. Allows for ordering, delivery, allocation and value analysis of stock, together with blind audit by stores and minimum quantity warnings. Enables 'cyclic stock' recording and Hotel(s) Audit of Stocks, including orders outstanding.

Multisite. All the modules are able to cater for one or a number of hotels on one computer system, with facilities to consolidate information centrally or by hotel and allow for such requirements as cross-hotel reservations, consolidated and individual ledgers, electronic mailing across the group, etc.

Security

Whatever the size or type of computer being utilized it will be important to make sure that the users of the system only have access to the applications, functions and data that they individually require to fulfil their work. There will, for example, be information that is confidential to some aspects of the operation, such as accounts, that needs to be kept away from staff who do not require access to these figures.

The hardware and software will therefore be designed to limit such information to the people who need access. This limitation of access usually works on a variety of levels.

Hardware. It may be a feature of the system that certain pieces of hardware are only permitted to perform certain functions. In effect, each department in the catering operation may be allocated menus of programs which refer specifically to their requirements. Each device, whether this be a VDU or printer, can be designated so that it only performs the functions of that department. For example, reception and cashiering programs are not required in the switchboard area, whilst most of the switchboard programs would be available to the reception and cashiers.

Software. Each operator on the system who has access will usually be provided with their own individual, and therefore unique, security password. The passwords may be entered daily by the supervisor at the start of a shift or they may remain constant for regular intervals, depending on the management's requirements and operational methods. All work performed by the individual operator is logged under their unique password. It is important that the system never displays the passwords in use.

The software will also provide the facility for the hotel management to impose on any program in the system a level of authority below which access is restricted. Even though a program may appear on an individual user's program menu, access to it may require a higher level of authority for the program to proceed. Each individual may require an authority code in addition to their own unique password or they may be barred totally from the specific program. A typical representation of levels of authority might be as follows:

- supervisors' authority
- managers' authority
- general managers' authority

References

Banking World, September 1986. A survey of software for banks.

Bennett, Robert, May 1985. Hotel communications: going private. *Communications/Communications International*.

Breen, Terry, 12 January 1987. Hoteliers select most valuable high-tech features. *Hotel & Motel Management*.

Bushman, John A. (FFARCS, FInstMC, MBCS, Member of British Computer Society, Deputy Director, Research Department of Anaesthetics at the Royal College of Surgeons). VDU readers – read and relax. *Mind Your Own Business*.

Hammond, Carol, June 1986. The hazards of VDUs. *Practical Computing*.

Hanks, Keith, October 1986. Laser printers create a revolution. *Mind Your Own Business*.

Hotel & Catering Technology, April 1987. BA goes live into Sahara.

Mable, Cynthia A., 12 January 1987. New property management systems offer many features. *Hotel & Motel Management*.

Marko, Joseph A. and Moore, Richard G., August 1980. How to select a computing system. *Cornell Hotel and Restaurant Administration Quarterly*.

Tougas, Jane Grant, 25 June 1986. Why computers make dollars and sense. *Restaurants & Institutions*.

Turner, Annie, April 1987. The second hand computer market. *Computer Systems*.

Which Computer, June 1984. Stars of the silver screen.

Which Computer, October 1984. Multi-user buying guide.

Whitaker, Marian, November 1986. *Survey into the Use of Information technology in the Hotel and Catering Industry*. Brighton Polytechnic.

Whitehall, Bruce, 23 October 1986. Hotel systems: pros and cons/All systems go! *Caterer & Hotelkeeper*.

6 Overcoming Computer Jargon

'COMPUTERSPEAK'

The computer industry has developed so quickly that our existing vocabulary, which has served us so well over so many centuries, has been forced to absorb a large number of new terms at a seemingly indecent rate. Indeed the new terminology has been essential to keep pace with the discovery of new technology.

Every industry has its own peculiar method of communicating its intricacies and technicalities. Just as every country around the world has its own language and regions within each of those countries have their own dialects, the computing industry has its own peculiar terminology that can be daunting to uninitiated outsiders, who may feel that they have been exposed to and confused by a whole new language.

Computer buffs often seem to abbreviate their way of speaking, often managing confusingly to combine their words, and indeed they have created a language largely of their own as new technology has progressed. Sometimes this language is referred to as *Computerspeak*.

This is certainly no exaggeration and the unfortunate consequence is that many of us who have come across computers for the first time have often been discouraged by the enthusiastic computer salesmen purely because they are incomprehensible. Even the copious literature that is churned out by the purveyors of software and hardware contains a large amount of technical computerspeak that makes little sense to the layman.

When one combines terminology with the similarly introverted world of the caterer then there is an obvious opportunity for misunderstanding. Caterers are largely people in a hurry operating against instant deadlines and they possess little patience or indeed opportunity to actually sit down and fathom out what this baffling new technological language actually means.

When caterers are confronted by the enthusiastic salesmen it is essential to ensure that they actually grasp the technical phrases that are being fired at them. It is no exaggeration to say that computer salesmen can be quite frightening when they get into full swing and are intent on selling their machine. Large quantities of jargon and statistics may be used and caterers should be inquisitive and not allow the salesman to leave them behind.

It is important for the caterers to realize that they are first and foremost caterers and that the computer is just another piece of equipment that will allow them to serve their customers more efficiently, and therefore they do not have to become knowledgeable computer experts. They just need to know what the computer will do for them.

Many caterers will have been lucky enough to have been exposed to personal computers throughout their education. For those who have had new technology thrust upon them since entering the industry, many terms and pieces of jargon are explained in the following pages that hopefully will help shed some light on the subject.

It is therefore the intention this part of the book to give a synopsis of some of the commonest computer terms so that the average caterer may have some chance of cracking what can appear to be the incomprehensible and infuriating code otherwise known as computerspeak.

Before getting immersed in the jargon of computers as it applies to hotels we should refresh our minds with the knowledge that not everybody feels that computerspeak is as serious as it is made out to be:

An alternative glossary

ABORT	An arguable way of avoiding the inevitable.
ADD-ON	Used by salesmen, as in 'ADD-ON a couple of noughts for that bit of gear'.
BACK-UP	Used in the phrase 'This really puts my _____'.
BENCHMARK	Scuff marks left by clumsy handling of hardware.
BUG	Found in all personal programming and general software, another way of saying 'I dunno what's gone wrong with the thing – must be a BUG'.
CAD	A bounder who uses a machine instead of a T-square to do his technical drawing.
CHIP	A chance for the office wag to make a couple of Music Hall Gags.
COBOL	A terribly difficult language invented by the Aboriginals of Arnhemland.
COMPUTER	An incredibly fast idiot.
CRT	A television.
DEBUGGER	The person who wrote the program in the first place.
DIGITAL	A one finger salutation to the system after a trying day.
EMULATION	The sincerest form of flattery.
ERROR	A constant reminder of your inability to operate a simple piece of machinery.
FLEXIBLE DISC	A disc that can be folded in half to fit in your pocket.
FORTRAN	Another language from those Aboriginals.
GOTO	A string put to the computer as in 'You can GOTO . . .'.
HEADCRASH	The movement made by the operator in despair gently against the screen.
JOYSTICK	A misnomer in Games, blamed for everything.
KEYPUNCH	Final attempt to make a particular command understood.
LOOP	Something you will eventually hang yourself with.
MSDOS	A household cleaner.
PASCAL	Language written in Mandarin this time.
PASSWORD	Something you forget.
PROGRAMME	Misspelling of PROGRAM.
SILICON VALLEY	A breast enlargement centre.
TERMINAL	The condition of any operator living near a computer.
VIEWDATA	An expensive con by telephone.
WINCHESTER	A disk that is difficult to remove and when you do it won't work again.
ZILCH, ZIPPO, ZERO	What you get on the screen when it crashes.

Which Computer, 1983.

HOW TO CONQUER 'TECHNOFEAR'

Technofear is the feeling that many uninitiated people suffer when confronted by what appears to be the baffling technology involved in computer systems. It is quite apparent that computers have generated both resentment and misunderstanding in many people who have innocently contemplated their use but thanks to the shroud of mystery encouraged by the liberal use of the new technology's own language, have been alienated.

As discussed at the beginning of this section, computerspeak, or the jargon of computers, in itself serves to scare many people away from the very concept of actually making use of new technology. It is therefore essential that any potential user at least realizes that there is nothing mystical about the way computers work or the way they are described.

If caterers are worried about the jargon they should comfort themselves by thinking how the computer expert would cope with the terminology of the catering industry. Caterers themselves have their own jargon and take it for granted, for example, that the terms in a classical French menu will be understood by outsiders. It is reassuring to know that if some computer experts were confronted with phraseology such as 'There were so many no shows and a lack of chance that we didn't achieve our income occupancy', they would be equally as confused as the caterers who try to cope with their computerspeak.

Amstrad were one of the first companies to assist in overcoming this fear by introducing their ultra-cheap word processing system which they marketed as an enhanced typewriter. All the technicalities were smoothed over by using down-to-earth language in the instructions of their admittedly cheap systems and immediately sales of their equipment increased dramatically especially in the home market. The company overcame technofear in the sensitive home market by minimizing the use of computerspeak and thereby exposed many more people than before to the uses of computers.

Make use of training films

One of the direct methods of becoming aware of computers and their uses is to view a well made training film. Expert in this line is Video Arts, a film company formed by John Cleese, which has made some very successful and useful films on computers and their impact. *What is a Computer?* and *How does a Computer Work?* are two excellent films which make employees aware of the ways in which a computer can help and benefit them. The films are deliberately addressed at the employee with no computer experience at all and avoid computerspeak entirely. They are also totally free of any sales pitch that a film made by a manufacturer might include. More recent films include *What is a Word Processor?*, which follows the same format and may prove very useful in breaking the ice where familiarization with computerization is concerned. A well produced training aid, such as a film, may be a useful way of helping a person overcome technofear.

Resistance to change is quite natural

One must not forget in installing a new system that many of the staff are, through human nature, going to be resistant to change. Over a period of time they will have become used to their existing systems and may not therefore be totally committed to a changeover. This situation can also occur when changing from one computer system to another.

Staff may be fearful that their jobs may be under threat from a computer or a new replacement system. This may have been caused because they felt left out and therefore they may automatically be against the new system. In fact, not that many jobs are lost through computerization but jobs may well change. It has been asserted, for example, that a computer may take over the more interesting parts of a clerical job and leave the member of staff as purely a keyboard operator. Dealing with this type of assertion will require good management skills.

The staff, particularly those who are older and therefore have not grown up with computers, may fear that they are not going to be able to learn the system. The answer here is to make sure that the staff realize that they will be in control of the computer and not vice versa. Computerization can sometimes remove the existing hierarchical system of status and this too may cause anxiety. The physical loss of a colleague who has been moved from the adjoining desk to another part of the office may cause concern, and whilst this is on the surface trivial in practice it may lead to employee problems.

Not only will a gradual, fully involved, installation process be required but it will also be essential that the new system is 'sold' to existing staff so that they can see the future advantages. This is a very necessary part of overcoming technofear.

Try playing games

Well designed interactive games can provide a useful function in introducing staff who might suffer from technofear to the use of computers. Cultivating the image of the home computer as the modern equivalent of the train set – something that parents and children can both enjoy – has great benefits in that the initial stage of learning to operate the system does not discourage people, many of whom suffer from feelings of inferiority when faced with new technology.

It is therefore common on good software packages, whether these be designed for mainframe, mini or microcomputer use, to find built-in games that serve just this purpose of familiarizing staff with equipment well before they are exposed to complicated and apparently intimidating business applications.

THE IMPORTANCE OF TRAINING

There is little doubt that the effective operation of computer systems depends largely on the training given to staff. Training, though, is sadly one of those areas often economized on by caterers in general, and as a consequence many of them do not appreciate the benefits when it comes to computer installation and operation.

How are caterers trained to use their computers?

There are several different ways in which it is possible for catering staff to be trained to use their computers. Figure 6.1, taken from recent research (Whitaker, 1986), shows the relative popularity of the various methods up to now.

The same research also established the ways that existing members of staff had received their computer training, or information technology (IT) training as it was referred to in the questionnaire.

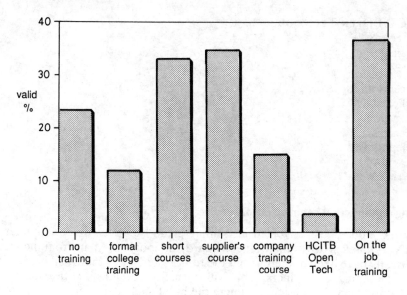

Figure 6.1 *IT training in catering*

Staff attending various training options

COLLEGE:
- computer managers
- assistant managers
- directors
- accounts clerks
- catering managers

SHORT COURSES:
- accountants
- secretaries
- assistant managers
- office staff
- accounts clerks
- managers

COURSES RUN BY SUPPLIERS
- secretaries
- receptionists
- computer managers
- chefs
- accounts clerks
- managers
- word processor operators

COMPANY TRAINING COURSE:
- managers
- office staff

HCTB OPEN TECH COURSE:
- directors
- managers

ON THE JOB TRAINING:
- receptionists
- office staff
- managers
- cashiers
- telephonists
- new staff

(Whitaker, 1986)

Training on the actual catering premises

One of the hidden costs involved in training given by the computer supplier on the caterer's premises involves the trainer's board and lodging. Apart from the fee, which will normally have been quoted within the total system cost, there will be the problem of accommodating the trainers. This will normally be laid on with ease by a hotel where rooms can be kept aside, although the hotel must allow for the consequent loss of revenue if the rooms could otherwise have been let to customers. Equally, food should be no problem in a hotel as the opportunity exists to make use of one of the restaurants. In the case of an establishment without accommodation, such as an industrial caterer, hotel rooms will have to be booked and meals out of hours arranged.

CASE STUDY NUMBER 9

TRAINING REGARDED AS AN IMPORTANT ELEMENT OF INSTALLATION

A company that operates eight hotels recently embarked on a policy of total computerization both for those hotels already within the group and those proposed in the future. The priority requirements of the chosen system were reliability, good support, user-friendliness and a competitive price.

'Support and back-up was essential', said the group's development executive, 'and we wanted a company that would provide a whole service, not that time-wasting and costly conflict between hardware and software support.' It was a requirement that the final quotation included a certain amount of training which along with configuration costs, cabling and installation was regarded as essential.

'We learned the best installation procedure by experience!' said the group development executive, 'and feel fairly well versed now in terms of disruption and staff training.'

It was apparent that although the hotel staff were apprehensive they were also positive about computerization and the computer company's experience in training and smooth installation paid off. 'The importance of pre-live, on-site training can't be over-stated', she said. 'A conference room was set aside in each hotel with a dummy-run system which the staff, left to their own devices for two weeks following an initial training session, could play with at their leisure.'

'Another advantage of choosing a well-known system', she added, 'was the fact that some of our staff were already familiar with it. I've found from experience that it's more difficult to train members of staff away from one system to another, than it is to train them from scratch.'

As well as organizing the programme for installation a representative of the computer company, who was allocated to the hotel group full-time, visited each hotel to assess how much training would be necessary and to set a diary for training dates.

Once the systems went 'live' the company gave full 24-hours-a-day support until the hotel staff were confident they could manage. There has subsequently been a regular weekly check from the computer company to ensure that staff are happy with the systems.

The company are very pleased about the choice of their computer company with the development executive explaining that, '99 per cent of the staff in our hotels are very happy with the system'. Perhaps this is in no small way due to the comprehensive training given at the outset.

(*Hotel & Catering Technology*, 1987)

The benefit of user-friendly software

Some computer systems are much easier for staff to train on than others. These tend to be the systems that are described as user-friendly as they have software that has been designed with the user in mind, not a computer scientist.

It is always a great advantage where ease of training is concerned if the system boasts a HELP facility that gives advice to users who find themselves unable to progress with an application. On pressing the relevant help code the user will be presented with a display that facilitates the solving of the problem through questioning and allows the user to continue. A good help facility is therefore essential so that staff can, in effect, train themselves by solving their own problems. It is also argued that user-friendly software leads to the learning curve for new staff being considerably reduced, thereby providing competent staff at a lower cost.

Should all the staff be trained?

Some computer suppliers prefer to train a limited number of the caterer's staff rather than the entire staff. Indeed some purchase agreements for systems include training for a maximum of six members of the caterer's training staff or key personnel free of charge. It is argued that this form of training has proved more effective in meeting the long-term objectives of a caterer's business, rather than the more traditional methods where the computer supplier attempts to re-train all the staff in the new method of operation.

References

Hotel & Catering Technology, January 1987. Friendly about their system.

Whitaker, Marian, December 1986. *Survey into the use of Information Technology in the Hotel and Catering Industry*. Brighton Polytechnic.

Appendix
Glossary of computer jargon

Access Time   The length of time taken to communicate with the computer memory. This is also the time between making a request for information from the computer and it becoming available.

Acoustic Coupler   A device that accepts a telephone handset and converts the computer's digital signals for transmission along telephone lines.

Address   A number that designates a specific storage location in the device.

AFC   See Automatic Frequency Control.

AGC   See Automatic Gain Control.

AGRS   Automated Guest Registration System, such as the 'Night Clerk', which allows guests to check-in themselves by credit card after hours or when there is a queue at the front desk.

AI   Artificial Intelligence.

ALGOL   ALGOrithmic Language is an algebraic computer language.

Algorithm   A set of procedures for solving a problem.

Alphanumeric   A way of describing a set of characters consisting of alphabetic, numeric and special characters including punctuation marks in some cases.

Alphanumeric Keyboard   A keyboard containing both number and letter keys.

Application Program   A set of computer instructions written for a specific user application.

Applications Package   *See* Application Program.

Architecture   A term given to the internal design of a computer.

Archive   Long-term storage.

ASCII   American Standard Code for Information Interchange. A standard code for communications.

Assembler   The software that translates an assembly language into a code that is machine-readable.

Assembly Language   A 'low level' or elementary language used by professional programmers.

Asynchronous Transmission   When the transmission of data between processor and peripheral is sent at irregular times.

ATM   Automated Teller Machines.

Audioconferencing   A facility on a computerized telephone switchboard that allows a number of telephones or extensions to be linked together allowing a number of people to communicate with each other simultaneously.

Automated Guest Registration System   *See* AGRS.

Automatic Frequency Control (AFC)   The means by which a satellite TV station is kept tuned once located.

Automatic Gain Control (AGC)   The automatic adjustment of amplification of a signal to give constant output if there is variable reception with satellite TV.

AV Output   The video signal needed by a TV set that is also a monitor.

Azimuth   When referring to satellite TV, the position of the satellite expressed as a compass bearing.

Background   *See* foreground and background.

Back-up   A copy, usually taken for reasons of safety, so that accidental loss of one set of data does not mean total loss.

Baseband Output   The type of video output that is necessary if a receiving system requires a decoder.

BASIC   Beginner's All-Purpose Symbolic Instruction Code. A programming language often used with microcomputer systems. By the use of a compiler device instructions may be fed in using English as opposed to code. This is a 'high level' language.

Batch Mode   A way of inputting data into the computer for an application in a continuous stream. When the input has been

Batch Mode – *cont.*
completed the program is run and all the information processed.

Batch Processing *See* batch mode.

Baud A measurement in bits per second of the speed of transmitting data.

Benchmark Testing Testing hardware or software against fixed standards, or benchmarks.

Binary A system of numbers in base 2, which means it has only two digits – 1 and 0.

Bit An abbreviation for a binary digit. A single binary digit is usually represented by '1' or '0'. A bit is the smallest unit of stored data.

Bits Per Second (BPS) The speed or baud rate at which data can be transmitted.

Boot Up A term or euphemism for switching on the computer or for reading in the operating systems software from disk.

BPS *See* bits per second.

Buffer A device used to hold data temporarily during data transfer. This is commonly between internal and external elements of a system such as between the computer itself and the printer.

BUG An error in a program causing that program to give incorrect results. American US Navy computer expert Grace Hopper is said to have originated this phrase when a grasshopper emerged from the circuitry of her experimental computer having created a fault.

Bus The wiring that carries data between the processor, memory and store on a microcomputer.

Byte A sequence of eight binary digits which may be used to represent a single character of information.

CAD Computer-Aided Design.

CADCAM Computer-Aided Design and Manufacturing.

CAL Computer-Assisted Learning.

Capacity The capacity of a computer is normally measured in bytes and shown as 32K, 256K, etc. This is the number of units or characters which can be processed on a regular basis by the computer.

Caps Lock Key The key that keeps all keys in upper case.

Capturing A function within data processing when data is captured for input.

CAR Computer-Assisted Retrieval of information stored on microfilm.

Carrier-to-Noise Ratio *See* C/N ratio.

Cassette The store on small microcomputers, identical to a music cassette tape.

Cathode Ray Tube (CRT) The electronic tube that produces the visual display of data. A common integral part of a television. In the USA this is an alternative term for a VDU.

Cell Display area within a spreadsheet, or a segment of a mobile telephone network.

Central Processing Unit *See* CPU.

Character A letter, digit, symbol or punctuation mark that a computer can readily store.

Character Set The set of characters that a computer can produce such as ASCII on most microcomputers.

Chip The piece of silicon that holds the various electronic circuits which facilitate the memory and processor functions.

C/N Ratio Carrier-to-Noise Ratio. The way in which interference is measured on a TV signal.

COBOL Common Orientated Language which is devised to handle business system problems.

Code Presenting data within a computer using a system of symbols.

COM Computer-Output to Microfilm.

Compatibility The ability of two or more computers to run the same program without modification even though the program might have originally been created for a different computer system.

Compiler The software that allows a high level language program to become machine-readable.

Computer A machine that is able to perform problem solving and data processing.

Computer-Dependent A term referring to a business that cannot operate without a computer.

Computer Memory The internal store of the computer.

Computer Service Bureau An external source of advice and practical assistance run by computer experts.

Configuration The layout of the components of a computer system.

Consumables A term familiar to caterers with broadly the same meaning. In the case of the computer consumables refers to the paper, disks, ribbons, cleaning materials and accessories that are used by the computer.

Converter A piece of hardware that translates one computer language into another.

CP/M Control Program (for) Microcomputers. This is a commonly found program that organizes the internal operation of the computer. It is therefore an operating system and was developed by Digital Research Inc.

CPS Characters Per Second. A term used to describe the speed of a computer's printer.

CPU Central Processing Unit. This is the heart of the computer and can also be called the Processor. It is usually housed within the System Unit (SU) and consists of the processor, main memory and input/output controller.

Crash The term given to the failure of a program or part of a computer system.

Cursor This is the indicator symbol in the form of a line or square that appears on the VDU screen to indicate where the next input will take place, the next command originated or the next entry made.

Daisy Wheel Printer A high-quality printer of slow speed.

Data Information. This is the raw material, or items of fact, that the computer processes. Data is made up of characters, words, numbers and pictures.

Database A collection of information organized within a defined structure that may be accessed in a specific way.

Database Management System A collection of software instructions constructed to ease the job of linking complex sets of data.

Data Processing The manipulation of data through the execution of a sequence of instructions.

DBMS DataBase Management System.

DBS Direct Broadcasting by Satellite. The method of transmitting TV signals from a satellite.

Debug To remove errors in a program once they have been identified.

Dedicated Chip A chip that performs one task only.

Digital The description of data in digit form such as in binary, i.e. 0 to 1.

Disk A flexible disk coated with a magnetic material that stores information; sometimes called a diskette or floppy disk. *See also* Hard Disk.

Disk Drive The equipment that holds the magnetic storage disks and reads from and writes on to them.

Disk Operating System *See* DOS.

Dongle A small device supplied with a software package to protect it from unauthorized copying.

DOS Disk Operating System. This is the part of the computer that controls the operation of the disk drive. This covers loading the software, if necessary, as well as disk management functions.

Dot Matrix A pattern of dots that make up an image on the VDU screen or on paper output from a printer. There are consequently Dot Matrix printers too.

Dot Matrix Printer *See* Dot Matrix.

Down Convertor The piece of electronics that converts microwave signals down to TV frequencies.

Downloading The process of moving information or software from one system to another.

Downtime The time for which the computer is 'down' or out of action.

Dump A term used for the transfer and storage of data on a back-up storage system outside the main memory.

EBMS Electronic Bar Management System.

EDD Electronic Drink Dispensing System.

Edit The modification of information by inserting, eliminating or changing characters.

Editor A program that allows the user to edit data.

EFT Electronic Funds Transfer.

EFTPOS Electronic Funds Transfer at the Point-Of-Sale. A computerized facility by

EFTPOS – *cont.*
which customers may have their bank account debited direct without signing a cheque when settling a hotel or catering bill.

Elaz Mount   The mounting point of a satellite TV dish that allows it to swivel up and down as well as sideways.

Electronic Mail   A facility that allows communications or 'memos' to be sent and responded to throughout a computerized electronic office system.

Electronic Office   The integration of office functions that is reliant on a computerized system.

Encryption   A scrambling system that allows satellite TV signals to be received only by those sets that have a decoder fitted.

End User   The individual who makes use of a computer system.

EPOS   *See* Point-Of-Sale.

EPROM   Erasable Programmable Read Only Memory. A ROM memory that can be erased and programmed.

Erase   To remove information stored in the memory or on other storage media.

Ethernet   Local area network system of Xerox Corporation.

Eutelstat ECS F-1   A European communications satellite whose transmissions are received in the UK.

Execute   To undertake the program instructions.

Facsimile Machines (FAX)   A machine capable of transmitting and receiving exact copies of documents or photographs along telephone lines.

FAX   *See* Facsimile Machines.

Feedhorn   The piece of the satellite TV receiver that takes the signals reflected from the dish on to the aerial and focuses them.

Field   An item of data stored within a data-base.

File   A collection of related data or groups of facts.

Financial Modelling   A software package that allows detailed financial analysis and forecasting.

Firmware   Instructions for the computer stored in ROM.

Flexible Manufacturing System   An automated production system utilizing equipment which can be readily reprogrammed to construct a different product.

Floppy Disk   *See* Disk.

Footprint   The ground area within which satellite TV transmissions can be received.

Foreground and Background   The colour on the VDU of the text and screen itself.

Formatting   The preparation of a virgin disk to take data or programs.

FORTRAN   FORmula TRANslation is a computer language in scientific and mathematical use.

Function Key   Keys on a computer keyboard that carry out a specific task when suitably programmed. Also called User-Programmable keys.

Gateway   The link that a computer has with external networks such as Prestel.

Grid   A visual display of a spreadsheet program in rowcolumn format.

Handshake   The communication that takes place between two or more parts of a computer system. Handshaking means that they are ready to transmit and receive data.

Hard Copy   The print-out produced in document form by the computer printer.

Hard Disk   A permanent disk of large capacity usually contained within a computer. *See also* Winchester disk.

Hardware   The operational equipment such as the keyboard and screen that makes up a computer as distinct from the software. Without the software programs the hardware cannot function.

Head-End   The control room of a cable television network from which the television transmissions on the various channels are originated.

High Level Language   A computer language such as BASIC that uses English and mathematical notation.

High Resolution   The high-quality graphical picture possible when individual dots on the VDU screen can be identified.

HIS   *See* Hotel Information System.

Hobbyist   A somewhat unfair term for a person who uses a computer at home.

Hotel Information System (HIS) The arrangement of hotel information into a regulated flow that allows effective management.

IBM Compatible Machines from manufacturers other than IBM that will operate software designed for IBM equipment.

IC *See* Integrated Circuit.

Information Technology (IT) A term for the communicating of information by computer.

Ink-Jet Printer A printer that uses jets of ink to construct the printed image.

Input The entering of data into the computer.

Input Unit The terminal that allows data to be put into the computer.

Integrated Circuit (IC) A component of a computer system that is solid state.

Integrated Network A computer system involving a shared main computer database available to a number of users.

Integrated Services Digital Network (ISDN) A national switched digital network to be introduced by British Telecom.

Intelligent Terminal A computer terminal that can undertake some local functions within its own processor.

Intelstat VF-10 A communications satellite commonly used in the UK.

Interactive Display A display that allows the user to put in further data in response to information already displayed.

Interactive Video The linking of a computer with a video allowing the user to progress through a regulated decision making process at their own speed. Ideal for training applications in learning situations.

Interface The physical link between two computers that allows the transfer of information.

Interpreter A program that converts a high level language into a code that is machine-readable.

Inverse Video The ability of a computer to display characters in 'negative' on a screen.

I/O Input/Output. A port or connection through which the computer communicates with its peripheral devices such as the printer.

I/O Ports Input/Output Ports. Sockets in a computer where leads from peripheral equipment may be connected.

ISDN *See* Integrated Services Digital Network.

Kilobaud In the transmission of data this means one thousand bits per second.

Kilobyte (Kb) A measurement of computer capacity or memory. Kilo is normally the abbreviation for 1,000 but not as far as computer memory is concerned. One Kilobyte = 1,024 bytes.

LNO *See* Low-noise convertor.

Load To input information from a peripheral store into a computer.

Low-noise Convertor (LNC) A satellite TV 'down convertor' fitted to most receiving dishes to convert microwave signals from the satellite into TV frequencies.

Machine Code 0s and 1s or numeric codes that the Central Processing Unit can understand.

Macro Programming Programming of a very high level.

Magnetic Core A type of computer memory store.

Magnetic Disk A type of computer memory store.

Magnetic Drum A type of computer memory store.

Magnetic Tape A type of computer memory store.

Magnetic Wire A type of computer memory store.

Mainframe Computer A very large computer with a comprehensive array of applications.

MATV System Master Television system used in hotels to distribute television signals from a central receiver to all the television sets.

Megabyte (Mb) Mega is the abbreviation for 1 million but in computing memory terms it is 1,024,000 bytes. The term is used for gauging the capacity of hard disks. 1 Megabyte = 1,024,000 bytes.

Megastream A dedicated digital communication system that can be leased.

Memory The part of the computer system that stores data and programs.

Menu The list of options displayed on the VDU screen.

Metal Oxide Semiconductor Technology (MOS) The computer-aided design technique that allows circuitry layouts to be reproduced photographically on to a very small silicon chip.

Microcomputer A small computer using a microprocessor as the central processing unit. Also called a personal computer or a desk top computer.

Microprocessor The electronics within a single chip that perform data manipulation. It is in itself a comparatively small processor but it has a relatively large capacity.

Microprocessor Unit (MPU) The microprocessor that controls a microcomputer.

Microsecond One millionth of a second.

Microwave A very high frequency electromagnetic wave used for satellite transmissions. The same as used in microwave ovens but too weak to be dangerous.

Millisecond One thousandth of a second.

Minicomputer The middle range of computer that is neither mainframe nor micro.

MODEM MOdulation/DEModulation device. An electronic device that permits computer communication via the telephone or similar lines. *See* also Protocol.

Monitor The device that displays video signals from the computer. Also known as VDU or screen.

MOS *See* Metal Oxide Semiconductor Technology.

MPU *See* Microprocessor Unit.

MS *See* Millisecond.

MSDOS MicroSoft Disk Operating System. The control program for IBM computers and compatibles.

Multi-Access or Multi-User A computer capable of allowing more than one person to use it simultaneously is described as multi-access or multi-user. This is normally achieved by having a number of separate terminals but is not easy with small computers.

Multi-Programming This is a facility on some computers whereby several programs can be within the computer memory and simultaneously share available processor time and peripherals.

Multi-tasking A computer able to handle a large number of user requests at the same time.

Nanosecond One thousand millionth (one billionth) of a second.

Near Letter Quality (NLQ) A term for the printed documentation that a computer produces that is not quite of good enough quality to be used for a letter.

Network The formal linking together of several computers or peripheral devices.

Non-Volatile Memory Memory that is retained even when the power is cut off.

Numeric Keypad A computer keyboard with only number keys.

OA Office Automation.

OCR Optical Character Recognition.

OEM Original Equipment Manufacturer. A company that buys equipment and repackages it into a resaleable product.

Off-Line This is where the main processor is not in control of a peripheral or other piece of equipment.

Offset Focus The way in which the 'low-noise convertor' is mounted away from the centre of a satellite TV dish so that its signal shadow is less likely to cause problems with reception.

On-Line This is where the main processor is directly connected to a process or a peripheral and is functioning.

Operating System The program that organizes internally the operation of the computer.

Original Equipment Manufacturer *See* OEM.

Output The data that the computer produces.

Output Unit The terminal device, normally the VDU or printer, which allows information to be presented in visual or document form.

Package The set of programs related to a specific application.

Packet Switched Data Network *See* PSS.

Paperless Environment The environment that is possible within a business where only information of a legal nature is kept on paper. The rest is held within the computer memory.

Parabolic The curved design of a satellite TV dish.

Parallel The transmission of signals simultaneously.

Password A security code given to computer users to restrict information to specific persons.

Patch A programmers' term for an alteration to a program usually required to overcome a bug.

PBX A type of telephone switchboard.

PC Personal Computer.

Period An American term for full stop.

Peripherals All the computer devices that are attached externally to the main processor such as VDU, and printer.

Petalized A type of satellite TV dish that is segmented into 'petals' so that it can be transported with ease.

Pixel The individual dot, a number of which create the characters on the VDU screen.

Plotter A peripheral printing device used for reproducing graphics or pictures.

PMS Property Management System. A term originating from America to describe an integrated computer system utilized throughout a hotel.

Polarity The way in which the 'low-noise convertor' on a satellite TV dish is set up to handle either vertical or horizontal signals.

Polarotor An electronic device that turns the 'low-noise convertor' block on a satellite TV dish to change polarity.

Point-Of-Sale (POS) The place at which a sale is made, often far removed from the central processor.

Port The terminal or socket through which the processor communicates externally and into which leads from peripheral equipment are plugged.

POS *See* Point-Of-Sale.

Prime Focus A satellite TV dish where the 'low-noise convertor' is mounted directly over the centre.

Printer The computer device that produces printed output or hard copy.

Print-Out Output or hard copy from a printer.

Processor The part of the computer hardware that carries out operations to produce information from data.

Program The coded instructions that tell the computer to perform specific operations.

Programmable Read Only Memory *See* PROM.

Programmer The individual who creates a program.

PROM Programmable Read Only Memory. A chip that is programmed once and then cannot be altered.

Prompt A symbol that appears on the computer's screen when it requires information from the user.

Property Management System *See* PMS.

Protocol The linking software that allows two computers to communicate between each other.

PSS Packet switched data network. The network of telecommunications lines especially constructed for information transmission and controlled by British Telecom in the UK.

PSTN *See* Public Switched Telephone Network.

Public Switched Telephone Network (PSTN) The telephone system provided for general public use by British Telecom.

Pulse A sharp fluctuation in electrical voltage.

Punch Card A standard card bearing a pattern of punched holes that can be 'read' by a computer equipped with the appropriate reader device.

Punched Tape As for 'Punch Card' but a paper tape replaces the card.

QWERTY The name given to the standard layout of typewriter and computer keyboards, so named after the letters in the top left-hand row.

RAM Random Access Memory. Memory made up of operating system, and 'user memory'. Access to the information stored is not restricted and is therefore 'at random'. Size is expressed in bytes, for example, 64 Kb = 64,000 characters or bytes.

Random Access Memory *See* RAM.

Rapid Order System Point of Delivery *See* ROSPOD.

Read To/Into Entering information into the memory or store.

Real Time Expressed in seconds this is the ability to access, retrieve and update information instantly.

Record A single complete set of information contained within a database.

Register A fast storage device within the MPU that stores temporarily small quantities of data.

Remote Polling The ability to obtain information from a remote terminal or point-of-sale via telephone lines for the use of a central computer.

Reverse Video *See* Inverse Video.

RF Output The standard TV signal produced from the satellite transmissions by the receiver.

ROM Read Only Memory. Memory which is pre-determined and cannot be changed as it is protected from any inadvertent override.

ROSPOD Rapid Order System Point of Delivery. A holder situated in a restaurant that accepts a handheld terminal and then allows the information contained within the terminal to be communicated to the host computer.

Routine A program or part program that performs a single specified action.

Run A term given to the operation and completion of a computer routine or program.

Scart A standard European socket for connecting electronic equipment, especially where satellite TV is concerned.

Screen Format The number of characters that will fit on to a screen.

Screen Height The number of characters that appear vertically on the screen.

Screen Width The number of characters that appear horizontally on the screen.

Scrolling The method by which the display on a VDU rolls from one page to another.

Service Bureau An organization that provides computer services for other organizations.

Shadow Anything that obstructs microwaves between the satellite and the

receiver where satellite TV is concerned.

Soft Copy The display of information on a VDU screen.

Software The programs that tell the computer how to carry out useful tasks. Sub-divided into Systems, Manufacturers' and User Software.

Software House A company specializing in the development of software.

Software Package Programs available already developed and ready to run.

Spreadsheet A program where figures may be added to grids similar to standard accounting layouts. Calculations can then be programmed for each space on the grid to produce results such as budgets and forecasts.

Stand-Alone System A computer system that can function without other computer systems.

Store *See* Memory.

Sub-Routine An operation within a computer program.

Switched Star System The type of cable TV network that uses an intelligent video switch in each geographical area to control TV signals entering subscribers' premises. Allows interactive communication.

Synchronous Transmission In data transmission this means that the time intervals between signals are regular.

Systems House A computer company which produces a complete computing system under its own name having bought in the hardware components and then added its own software.

Systems Software or Manufacturers' Software The programs necessary for the computer to physically function.

Technofear The dread that uninitiated computer users feel when confronted by equipment and programs that they find difficult to comprehend.

Teletex Modern telex facilities. (Do not confuse with teletext.)

Teletext *See* Videotex.

Television Receiver Only *See* TVRO.

Template A list of commands that cause a spreadsheet program to undertake a particular job.

Terminal The device used to input data to and output information from the processor.

Threshold Extension A method of improving signal quality where satellite TV is concerned.

Time Sharing The way in which a computer controls its multiple use by a number of users.

Track A path of pulses on a disk, tape, core, drum or wire.

Transponder The electronics within a TV satellite that receive ground signals and then re-broadcast them.

Tree & Branch System Cable TV network that sends *all* TV signals to each subscriber's premises and the tuner facilitates the viewing choice.

'Turn-Key' System A computer system that is supplied ready to use instantly at 'the turn of the key'.

TVRO Television Receiver Only. A TV receiver that is 'dumb' or cannot transmit.

UNIX An operating system for 16-bit computers.

Upgrade To increase the capability of a computer.

User A person who uses a computer.

User-Friendly A term to describe a computer system, and particularly software, that a user finds simple and easy to follow.

User-Programmable Key *See* Function Key.

VDU or Visual Display Unit The television-type screen that displays video information stored in the computer. Also called a monitor.

Videotex The display of computer-based material on a domestic television screen. Same as Teletext or Viewdata.

Viewdata *See* Videotex.

Visual Display Unit *See* VDU.

Voice Input Controlling a computer directly by speech instead of by keyboard.

Volatile Memory A memory in which the content is lost when the electricity is cut off, as is the case with most RAM.

Winchester Disk A type of hard disk that cannot be removed from its housing.

Wind Loading The wind pressure on a satellite TV dish.

Word A collection of bits. Same meaning as a byte.

Word Processor A computer system for manipulating text.

Worksheet *See* Template.

Wrap This is the way the computer starts a new line when text proves too long on the screen.

Zap North American term for destroy or erase.

Index

Note: numbers in *italic* refer to Figures and Tables.

abbreviated audit, telephone information 179
abbreviated dialling 172, 173
access
  limitation of (computers) 313
  prevention of 191
accommodation, current and future
    availability 107
account histories 144–5
accounting 16
  catering information system (CIS) 70
  open-time 157
accounting applications, computerized 157
accounts 160, 271
  updated statements 161
  and word processing 291
acoustic modems 294
Activity Report, bars 92
administrative functions, centralization
    of 298
advance reservations 270
advance reservations credit account
    control 161
AGCS *see* guest check-out system, automated
AGRS *see* guest registration system,
    automated
alarm services, cable TV 220
American date format 113
American Express (Amex), hotel reservations
    system 108–9
Amstrad, cheap word processing systems 317
anti-glare screens 278
antistatic carpets/mats 244
applications software 308–9
audit trail, full 163
authorization cards (magnetic strip) 195, 196
auto-call systems 46, *47*
auto-repeat facility, keyboards 275
automated check-in and check-out 129–33
automated checking, previous accounts 30
automatic call-back verification system 119
automatic cheque production 157
automatic computerized fire systems 185,
    187–90
automatic detector Energy Management
    Systems 207–8

automatic personal debt collection
    correspondence 155
automatic recall 171

baby listening 173
back office computerized accounts 157–70
  budgeting and forecasting 162
  computerizing the payroll 163–7
  financial modelling 160
  general ledger 159, 162
  management information 159–60
  night audit 162–3
  purchase ledger 157–8
  sales ledger 160–2
  time accounting by computer 167–70
back office management linked to front office
    systems for billing 43
  reports received 43
back office systems integrated with POS
    terminals 42
back-up
  integrated 268
  necessity for 304–7
  store away from system 306
back-up copies 283
back-up systems 235
balance sheet and profit and loss account 159
banqueting events 143
bar codes, and automated data collection 64–
    5
bar control 22
bar extensions 155
bar point-of-sale accounting 90–3
bar stock control, electronic bar management
    systems (EBMS) 93–4
bar stock package 97–100
bar stocktaking 100–1
  transfer of information 101
bars 247
  and computers 89–101
  transfer of information to breweries 93
beer dispensing, problem for EBMS 94
bespoke software 240, 310
bill printers 133, 171
  attached to television sets 127

billing 122, 123, 126–7
  itemized 91
  for telephone calls 176, 177, 178
billing routine 126
black lists 140
bookings
  block and group 112
  conference management system 154–5
bought ledger 312
breweries
  and energy management 206
  viewdata systems 229
British Association of Hotel Accountants
    (BAHA), survey of hotel computer
    use 26
British hotels, scope for computerization 20
budget alarm 173
budget generating facility, linked to general
    ledger 162
budgeting and forecasting, back office
    computerized accounts 162
Burger King, computerization 31
business graphics 277
business guests, in-room entertainment 210–
    11
business, origin of 143
business software 16
buyer pattern feedback, instant 155

cable television 202, 210–11, 214–15
  Westminster Cable Television 215–21
call accounting systems *see* telephone
    monitoring systems
call barring 172, 173
call costing 173
call diversion 172
call pick-up 172
call stations 48
call waiting tone 172
cancellations 112
cancellations report facility 154
cards
  and guest activated technology 35
  for vending machines 101
  see also charge cards; credit cards;
    keycards; magnetic cards, secure; smart
    cards
carpets, static electricity and static
    discharge 243–4
carriage width, printer 286
case studies
  computer rules Roux restaurants 57–8
  computerized reservations, distrust of 117
  hotel computer saves time but memory too
    small 280–1

managers given time to manage by
    restaurant computer, large London
    Hotel 55–6
New York Hilton 123–4
not all systems allow necessary
    flexibility 113
old pub benefits from new technology 90
restaurants benefit from in-house
    computer 44–5
training an important element of
    installation 320–1
cash control 42
  and EBMS 94
cash control terminals 94
cash loaders, advantages of 103
cash registers
  networked 53
  programmable 34
cash-flow 157
cashiering system, computerized 126
cashiers 127, 270
cashing up, point-of-sale tills 92
cashless vending *35*, 102–5
  benefits of 104–5
caterers, disappointments with computer
    technology 19
catering, computerization of slow 18–19
catering computers, evolution of 18–37
  fast-food outlets 31
  the future 34–7
  history and significant development 19–25
  hotels 26–30
  industrial catering 33
  pubs 34
  restaurants 32–3
  welfare catering 33–4
catering control, computer terminal/cash
    register 52
catering hardware 268
catering information system (CIS) computers,
    controlling food production 65–70
catering information systems (CIS) 40–1
  in hospitals 71–88
catering management computer systems, in
    hospital 60
catering management information system,
    linked to conference management
    system 155
central processing unit (CPU) 274
central reservations facility 298
CHAMPS, modular integrated system *126*,
    312–13
chance arrivals, and automated guest
    registration systems 129
change, resistance to 235, 317–18

charge cards, used in EFTPOS terminals 134
check-in
  automatic *see* guest registration systems,
    automated
  hotel switchboard 173
check-in hotel systems overview *311*
check-in machines, electronic 25
check-in time, reduced 136
check-in/check-out
  automated 129–33
  procedures 21
check-out, and telephone information 180
cheques, automatic production of 157
CIS *see* catering information system
Citel reservation system 109
city ledger 162
cleanliness and computers 243
coaxial cabling 295, 297
cocktail bars and EDD systems 96–7
collation package, sales and marketing
    system 151
colour coding, POS keyboards 91
commissions, sales manager's decisions 152–
  3
communications 302–4
compatibility 267–8
computer applications, in hotels 27
computer configurations 268–71, 305–6
computer exhibitions, usefulness of 239–40
computer facilities, updating of 37
computer maintenance, importance of 256–
  60
  cost of 259–60
  third party maintenance 260
  type of contract 257–9
computer memory, importance of 279–81
computer networks 295–302
computer service bureaux 240
Computer Services Associations (CSA) Third
    Party Maintenance Group 260
computer speed 266–7
computer suite 242–3
computer suppliers 238–41
  purchasing considerations 240–1
computer systems
  countdown for a restaurant
    installation 245–55
  fully integrated
    appreciation of 272–3
    situation in the UK 273, *274*
    usefulness of 271–2
  initial investigation 236–7
  installation of 241–2
  integrated 174–5
  single and dual processor 306

specification, requirements analysis 237–8
support for 255–6
computer systems, selection of 231–63
  clean electricity 244
  computer installation 241–2
    necessary physical alteration 242–4
  countdown for installation 245–55
  impartial advice 260–3
  importance of computer maintenance 256–
    60
  selection process 235–8
  suppliers 238–41
  support 255–6
  why use a computer 232–5
computer technology, use of 28–30
computerization
  benefits of 232–5
  and telephones 170–83
computerized keys 129
computers
  as an aid to sales and marketing 141–53
  and back office accounts 157–70
  and bars 89–101
  capital cost dropping 30
  cost-effectiveness of 233–4
  equipment installed *17*
  fallibility of 304
  and fire security 187–90
  in food and beverage 39–105
  and the front desk 121–33
  in hospital catering 71–88
  and the housekeeping department 200–1
  inherent problems with 235–6
  and kitchens 59–70
  linked via analogue telephone lines 293
  linked via digital core networks 293
  and reservations 107–21
  in restaurant operation 41–58
  and vending 101–5
computerspeak 315–16
  an alternative glossary 316
conference and banqueting, and word
    processing 291
conference calls 172
conference diary 153–4
conference and functions business, handled
    well by computer 147
conference management 153–7
  teleconferencing 156–7
conference management system 153
consultants 260–1
containers, returnable 40
cook-chill/cook-freeze methods, suited to
    computerization 65–70
corridors and public areas, heating of 208

costings options 248–9
credit cards 35, 36
  account payment from hotel room 126–7
  approval during registration, automated 30
  authorise payment through video
    checkout 126–7
  doubling as room keys 200
  used in automated guest registration
    systems 129, 130, 131
  used in EFTPOS terminals 134
credit control 22
credit control system 161
credit customers 123
credit limits 128
credit worthiness 140
crime, reduced by automated guest
  registration systems 130
Cumberland Hotel 19
currency conversion module 127, 128
customer/staff communication 18, 48

Daily House Cash Report, bars 92
Daily Server Report, bars 92
daily usage, stock items 39
daisy wheel printers 285–6, 288–9
data cables 252
data capture
  at point-of-sale 49–52
  for billing 21
  kitchen stock control 63–4
data communications, timecard network 169–
  70
Data Protection Act 140–1, 167
data transmission speed, modems 294
database programs 308–9
databases
  for a catering information system 41
  market research 155
  marketing 141–5
  recipe 60–1
Datel 303
debt collection correspondence,
  personalised 161
delivery notes 70
delivery and refill system, EDDs,
  microprocessor controlled 95
Delphi (Hilton International sales
  management system) 143–7
deregulation, telecommunications, USA 23
desk top computers *see* microcomputers
device housings, customization of 248, 250–1,
  252–3
diet history 60
diet validation 73, 83
digitizers, flexibility of 80–2

Diplomat Hotel 109
direct connect modems 294
direct debit loader, access to wage or salary
  account 104
direct diagnosis 257, 259–60
direct mailing 148
disasters, planning for 307
dispense bars 247
  and point-of-sale systems 93
dispensing systems, automatic, need for
  checking 63
distributed processing 268
do not disturb 173
DOARS network, TWA 109
door locking systems, computerized 192–200
dot matrix printers 285–6, 287–8
drinks dispensing
  automatic systems 34
  need for EBMS 93
dual processor computer systems 306

EBMS *see* electronic bar management system
EDD *see* electronic drink dispensers
educational services, cable TV 220
EFTPOS 133–6
  Northampton Paypoint trial 25
  operational problems 135
EFTPOS terminals 35
  on-line 135
  operation of 133–5
  store and forward 135
electrical installation 250, 252
electrical surges, and computer faults 244
electricity, clean 244, 247, 250, 252
electricity purchase, scheduling of 209
electronic bar management systems 93–4
electronic cash registers 94
electronic door-locking systems *see* door
  locking systems, computerized
electronic drink dispensers 94–7
electronic funds transfer at point-of-sale *see*
  EFTPOS
electronic keycard systems 186
electronic mail 215, 227, 228, 302, 303–4
electronic newspaper, local 218–19
electronic point-of-sale *see* EPOS
electronic reservations 228
electrostatic field, VDUs 278
emergency calls 173
employer and staff details, integrated payroll
  systems 165
EMS *see* energy management systems
encoders, for magnetic strip key cards 192,
  195, 196–7

end-of-day procedure, with point-of-sale systems 92–3
end-of-day routines 128
energy conservation 204–9
energy management, remote 206
energy management systems (EMS) 204–9
    integrated 205–6
energy waste 205
enquiries 271
    conference management system 153
enquiry, telephone information 180
epilepsy and VDUs 277
EPOS machines, customer billing and cash control 42
errors
    in computer systems 108
    human, reduced by computerization 233
Ethernet networks 297
Eutelstat 221
exception reports 165, 169
exchange and operator efficiency 175
existing users, enquiries to 246
expandability 44
express lifts 191
Express Reservations Space Bank (Amex) 108–9
extension status display 171
extension to extension calls 171
external (backing) store 280
eyesight and VDUs 277–8

false fire alarms 189
fast-food outlets, use of computers 31
fax 302–3
fibre optic cabling 44, 215, 218
finances, of satellite television systems 224–5
financial accounting program 157
financial control, computer terminal/cash register 52, 53
financial information, guest access to 211
financial modelling 111, 160
financial operations 16
financial status of hotel, fast access to 163
fire alarm, sequence of events 189–90
fire detection and control devices 188
fire escapes, alarm system for 191
fire extinguishing gas 243
fire prevention, and computers 243
fire security 183–6
    and computers 187–90
    lack of 183–4
floppy discs 280, 282
    double-density 281
    safe-guarding information 283
    taking care of 283

flow-meters, insufficiently sensitive 94
food and beverage, and word processing 291
food and beverage computer systems, general features 39–40
food production, controlled by computer 65–70
food service areas, remote, and radio-controlled hand-held terminals 48
food stock control 63
food waste 33, 79, 82
forecasting 233
foreign currency converter 127, 128
foul air/pollution detectors 208
free-vend sessions 101, 103
front desk 270, 312
    computerized 121–33
        automated check-in and check-out 129–30
        guest check-in 125–6
        guest check-out 126–7
        posting guest charges 127–9
    controlling mini-bars 203
    integrated reservations system 110–11
front desk package 122–3
front desk reports 123
front hall *see* front desk
front office 159–60
    computers in 29
    and word processing 291
front office systems 22
front office terminal, and in-house movie system 212–13
full audit, telephone information 179
full travel keys 275
function list 154
function room availability 145

games playing, and computer familiarization 318
general ledger, back office computerized accounts 159, 162
ghost bar sales 204
graphics and colour on VDUs 277
group bookings 270
    potential 152
group business, and the reservations system 107
group check-in 125
guest account posting, automatic 161
guest charges, posting of 127–8
guest check presentation option 56
guest check-in 121–2, 125–6
    automatic 35, 36
    integrated systems 125–6

guest check-out 126–7
  automated 131–3
guest credit control 127
guest facilities, most attractive 273
guest history 115–16, 136–41, 163, 312
  affected by Data Protection Act 140–1
  and personalized hospitality 136–9
  use as marketing facility 139
guest history files 111
guest history module, interfaced with word
    processing module 139
guest history programs 136–7
  integrated 138–9
guest in-house 137–8
guest information 115–16
  displayed by automated guest check-out
    system 132
  using viewdata 228
guest information units 133
guest messages 123, 173
guest registration card 147
guest registration systems, automated 25,
    129–31
guest room key control 192–200
guest service, improved by
    computerization 233
guest service centres 25, 26
guest telephone handsets 180–1
guest telephone service, expenses of
    provision 176

handheld computers 63
handheld remote controllers 211
handheld stocktaking computers 100–1
  and bar stock packages 97
handheld terminals 25
  radio-controlled 48, 49
Happy Hours 39, 94, 101
hard discs 281, 283
hard-copy, from printer 284
hardware 240
  questions to ask 266–73
  second-hand 265–6
  security 313
hardware selection 265–306
  communications 302–4
  Hilton's in-house communications
    network 299–302
  importance of memory 279–81
  interfaces 283–4, 285
  keyboards 274–6
  local area networks (LANs) 297–8
  minicomputer or microcomputer 266–74
  modems 293–4
  multi-user computers and computer

networks, differences 294–7
  necessity for back-up 304–7
  printers 284–91
  processor 274
  storage 280–3
  VDUs (visual display units) 276–9
  wide area networks (WANs) 298
  word processing 291–3
hardware support 255
health and VDUs 277–9
heating services control 205
HI-NET (Holiday Inns) 156
hidden costs, of a computer system 241
Hilton International, in-house reservations
    system 109
Hilton International sales management
    system (Delphi) 143–7
Hilton, Las Vegas 23–4, 184, 190
Hiltonet network 109, 299–301
  using mainframe computers 300
Holiday Inns 117–18, 148
  in-house reservations system 109
  introduced teleconferencing 155
holiday pay 164
Holidex (I, II and III), in-house reservations
    network 117–18
Holidex III, in-house reservations
    network 148
Hoskyns, microcomputer-based front office
    system 22
hospital catering computers 33
hospital catering, using a catering information
    system 71–88
  production planning 84–8
  running the system 74–84
  setting up a system – key files 72–4
hospitality system, integrated 272
hotel and catering administration, computer
    applications in 107–229
  as an aid to sales and marketing 141–53
  back office accounts 157–70
  computers and reservations 107–21
  conference management 153–7
  electronic funds transfer at point-of-sale
    (EFTPOS) 133–6
  energy management systems 204–9
  the front desk 121–33
  guest history 136–41
  housekeeping department 200–1
  minibars/in-room refreshment centres 201–
    4
  security 183–200
  telephones and computerization 170–83
  television provision 209–29
Hotel and Catering Training Board (HCTB)

consultancy service 261
microcomputer training courses *263*
Open Learning scheme *262–3*
hotel choice, influenced by hospitality 136
hotel consultancy companies 260
HOTEL system, *CHAMPS 234–5*
hotels, growth of computer usage 26–30
house buying, cable television 219
housekeeping department 271
computerized 200–1
monitoring room status 201
housekeeping package 200
human element, and electronic door-locking
systems 199

IBM microcomputers (PCs)
and compatibles 24–5
and Roomfinder III 119–20
illicit call alarm 173
impact printers 285–6
in-house computers 20, 22, 44–5
in-house movie channels/system 202, 211–14
in-house telephone systems 170–1
in-room entertainment systems 202, 209–29
in-room facilities 36, 171, 201–4
use of 128
in-room refreshment centres,
computerized 201–4
in-room safes 191
industrial catering, use of computers 33
information channel, satellite TV
systems 223–4
information technology (IT)
recent developments in welfare catering 33
training 318–20
infra-red sensors 207
infra-red transmission, and hand-held
restaurant terminals 48
inhibit facility, keycards 196
initial enquiry, reservations 114–15
ink-jet printers 291
Innfinance, ADP 160
installation site visit, points raised 249–50
installations, for television services 211
insurance 249
integrated services digital network
(ISDN) 293
integrated software 309
intelligent workstations 295
Intelpost 303
Intelstat 221
interactive games, cable TV 220
interactive teleconferencing 156–7
interfaces 272, 283–4, *285*, 312
internal directory display 171

International Reservations Ltd 21
invoicing 22, 70
conference management system 155

jobs
suitable for computerization 236
threatened by computerization 318

keyboard keys, non-glare 275
keyboards 274–6
features for a catering computer
keyboard 275–6
point-of-sale 91
touch-sensitive 275–6
keycard usage analysis 196
keycards
magnetic strip 193–7
access levels 195
possibilities of 195–6
punched hole 197–8
temporary power down 197
time controlled 197
keys, computerized 129
Kilostream, British Telecom 229, 293
kitchen liaison 42–3, 45–9
auto-call systems 46, *47*
hand-held terminals 48
and networked cash registers 53
kitchens 247, 250
kitchens, and computers 59–70
controlling food production by
computer 65–70
nutritional analysis and computerized
dietary control 60–1
restaurant liaison 59
stocktaking 61–5

labour analysis, through payroll
computerization 166–7
labour costs 97
labour forecast 167
Las Vegas Hotel fires
effect on hotel guests 185–6
Las Vegas Hilton 184, 190
MGM Grand Hotel 183–4, 190
prompted research into computer
systems 22–4
laser printers 290
laser scanners 64
last number redial 172
LEO (Lyons Electronic Office) 19–20
L'Hôtel St Jacques 109–10
fully integrated computer system 21–2
lift attendants, for security 191
lighting, and VDUs 279

limiters in an EMS system 208
line printers 271, 290–1
liquor control, aided by computer 89–90
liquor stock control 61–2
local area networks (LANs) 295, 297–8
  in hotels 297
  mistakes made 245
location of goods 69
locks, reprogrammable 192
longest waiting indication 171
lost business tracking 145
'lost and found' modules 30
lost revenues 96
Lyons, J., Ltd 19–20

McDonalds, computerization 31
machine substitution 257
magnetic cards, secure
  additional uses of 105
  vending machines *102*, 103
magnetic tape cassettes, not useful 283
mail shots 152, 292
  personalized 148
mailing, and word processing 152
mailing lists 148–9
main memory (computers) 279–80
main processor, location of 247
mainframes 15–16, 119, 243
  in Hiltonet network 300
maintenance 200–1
  preventative 258
  printers 287
  timing of 304–5
maintenance agreements 239, 249, 255
  checklist 258
maintenance modules 30
malicious or unwanted calls 173
management
  by crisis 46
  efficiency and control increased by
    computerization 233
management centre 250, *254*
management control 21
  in restaurants 43
management information, back office
    computerized accounts 159–60
management information system,
    integrated 71
management reports 256
  regular consolidated, hospital CIS 74–80
  specialist 160
managers, freer to manage 56–7
manuals, need for 242
market analysis program (MHM
    system) 147–8

market research database, conference
    management system 155
marketing data source 150
marketing database 141
  sales and marketing computer
    systems 143–4
  segment, source, channel 142
  service history 144–5
marketing information, demanded by sales
    managers 141–2
marketing and mailing 155
Marketing Plan Summary 142
marketing records 150–1
marketing and sales, and word processing
    291
MATV (Master TV) systems 211
Maximum Demand Tariff 208, 209
media selection 149
Megastream, British Telecom 293
memory, microcomputers 267
menu analysis 79
  patients 79–80
  staff 83–4
menu choice and diet history 60
menu costings 40
menu planning 40
menu production 292
menu uptake analysis 52
menus, linked to patient category 82
merge facility 292
message switching device 300, 301
messaging service 171, 303–4
meter telemetry, cable TV 221
MGM Grand Hotel, Las Vegas 22–3, 24,
    183–4, 190
microcomputer vs. minicomputer, cost 255
microcomputers 17, 33, 34, 55, 119–20, 143,
    240
  integrated 34
  linked to POS terminals 43
  memory 267
  not so susceptible to temperature
    change 266
  in restaurant management control 49–52
mini-bar systems 202–4
  revenue sharing plan 202–3
mini-bars 21, 226
  computerized 201–4
  ghost bar sales 204
minicomputer or microcomputer 266–74
minicomputers 16, 21, 27–8, 33, 119, 120,
    143, 240
minors, denied access to alcoholic beverages
    in mini-bars 203
modelling, on the computer 233

modems 203, 255, 257, 259–60, 268, 293–4, 297
 down-loading bar stocktaking details 101
 half or full duplex 294
modular software 310, 311–13
modulation and demodulation 293
Motor Hotel Management (MHM) system 147–8
movement detectors 207
multi-site systems, and WANs 298
multi-user computers and computer networks, differences 294–7
multi-user operations 16
multisite modules 313
mutual-aid arrangements 260

national chains, and computerization 31, 32
National Health Service, encourages computerization 33
national reservations network, UK 20–1
network configurations 295
networked tills
 microcomputer included 50–2
 slow feedback 49–50
networks 17, 36–7, 43
new business, identification of 151
new revenues 96
New York Hilton, failure of early computer system 18, 20, 123–4
news service, satellite TV systems 224
night audit
 back office computerized accounts 162–3
 reports allow manual running of establishment 305
night audit package, integrated 163
'Night Clerk' 25, *130*
NLQ printers 285
nominal ledger 312
non-impact printers 286
North America, early computerization 19
nutritional analysis and computerized dietary control 60–1, *62*

Off-Sales 94
office administration 313
on-site maintenance contract 257
one-to-one communication, guest check-in 121
open-time accounting 157
operating systems 282
operating systems software 307–8
operational control, computer terminal/cash register 51
operator passcodes 114, 125, 129

opinion polling, cable TV 220–1
optic cables *36*
optical mark readers 82–3
order processing 22
ordering system, catering information system 66
overbooking facility 154
overseas guests 127, 128
 requirements of 21
overstocking 61
'own' software 310, *311*

PABX (Private Automatic Branch Exchange) switchboards 171, *172*
package software 17, 240, 255, 309–10
Packet Switched System (PPS), British· Telecom 37
packing and labelling, catering information system 69
Panamac reservations system 109
paper slew feed 286
parallel interface 284
parts and labour agreement 259
patients, acquisition of information from 80–3
pay TV, payment for 213–14
payroll
 computerization of, back office computerized accounts 163–7
 and personnel 312
payroll costs 21
payroll expenses analysis packages 166–7
payroll processing 165, 167, 169
payroll reports 165–6
payslips 164
performance to date, computer suppliers 238–9
peripherals 247
 configuration of 270–1
 connected in LANs 297
 increase cost of maintenance 259
 and interfaces 284
personal computers *see* microcomputers
personalized service 173
photovideotex 219, 229
pilferage 61, 89
PIN number (personal identification number) 37, 136
pixels 277
planning, catering information system 67
plate waste 82
PMS *see* property management systems
point-of-sale billing systems 297
point-of-sale cash register network, linked to microcomputer 49–52

point-of-sale systems
  bars 90–3
  fast-food outlets 31
  suitable for restaurant 44
point-of-sale terminals 42, 272
  incorporating bill printers 57
  staff keys 57
portable computers
  and guest telephone handsets 180–1
  in stock taking 63, *64*
portion sizes 73
POS *see* point-of-sale
posture and VDUs 278–9
precheck *see* VDUs, in restaurant computer
    systems
pregnancy, and VDUs 277, 279
preset keys, for non-sensor items *91*, 94
Prestel 37, 227
  'Room Service' 116
price changes, easy with food and beverage
    computer systems 40
price look up (PLU) number 49, 51, 53
price look up (PLU) table 128
print quality 284–5
printer noise level 286
printer ribbons 286
printer speed (cps or characters per
    second) 286, 287
printer stationery, single sheet or
    fanfold 286–7
printers 270–1, 284–91
  in front office 124
  Hiltonet network 300
  possible locations 247, 250
processors 267, 274, 306
production monitoring, catering information
    system 68
production planning, hospital CIS 84–8
production schedule, costed 84
professional advice 232
programmes, satellite TV systems 224
project leader, responsible for work on
    computer system 236
Promo channel 226–7
property management systems 30, 245
  early, failure at New York Hilton 20, 123–
    4
  interfacing with Holidex III 118
  interfacing with Roomfinder III 119–20
  linked to computerized switchboard 174–5
  telephone package 174
proprietary foodstuffs, nutritional content
    of 60–1
public switched telephone network
    (PSTN) 293

pubs, use of computers 34
pumps and fans, run by EMS 206
Purchase Day Book, hospital CIS 77–8
purchase ledger
  back office computerized accounts 157–8
  interfaced with word processing facility 158
purchase ledger reports 158
purchase orders, hospital CIS *87–8*
purchasing, catering information system 67

quotations and sales forecasting, conference
    management system 154
QWERTY keyboard 274–5

radiator heated zones 206
radio communication, hand-held terminals 25
Radio Frequency Interference (RFI) 244
radio telephones, for guests 181
radio-pagers, in kitchen liaison 46
RAM (Random Access Memory) 267, 279–
    80
Ramada Business Card 120
Ramada Hotels 118–20
Ramada International 118–20
Rapid Order System Point of Delivery
    (ROSPOD) 48
re-ordering report, bar stock packages 98–9
receive only teleconferencing 156–7
recipe database 60–1
recipe details, hospital CIS 73, *74*
recipes
  catering information system 67–8
  exploded to check stock 67
  individual *86–7*
refresh rate, VDUs 278
registration cards 136
relay broadcasting, fax 302
reliability, of computer system 44
remote links 268
repeat key 275
replica keys
  disposable 199
  re-usable 198–9
reporting, conference management
    system 155–6
reports, from mini-bar system 203–4
reprogrammable locks 192
reservation data collection 115–16
reservation sequence 114–16
reservations 16, 21, 22, 312
  computerized 107–21
  essential facilities 111–12
  from home via television 37
  Hiltonet network 299

reports 114
useful features 112
reservations systems 107–21
  bad design 113
  external networks 108–9
  in-house networks 109, 117–20
  integrated system 110–17
  single-site systems 109–10, 120–1
  various 109
Reservations World 109
restaurant chains, transmission of information
    to head office 43, 44
restaurant computer systems
  operating in a hostile environment 44
  using non-intelligent terminals 54–8
restaurant liaison 59
restaurant management control 49–58
restaurant ordering process, more
    efficient 45–6
restaurant sales, breakdown of 42
restaurant terminals, hand-held 48, *49*
restaurants
  operation by computers
    kitchen liaison 45–8
    management control 49–58
  use of computers 32–3
revenue control, food and beverage computer
    systems 39–40
revenue entry 167
revenue statistics 167
revenues, new and lost 96
ring back on busy 172
robbery and assault 186, 191
rolling diary 153
ROM (Read Only Memory) 267, 280
room allocation 122, 129
room availability 115, 145
  on screen 106, 125
room management, and telephone
    management system 175
room occupancy 107, 108, 163
room rack, eliminated 125
room records, stored by computer 125
room sensors 207–8
room service 226
  increased use of 211
room status 16, 199, 271
  monitored by computer 200, 201
room temperature control 206–7
room transfers 128
room types 112
Roomfinder I, II and III (personal computer
    network) 118–20
rooming list facility 125
'Roomservice', Prestel 116

SAHARA (SITA Airline Hotel Advanced
    Reservations Automation) 301–2
St John's Hotel, Solihull, in-house
    computer 22
sales action plan 151–2
sales details 151
sales ledger 312
  back office computerized accounts 160–2
  conference management system 155
sales ledger function, centralization of 298
sales and marketing systems 143, 149–53
  need for comprehensive word processing
    facility 147
sales and marketing, use of computers 141–3
  Hilton International sales management
    system (Delphi) 143–7
  Holidex III system 148
  integrated marketing system 149–56
  mailing lists 148–9
  media selection 149
  MHM system 147–8
  teleconferencing 156–7
sales and purchase ledgers, integrated 158
sales software package 149
satellite communications
  Holiday Inns 156
  for teleconferencing 155
satellite dish aerials 211, *215, 222, 223*
satellite television 202, 210–11, 221–5
  in London hotel bedrooms 24
screen character size 278
screen resolution/density 277
screen size and format 276–7
scrolling 277
search and sort capability 143–4
security 183–200
  for cashier 126
  of computer package 114
  computers and fire security 187–90
  during check-in 125
  fire security 183–6
  in guest charge posting 129
  guest room key control 192–200
  and payroll 166
  robbery and assault 186, 191
  of software 313
  and word processors 293
security password 313
security systems
  automatic computerized 24
  Roomfinder II 119
'Self-Chek' Guest Service Centre 25, *26, 132,*
    133
selling, using the telephone monitoring
    system 177

sensors, monitoring drinks 93
sequential broadcasting, fax 302
serial interface 284
server key, POS systems 90–1
server terminals 56, *254*
Serving Period Sales Report 55
shelf life 67
Sheraton in-house reservations system 109
single key dialling 171
single processor computer systems 306
single-site operation
  reservation systems 109–10, 120–1
  using microcomputers 43
SITA system 299, 301–2
smart cards 36, 135–6
  as room keys 35
software
  bespoke 240, 310
  for the caterer 309–11
  modular 310, 311–13
  'own' 310, *311*
  restaurant 44–5
  security 313
  standard 55
  tailored 310
  user-friendly 44, 45, 321
software enhancement 311–13
software failures 259–60
software requirements, hospital catering
    operation 71–2
software selection 307–13
  applications software 308–9
  integrated software 309
  modular software 311–13
  operating systems software 307–8
  security 313
  software for the caterer 309–11
software support 255
spelling checkers 292
spreadsheets 277, 308–9
stability, long-term, of computer
    suppliers 238
staff fatigue, lessening of 129
staff organization, conference management
    system 154
staff telephones, management of 181–2
standard letters 148
standard maintenance charge 259
standardization, of recipes 67
standby facilities 307
star networks 295, *296*
static discharge 243–4
static electricity 243–4
stationery costs 239
stock control

bars, with EBMS 93–4
with a catering information system 40–1,
    67
computerized, benefits of 63
food and beverage computer systems 39
hospital CIS 77, *78*
pubs 34
typical system 61–2
stock details, hospital catering information
    system (CIS) 73
stock item details 97, *98*
stock picking note 67, *68*
stock records, bar stock packages 97
stock register 313
stock reports
  bar stock packages 97–8
  hospital CIS *78, 79*
  consolidated 75
stock rotation 70
  stock storage, catering information system
    (CIS) 69–70
stock usage report, bar stock packages 99
stocktaking and computers, kitchens 61–5
storage (computer) 280–3
stores requisition list, hospital CIS 84, *85*
Strand Hotels 19–20, 110
Strand Palace Hotel 19
Sun Valley in-house computer 20
super-smart cards 135–6
superconductors 34
supplementary dictionary 292
supplier data 158
supplier details
  bar stock packages 98
  hospital catering information system
    (CIS) 72
supplier reliability 255
supplier visit 247
suppliers
  installation details 250
  and small hotels 30
switchboard 271
switchboard (computerized) facilities
  general 171–2
  hotel-specific 173–4
switched star system, cable TV 215
  Westminster Cable Television 215–21
System X 229
system controller, in-house movie channels,
    billing structure 212
system overhead 281–2

T-switch (LAN) 297
tailored software 310
technofear, conquering of 317–18

telebanking 219
telebooking 219–20
Telecom Gold 303–4
telecommunications network 156
teleconferencing 24, 156–7, 215
Telemax system, USA 108
telephone call logging system 271, 272
telephone calls, posting to room account 180
telephone charges, accounting for 176
telephone handsets
    built-in data ports 180–1
    controlling room facilities 171
telephone line, external 250
telephone management systems (TMS) 174–
    80
telephone monitoring systems 176–7
telephone system
    administration use of 175
    management of 178–80
telephone usage, staff telephones 182
telephones, linked to main processor 21
telephones and computerization 170–83
    guest telephone handsets 180–1
    making a profit from the telephone
        system 176–80
    management of staff telephones 181–2
    telephone management systems
        (TMS) 174–80
    voice messaging 182–3
teleshopping 219
teletypewriter circuits, Hiltonet network 301
television 37
television provision 209–29
    best of all worlds 225–7
    cable television 214–15
    free or pay TV 213–14
    in-house movie channels 211–14
    installation considerations 211
    satellite TV 221–5
    viewdata (videotex) 227–9
    Westminster Cable Television 215–21
telex 228, 302
    in Hiltonet network 299, 301
Telidon (videotex, USA) 227
terminals 16, 270–1
    Hiltonet network 300
    non-intelligent 54–8
    POS systems 90–2
    possible locations 247, 250
    VDUs 276–9
terminology, catering and computer 315
text manipulation 292
text printing 292
thermal transfer printers 291
thermostats 207

third party maintenance 260
time accounting by computer 167–70
    reports 169
time and attendance data 170
timecard network, automated 164, 167–70
timecard terminal 168
toll ticketing 179
touch pads 94
touch-sensitive keyboards 275–6
tours and groups 143
trading-in hardware 265
training 239, 249, 253, 255
    importance of 318–21
    on the premises, a hidden cost 320
    some or all staff 321
training films 317
transaction posting 128
travel agency and tour company
    business 152–3
Traveldex 117
tree and branch system, cable TV 214–15
TVRO (Television Receive Only) earth
    station 223
twisted pair cabling 295

ultrasonic devices as room sensors 207–8
Uniform Accounting System for Hotels 159
Universal Product Code (UPC) 64–5
USA
    hotel reservation systems 108–9
    property management systems 30
user comfort, keyboards 275
user-friendly software 44, 45
    benefits of 321

variable pricing policy, vending machines 101
VAT 40
    handling of 153
    in purchase ledger 158
    and service charges 128
VDU feature checklist 279
VDUs 270, 276–9
    in restaurant computer systems 54–5
vending, and computers 101–5
    cashless vending 102–5
vending machines and tills 104
Video Arts, training films 317
video checkout 126–7
video recorders 210, 211
videodiscs 132
    in guest information units 133
viewdata, and reservations 116
viewdata systems, networked, in
    breweries 229
viewdata (videotex) 227–9, 304

VISA, development of 136
visual display communication, restaurant/
    kitchen *see* auto-call systems
visual display units *see* VDUs
voice messaging 182–3
Voicebank, British Telecom 183
voided product report 58

wake-up calls 173
waste 33, 79, 82
    bars 89
    cutting down on 65
welfare catering, use of computers 33–4
Westminster Cable Television 215–21
    broadcast channels 217
    the future 218–21
    programme channels 216–17

text services 217–18
Whitney boards 113
wide area networks (WANs) 298
Winchester discs *see* hard discs
word processing 291–3
    80-column screen 276
word processing facility 147, 148–9, 158
word processing module 139
word processing software packages 152, 308–9
word-processing systems 155
    linked to sales ledger 161
working hours, and maintenance
    agreements 259

X-stream network 37
X-switch (LAN) 297